# PRISON WITHIN SOCIETY

Lawrence Hazelrigg is a graduate of the University of Missouri and Florida State University, where he received his B.A. and M.S. degrees respectively. He has been an instructor and the assistant director of the Institute of Contemporary Corrections and the Behavioral Sciences at Sam Houston State College, Huntsville, Texas, and has written articles for several professional journals. He is currently pursuing his doctoral studies at the University of Texas.

# PRISON WITHIN SOCIETY

*A Reader in Penology*

*Edited by*

LAWRENCE E. HAZELRIGG

*Department of Sociology*
*The University of Texas*

ANCHOR BOOKS

DOUBLEDAY & COMPANY, INC.

*Garden City, New York*

Grateful acknowledgment is made for the following material:

"External Setting and Internal Relations of the Prison" by George H. Grosser, from *Theoretical Studies in Social Organization of the Prison*, Pamphlet #15 (1960). Reprinted by permission of the author and The Social Science Research Council.

"The Social Functions of a Prison" by Johan Galtung, from *Social Problems*, Volume VI, No. 2. Reprinted by permission of the author and The Society for the Study of Social Problems.

"Achievement of an Unstated Organizational Goal: An Observation on Prisons" by Donald R. Cressey, from *Pacific Sociological Review*, Volume I (1958). Reprinted by permission of the *Pacific Sociological Review*.

"Conditions of Successful Degradation Ceremonies" by Harold Garfinkel, from the *American Journal of Sociology*, Volume LXI (1956). Reprinted by permission of The University of Chicago Press.

"Social Control in the Prison" by Richard A. Cloward, from *Theoretical Studies in Social Organization of the Prison*, Pamphlet #15 (1960). Reprinted by permission of the author and The Social Science Research Council.

"Correctional Administration and Political Change" by Richard McCleery. Reprinted by permission of the author.

"Socialization in Correctional Communities" by Stanton Wheeler, from the *American Sociological Review*, Volume XXVI (October 1961). Reprinted by permission of the author and the *American Sociological Review*.

"Effective Institutions for Juvenile Delinquents: A Research Statement" by Robert D. Vinter and Morris Janowitz, from the *Social Service Review*, Volume XXXIII (June 1959). Reprinted by permission of The University of Chicago Press.

"The Inmate Group in Custodial and Treatment Settings" by David Street, from the *American Sociological Review*, Volume XXX (January 1965). Reprinted by permission of the author and the *American Sociological Review*.

"The Correctional Institution for Juvenile Offenders: An Analysis of Organizational 'Character'" by Mayer N. Zald, from *Social Problems*, Volume VIII (Summer 1960). Reprinted by permission of the author and The Society for the Study of Social Problems.

"Action Theory and Research in Social Organization" by Frances G. Scott, from the *American Journal of Sociology*, Volume LXIV (January 1959). Reprinted by permission of The University of Chicago Press.

"Achieving Change in People: Some Applications of Group Dynamics Theory" by Dorwin Cartwright, from *Human Relations*, Volume IV (1951). Reprinted by permission of Plenum Publishing Corporation.

# PREFACE

Since the appearance of Donald Clemmer's *The Prison Community* just over a quarter of a century ago,[1] the literature dealing with the correctional organization has multiplied many times over. A major theme running throughout much of this literature has been the treatment of the prison as a *formal* or *complex organization*, a large-scale, multigroup organization characterized by a task orientation, functional specialization, and role-reciprocity. The prison is seen not within the narrow perspective of an isolated, discrete type of organization but within a larger analytic framework which allows the utilization of insights gained from other, more fundamental perspectives, including those of sociology, psychology, social psychology, political science, and administrative science.

The corrections professional should be one of the prime beneficiaries of this growing body of increasingly sophisticated literature, in as much as it would assist him in understanding the complexities of the organizational setting in which he works. Unfortunately, however, most of the literature dealing with the prison as a social organization has appeared in scholarly journals that are seldom read by correctional people—for example, *Administrative Science Quarterly*, *American Sociological Review*, *Human Relations*, and *Social Service Review*.

*Prison Within Society* is intended to serve as a partial remedy to the inadequate flow of information from the research scientist to the correctional practitioner by providing the latter individual with an integrated and more readily accessible collection of some of the most important studies of the correctional organization. Obviously this kind of solution can be little more than a holding action, since articles that are relevant to the correctional institution appear in the several scholarly journals on a regular basis. It would be better if the correctional worker made frequent use of the journals as original sources of pertinent information, instead of relying upon a collection of articles that have been selected by an intermediate as "the most important" or "among the most important" articles available. In the meantime, edited collections such as this one, *The Prison*,[2] and *The Sociology of Punishment and Correction*[3] will hopefully introduce more of the literature to those who are interested in correctional institutions.

The twenty-four articles included in this volume are divided into three major sections, each with its own introduction: "Prison within Society," with eleven selections; "The Therapeutic Function of Prisons," with seven selections; and "Problems of Organization Within the Prison," with five selections. The textual material is concluded by "A Final Note," an intriguing essay which brutally depicts the need for additional studies of the kind found in this volume. A "Selected Bibliography" is appended.

First acknowledgment is due the authors and publishers for permission to use the articles which appear in the following pages. Individually, I would like to thank three persons: Delos Fulton, for aiding immensely in the preparation of the manuscript and compilation of the bibliography; Loretta Barrett, of Doubleday & Company, Inc., for the editorial assistance without which no writer, at least not this one, could work; and Jo, my wife, for readjusting domestic time schedules, assisting with the proofreading chores, and for helping in many other ways too numerous to document. In many respects, this book is as much the product of their efforts as it is of mine.

LEH

## NOTES

1. Boston: Christopher, 1940 (Reissued edition, New York: Holt, Rinehart & Winston, 1958).
2. Donald R. Cressey, editor, *The Prison: Studies in Institutional Organization and Change* (New York: Holt, Rinehart & Winston, 1961).
3. Norman Johnston, Leonard Savitz, and Marvin E. Wolfgang, editors, *The Sociology of Punishment and Correction* (New York: John Wiley & Sons, 1962).

# CONTENTS

---

## THE THERAPEUTIC FUNCTION OF PRISONS

## A FINAL NOTE

# PRISON WITHIN SOCIETY

# INTRODUCTION

Until recently, studies of the prison generally ignored the organizational context within which the stated goals of imprisonment are either fulfilled or defeated. Instead, emphasis was assigned to the inmate alone, as if he were isolated not only from the outside world but also from the society supported agents of the institution itself. To understand "inmate behavior," one looked at the inmate—his psychology, his experiences, his relations with other inmates, at one time even his genetic endowment and his physique. The total organizational context of the prison as *a* social system which includes inmate-staff and interstaff relations as well as interinmate relations was ignored. As one of many consequences of this mentality, if staff efforts at reformation failed, the burden of guilt fell automatically upon the inmate. This kind of thinking has a subterranean but nonetheless predictable influence upon both the means and rationale of the reformation goal.

Anyone exposed to recent literature in professional journals such as *Administrative Science Quarterly, American Sociological Review, Law and Contemporary Problems,* and *Social Service Review,* to cite a few, is no doubt aware that circumstances have changed. The academic disciplines that examine human behavior have discovered the prison as a major source of information which is relevant to theories of social organization. Along with this discovery we have learned more about the intricacies of the patterns of life in the prison than in all previous years of the prison's existence. Now, for example, it is recognized that if the actions of an incarcerated person are to be understood, he must be considered in his interrelations with all other individuals who are of immediate social reality to him. And if a particular program designed to reform patterns of human action fails, the burden of failure (guilt seems to apply only to inmates) rests with the program and, to the extent it is critically influential, with the organizational structure of the prison itself. Techniques of inducing change in human behavior can be no better than the quality of the interpersonal context within which they exist.

The first eleven selections of this book consider the organizational character of the prison or correctional institution. Some of the selections are of a more general nature than others; that is, some are concerned more with the generic dimensions of complex social organization than with the character of the prison *per se*. It should be understood, however, that all of the selections pertain to the prison as an ongoing social organization.

The opening selection, Grosser's "External Setting and Internal Relations of the Prison," provides an introduction to the prison as a social system through a general discussion of its relationship to larger society, its internal dynamics, including patterns of deviance and control, and some implications of its organizational structures to the stated goal of treatment.

Following Grosser's introduction, Galtung analyzes the social functions of the prison. He brings to his work the necessary academic scholarship in the social sciences plus the direct experience of his incarceration in a Norwegian prison as a conscientious objector. Galtung states the significant sociological problem of the prison as the determination of "what limitations this one critical function of resocialization sets for the choice of prison structure," and whether these limitations are such that resocialization and the remaining functions of the prison are "not obtainable simultaneously by means of the same structure."

It is worth noting that Galtung makes a distinction between resocialization and the more popular term, rehabilitation. By the latter, the individual abstains from criminal acts simply because the opportunities for such acts are not prevalent in his general sphere of action. Resocialization, on the other hand, means that the individual does not engage in criminal acts even when the opportunities are present. Newly internalized normative constraints prevent him from engaging in such acts that would violate his own new standards of proper and expected behavior. According to these respective definitions, one might conclude that the majority of our direct correctional efforts end at best in rehabilitation, since resocialization implies a level of efficacy in techniques of induced change that the social, psychological and psychiatric disciplines have yet to offer.

Cressey, in selection 3, examines the existence of a relatively new and unrecognized goal of the contemporary correctional institution: the protection of inmates from society. He notes the variations in achievement of this goal between the treatment- and the custodial-oriented institution and suggests that the variations reflect opposed conceptions of deviance: deviance as the *inability* to conform (the treatment view) versus deviance as *intentional* nonconformity (the custodial view).

Garfinkel's trenchant analysis of "status degradation ceremonies" in the fourth selection affords the reader a background against which subsequent discussions of social control, deviance, and the therapeutic process acquire added significance. He succinctly describes what the inmate has experienced by the time he reaches the prison door: he has been publicly denounced and degraded. This denouncement, as Goffman has illustrated elsewhere,[1] does not cease with imprisonment. As one consequence of the degradation, the inmate's status has been reduced to such a level that it becomes ever less psychologically painful to reduce him still further. Conceivably he may be lowered to a subhuman level in society's eyes, and thus deprived of human status, he can become the justified target of any activity deemed necessary. In this world of the prison inmate, the end *does* seemingly justify the means.

In selection 5, Cloward proceeds to demonstrate the "pressures toward deviance" which emerge from status degradation ceremonies and, especially, to suggest the thesis that social control processes in the prison often "generate the very behavior they were intended to avert." A system of incentives, intended as inducive and supportive of conformity, actually induces and supports deviant behavior simply because these incentives are unattainable for the majority of inmates.

The next selection also considers processes of control in the prison, but whereas Cloward focuses on the function of the inmate system to the maintenance of the total organization, McCleery considers systems of authority and control as they are influenced by processes of change. In his monograph, *Policy Change in Prison Management*,[2] McCleery documented the complex changes in the power structure and communication patterns of Oahu Prison (Hawaii) as the prison's management shifted from a punitive, authoritarian stance to a more liberal and rehabilitative orientation. By 1955, the new operational philosophy had become an accomplished fact, and Oahu Prison had been transformed into an exceptionally open, experimentally oriented correctional institution. During 1960, however, the newly established system of authority and control collapsed in a climax of insubordination by top prison officials and one of the most violent riots in the history of American corrections. In selection 6, McCleery attempts to account for the series of events that led to the collapse of an entire system of social control by turning to the broader analytical framework of policy change at the societal level. His analysis not only further explores the thesis that communication patterns can serve as functional substitutes for force in systems of control, it also illustrates once again the dependence of social institutions upon the context of larger society.

In selection 7, Wheeler re-examines the problem of how and to what extent the newly admitted inmate integrates into the general inmate social system. Through empirical tests of the socialization process, he suggests refinements of Donald Clemmer's original concept of "prisonization" and relates the resulting reformulation to other characteristics of the prison. As one of the central conclusions of this study, Wheeler found that the level of inmate integration does not increase in simple linear fashion as the inmate passes through his prison term but responds curvilinearly: low at entrance to the institution and again when release is anticipated; high during the middle phase of the prison term.

The next three selections also report empirical investigations of prison organizations, dealing with the correctional institution for juvenile delinquents. In selection 8, Vinter and Janowitz outline a field research project that analyzed the problems involved in the development and implementation of effective behavioral change programs. This project served as an umbrella for several different but related studies conducted by students of the authors. Two of these studies comprise selections 9 and 10. Street's investigation of variations in the organizational goals of seven juvenile institutions suggests that the inmate social system is not necessarily one of sustained opposition to staff or societal norms. Rather, it performs essentially a problem-solving function and, depending on the "balance of gratification and deprivation and patterns of staff authority and control," it may or may not assume an oppositional stance.

Zald relies upon the same seven institutions for an analysis of the "character" of an organization: its goals, its relationships to the larger community and its internal structure. According to Zald, a "character analysis" will not only explain the differences among various correctional institutions but also the patterns of similarity and dissimilarity between correctional and other organizations. This may make it possible to synthesize existing knowledge, identify research needs, and formulate generative concepts which will eventually lead to the construction of a more comprehensive theory of formal organization.

In the concluding section, Scott offers a theoretical framework for the study of those formal organizations which perform an integrative function in society and illustrates the utility of this approach with an analysis of two such organizations, the prison and the mental hospital.

## NOTES

1. Erving Goffman, *Asylums* (New York: Doubleday, 1961), esp. Chapter 1.
2. Richard McCleery, *Policy Change in Prison Management* (East Lansing: Governmental Research Bureau, Michigan State University, 1957), reprinted in Amitai Etzioni, ed., *Complex Organizations* (New York: Holt, Rinehart & Winston, 1961). Before reading the current selection, the reader should become familiar with McCleery's original monograph or with one of the somewhat revised versions of it: "Communication Patterns as Bases of Systems of Authority and Power," in Richard A. Cloward, *et al., Theoretical Studies in Social Organization of the Prison* (New York: Social Science Research Council, 1960), 49–77; and "The Governmental Process of Informal Social Control," in Donald R. Cressey, ed., *The Prison: Studies in Institution Organization and Change* (New York: Holt, Rinehart & Winston, 1961), 149–88.

# 1

## EXTERNAL SETTING AND INTERNAL RELATIONS OF THE PRISON

*George H. Grosser†*

The mandate given to the prison by society is to isolate those of its members who have been defined as refractory and threatening to the social order. It is natural, therefore, that many of the papers of this section should focus mainly on the control function of the prison. In general they agree that, no matter what the stated aims of a correctional system or prison administrator, the effect of imprisonment on the individual is frustration through the restriction of participation in the society and the imposition of special rules, among which the prohibition of freedom of movement is only one.

## THE PRISON AS A SOCIAL SYSTEM

As a social organization, the prison may be conceptually viewed in relation to society as a service organization, supported by the community largely for the purpose of maintaining order and not for the production of any goods which yield the individual or the community an immediate economic return. Like most other service organizations (such as mental hospitals and social agencies), the prison is a means of safeguarding other institutions of the society.

From the viewpoint of the prison as a relatively isolated social system, however, it is a structure composed of a ruling caste and a subordinate caste. The ruling group, save for the fact that its authority is almost total and not based on any

† George Grosser is an associate professor in the Department of Psychiatry at the Tufts University School of Medicine.

contractual relationship with the governed, might be likened to a managing bureaucracy. The term *caste* is more appropriate here, however, since there is no possibility of vertical mobility across caste lines in the prison and—unlike organizations of a bureaucratic type—the two castes do not share any over-all primary goal through co-operative participation in production.

Before the analogy with a caste system is stretched too far, one principal difference must be pointed out. Whereas in most caste systems behavior within and between castes is governed by moral obligations derived from an ideology largely shared by all members of the society, there is no reciprocal assumption of moral obligations by the two prison castes. Rather, it is assumed—and usually rightly so—that the inmates are devoid of a sense of moral obligation to the institution and its administration. This tends to create a special problem of control. . . .

While prison management defines its role largely in terms of institutionalized criteria of success, such as maintenance of order and wise budgetary management, and holds an achieved status characteristic of the occupational structure of our society, the prisoner caste is relegated to the enforced dependency of an ascribed status imposed for a stated period. Cloward has pointed out that in this situation there are few opportunities to harness even minimal self-interest of prisoners for the accomplishment of the wider aims of the institution as a whole.[1] Thus, the absence of both moral obligations and achievable goals accentuates the problem of social control in the prison.

It is the more remarkable, then, that prisons function as going concerns and succeed in doing so under a variety of regimes, ranging from the most authoritarian to the most modern. It seems worth while to cite the special conditions of accommodation that keep the symbiotic relationship of the two disparate groups—prison management and inmates—in a state of equilibrium. These conditions are by no means the product of the internal structure of the system alone, but are in part supported by the peculiar position of the prison in the society.

## Position of the Prison in the Community

In a society in which organizations compete either for economic resources or for the loyalty and support of group members, the prison has a unique position. It is noncompetitive in the sense that no other organization challenges it directly. The prison therefore need not, as ultima ratio of its existence, maintain competitive standards, adapt itself rapidly to technological progress, or respond to fluctuations of market conditions; nor is it as immediately dependent on the good will, benevolence, or loyalty of a group of sponsors or followers, as are many other nonprofit organizations. The prison justifies its existence by fulfilling a legal mandate which, like most legal mandates, sets a floor below which achievement cannot fall but does not require the achievement of ever higher aims. This gives prison management a certain latitude in decisions, for the organization is relatively independent of the intensive public scrutiny or success standards that often govern the existence of other institutions.

Furthermore, members of the larger society (except for the relatives of inmates) have no direct stake in the prison in terms of ownership, goods, services, or reciprocal relations of any kind; and this remoteness from the organization gives even the concerned taxpayer very few criteria with which to judge the efficacy of the correctional system.[2] Thus, the prison is relatively protected from outside scrutiny. Since the prison administrator generally holds a monopoly of the channels of communication with the outside world, he can keep much information that is deemed detrimental within the walls as long as he can count on the loyalty of his staff. If this seems inconsistent with the fact that public indignation about the prison system is periodically aroused, the contradiction is more apparent than real. Public cries for reform and shake-ups in the prison system are rarely, if ever, an immediate response to the day-to-day operation of the relatively static prison community, but are usually the work of outside interest groups.

In its relative independence, then, the prison administration may turn its attention to internal organization, enjoying a position that rests ultimately on its monopoly of the exercise of force and channels of communication, and the reasonable certainty of continuing financial support. It is perhaps because of this independence that prisons display such a variety of forms of management, control, and internal conditions.

## Internal Relationships

Both to students of social organization interested in system maintenance and to persons concerned with prison reform, the most significant aspect of internal structure is the social organization of the inmate population. While from the administration's viewpoint the inmates are social equals (except for a few privileged positions that may be earned) the inmate social system exhibits all the earmarks of a subsociety within the institution. The inmate society maintains a value system, more or less rigidly adhered to; a system of stratification with statuses and roles peculiar to itself; and a system of social controls independent of the official controls maintained by the administrative hierarchy. . . . It is generally agreed that the inmate social system contributes toward maintenance of the institution, despite the fact that the norms explicitly governing and justifying the inmate hierarchy are predominantly opposed to the aims of the administration.

A number of interesting questions concerning the content of the inmate code or the ideology of the prisoner may be raised, although most of them must await future research for their answers. Part of the ideology of the inmate is imported into the prison from the value system he and his group held outside. This fact might give the inmate code an antagonistic tinge regardless of the frustrating conditions within the prison. The low valuation given the lower echelons of the administrative hierarchy and the belief in the venality and arbitrariness of legal authority are notions imported from the criminal world and quickly applied to the prison administration. Imported also are a belief in the widespread dishonesty of so-called law-abiding society and a conviction that at least minor deviations from established rules are perfectly justified if one can get away with them. Thus, the foundation for a hostile ideology, mistrust of the administration, and an interest in rule breaking exist from the time of admission.

To this foundation must be added the needs that imprisonment itself creates. The need for management of aggression deserves special emphasis, for their social background and way of life have led many inmates to accept the overt expression of aggression as an essential feature of their existence. Since many prisoners bring their belief in the efficacy of threats and violence into the prison, where in the interest of order and control the expression of violence tends to be countenanced by neither the administration nor the inmate population, a serious problem in management of aggression arises. It is further to be assumed that the frustrations of prison life—monotony, sexual deprivation, lack of privacy, and daily forced association with the same people—augment aggressive tendencies. In these conditions occasional outbursts and riots are not incomprehensible; only their rarity is surprising.

It would seem, then, that the inmate social organization finds a way of channeling the aggression short of mass outbreaks of violence or rebellion against the prison. The way in which this is done stands in contrast to the alternative solutions more frequently attempted by organized social groups under prolonged conditions of stress. Such groups often develop a revolutionary ideology (to be differentiated from mere hostility), but no such movement is manifest among prisoners. The conviction that the prison system is stronger than any possible combination of inmates, and that a victorious revolution and abolition of the system cannot be achieved, probably is an accepted part of the inmate system of beliefs. Another reason for the absence of a revolutionary ideology is that the prisoner has no cause, beyond his own immediate welfare, for which he would think it worth while to fight; just as he has previously accepted the social order (without strong conviction) as something with which he had to reckon, he now accepts the existing order in prison.

. . . Why does prison society not adopt an ideology of submission and acceptance, as some groups under total slavery have done, or an ideology of self-criticism, such as that exhibited by Alcoholics Anonymous? In short, what prevents the inmate population from turning the aggression inward against themselves, as some individual members do? A definitive answer is not possible at this time, but it is likely that the solidarity of the inmate organization, coupled with the fact that its leaders and many of its members usually are persons with poor superego development who disseminate the myth of guiltlessness, helps to prevent the inward turning of aggression. In consequence, aggression must be partly restrained and partly displaced and projected, both onto *rats* and other unreliable inmates and onto a variety of out-groups within and outside the walls, thus helping to sustain the hostile attitude of the inmate in-group.

It has been noted that certain roles occur in so many prisons and are so well known that argot terms have been developed to designate them.[3] The maintenance of these roles stems in part from a stereotyping and selective perception of one another by inmates and guards, but must rest also on the prevalence of personality types to which these roles give adequate expression. The frequency of such roles may be governed by the frequency with which certain personality types are found in the criminal population, or perhaps in the population at large; or the selective process of imprisonment may funnel into the prison personality types that take on the argot roles. Or it is possible that the prison community shapes personalities in accordance with the requirements of living among inmates, just as a bureaucratic structure fosters certain personality characteristics among its officeholders.

Political theorists are well aware of the influence of length of time in office on the establishment of a power structure. This influence is inherent in the prison situation, where long-term inmates tend to find themselves in positions of leadership. Their control is the more secure because a good part of the inmate population changes much more rapidly and thus cannot entrench itself or challenge the existing power structure. This differential turnover of personnel guarantees continuity of leadership to the inmate social system; it is this continuity that sets the tone of the organization. If the inmate organization is compared with that of a college class, which will move out *in toto* at a foreseeable time, making way for an entirely new group, the significance of the differential rates of personnel change becomes clearer. The code of the student body can be maintained because of the overlapping of classes; but if the leadership of a new class were moved to change the student code, this could be done relatively easily.

It might be worth while to experiment with classification and segregation of inmate populations, by placing together short-term inmates with approximately the same length of sentence and preventing any contact with long-term prisoners. It is possible that no entrenchment of leadership would take place in those circumstances.

As Cloward has pointed out, such informal relationships as the inmate social organization exhibits are a natural consequence of any large-scale organization.[4] A degree of solidarity, a system of stratification, and an inmate code will emerge under widely different conditions of prison life; and the tendency to reach an adaptive equilibrium within the prison appears, as McCleery has shown,[5] under various conditions of administrative control. A question of primary importance, to be answered by future research, is whether the inmate social system always, under any prison conditions, will embody features of hostility to the administration to the degree indicated by past research, i.e., whether the mere fact of imprisonment itself, even under the most enlightened and humane conditions, always will produce an in-group that constitutes a reference group hostile to the society and its representatives in the prison administration.

### Mechanisms of Control

The fact that life in the ordinary prison has to be lived wholly within walls extends the authority of the administration to the regulation of functions that in most other social organizations are left to the individual's discretion.[6] Even eating and sleeping tend to become routinized in the prison. The discipline extended to every aspect of the prisoner's multiple roles leaves little scope for nonregulated or unsupervised activity. Historically, this development was based on the belief that discipline *per se* is a good and that its enforcement will have benefits beyond the prison walls in the habits inculcated in individual prisoners.

The routinization of prison life is also traceable to: (1) the punitive philosophy, which tends to be expressed in over-elaboration of the necessary routines of living so that prisoners "don't have it too easy"; and (2) the imperatives of any functioning institution, which cannot leave time schedules, allocation of resources, etc., to the discretion of each individual. The ways in which the personality of inmates is affected by this routinization have been discussed. It is apparently conducive not to self-direction, but to a reliance upon authoritative initiative, so that prisonization, like hospitalization, results in dependence rather than independence. This dependence does not merely make the inmate subservient to authoritative rule by the administration, but can be exploited equally well by the leaders of the informal inmate groups to recruit convicts and to dominate them. That routinization beyond a minimum necessary for organizational functioning is not essential for the maintenance of the prison as a system has been demonstrated where prisoners have been given more scope for self-direction. Cressey and McCleery have shown that prison management of the latter type is more fraught with anxiety for the administration and requires greater adaptability on the part of personnel.[7] These conditions, however, do not necessarily impair the essential functioning of a prison.

The application of force and the threat of force are, of course, prominent features of both administrative rule and inmate dominance. In the former, the use of force is legitimized by the legal mandate and the assumption of recalcitrance on the part of prisoners. In the latter, force is indispensable for the exercise of leadership and the prevention of defections from the inmate group, in as much as the inmate hierarchy and most of its activities are not sanctioned by the official code, and there is therefore no recourse to arbitration by the prison authorities or any kind of judicial process.

Despite the omnipresent threat of force, however, it cannot be considered the prime mechanism producing compliance on the part of prisoners.[8] In a number of areas both the prisoner's self-interest and his normative orientation are decisive in guiding his behavior. The prisoner attempts to make his imprisonment as bearable as possible, and if satisfaction of this kind of need must be "purchased" by adherence to some official norms, he will comply and thereby make the application of force unnecessary. Sykes has pointed out that the adherence by the prisoner to certain portions of the inmate code is not merely a matter of verbal consensus but an obligation imposed on him by the solidarity of the inmate society. The extent to which prisoners yield to force, act in their own self-interest, or conform because of their own normative orientation might well be studied, to throw light on what Redl has called the "delinquent ego,"[9] and on the extent and content of the "criminal superego."[10]

It is clear that in contrast with industrial and educational organizations, for example, the aims of the corrective organization are not such as to harness the self-interested motivation of inmates. In the prison self-interest is directed toward leaving the organization at the earliest possible moment or, failing that, satisfying one's needs within it irrespective of the goals of the organization. There is no identification of the individual's own effort with the achievement of an over-all objective.

## Deviance from Official Norms

It has been pointed out that along with conformity in prison, there is deviant behavior—deviant, that is, from the standpoint of the official norms. It is hard to assess its extent, since anecdotal material and autobiographies of ex-convicts are biased in one way or the other, but it is clear that deviant behavior flourishes, at times openly. Some contend that it constitutes a safety valve for the convicts and, so long as it does not threaten the institution as a whole, in effect aids the custodial aims of the administration. On the other hand, by creating closer solidarity, a conspiratorial air, and a potential for denunciation and blackmail, deviant behavior reinforces the inmate social system and its values.

The relationship between conformity to official rules and deviant behavior is an interesting facet of prison life. Conformity often serves the convicts as a means of ensuring a predictable atmosphere in which they can better organize and practice their deviant behavior. This is evident in the many admonitions not to *bring on the heat*. Prisoners capitalize on the administration's desire for order and stability. One suspects that administrative personnel, especially the lower echelons, similarly capitalize on the great need for pacifying the convicts and develop short-cuts and deviations of their own. Thus there develops a peculiar symbiotic relationship, which is found in other organizations as well: a tacit understanding that certain deviations from official rules will be accepted. One might even say that such deviations become regularized expectations and are tantamount to new rules.[11]

In summary, the prison runs neither by force nor the threat of force alone, but largely by virtue of acceptance on the part of the inmates and their voluntary adherence to rules. These rules are partly the official rules of the prison, partly the mores of the inmate culture developed in the adaptation of many generations of convicts to the official code.

Drastic changes in administration which alter the power structure or lines of communication in the prison have an unsettling effect on its routinized ways, whether the changes are in the direction of a more repressive regime or a less repressive one. It is at such times, when routinized ways of behavior are disrupted and expectations do not materialize, that the functions of the inmate social system in maintenance of order come to the fore. The increase in violence, often the result of a struggle for power among inmates and the disappointment of many of their expectations, demonstrates that the forces that have bound their aggression have weakened, and a kind of disorganization of the inmate social system appears. If the administrative change has been in the direction of greater leniency, the ensuing violence may lead the public to believe that it is a mistake to treat convicts leniently; yet the disruption ceases as soon as a new system of informal relationships develops on a different basis. The disorganization is to be attributed to disruption of routine rather than to either repressiveness or liberalism.

## SOME IMPLICATIONS FOR TREATMENT

A social system may be discussed as a going concern in terms of the functional contribution of each part to the organization as a whole; but mandates or goals of the total organization may thereby be temporarily overlooked. The prison's mandate from the community in recent years increasingly includes the demand for treatment and reform of inmates through modern psychiatric and social work techniques. These objectives are added to, but not expected to replace, the prison's custodial aims, which remain partly for punitive reasons, partly for society's protection from potentially dangerous criminals.

There is little to say about the performance of the custodial function. Several analyses have shown that here the prison does well but at a considerable price.[12] Before considering this price, we may note that McCleery[13] and corroborative observations have shown that the custodial function can be performed equally well in an authoritarian organization and in one that grants more scope and self-determination to the prisoners. If repressive and more humane methods can serve equally well[14] to safeguard the community and isolate prisoners, then according to the values of our society the more humane system is preferable.

The more humane prison, on the other hand, is not necessarily to be confused with one more oriented to treatment, although it is true that modern treatment orientation, in the psychiatric and social work sense, is incompatible with an authoritarian maximum-security prison. More self-determination and more humane treatment of prisoners do not necessarily reform their characters or change their values from criminal to noncriminal. This appears to be an important implication of the following papers, for several reasons: (1) The informal inmate culture, with its code and group organization, appears in these papers as a necessary consequence for any large congregate prison. (2) The potency of this group as a reference group persists for most prisoners, both for psychological reasons and because there is no other reference group that competes, with suitable incentives and assurance of acceptance, for their loyalty. (3) Even in the most lenient prison, the fact of imprisonment and its attendant frustrations, as well as the symbolism of caste distinction, tends to keep the offender's self-image *as convict* highly salient. Thus, in effect, incorporation of a lenient philosophy and even the employment of a treatment and training staff cannot be interpreted as more than a professed change in ideology in the direction of treatment orientation.

In performance of the custodial function and in the employment of incentives primarily to that end, the prison jeopardizes its potential as a treatment agency. Hence any attempt to maximize custodial and treatment orientations simultaneously can only fail to do justice to treatment. Such an attempt imposes conflicting demands on personnel. The organization cannot simultaneously maintain regimented discipline and a therapeutic atmosphere characterized by permissiveness and maximum regard for individual needs. Even if all prison personnel were skilled in modern therapeutic methods, some role conflict would be inevitable, whether between segregated roles represented by separate custodial and treatment staffs, or within individuals attempting to carry on the two types of roles simultaneously.[15]

The inmate social organization . . . is a still more formidable obstacle to any basic change of character among inmates, for this organization produces, in response to their psychological needs, precisely the conditions that make identification with noncriminal values highly improbable. It is the isolate and the precariously adjusted prisoner, holding at best a marginal position between the inmate group and the administration, who is most likely to be open to rehabilitative influence. Since this influence is often not forthcoming, or the prisoners are intimidated by the power of the inmate organization, their stability is more often jeopardized than reinforced.

As long as the inmate social organization presents the only reference group powerful and accessible enough to offer the recruit some sense of security, a change in his values can hardly be expected. This statement has another implication for treatment. The notion that the informal inmate organization might be used in treatment is beginning to emerge in discussions of penology, especially with reference to juvenile institutions.[16] With other deviants, such as alcoholics and emotionally maladjusted persons, the use of groups for therapeutic purposes has been explored and attempted. In the prison, however, there has been an understandable reluctance to recognize this potential of the inmate group, first, because its organization—like that of a hostile group in any social order—is thought to present a threat to the administration. Second, it is generally assumed that criminality is fostered by the group, that criminal techniques are spread through group affiliation, and therefore that criminals have nothing good to teach one another. Third, treatment orientation emphasizes individualization of treatment on the grounds that the problems causative of criminal offense are peculiar to each person and require individual solution.[17]

The first two reasons for the reluctance to recognize any therapeutic potential of the inmate organization are based on practical experience, which has always furnished administrators with adequate arguments for upholding the injunction to prisoners to do their own time and avoid group entanglements. The third point stems from a somewhat mistaken interpretation of the word "individual" with reference to problems of causation and methods of treatment. As Sutherland asserted: ". . . from the therapeutic point of view, attempts to change individuals one at a time while their groups and their culture remain unchanged is generally futile. The policy of individualization as practiced in most penal and reformatory institutions has had a stated ambition to study each prisoner, develop a program for him as an individual, and reform him by a program adapted to what was found in studying him. This description and also the practice have frequently gone on as though the individual prisoner lived in a vacuum."[18] Such an atomistic view of the prisoner is false for two reasons. The prisoner maintains relations with the community—or, better, his subculture—even if direct communication is interrupted; and he maintains relations with others in the inmate culture.

All these relations have a continuing influence on his values, loyalties, and self-image. Even if an attempt to alienate him from these groups were successful, he would remain an unstable, alienated individual, a marginal man, upon emergence from prison. But the chances are greater that he would try to maintain his group attachments and thereby emerge unchanged.

The success of individualized treatment in psychiatry and social work is attributable to the fact that the therapist represents group values and tries to adjust the individual to a group that is socially acceptable. In social work, this is generally affirmed explicitly. In prison, on the other hand, the caste system means that there is no such reference group available for the prisoner outside the inmate culture. If, as McCorkle and Korn state, the prisoner is intent on rejecting his rejectors,[19] individual therapy could succeed only if the rejection by society and the degradation of the prisoner were eliminated. Individuals do not attach themselves to a new reference group unless they are strongly motivated to do so. The prison, as constituted, does not furnish sufficient motivation. On the contrary, motivational pressures generally work toward attaching the new recruit to an inmate organization which is hostile to rehabilitation. Individualization of treatment, then, interpreted narrowly as individual therapy or individual contact between treatment personnel and prisoners, would be likely to meet strong resistance even if it were possible on a large scale. This proposition cannot be tested, however, for the problems of maintenance of the organization and the practical obstacles of inadequate budgets and unavailability of trained personnel prevent true individualization of treatment.

If treatment, then, is not to be carried on in a vacuum, a positive reference group must be found to attract the allegiance of the prisoner. Since he is already confronted with one reference group that is powerful and close at hand, strong motivation undoubtedly would be required to help him change his self-image. Reports in the literature, especially in autobiographical materials, generally indicate that individuals with unusual gifts that had hitherto been dormant, or those with strong conflicts concerning their criminality in the first place, were motivated to dissociate themselves from the inmate group through orientation to a new goal or insight into their own conflicts. The great majority of prisoners, however, have neither any special talents nor the ability to achieve insight into their basic conflicts. For them, adjustment means attachment to, or at least acceptance of, the inmate group.

The role of the inmate social system is far more significant and exerts far deeper influence on the personality of its members than is implied by the superficial notion that criminals teach each other bad habits. Recognition of the extent of this influence is the first prerequisite for reconsideration of the problems of the prison. Treatment orientation and reform have to reckon with the prisoner *as a group member* and all that this entails. The correctional system should be organized to make socially acceptable reference groups available to more prisoners;[20] or the existing inmate social organization should be utilized as a reference group of a different sort—one that to some extent would aid the prisoner in his transition to law-abiding society. To move in this direction, much thinking and research will have to be done. The basic idea of what classification and diagnosis should comprise may have to be reformulated. Some segregation of prisoners in smaller units, organized around a combination of personality types and abilities, and perhaps complete segregation of life and long-term inmates from short-term inmates may be indicated. However, the custodial and deterrent functions of the prison cannot be ignored.

A few words concerning the place of the prison in the total social structure may be in order. The position of the prison can be clarified by comparing its functions with those of other service organizations. In a functional perspective, the total process of apprehension and adjudication of the criminal can be seen as a well-regulated process of status attribution. An individual is singled out and forcefully given minority status by representatives of the society. Thus the prison not only segregates its inmates physically and almost completely interrupts the interaction of each with others in the larger society, but also systematically reinforces the ascribed low status of "criminal." Illness, too, is an ascribed status. The hospital and the sickbed are places of quasi-isolation for people who are given this status. Yet the hospital is oriented toward protecting the individual from the demands ordinarily imposed by his social roles and thereby helps him maintain his social status, ready to be resumed as soon as he can emerge "cured." The prison, on the other hand, functions largely for the protection of society and its interests by downgrading the prisoner, rather than protecting his social status. The difference, of course, is largely based on the difference between the conception of illness as involuntary and accidental, and the attribution of freedom of the will and moral turpitude to the criminal.

Analysis of other service organizations in a society with relatively fluid vertical mobility would probably reveal that they function either to preserve or to enhance the individual's status. Thus in this respect, also, the prison occupies a unique position in our institutional network. A society that is becoming more and more conscious of the operation of its institutions and increasingly desirous of improving them will, it is hoped, face this fact realistically in the future and deal with the crucial questions: whether degradation of the offender's status is an inevitable consequence of the outraged sentiments of society, and whether making prisoners a minority group is the best means to their reformation.

## NOTES

SOURCE: *Theoretical Studies in Social Organization of the Prison* (New York: Social Science Research Council, Pamphlet #15, 1960), 130–45. Editorial adaptations.

1. Richard A. Cloward, "Social Control in the Prison," *Theoretical Studies in Social Organization of the Prison* (New York: Social Science Research Council, Pamphlet #15, 1960), 20–48.

2. However, Ohlin points out that certan interested groups do maintain a check on the activities of the prison administration. While the prison is vulnerable to criticism from these sources, it is not as sensitive as other organizations and tends to react slowly except in crisis situations. Lloyd E. Ohlin, "Conflicting Interests in Correctional Objectives," *Theoretical Studies . . . , op. cit.*, 111–29.

3. Gresham M. Sykes and Sheldon L. Messinger, "The Inmate Social System," *Theoretical Studies . . . , op. cit.,* 5–19.
4. Cloward, *op. cit.*
5. Richard McCleery, "Communication Patterns as Bases of Systems of Authority and Power," *Theoretical Studies . . . , op. cit.,* 49–77.
6. See Erving Goffman, "The Characteristics of Total Institutions," in *Symposium on Preventive and Social Psychiatry* (Washington: Walter Reed Army Institute of Research, 1958), 43–84. (Editor's note: An expanded version appears as Chapters 1 and 2 of Donald R. Cressey, editor, *The Prison: Studies in Institutional Organization and Change* [New York: Holt, Rinehart & Winston, 1961], 15–106.)
7. Donald R. Cressey, "Limitations on Organization of Treatment in the Modern Prison," *Theoretical Studies . . . , op. cit.,* 78–110; McCleery, *op. cit.*
8. Herein may lie the most important difference between the control mechanisms of the prison and those of concentration or slave-labor camps. Unlike administrators of such camps, wardens of modern prisons are limited in the use of force. They are not dealing with human material that is viewed as expendable. See Donald R. Cressey and Witold Krassowski, "Inmate Organization and Anomie in American Prisons and Soviet Labor Camps," *Social Problems,* 5 (Winter 1957–58, 217–30).
9. Fritz Redl and David Wineman, *Children Who Hate* (Glencoe: Free Press, 1951), Chapter 4.
10. The orthodox psychoanalytic formulation, which is still widely upheld, denies the development of a superego in criminals. No account is taken in this formulation of the fact that most active criminals adhere to many norms of the law-abiding population. Conversely, there has been no adequate study of superego formation in random population samples which might provide a control group. All observations indicate that prisonization is a socializing process which leads not only to the learning of a repertory of ego-controlled behavior but also to the internalization of norms, a process similar to assimilation in the sociological sense.
11. Such phenomena have been observed in industrial establishments, where "no smoking" rules or certain safety rules, for example, are systematically broken or adhered to only when inspection is announced. See Alvin W. Gouldner, *Patterns of Industrial Bureaucracy* (Glencoe: Free Press, 1954), 182–93. Relaxation of rules is an important element in the adaptation of individuals to a social system—the oil that reduces friction in the mechanism.
12. See *Theoretical Studies . . . , op. cit.*
13. McCleery, *op. cit.*
14. It is not clear whether this holds true for all prisoners. Detailed studies of conduct records of various types of individuals under different prison regimes will have to be made, but enough observations are available to indicate that most prisoners could adjust to less authoritarianism than now exists in most prisons.
15. The optimum conditions have yet to be explored, for too few prisons have been in a position to employ trained treatment personnel in sufficient numbers.
16. See F. Lovell Bixby and Lloyd W. McCorkle, "Guided Group Interaction in Correctional Work," *American Sociological Review,* 16

(August 1951), 455–59; George H. Grosser, "The Role of Informal Inmate Groups in Change of Values," *Children,* 5 (January-February 1958), 25–29.

17. Donald R. Cressey, "Changing Criminals," *American Journal of Sociology,* 61 (September 1955), 116–20; and "Contradictory Theories in Correctional Group Therapy Programs," *Federal Probation,* 18 (June 1954), 20–26.

18. Edwin H. Sutherland, "The Person and the Situation in the Treatment of Prisoners," in Albert Cohen, Alfred Lindesmith, and Karl Schuessler, editors, *The Sutherland Papers* (Bloomington: Indiana University Press, 1956), 162–63, reprinted from *Proceedings of the Sixty-Seventh Annual Congress of the American Prison Association, 1937.*

19. Lloyd W. McCorkle and Richard Korn, "Resocialization Within Walls," *The Annals,* 293 (May 1954), 88.

20. The availability of such groups is, of course, the great advantage that the offender on probation or parole enjoys. However, in the case of the parolee, prisonization often has done its work already.

# 2

## THE SOCIAL FUNCTIONS OF
## A PRISON*

### *Johan Galtung†*

The prison is a social institution designed to meet a multiplicity of functions. Some of these functions are very explicitly expressed by legislators, court decisions, and prison officials, whereas others must be inferred. In most debates concerning the effects of incarceration, etc., the discussion is centered around the compatibility or incompatibility of the function of resocializing the inmates, on one hand, and all the other functions generally imputed to the prison, on the other. It is our belief that only a careful study of what happens to an incarcerated violator of a legal norm can give us an answer to the problem. As the author happened to be imprisoned for a period of six months in Norway's largest prison (maximum prisoner population around 350) as a conscientious objector, he was given ample opportunity to reflect on the question. The conditions for participant observation were unusually good, and the data thus collected were later (after release) supplemented by systematic interviews of 35 prisoners and 20 guards, questionnaires to 30 of the guards, and long informal interviews with prison officials. The samples are small and not entirely representative (because the interviewing was on a voluntary basis), but it is felt that the general lack of sociological studies of non-American prisons justifies the presentation of data that do not satisfy all methodological standards. Our data do not constitute proofs of any hypothesis, but may be regarded as illustrations of our theoretical analysis.

† Johan Galtung is Professor of Sociology and Director of the International Peace Research Institute at the University of Oslo, Norway.

**1. Introduction.** When we say that human life is normatively regulated, we do not only mean that boundaries are set for human action—but also that human imagination is able to transcend these boundaries, and that some actions actually fall outside the boundaries. It seems that we could supplement the old "exceptions prove the rule" with "deviant acts prove the norm." But human imagination is capable of transcending more boundaries than normative ones, and to create a complete *universe of conceivable actions,* U, for any person, P.

In this set, or action-space, different *constraints* operate, and we suggest that there are three kinds of them:

1. *Physical constraints* which eliminate actions because of nonsocial conditions external to the individual. An example is a properly designed safety vault for a would-be bank robber or that there are no banks where he lives.
2. *Biological constraints* which eliminate actions because of the organic limitations of the individual. An example is the bank robber who changes to a new occupation because he has lost the agility he had in his youth.
3. *Normative constraints* which eliminate actions because negative sanctions are anticipated if the actions are carried out. As there are two possible sources of sanctions—the social system P is a member of, and the personal system P itself—there are two kinds of normative constraints:
   (a) *Institutionalized norms*—these are norms from other members of the social system to P, with informal or formal sanctions in the social system, anticipated by P.
   (b) *Internalized norms*—these are norms from P to himself with sanctions in the personal system (bad conscience, etc.). They can be norms against letting a deviant act enter the action-space ("you shall not even think of pinching a book in a bookstore")—or norms with personal sanctions after the act has been carried out, anticipated by P.

For a norm to be institutionalized, it must perhaps be internalized by at least some of the norm senders and it may even be internalized by P himself. The constraints in his action-space, however, are neither the norms nor the sanctions but the anticipations of the sanctions. When all the different constraints have operated in the action-space, a subset of physically, biologically, socially, and psychologically possible actions is left.

Some institutionalized norms are legal norms, and violation of them may lead the violator into the three-stage process of detection-trial-punishment if the constraints have not excluded the act from the set of possible actions. Eventually, the process may lead to incarceration in a prison, the functions of which we want to examine.

**2. The Social Functions of the Prison.** We can distinguish between two groups of social functions of the prison, where the common factor of the six functions in the first group is the *prevention of crime*, i.e., the provision of constraints in the action-spaces of the violators of legal norms, and of others. If we now make use of the general analysis of types of constraints above, the possible functions of this type attributed to the prison can easily be outlined.

First of all, we get

> $F_1$: *The prison as a physical constraint.* Incarceration in an efficient prison obviously concentrates the future violations of the convicted violator to a small area—the prison—because of the prison walls. This does not prevent the inmates from illegal acts, but the very high rate of criminal acts within the walls is not so immediately dysfunctional to the society as a whole because of the very low degree of visibility for members of the society outside the prison.

> $F_2$: *The prison as a biological constraint.* Incarceration can imply that the prison turns out an older and somewhat physically reduced violator after his period of incarceration—at least if the sentence is sufficiently long.

However, the prison is usually thought of as an institution that reinforces normative constraints or introduces them to the prisoners. Normative constraints can be introduced in the action-space of the *offender* or in the action-spaces of *others,* "the potential offenders," who are holders of the same status(es) as the offender, e.g., citizen, civil servant, etc. Further, the normative constraints can, as mentioned above, be of two kinds, based on internalized or institutionalized norms. These two dichotomies yield the following fourfold table with the next four functions of the prison.

TABLE 1
THE PRISON CONTRIBUTES TO NORMATIVE
CONSTRAINTS

|  | By means of Internalized norms | By means of Institutionalized norms |
|---|---|---|
| in the violator | $F_3$: *Resocialization* | $F_4$: *Deterrent* |
| in the other holders of his status | $F_5$: *Formation and enforcement of mores* | $F_6$: *Collective Deterrent* |

The horizontal division corresponds to the classical distinction between individual and general prevention and the vertical division to the old ethical problem of whether an individual abstains from an action because he thinks the action is wrong, or for fear of the (social) consequences.

In the other group of functions there is no common theme, but they should be mentioned to give a fuller picture of what the prison does or might do for a society. We suggest:

$F_7$: *Retribution*—the punishment shall equal the offense in negative value, to satisfy the offended party or generalized norms of justice in the culture.

$F_8$: *Outlet for general aggression or sadism* in parts of the population, i.e., those who press for severe punishment.

$F_9$: *Satisfaction of masochistic needs* and general needs for expiation and atonement, both in the prisoners and in others who feel that the prisoners expiate for them.

$F_{10}$: *Provision for cheap labor force* through prison labor.

$F_{11}$: *Social sanitation* by decreasing to zero the visibility of selected types of deviants.

$F_{12}$: *Reinforcement of the symbols of the power holders,* and particularly of their power.

This list could easily be extended, but we feel that the list of the first six functions (that have to do with the prevention of crime) is in a sense logically and empirically exhaustive. Many of these functions apply to other forms of punishment as well, or to "punishment" in general. To what extent the functions are *manifest functions* in Merton's sense depends on whether they are intended and recognized, and whether they are actual consequences, not only intentions. These are two distinct and important empirical problems.

At first glance, it seems impossible for one relatively simple social institution to fulfill all these (twelve) functions at the same time. However, it is remarkable how efficient the prison may be in fulfilling all functions except the internalization of norms in the violator. Maximum security prisons with very long sentences especially for young offenders, would be highly instrumental to the first two functions mentioned and to varying degrees to all the others except the function of resocialization. At the same time, this function has become increasingly manifest and is given a higher relative weight among the different functions.

**3. Resocialization vs. Rehabilitation.** The sociological problem is to find out what limitations this one critical function of resocialization sets for the choice of prison structures, and whether these limitations make the function incompatible with the other functions. ("Incompatibility" is here not to be interpreted in the logical sense of "contradiction" but in the empirical sense of "not obtainable simultaneously by means of the same structure.") There is, however, one important methodological problem. To evaluate prisons, we cannot simply compare measures of recidivism for prisoners released from different types of prisons, matched on a high number of relevant conditions. Penologically and socially the most important fact is whether a released convict commits a new crime or not. If he does not, *rehabilitation* may be said to have taken place, but this is not the same as resocialization. *Resocialization* means that he abstains from criminal acts when these acts are in his action-space, but are excluded because of the constraints from anticipated personal sanctions. Thus, resocialization implies rehabilitation, *but the converse need not be true.* According to our scheme, there are three other ways in which the criminal acts may be excluded, but more significantly: *Rehabilitation may result from the disappearance of the illegal acts from the action-space.* This follows from the logic of our analysis and is probably the simple explanation why so many crimes are *not* committed—lack of training, of awareness of the possibilities of the situation or of imagination may result in an innocent action-space. But almost daily exposure through mass media to criminal acts committed by others, not to mention the exposure in the prison, necessarily must have the opposite result.

The most significant way in which a criminal act may disappear is probably if the ex-convict has found some functionally equivalent acts that can take the place of the crime in his action-space, because they satisfy the same needs. What these functional equivalents are is perhaps the greatest problem in modern criminology, and the answer depends on the meaning of the crime for the criminal—whether it is a means to economic or sexual gain; to power; a way of achieving high status as a skilled person; a means to obtain belongingness in a primary group; to demonstrate mastery of an adult sex role; to obtain new experience; to punish society or particular status-holders; etc. But we are mainly interested in the particular way of achieving rehabilitation called resocialization, and whether contemporary prison-structures are instrumental to this function. As we cannot infer from statistics of recidivism to what extent resocialization takes place we must take the point of departure in a fairly detailed analysis of what to us seems to be relevant aspects of the prison community.

**4. The Expectations in the Prison.** In the prison community there are three main statuses: The prisoners, the guards, and the administration. Each of the groups sends and receives expectations to and from all the three groups. This gives us a suitable point of departure for the analysis of prison culture:

| NORM-SENDERS | NORM-RECEIVERS | | |
|---|---|---|---|
| | *Prisoners* | *Guards* | *Administration* |
| Prisoners | P → P (P) | P → G | P → A |
| Guards | G → P | G → G | G → A |
| Administration | A → P (A) | A → G | A → A |
| TOTAL | The status of the prisoner | the status of the guard | the status of the administration member |

The last row gives us the three statuses, when defined as the sums of other-expectations. We shall only deal with two of these systems in detail and have indicated simplified symbols in parentheses. Along the main diagonal, we have the expectation systems of the three subsystems of the prison community: the prisoners' community, the guards' community, and the administration. The administration partly reflects the expectations of pressure groups outside the prison (from the police: "do not let him escape, we had so much trouble catching him"; from the offended: "let there be a real retribution"; from the public, the press: "let him suffer to deter others from the same action"; from the probation leagues and others: "resocialize him!"), and partly has expectations emerging within the prison community reflecting its particular structural problems.

There is an interesting analogy between attitudes we find reflected in the expectation system, A→P, and the expectations to a patient as given in Parsons' analysis.[1] The expectations of the administration can be expressed by these norms directed to the prisoner:

A₁: You shall recognize that you are guilty!

A₂: You shall recognize that it was correct to take you out of your social context and imprison you!

A₃: You shall perceive your status as a criminal as undesirable!

$A_4$: You shall do your best to "pull yourself together"!

$A_5$: You shall perceive the stay in prison and the services offered as means to rehabilitation, and utilize the possibilities maximally!

$A_6$: You shall obey the prison regulations!

Apart from the last one, these norms were only weakly institutionalized, except in a negative sense: if a prisoner visibly did the opposite of the normatively prescribed action (e.g., if he said openly that he "preferred to be an honest criminal") negative sanctions would in most cases be entailed. It is hardly necessary to add that for the experienced prison official these norms were normative expectations only and not cognitive expectations. If a prisoner acted visibly in accordance with all six, he would be almost sure to obtain some form of positive sanction if it were not too obvious that he did it for the sake of the sanctions only (a trusted job within the prison, recognition by superiors, a better chance of parole) and not for the sake of resocialization, or *therapy,* to use a term that covers both the administration-prisoner and physician-patient role relationships.

**5. The Prisoner's Situation.**  Like the patient, the prisoner is exempted from his usual status obligations. But from this point on, the dissimilarities are more striking than the similarities. First of all, the deviant actions of the patient are culturally defined as *caused* by external or organic factors, and hence perceived as involuntary. But the deviant actions of the prisoner are culturally defined as *voluntary.* Or, to express this more precisely: *we recognize* in both cases sets of *necessary* conditions for the deviance, such as exposure to contagion or being brought up in a highly delinquent subculture. These conditions may be deterministically or stochastically linked together with the deviant act. The difference is that in most cases of illness these conditions (extrinsic to the deviant, the patient) are defined in our culture as not only necessary, *but also as sufficient.* But in the case of the criminal deviant, these extrinsic conditions are believed to be *necessary only,* and a voluntary decision must be added to them to make a sufficient condition for the deviance. (Hence the norm $A_4$, which is not found in the case of the patient.) Even though the current trend is to bridge the gap between the two forms of deviance, there is still a substantial difference. And this makes it by far easier for a deviant to recognize his illness than his guilt, and hence to be prepared for therapeutic help in a hospital than a prison. This preparedness can make the patient suffer negative experience in the hospital ritual and be convinced that it is instrumental to his rehabilitation, but the prisoner will have enormous difficulties in perceiving all *he* must suffer as relevant to his resocialization. He will rather interpret it as instrumental to one or more of the eleven other functions.

And what then are the prisoner's frustrations? The prisoner is not exposed to direct physical violence, due to the influence of the "humanitarian" trends in the last centuries, but he lives in a situation that is overwhelmingly frustrating. The main frustrations are the following:

1. *The relation to the deviant act.* The presence of guilt, or remorse that he was technically unsuccessful.
2. *The relation to trial and punishment.* The feeling connected with "being one who is tried and punished."
3. *The relation to the outside world,* especially the belongingness he has lost, the pleasures he does not experience, and most significantly: the *time* element; he is put out of the time sequence.
4. *The relation to his sexual life,* the complete and unvoluntary absence of heterosexual satisfaction, and more significantly for a predictable period of time.
5. *The relation to his own development,* the observation of how he is gradually reduced physically, psychologically, and socially. It may be that others do not agree with him in his subjective judgment of his own degeneration, but that does not necessarily alter his perception substantially.

These frustrations are mostly felt during the 40 per cent of the week when he is alone in his cell and awake. Of all of them, we suggest that the factor of "losing time" is perhaps the most important, for beings with a life-expectancy slightly above seventy years. This was reflected in our data by two-thirds of the prisoners, who were willing to decline most or all of the more positive elements in prison life such as radio, letter-writing, visits, most of the food (if they could only retain bread and water), prison work, books to read and even tobacco, if this could shorten their sentences. For most persons, any one of the frustrations would be enough to necessitate some kind of readjustment. For the prisoner this is an absolute necessity; he must work out some solution on the individual or group level to reduce the pressure. But these solutions are highly limited by the physical and social constraints set by the prison, so most of them have to be inner-directed. The usual psychological defense mechanisms are resorted to by nearly all prisoners, especially retrogression to infantile behavior. More interesting, however, are what we call the *prisoner's escape reactions*. In this prison he had several main possibilities of escape, in addition to the sociologically more trivial of real escape (very rare) and parole. The reader will recognize some of the thoughts in Bettelheim's study.[2]

6. **The Escape Mechanisms.** Firstly, he can escape *into the prison community,* by becoming a part of it, vividly interested in technical details as the distribution of food to the prisoners or the sanitation, with friends everywhere among prisoners, guards, and officials. The prison becomes his world. He does not necessarily always conform to the prison regulations, but he is seldom a major cause of trouble. By accepting the prison as the place in which he must live for some time, he reduces the effect of the pressure. In many cases, this prisoner will adopt the ideology of the guard or administration, and may become a "squealer."

*The Prisoner Community.* Secondly, he can escape *into the prisoners' community* with its peculiar subculture. This culture is particularly shaped to protect him against all the frustrations, and its emergence can be very well described along the lines Albert Cohen suggests: "I may stick my neck out, just a little way, but I will quickly withdraw it unless you, by some sign of affirmation, stick *yours* out."[3] In this community the prisoner regains his lost belongingness to a primary group if he had one; or he experiences it, perhaps sometimes almost for the first time in his life. The prisoner community assures him that the necessary conditions for a criminal act are also sufficient conditions (the society is far more to blame than he is), or that it is all due to the conspiring of the upper classes with the police to crush the exploited elements in the society. In this prison, the more sophisticated of the older prisoners felt a kind of cause they were imprisoned for—the cause of the man who has rebelled against the existing social order through his illegal actions, with no clear conception of what he would substitute for it. This solution is an example of a more general solution offered by the prisoners' community, where deviant acts are perceived as *pro*scribed acts, but at the same time as *pre*scribed acts according to some other norms ("Thou shalt rebel!") they place higher in their norm hierarchy. The most common solution, however, is to deny that a criminal act was performed at all or that it was grossly exaggerated by police and court. Twenty-seven of the thirty-five prisoners reported in the private interview that they were innocent.

The leaders in Norwegian prisons do not nearly play the same role as in American prisons.[4] To become a leader, there are some crimes the prisoner must not have committed, e.g., petty thefts, sexual offenses, or political crimes (another thing is that a political criminal may have power, but his power is not likely to be recognized by the others). He must come from the strata in society from which the majority of the prison population is mostly recruited. He must have prison experience or a long sentence, and must be capable of performing instrumental actions (particularly of exploiting guards and officials) and expressive activities (comforting, supporting a prisoner's self-image by presenting him with an almost identical other-image, "of course you did not use the knife, she used it against herself," "of course, they will give you parole, they are afraid of you because you know something about them!").

The following norm system gives a picture of the culture of the prisoners' community as we experienced it:

$P_1$: You shall not ask another prisoner why he is here!

$P_2$: You shall never openly say that you are guilty!

$P_3$: You shall never moralize!

$P_4$: You shall never claim that you are morally superior to other prisoners!

$P_5$: You shall never openly say that the sentence was correct!

$P_6$: You may say that your status as criminal is undesirable, but not that the prison is a means to resocialization!

$P_7$: You shall say that the prison either has no effect on you or harmful effects only!

$P_8$: You shall express as your opinion that the guards and partly the officials are inferior human beings!

$P_9$: You shall be on the prisoner's side in all conflicts!

$P_{10}$: You shall exploit the prison to your own advantage!

$P_{11}$: You shall not be an informer!

$P_{12}$: You shall never directly contradict another prisoner in his interpretation of his own situation, if he likes his own interpretation!

$P_{13}$: You shall tolerate deviance from usual social norms but never deviance from these norms! (Refers above all to deviation from sex norms.)

$P_{14}$: You shall talk about the outside world in such a way as not to increase the frustrations for other prisoners!

$P_{15}$: You shall not be different from other prisoners!

It is easily seen how all these norms are conducive to the reduction of the different kinds of frustrations we have mentioned. We do not know enough to rank the norms in saliency, so as to be able to predict what would happen in a norm-conflict situation.

Thirdly, he can escape *into isolation from both the prison community and the prisoners' community;* by never associating with other prisoners or with guards and officials except for the enforced minimum; by conforming to avoid trouble; by keeping maximum contact with the outer world through radio, papers, letters, visits—in short: by being only physically present in the prison. This is often the white collar prisoner's form of escape—he has promised himself to reduce all effects of the prison stay to a minimum and may be able to enclose this period in his life in parentheses.

Fourthly, he can escape *into his own case*. Because of the structure of our legal institutions, he almost never has to confront the offended party. A third party—"the people," "the state," "the government"—enters between him and the offended party, and the direct relation is transformed to a more technical relation to the legal system. This peculiarity of our legal heritage is exploited fully by many prisoners. The deviant act does not exist, only the technicalities of the legal procedure. He becomes an expert, continuously studying, writing petitions. This keeps him busy, and at the same time reduces the other frustrations.

Fifthly, he can escape *into expiation*. He can refuse the small advantages the prison may give him, and indulge in his suffering. By increasing the burden of the last three frustrations, he reduces the burden of the first two. When he is finally released, he will have a strong feeling that he has made restitution to society and has re-established a moral balance, perhaps even a balance in his own favor, which he feels society should repay.

Sixthly, the prisoner can escape *into violation of the prison regulations*. Apart from the obvious factors that make this an escape from his frustrations—the change in the daily rhythm, the release of aggression, particularly on guards—there is a sociologically more interesting factor: by violating a prison regulation, and thus inflicting punishment upon himself, he enters a new situation where he is punished by the offended party, with no third party intervening between him and his victim. The punishment and the expiation become more meaningful to him, as was suggested by many comments.

*The Prison Hospital.* Seventhly, and finally, he can escape *into illness*. The illness rate is high, and the illnesses range all the way from genuine illnesses to simulations and directly contrived diseases (especially by eating indigestible things such as nails, parts of carpets; or cutting veins, etc.). The extreme among this dimension, the final escape, is the successful suicide. Apart from the obvious factors that make illness an escape reaction from his frustrations—the change in the daily rhythm, the more individualized and less severe treatment, the chance to see women (nurses), the release of aggression by causing trouble (one prisoner kept systematic track of the expenses he had caused by his self-inflicted diseases)—there is again another sociologically more interesting factor: in the moment the prisoner is moved from the prison cell to the prison hospital he can change his status from that of a prisoner to that of a patient and insist on being treated as a patient. Further, he enters a therapeutic process to some extent analogous to the one he is expected by the prison administration to be a part of as a prisoner, but with considerably more chance of success. We suggest that a kind of transfer may take place in him: his rehabilitation as a patient may at the same time symbolize the rehabilitation as a prisoner he is more or less consciously longing for. This puts the hospital staff in a difficult situation which can serve as a paradigm of the whole conflict inherent in the prison system: they may yield to the prisoner's desire to escape into the status of a patient and get negative sanctions from the prison staff (and prisoners!)—or they may find an uneasy compromise between the two role relationships, possibly at the expense of the efficiency of the medical therapeutic process. In this prison hospital the conflict was relieved somewhat in the usual way: there emerged a division of labor in the hospital staff, with some members playing guard roles and some members playing physician —and nurse—roles. Thus, the conflict was moved from the personal system to the social system, and the members could to some extent preserve their integrity. The conflict in the social system of the prison hospital, however, led to a certain polarization of attitudes which was dysfunctional for the prison hospital as a whole.

**7. The Institutionalized Uncertainty.** These seven reactions are resorted to more or less by most prisoners. In addition to them, it is strange to notice that the prison itself offers an escape mechanism to the inmates, viz., the pattern of "institutionalized uncertainty." In principle, the prisoner's life is predictable to an extent very few persons experience. The daily, weekly, monthly, and yearly rhythms of prison life are known to him to the most minute detail, and the first thing he does when he enters his cell is to calculate (for the nth time) exactly when he will be released. This predictability is unbearable, and not all prisoners have the imagination needed to create a phantasy world where the "need for new experience" can be satisfied. But the prison comes to his assistance when the administration gives him a more optimistic view on the chances for parole, transfer to another prison, to another kind of work inside the prison, etc., than statistics should warrant. For the administration this serves the function of protecting them against the highly observable despair and aggression of the prisoner when he is turned down, and for the prisoner this makes prison life less predictable, and hence less unbearable. There seems to be a general principle involved here: that predictability is only functional to the system concerned up to a certain point, and that a further increase in predictability will cause a need for uncertainty that can manifest itself in evasions of the norms, and these evasions may sooner or later become institutionalized in counternorms (although on a more informal level than the norms they are evasions from).

8. The Guard's Situation. We have dealt at some length with the problems facing the prisoner and how the structure of the prison is made use of to relieve him of his frustrations, to some extent. But how is the situation for the guard? He is subjected to expectations from the prison administration as well. These expectations vary somewhat from prison to prison, but we suggest that they can be summarized by making use of Parsons' pattern variables in the following way: the prescribed role for the guard in his behavior toward the prisoner is highly *universalistic* (only intersubjective properties of the prisoner shall be utilized in his orientation to him), highly *specific* (only very few properties are defined by the prison administration as *relevant* in the guard's orientation toward the prisoner), *performance-orientated* (it does not matter *who* the prisoner is, his behavior in the prison is highly relevant) and *affectively neutral* (the guard is supposed to evaluate be-

fore he goes to "release into action," and to restrain his emotions). In addition to this pattern the orientation is *collectivistic,* the guard shall in principle act in such a way as to further
collective ends. To summarize: this is the typical collectivistic,
secondary relationship type role which we find in so many
professions where interaction with other human beings is a
part of the function. The manifest function of his role definition is to achieve *justice*—prisoners with the same relevant
properties shall be treated in the same way—and the most
relevant properties a prisoner can have are the nature of his
crime and the sentence he has been given.

The guards, however, have very little if any training for
their profession (except the kind of training that is necessary
to achieve F, above). They draw a poor salary, and they have
a peculiar kind of job which is strenuous exactly because not
very much happens for long intervals—but something *may*
happen, and this something may be dangerous. They want to
feel that theirs is a profession that requires particular skills.
But such skills must be defined in relation to the specific properties of the prisoners they are asked to be oriented toward.
And which are these properties?

In addition to those defined by the court, several properties
have been suggested as nuclei around which the roles of the
guards can crystallize. The prisoners are *dangerous*—one must
be careful, constantly on guard against them. But this obviously does not apply to the old loiterer or the young embezzler, or the executive who drove his car with more than
0.05 per cent alcohol in his veins. The easiest property then
is centered around the concept of *discipline*—do the prisoners
conform to the prison regulations? The guard may very well
fill his working day watching whether the action carried out
by the prisoners fall in the region of prescribed, permitted,
or proscribed actions, relative to the prison regulations. But
in this prison it became clear from interviews with the guards
that this was not satisfactory. To many of them the conformity
to prison regulations had become an end in itself. But most
of them were dissatisfied. It was so clear to them that if conformity was supposedly instrumental to rehabilitation, then
this supposition was wrong—because 75 per cent of the in-

mates had been in prison before, most of them in the same prison. The guards had lost their belief in discipline and were looking for something new.

And in their search for a new role they became deviants from their prescribed role. Instead of collectivistic, secondary relationship they tended toward a collectivistic (or sometimes individualistic) primary relationship type role. They extended the range of relevant properties to a more diffuse orientation, and they permitted their own judgment to enter and form a particularistic orientation to the prisoner, without asking for consensus. One reason for this is sociologically interesting: some of the guards had noticed how unjust a universalistic orientation is—because intended equality in treatment does not necessarily imply perceived equality. The "toughs" were so much better off than some of the novices, and that made it impossible for the more sensitive guards to "give the same kind of shoes to all of them." But only in a more primary type relationship could they develop the sensitivity and insight necessary for a more particularistic treatment. And only this kind of relationship could make it possible to come to the assistance of some of the prisoners, in small, relatively trivial problem-situations.

Thus the guards were in a dilemma not too different from that of the prisoners. If they had a secondary relation with the prisoners, they conformed to prison expectations and some of them felt they had a real occupation. If they had a primary relation with them, they might be more able to help them ("all they ask for is a little bit of friendliness"), might correct for the iron rule of universalism, but at the risk of receiving negative sanctions from guards and officials higher up in the prison hierarchy. To some extent the problem was solved on the personality level by a division of labor and group formation around the two types of orientation (very similar to the situation in the prison hospital). Another solution was to make visible, when they interacted with the prisoner, whether they were in the *formal* (or external) system or in the *informal* (or internal) system. This was often done by taking off the cap—thus symbolizing that "we are now in the informal system, let us change from universalism-specificity to particular-

ism-diffuseness!" But this change in the prescribed role relationship, by both partners, happened only when they believed
themselves not to be observed.

When given a set of statements about treatment of prisoners, the guards proved to vary considerably in ideology, as
we should expect from the above. But they agreed on statements stressing the social significance of their occupation and
expressed a strong desire for more training for what they held
to be a "very complicated job."

There is no wonder that the interaction between the prisoner
and the guard is somewhat confused and that their role expectations very often are not complementary, to some
extent because of lack of knowledge of alter's expectations.
The informal expectations are built around the desire to preserve self-image and to preserve one's role definition (e.g.,
from the prisoner to the guard: "Do not force me out of my
escape reaction!" and from the guard to the prisoner: "Do
not force me out of my primary (secondary) relationship with
you!"). Sociologically interesting is the sanction system. There
is no difficulty in finding negative sanctions: the guards could
punish by enforcing regulations and withdraw into a strictly
universalistic role, and the prisoner could increase the work
burden of the guard by all kinds of tricks the more "prisonized" among them would be only too glad to inform him
about. But positive sanctions as we think of them are scarce
in this closed social system. They are not allowed to exchange
gifts and praise, and laudatory comments are mostly proscribed as being indicative of a primary relation. What they
did was to lower the standards for positive sanctions. The
guards rewarded by not enforcing the regulations,[5] i.e., they
sanctioned positively by not sanctioning negatively. And the
prisoners did the same: they sanctioned positively by conforming to the prison regulations. In this way they were able
to play their games with each other, the confusing game of
role partners in an interaction both parties have difficulties in
interpreting as functional.

9. **Consequences for Possible Forms of Resocialization.**
This description does not pretend to be a picture of more than
one prison, but the literature on prisons gives reason to be-

lieve that the kinds of conflicts indicated are fairly universal and necessary results of institutions with the functions outlined above. The basic question is again whether resocialization is probable, possible, or impossible in a system with these characteristics. It seems to the present author that if resocialization is to take place in a prison at all, a prerequisite is that the prisoner internalizes norm system A above. This may be possible if the prisoner has reason to believe that there exists a therapeutic process in the prison. But if he thinks, as the majority of our respondents did, "that society may think prison makes us better, but it only makes us worse," internalization of system A will only increase the frustrations. If this conviction is contrary to what he hoped the prison would be, he feels deceived, cheated, and the chances of therapy preparedness are very small. Hence, it is much more likely that they will revert to one or more of the escape mechanisms, and we believe that all of them are dysfunctional or at best nonfunctional to resocialization (except, perhaps the escape into the prison community, under special conditions).

If resocialization is to be successful, it seems that it must take place by means of one or more of the following three mechanisms.

First of all, resocialization can take place much in the same way as it continuously takes place in all primary groups. But this presupposes that the prisoner is offered other primary relations than those he can obtain in the prisoners' community— and the only possibility seems to be primary relations with the guards, and this is proscribed. A decrease in social distance, however, may be dangerous for other reasons, as McCorkle and Korn point out,[6] it may lead to corruption. A prerequisite is incorruptible guards with very high human standards and ability to enter positive primary relations with sometimes extremely difficult human beings. Such guards would be obtainable at considerable cost only, or as "idealists" —and the latter solution is not acceptable to a formal organization (though it might be used more than is presently the case). A more severe difficulty, however, seems to be the ideological linkage in our culture of "justice" with universalism and specificity.

Secondly, the socialization process in the primary group (particularly in the family) may become sufficiently known and codified in such a way that a professional role (collectivistic, secondary relation type) may be built around it. We have such roles today; the psychiatrist, the psychoanalyst, the counselor, or to some extent the priest are examples, and they are made use of in prisons to take care of more extreme cases. However, it seems that therapy is hardly possible in an antitherapeutic atmosphere, and that it is very optimistic to believe that resocialization can take place in the therapist's office if the prisoner lives in the prison climate described above for 166 of the hours in a week when he is not being "resocialized."[7] A therapeutic atmosphere presupposes that a large part of the guards' actions are directly and manifestly geared toward resocialization, and this again presupposes that new, relevant properties of the prisoners are defined. Further, these properties must not require the kind of training we designate as "academic"—but rather make the role of the guard stand in the same relation to the role of the psychoanalyst as the role of the nurse stands to that of the physician. The present recruitment pattern of our prisons makes socialization into the layers in the social stratification from which academic people are recruited less desirable.

Thirdly, the socialization process may be a by-product of life in the prison community, if the prison community is a small scale model of the society the prisoners are released into. This has been the content of many prison theories; if we build our prisons around the personality properties we want to develop in the inmates, there will be a carry-over from habits in the prison community to habits in the society. Hard labor, a regular life, and strong discipline combined with the learning of certain skills have been particularly popular. However, these structural characteristics have at the same time served other functions as deterrent, retribution, and provision for cheap labor—and have been perceived as such by the prisoners. And, what is more important, they cover only a very small range of the problems the released prisoner is likely to encounter. Role-playing is a significant step in the direction of training for social life—but can be met with the same argument, that it takes place in an atmosphere which is hostile to therapy. The ideal seems to be a prison that is a kind of continuous role-playing session, with some of the varieties and irregularities of real social life built into it.

In the prison we have examined, primary relationships between guards and prisoners are proscribed, properties of the prisoners relevant for resocialization are either not known or not transmitted to the guards, and the prison community is more of a caricature than a real model of the Norwegian society. This, together with the descriptions we have given of the prisoners' and guards' situation, make *resocialization* in the sense we have defined it highly improbable, and the prisoners' own evaluation of the effects of the prison very reasonable. This, however, does not preclude the possibility of *rehabilitation* for one or more of the other reasons outlined above—and we suggest that these reasons in some combinations explain the majority of cases of nonrecidivism. On the other hand, there is no doubt that the prison is excellently fit for the functions of providing *physical constraints* for a limited time (not of providing biological constraints; sentences in Norway are not sufficiently long, nor are the prisons sufficiently detrimental to health), of *retribution* by means of the frustrations mentioned and of *social sanitation*. And a study of the relative impact of the pressure groups on the prison authorities and of the authorities' behavior in conflict situations (e.g., when a prisoner is not released [at the time] he should be, even though he may be said to be resocialized and a longer stay may have very detrimental effects) gives us reason to believe that the function of resocialization is given less weight than these other three. However, the presence of the resocialization function on the manifest level serves, in our cultural climate, to justify the presence of the other three (or eleven)—and to make partly latent the culturally difficult function of retribution. Thus, what happens to prisoners in Norwegian prisons is now very often referred to by the prison authorities by means of the eulogism "treatment."

**10. Conclusion.** The structure of the prison is in an uneasy balance between the different functions it is designed to meet. As a prisoner expressed it: "This prison is neither harsh enough to make me repent or to fear it, nor is it good enough to make me accept society." The problem was easier some generations ago, when it was sincerely believed that the same austere treatment could satisfy as diverse functions as retribution and resocialization. But the trend today is toward an increasing belief in rewards as superior to negative sanctions, punishment in a (re)socialization process. And this is the fundamental dilemma: retribution points to negative sanctions, socialization (at least partly) to positive sanctions and conditions under which it is possible for the deviant to internalize a therapeutic attitude without increasing his frustrations.

It is the contention of the present author that society must make a choice between an institution designed for resocialization and an institution designed to meet all or most of the eleven other functions we have examined, and not try to combine them within one set of prison walls. This is not to suggest that the other functions are not important to many people, and some of them perhaps even close to being functional requirements of any society. But the functions do not unambiguously determine the structures, and it is quite conceivable that a sequence of institutions might be the solution, with a division of labor where each institution is allocated one or a few of the various functions, if society wants to retain them. One of these institutions might be designed to meet the resocialization function only, or possibly together with the function of providing physical constraints.

However, how it is possible to avoid the interpretation of any closed institution as a kind of retribution at the present low level of knowledge, ritual and success in resocialization processes, and thus to enter the vicious processes outlined above, is not clear. And it might be that the problem of preventing crime is mostly the problem of working against the *necessary* causes of deviance, and of removing the criminal act from the action-spaces by providing for a rich assortment of functional equivalents, and not the problem of internalizing norms. At this point the recent experience with drug-addicts, who deliberately undertake a cure so that the tolerance level for the drug is sufficiently reduced to make a new "honeymoon" with the drug possible, is sociologically and penologically important. Could it be that internalization of norms against a criminal act could make the act more exciting and be deliberately pursued for this effect? Though some prisoners gave indications that this might be the case, we do not know but suggest that this possibility of a vicious circle be further explored, because it might throw some new light on the subject of treating criminals.

## NOTES

SOURCE: *Social Problems,* VI (fall, 1958), 127–40.
* This paper was read at the Eastern Sociological Society meeting in Philadelphia, April 19–20, 1958. It is a highly condensed version of the author's thesis *"Fengselssamfunnet"* (The Prison Community), in Norwegian, mimeographed, Oslo, 1957 (to be published). I am indebted to Professor Robert K. Merton for many valuable suggestions.
1. Talcott Parsons, *The Social System* (Glencoe, Ill.: The Free Press, 1951), 436.
2. Bruno Bettelheim, "Individual and Mass Behavior in Extreme Situations," in G. E. Swanson, T. M. Newcomb, and E. L. Hartley, editors, *Readings in Social Psychology* (New York: Holt, 1952).
3. Albert K. Cohen, *Delinquent Boys* (Glencoe, Ill.: The Free Press, 1955), 60 f.
4. Lloyd W. McCorkle and Richard Korn, "Resocialization Within Walls," *The Annals of the American Academy of Political and Social Science,* 293 (May 1954), 89 f.
5. Gresham Sykes, *Crime and Society* (New York: Random House, 1956), 105 f.
6. Lloyd W. McCorkle and Richard Korn, *op. cit.,* 93.
7. Lloyd E. Ohlin, *Sociology and the Field of Corrections,* (New York: Russell Sage Foundation, 1956), 35.

# 3

## ACHIEVEMENT OF AN UNSTATED ORGANIZATIONAL GOAL: AN OBSERVATION ON PRISONS

### *Donald R. Cressey†*

It is customary for both sociologists and correctional workers to adopt the viewpoint of society, rather than of the prisoner, when discussing the goals of prisons and other correctional institutions. In general, prisons, like mental hospitals,
are seen as performing an integrative function for society.[1]
Usually, they are said to do this by incapacitating criminals,
thus directly protecting society from them; by punishing them,
thus protecting society both by reinforcing the system's anticriminal values and by deterring potential criminals; and by
reforming them, thus protecting society by restoring social integration.[2] In short, a society assigns *incapacitation, retribution, deterrence,* and *reformation* goals to prisons.

## THE GOALS OF PRISON

The goals of prisons also can be considered from the
viewpoint of the criminal. In the past fifty years America has
witnessed increasing concern for the welfare of prisoners.
Probably on the theoretical ground that confinement behind
bars is sufficient for incapacitation, punitive, and reformation
purposes, efforts have been made to improve sanitary conditions and facilities, medical and health programs, and food.
Also, numerous "amenities," as Reckless calls them,[3] have
been introduced: smoking privileges, radio, movies, sports,

† Donald Cressey is Dean of the College of Letters and Science at
the University of California at Santa Barbara.

and hobbycraft are among these. Moreover, the conception of the criminal has been slowly changing. Under the leadership of "professional" personnel such as social workers and psychiatrists, the conception of the criminal as a bad man or outlaw is giving way to conception of him as a needy or sick person who deserves help. Both these changes are expressions of concern for the welfare of inmates and have led to the assignment of a new goal to prisons—protection of inmates from society. Although criminology textbooks and institutional policy statements are silent regarding this relatively new goal, contemporary prisons are expected both to protect society from inmates and to protect inmates from society.

In the course of a year spent observing the structure and functioning of two prisons,[4] we are able to document such an extension of the protective goal, just as it has been documented in reference to mental hospitals and in the area of probation and parole.[5] This was done by extensive interviews with samples of all categories of employees and a sample of inmates and by firsthand observations of the institutions in action. Although neither institution had an explicit policy regarding protection of inmates, the staffs showed considerable concern for protecting them. This protection took two principal forms.

First, there was concern for protecting inmates from the ostracism, ridicule, exploitation, and even physical attack which they might have experienced had they been left in the free community. Criminals whose cases were well publicized and whose crimes were horrendous were viewed as in most need of such protection, but some interviewees in both prisons said that all prisoners should be protected (a) from exploitation by gangsters, high pressure salesmen, overzealous attorneys, and other individuals; (b) from ministrations of amateur "reformers" or "researchers"; and (c) from observation and ridicule by the morbidly curious. One guard pointed out, for example, that in some states criminal statutes prohibit the "exhibition" of criminals.

Second, over half the interviews in each prison indicated, and personal observation verified, that in both institutions con-

certed effort was made to protect inmates from each other
and from staff members. This included protection from dishonesty, ridicule, and physical harm.

Generally speaking, both institutions efficiently provided the
two kinds of protection. For example, individual inmates were
protected in many ways from individuals who wanted to
"study" them, "reform" them, or use them in some way.
Similarly, inmates were efficiently protected from dishonesty
and physical violence on the part of staff members and other
inmates. Both prisons had rules stating that no employee is
to touch an inmate except to search him or to subdue him
if he attacks another inmate or an employee. Despite popular
beliefs that prison guards and officials are likely to be "brutal"
or "sadistic," no behavior of this kind occurred during the
year of observation. Also, inmates were carefully policed to
ensure that they did not steal from each other or fight with
each other. Crime rates were low in both institutions.

Such similarities between the two prisons indicate that both
are organized, at least unofficially, for the protection of inmates. Even though unstated, this goal is achieved with considerable efficiency. However, some differences were observed
between the two institutions in the kind and amount of protection offered. As we shall show below, inmates in one prison
were more effectively protected from observation by curious
outside groups, while inmates in the other were more effectively protected from ridicule by staff members. These differences are of greater sociological significance than are the
similarities, for their presence illustrates three things of concern to students of social organization: (1) the effect of official
policies on accomplishment of unstated organizational goals,
(2) the effect on organizational behavior of relationships
which must be maintained with authority outside the system,
and (3) the effects on both official and unstated goals of officially substituting informal control mechanisms for formal
ones.

## VARIATIONS IN OFFICIAL POLICY

The two prisons are located in the same state, but their institutional "climates" were quite different. One was characterized by a "relaxed discipline" for inmates and staff alike. The administrators were "professional" persons and viewed inmates as men in need of "treatment" rather than, or in addition to, punishment and close supervision. Generally speaking, guards and other employees were expected to *understand* inmates, to help them with their problems, to avoid being "rigid" or "punitive" and to refer inmates with serious problems to professional personnel for therapy. Thus in this prison, which is for youthful offenders, official emphasis was on the fourth goal which society assigns to prisons: the reformation of criminals. Although the institution's walls, gun towers, bars, locks, and lines of marching inmates revealed official concern for protecting society, the stated policy was to "coordinate all the institution's facilities in a program of individualized treatment."[6]

The other prison housed older but not necessarily more dangerous offenders and its routine was not as "relaxed." Inmates were officially viewed as dangerous and conniving and, accordingly, were expected to obey explicit rules which were stated in advance. The principal duty of guards and other employees was to maintain "discipline" among inmates by enforcing rules. While administrators expressed and implemented concern for rehabilitation and treatment, the institutional routine attempted to ensure that a maximum number of inmates were under close surveillance at all times. Official emphasis was on the first goal which society assigns to prisons: the *incapacitation* of criminals. The official policy of this prison was stated as follows: "First of all, our purpose is protection of society; that is first and foremost."

Although the policy statement of the first prison specifies a single goal, treatment or rehabilitation, and that of the second prison indicates the possibility of multiple goals, it must be emphasized that both statements are expressions of the *priority* to be given to the rehabilitation goal and to the in-capacitation goal. Both institutions had both a rehabilitation and a custodial goal. In the first there was greater official emphasis upon meeting inmates' needs by "individualized treatment" in an effort to reform them.[7] In the second there was more emphasis upon protecting society from inmates. Because the difference is one of emphasis, we have called the first institution a "treatment-*oriented*" prison and the second a "custodially *oriented*" prison.

However, the differences in official policy had important implications for achieving the unstated goal of protecting in-mates. Despite the fact that the treatment-oriented institution had to protect society, the commitment to individualized treat-ment required that inmate deviations within the prison, like criminal acts themselves, be interpreted as a consequence of *inability* to conform rather than as *intentional* and *delib-erate* violation. This view is highly significant, for in our culture when nonconformity is perceived as unintentional the response to it is one of "treatment" or "education," indicating immediate concern for the individual deviant rather than for the society or group disrupted by the deviation.[8] This same response is found in criminal law theory, which exempts from official punishment insane persons and very young children who are viewed as not intending the consequences of their acts, even if they are harmful. The official concern for "treatment" in the treatment-oriented prison, then, necessarily placed emphasis upon inmate welfare and, more generally, upon protection of inmates from conditions which might inter-fere with the "treatment." The trend toward the "professional" view that criminals are sick rather than bad has had as one of its consequences the kind of policy characterizing the treatment-oriented prison and the attendant concern for in-mates rather than, or in addition to, concern for society.[9]

On the other hand, in our culture when deviation is per-ceived as *intentional* or *deliberate* the reaction is punish-ment and/or close surveillance. In the administration of the criminal law, for example, we traditionally have assumed that most deviation is deliberate and, accordingly, a proper sub-ject of punishment or control by force. Our conceptions of justice and civil liberties, in fact, have been constructed on the assumption that both the pain and the close surveillance which ordinarily characterize imprisonment are to be inflicted only on men who *deliberately* violate the law—on men who are "guilty."[10] Since criminals are "guilty," society is more deserving of protection than are prisoners. It is this principle which is emphasized in the custodially oriented prison. Although some inmates are to be "treated" and all are to be handled "humanely," the goal of protecting society from the majority of inmates is the one emphasized in the official policy statement.

The observed difference in official policies was found to be reflected in the degree to which inmates in the two prisons were protected from ridicule and humiliation by outsiders. In the state in question, as in others, a large number of citizens want to tour penal institutions in order to "educate" themselves or, perhaps more realistically, to "amuse" themselves. During the year of observation, inmates at the treatment-oriented prison were more carefully protected from such curious tourists than were those at the custodially oriented prison.

A decade ago almost any individual presenting himself at the gate could "go through" either institution for a small admission fee and tours were conducted almost every hour during the working day. During this period, tours for organized groups also were conducted. The tours for individuals "just passing through town" are no longer permitted in either institution, but organized associations of adults can still arrange in advance for conducted tours.

Such tours are much more frequent at the custodially oriented prison than they are at the treatment-oriented prison. During one month in a recent year over one hundred man-hours were devoted to guiding about one thousand visitors through the custodially oriented institution. Inmates complained about being put on exhibition, guards complained about the threat to security, and the administration found it necessary to maintain in the central lobby a large sign reading "Visitors must not speak to or point out prisoners." In the treatment-oriented prison, on the other hand, groups other than college classes or members of professional organizations somehow related to penology rarely were taken on tours. While nonacademic and nonprofessional groups were not prohibited from touring this prison, they were somehow discouraged from applying for tours.

The official policy statements, thus, had important consequences for accomplishing the unstated goal. The official emphasis upon treatment and the concomitant view that deviation is unintentional meant that inmate welfare, including protection from curious tourists, had to be given high priority, while the official emphasis on protecting society from inmates made this unnecessary.

## VARIATIONS IN RELATIONS WITH OUTSIDERS

The degree to which inmates as a class were protected from the stares of organized tourists also was affected by the kinds of external groups providing each of the prisons with its resources. Unlike most other organizations, a prison's official policies are always determined by various outside groups having direct interests in the institution's operations. The official policies, in turn, have definite implications for the criteria to be used in officially measuring the institution's success.[11] Similarly, achievement of unstated goals, such as protection of inmates, is affected by these external groups. However, most kinds of inmate protection involves only screening them from *individuals,* and it was in reference to these kinds of protection that the two prisons were very similar—protection from unwanted visitors, amateur reformers, exploiters, other inmates, etc. Protection from individuals can be offered and achieved without seriously threatening a prison's alliances with external interest groups. On the other hand, admission or refusal to admit organized groups can affect an institution's "public relations." Accordingly, variations in protecting inmates from curious groups of citizens should be a function of the kinds of external groups making up the principal "publics" of the two prisons.

Since we do not have space for documentation, we can only state that the significant external groups of the custodially oriented institution were police, judges, prosecuting attorneys, and other groups having custodial goals. This prison's "public," thus, was made up principally of groups emphasizing the institution's job of protecting society from criminals. Further, the prison operated according to a conception of public service expressed in a proposed code of ethics for employees and officials of Arlington County, Virginia: "Those holding public office, *as servants of the public,* are not owners of authority but agents of public purposes."[12] This conception of public service views "the public" as a *general* body, somewhat synonymous with society. It also has been expressed by an author who stresses "the utmost importance" of letting "the people decide for themselves what policies and objectives the public service shall have."[13]

If alliances with this kind of "public" are to be maintained, and if this conception of "public service" is to be implemented, a prison's affairs must be on open display and subject to scrutiny by almost all organized groups. "The public," defined in a general sense, should be invited to "see the institution for themselves." Exhibiting inmates to groups, then, is rather coincidental to proving that "the institution has nothing to hide" and to exhibiting an efficient organization for giving "the public" what it wants—protection from criminals, with rehabilitation as a subsidiary goal.

On the other hand, treatment-oriented prisons are likely to maintain alliances with a different public and administrators are likely to hold an alternative conception of "public service." While "the public" and "the taxpayers" may sometimes be considered a general group, it is explicitly recognized that members of this group are not of equal significance to a prison's welfare. "Professional" groups with power to measure "treatment" success and degree of conformity to professional ideology, and to institute personnel and other changes, are more important than the general protectively oriented "public." Consistently, the conception of public service implemented is one holding that government employees must have their own views of their purpose, of policy, and of appropriate means for achieving goals.[14] These views, in the treatment-oriented prison studied, were related to the notion that inmates are to

be professionally "treated," not merely confined. The work of
the prison's staff, then, was considered technical and "professional." The concomitant view was that it is to be judged by
members of the technical or professional groups involved, not
by "the public." Accordingly, professional groups such as psychiatrists and social workers, and technical groups such as
visiting wardens and foremen of prison industries, made up
the significant public of the treatment-oriented prison. This
left evaluation of professional or technical competence in the
hands of professional workers or technicians, not in the hands
of the uninformed taxpayer.[15]

In sum, it appears that the varying practices of the two
prisons in reference to the unstated goal of protecting inmates
from curious tourists were related to differences in dominant
conceptions of public service and, consistently, to differences
in the kinds of groups looked to for support. The treatment-
oriented prison could discourage, or not encourage, tours of
all but professional and technical groups on the ground that
inmates were being treated "professionally" and that tours by
others would interfere with treatment. This could not easily be
done in the custodially oriented prison, which had to look to a
broader "public" for support.


## VARIATIONS IN STRUCTURE

Because the custodially oriented prison's official policy and
relationships with external authority stressed the importance
of protecting society, a maximum number of treatment, educational, and industrial activities were made subservient to
custodial routines. Consistently, guards were expected to follow rules which had been designed to maximize safe custody
of inmates. For example, they were not expected to use "discretion" in deciding whether or not behavior was an infraction
of rules. One rule for guards was as follows: If a new prisoner
violates a minor rule, inform him of the rule and warn him
against future violations. Another rule was: After a "warning"
has been given or when there is other reasonable ground (e.g.,
the offense is a serious one, such as fighting) for believing an

inmate knows the rule, formally report infractions to the central disciplinary court for formal action.[16] Failure of a guard to follow such rules could be a serious offense with dismissal or refusal of a pay raise as its consequence.

Thus, the system of control was formal. Employees were trained to view inmates as dangerous and conniving men from whom society must be protected even at risk of life. They were to maintain social distance between themselves and inmates at all times and, like inmates, were to follow rules which had been specified in advance. These rules were, generally speaking, instructions for "enforcing" rules for inmates. As indicated earlier, the general duty of guards was to "maintain discipline" among men who were, by definition, inferior to them and in need of control. "Enforcing rules" and "maintaining discipline" meant that guards were to report deviations to the central court in a routine way; captains and lieutenants gave demerits to guards who were caught deviating from this formal procedure. In a sense the prison was organized to emphasize inmate inferiority to guards and guard inferiority to officers and administrators. Although some guards occasionally withdrew from this formal system and entered into co-operative alliances with inmates, such behavior did not seem to be as extensive as it was in the institutions observed by McCorkle and Korn, and by Sykes.[17]

Stated in another way, emphasis upon protecting society from inmates led to implementation of a system for controlling men who were feared. Just as a community hires policemen because it fears unapprehended criminals, it maintains prisons in part because it continues to fear these men after they have been apprehended and convicted. Within a prison which emphasizes protecting this outside community, the organizational response is a formal system designed to minimize inmate autonomy and to minimize opportunities for inmate rebellion. To this end, guards and others were trained to be alert to conditions which might stimulate inmate retaliation of either an individual or collective nature. One such condition, administrators believed, was informal relations with inmates. Again, control systems were to be formal and emotionally neutral. For example, even if ridiculing inmates works as a

short-term control measure, in the long run ridiculing men
who are in a system which defines them as bad and dangerous
can only be an irritant leading to individual or collective violence, both of which threaten institutional security. Further,
if controls are formal any inmate hostility might be directed
toward "the system," but informal control by ridicule might
direct hostility toward the ridiculer and thus be personally
dangerous.

At the treatment-oriented institution, on the other hand, employees were expected to view inmates as essentially maladjusted or "sick," as not entirely responsible for their actions,
and as in need of individualized "treatment" rather than, or in
addition to, "discipline." This individualized treatment policy
has definite organizational implications. Most significantly, it
calls for a "relaxed discipline" in which nonprofessional employees assist professional treatment personnel with the task of
treatment. There were two principal conceptions of what
guards, as members of a treatment organization, should do.
First, they were to act as referral agents for the professionally
trained staff. They were to discuss inmates' problems with
them and, in a broad sense, to diagnose surface problems of
adjustment. On the basis of these diagnoses, inmates were to
be referred to the proper professional personnel for clinical
handling. Second, guards were to participate more directly in
treatment. Under the direction of the professional staff they
were to handle inmates' minor emotional problems themselves,
to counsel and encourage inmates to "talk out" their problems,
and to inspire them by personal example.

In either case, guards were expected to be receptive, passive, and relaxed. They were to think for themselves, use discretion in deciding whether an action is a rule violation and
be "professional." Relationships with inmates were to be personal and friendly rather than formal. In their roles as treatment agents, guards were expected informally to give rewards
to inmates showing signs of improvement.

At the same time, however, guards had to function as
guards. While they were relaxing in their relationships with
inmates so as to contribute to rehabilitation, they were to
maintain order and ensure that inmates performed the work

tasks which had to be performed if the institution were to continue operating. Although institutional policy and reference groups stressed inmate welfare, guards were expected to help protect society. Because of this obligation to *guard,* to maintain peaceful routines, and to utilize inmate work crews efficiently, guards could not behave like archetypical treatment agents. They could relax and enter into informal relations with inmates, but they could not give unqualified support to meeting individual inmate needs for a relaxed "therapeutic climate." To do this would jeopardize their effectiveness as protectors of society. At the same time, to give unqualified support to a formal system of custodial control at the expense of therapeutic climate would jeopardize their effectiveness as treatment agents.[18]

The dual role of the inmate—as patient in need of treatment and as prisoner in need of control—thus brought into being a treatment-*oriented* organization in which it was extremely difficult for the guard to behave ideally in respect to the institution's official goal. The presence of the subsidiary goal, repression of inmates, meant that the discretion granted employees so that the organization would be therapeutic was not always used for therapeutic purposes. Rather, official decentralization of decision-making, introduced so that individualized treatment could be effected, had as one of its consequences the decentralization of *punishment.* In this institution, guards and other employees could not routinely refer inmates to a central court for disciplinary action because this would be evidence of "rigidity" and poor treatment practices. Faced, then, with the perceived need for stimulating conformity in a situation in which use of formal control mechanisms was denied them, guards used unofficial rewards and punishments to get the conformity they needed. Inmates occasionally were given duty which was dirty or unpleasant, deprived of recreational privileges or demoted from higher status jobs without ever going to a professional treatment specialist or to a disciplinary court. Probably there were few guards who did not informally use punishments in order to protect the institution and society, even if they subscribed to the notion that inmates should be understood rather than punished.

These variations in the structures of the two prisons were reflected in differences in the degree to which the unstated goal—protection of inmates—was achieved. In contradiction to the direction of the difference in protecting inmates from curious outsiders, protection from ridicule, humiliation, and even physical contact by staff members was more complete at the custodially oriented prison than at the treatment-oriented institution.

While some employees in both prisons probably ridiculed and attempted to humiliate some inmates, this practice was very rare in the custodially oriented prison but occurred occasionally at the treatment-oriented institution. At the former but not the latter all guards were frequently and carefully warned by the chief custodian against "needling" inmates. Further, at the custodially oriented prison guards were discouraged from holding any but very short conversations with inmates. Although they were permitted to talk briefly to inmates who came to them with questions about their work or who came to them for advice on some problem, they were not to engage in friendly or relaxed chats or to "joke" with inmates. One stated rationale for this rule was that friendly conversations and "joking" would lead to ridiculing inmates and this, in turn, might be misunderstood and lead to security problems. The investigator never heard an employee of the custodially oriented prison call an inmate names or otherwise deliberately ridicule him about his presumed low status in either the outside community or the prison.

At the treatment-oriented prison, on the other hand, guards were encouraged to engage in conversations with inmates, and the investigator occasionally heard inmates called "no good punks," "bums" and other names to their faces. One important employee always referred to inmates he didn't like as "rum dumbs," even when they were present. Ordinarily, however, such ridicule as occurred was in the form of "joking" with the youthful inmates about their presumed inability to hold a job or earn a living outside the institution. When courts open for fall terms there always is a sudden increase in the number of men entering prisons. Probably all guards at the treatment-oriented prison recognized this relationship between the operation of the courts and the rise in institutional population but rarely admitted it to inmates. Instead, a new inmate might be greeted with a "joke" going somewhat as follows: "Well, I see that the cold weather has frozen up the garbage cans so you had to come in [come back] to get something to eat." During the summer months the same idea was expressed as follows: "We will have some of your pals in here when the garbage cans begin to freeze up." A man going out on parole in the spring might hear, "Maybe you will make it until fall; the garbage cans are beginning to thaw out." Another theme of ridicule was in reference to sexual prowess. The youthful inmates tended to exaggerate their prior successes with women and a few guards ridiculed them by pointing out their immaturity in sexual matters.

It may be concluded that the lower degree of protection of inmates from ridicule by employees in the treatment-oriented institution was a function of the kind of controls guards were expected to exert. In the custodially oriented prison it was the duty of guards to maximize use of a formal system of control in order to protect society, and this formal system operated in such a way that the unstated goal was efficiently achieved. In the treatment-oriented prison decision-making was decentralized so guards could contribute to inmate rehabilitation, but the consequent informal control mechanisms were sometimes used for the nontherapeutic purpose of protecting the institution and society. The informal control mechanisms included unofficially administered rewards and punishments. Among these were ridicule and humiliation and, generally, the granting or withholding of friendship, affection, and esteem as reward or punishment. Grusky has made this point succinctly and well:

When relationships between members of an organization who are on different authority levels are affectively based, extensive pressures for the legitimized social control functions of the organization to become informalized arises. . . . The boss (or the guard or the attendant) now tends to be compelled to overlook the formal rules when interacting with the worker (or inmate or patient)—the superior-inferior relationship

embedded in the formal norms and in the formal role structure is supplemented by a new friend-to-friend type interpersonal relationship based on informal norms. *When this is
the pattern of interpersonal relationships in the organization
we find that social control then becomes largely dependent on
the deprivation of affection rather than on strong physical
controls.*[19]

The differences in the structures of the two institutions also
were reflected in more extensive physical contact between inmates and employees in the treatment-oriented institution. As
indicated earlier, even the touching of inmates was officially
prohibited in both institutions. In the custodially oriented
prison this rule was interpreted literally and no guard was observed touching an inmate except under the stipulated conditions. In the treatment-oriented institution, however, the rule
was interpreted to mean that an inmate was not to be touched
in connection with *custodial* duties and this interpretation of
the rule was not violated. Although there was no touching in
connection with the "minimal" number of formal relations between custodians and inmates which were present, "horseplay"
involving reciprocal punching and poking between guards and
inmates was common.

"Playing," like "joking," with inmates is a system for granting or withholding affection. In the custodially oriented prison
the formal structure made such behavior unnecessary and it
was considered extremely dangerous. Even the rule against
touching inmates seemed to be based, at least in part, on fear
of attack. Although the "no touching" rule also reflected concern for the dignity of inmates as human beings, direct force
was used much less frequently than seems to be the case in
mental hospitals,[20] probably because of the danger of reciprocity. Employees here did not informally engage in horseplay with inmates because such action might stimulate retaliation and, in the long run, result in failure of the institution to
protect society from criminals. Employees of the treatment-
oriented prison, however, could control inmates by expressing
affection through horseplay and disapproval by refusal to play.

## CONCLUSION

Historical trends and the concern of staff members in the two institutions studied for protecting inmates from the public, from each other, and from the staff indicate that an unstated goal of prisons is the protection of inmates. This unstated goal was efficiently achieved in both institutions, but two principal differences were present. Inmates of the treatment-oriented prison were more carefully protected from the stares of organized groups of tourists than were inmates of the other prison, and inmates of the custodially oriented prison were more carefully protected from ridicule by employees than was the case in the treatment-oriented prison. Analysis of these differences suggests: (1) that an organization's official, formal, policy has important effects even on achievement of unstated, informal, goals, (2) that an organization's arrangements with the larger social system maintaining it both determines and affects the accomplishment of unstated as well as official goals, and (3) that official substitution of informal for formal control mechanisms in an organization does not necessarily produce increased efficiency in accomplishing informal, unstated goals.

## NOTES

SOURCE: *The Pacific Sociological Review,* I (fall 1958), 43–49.
1. See Talcott Parsons, "Suggestions for a Sociological Approach to the Theory of Organizations, II," *Administrative Science Quarterly,* I (September 1956), 225–39.
2. For discussion of these institutional goals, which are sometimes called *functions,* see Edwin H. Sutherland and Donald R. Cressey, *Principles of Criminology,* Fifth Edition, (New York: J. B. Lippincott, 1955), 460–62.
3. Walter C. Reckless, *The Crime Problem,* Second Edition, (New York: Appleton-Century-Crofts, 1955), 572–73.
4. This paper is based on field research conducted between July 1955 and September 1956, when the author was attached to the Center of Education and Research in Corrections, University of Chicago. The results of this research project are now being prepared for early publication and are being integrated with the results of other re-

search conducted at the center during the years 1953–56. The author is greatly indebted to Lloyd E. Ohlin, director of the center, to Donnell M. Pappenfort and Herman Piven, who were research assistants, and to the Russell Sage Foundation, which financed the center.

5. Alfred H. Stanton and Morris S. Schwartz, *The Mental Hospital* (New York: Basic Books, 1954), 48–55, 233–34; Lloyd E. Ohlin, Herman Piven, and Donnell M. Pappenfort, "Major Dilemmas of the Social Worker in Probation and Parole," *National Probation and Parole Association Journal,* 2 (July 1956), 211–25.

6. For discussion of some of the limitations on implementing such a policy, see Donald R. Cressey, "Social Organization of Correctional Institutions" (paper read at the Annual Meetings of the American Sociological Society, 1956); and "Rehabilitation Theory and Reality, II, Organization and Freedom," *California Youth Authority Quarterly,* 10 (summer 1957), 40–47.

7. This theory of rehabilitation is not necessarily correct. See Donald R. Cressey, "Changing Criminals: The Application of the Theory of Differential Association," *American Journal of Sociology,* 61 (September 1955), 116–20; and "Contradictory Theories in Correctional Group Therapy Programs," *Federal Probation,* 18 (June 1954), 20–26.

8. See Alvin W. Gouldner, *Patterns of Industrial Bureaucracy,* (Glencoe: The Free Press, 1954), 159–61, 176–80, 215–19, 232–34.

9. See Donald R. Cressey, "Rehabilitation Theory and Reality, I, The Pain of Restriction," *California Youth Authority Quarterly,* 10 (spring 1957), 6–9.

10. Juvenile court procedures are a noteworthy exception. On the assumption that children's deviant acts are unintentional and indicate a need for the "help" which the juvenile court has to offer, children have been effectively deprived of most constitutional "due process" safeguards, such as the right to an attorney, to confront witnesses, and not be a witness against one's self. See Paul W. Tappan, *Juvenile Delinquency,* (New York: McGraw-Hill, 1949), 204–5.

11. See Lloyd E. Ohlin, "Interest Group Conflict and Correctional Objectives" (paper read at a meeting of the Social Science Research Council Conference Group on Research in Correctional Organization, Princeton, June 1956).

12. O. Glenn Stahl, "Democracy and Public Employee Morality," *Annals of the American Academy of Political and Social Science,* 297 (January 1955), 90–97. Italics not in the original.

13. Gordon R. Clapp, "A Credo for the Public Servant," *Public Personnel Review,* 12 (January 1951), 14. See also Harold J. Laski, "The Limitations of the Expert," *Harper's Monthly Magazine,* 162 (December 1930), 101–10.

14. See Phillip Monypenny, "The Control of Ethical Standards in the Public Service," *Annals of the American Academy of Political and Social Science,* 297 (January 1955), 98–104.

15. Caplow has pointed out that it is characteristic of professions that evaluation of merit is entirely in the hands of professionals, at least in principle. Theodore Caplow, *The Sociology of Work* (Minneapolis: the University of Minnesota Press, 1954), 110.

16. These expectations are not formally listed in any "Rule Book For Employees" but were rules nevertheless. Employees were informed of them in in-service training sessions and in everyday interaction with senior officers.
17. Lloyd W. McCorkle and Richard Korn, "Resocialization Within Walls," *The Annals of the American Academy of Political and Social Science,* 293 (May 1954) 88–98; Gresham M. Sykes, "The Corruption of Authority and Rehabilitation," *Social Forces,* 34 (March 1956), 257–62.
18. See Cressey, "Social Organization of Correctional Institutions," *op. cit.*
19. Oscar Grusky, *Treatment Goals and Organizational Behavior: A Study of an Experimental Prison Camp* (unpublished Ph.D. dissertation, University of Michigan, 1957), 9. Italics not in the original.
20. Stanton and Schwartz, *op. cit.,* 51.

# 4

## CONDITIONS OF SUCCESSFUL
## DEGRADATION CEREMONIES*

### Harold Garfinkel†

Any communicative work between persons, whereby the public identity of an actor is transformed into something looked on as lower in the local scheme of social types, will be called a "status degradation ceremony." Some restrictions on this definition may increase its usefulness. The identities referred to must be "total" identities. That is, these identities must refer to persons as "motivational" types rather than as "behavioral" types,[1] not to what a person may be expected to have done or to do (in Parsons' terms,[2] to his "performances") but to what the group holds to be the ultimate "grounds" or "reasons" for his performance.[3]

The grounds on which a participant achieves what for him is adequate understanding of why he or another acted as he did are not treated by him in a utilitarian manner. Rather, the correctness of an imputation is decided by the participant in accordance with socially valid and institutionally recommended standards of "preference." With reference to these standards, he makes the crucial distinctions between appearances and reality, truth and falsity, triviality and importance, accident and essence, coincidence and cause. Taken together, the grounds, as well as the behavior that the grounds make explicable as the other person's conduct, constitute a person's identity. Together, they constitute the other as a social object. Persons identified by means of the ultimate "reason" for their socially categorized and socially understood behavior will be said to be "totally" identified. The degradation ceremonies

† Harold Garfinkel is a professor in the Department of Sociology at the University of Califorina at Los Angeles.

here discussed are those that are concerned with the alteration of total identities.

It is proposed that only in societies that are completely demoralized will an observer be unable to find such ceremonies, since only in total anomie are the conditions of degradation ceremonies lacking. Max Scheler[4] argued that there is no society that does not provide in the very features of its organization the conditions sufficient for inducing shame. It will be treated here as axiomatic that there is no society whose social structure does not provide, in its routine features, the conditions of identity degradation. Just as the structural conditions of shame are universal to all societies by the very fact of their being organized, so the structural conditions of status degradation are universal to all societies. In this framework the critical question is not whether status degradation occurs or can occur within any given society. Instead, the question is: Starting from any state of a society's organization, what program of communicative tactics will get the work of status degradation done?

First of all, two questions will have to be decided, at least tentatively: *What are we referring to behaviorally when we propose the product of successful degradation work to be a changed total identity?* And *what are we to conceive the work of status degradation to have itself accomplished or to have assumed as the conditions of its success?*

I

Degradation ceremonies fall within the scope of the sociology of moral indignation. Moral indignation is a social affect. Roughly speaking, it is an instance of a class of feelings particular to the more or less organized ways that human beings develop as they live out their lives in one another's company. Shame, guilt, and boredom are further important instances of such affects.

Any affect has its behavioral paradigm. That of shame is found in the withdrawal and covering of the portion of the body that socially defines one's public appearance—promi-

nently, in our society, the eyes and face. The paradigm of
shame is found in the phrases that denote removal of the self
from public view, i.e., removal from the regard of the publicly
identified other: "I could have sunk through the floor; I wanted
to run away and hide; I wanted the earth to open up and
swallow me." The feeling of guilt finds its paradigm in the
behavior of self-abnegation—disgust, the rejection of further
contact with or withdrawal from, and the bodily and symbolic
expulsion of the foreign body, as when we cough, blow, gag,
vomit, spit, etc.

The paradigm of moral indignation is *public* denunciation.
We publicly deliver the curse: "I call upon all men to bear
witness that he is not as he appears but is otherwise and *in
essence*[5] of a lower species."

The social affects serve various functions both for the person as well as for the collectivity. A prominent function of
shame for the person is that of preserving the ego from further onslaughts by withdrawing entirely its contact with the
outside. For the collectivity shame is an "individuator." One
experiences shame in his own time.

Moral indignation serves to effect the ritual destruction of
the person denounced. Unlike shame, which does not bind persons together, moral indignation may reinforce group solidarity. In the market and in politics, a degradation ceremony
must be counted as a secular form of communion. Structur-
ally, a degradation ceremony bears close resemblance to ceremonies of investiture and elevation. How such a ceremony
may bind persons to the collectivity we shall see when we take
up the conditions of a successful denunciation. Our immediate
question concerns the meaning of ritual destruction.

In the statement that moral indignation brings about the
ritual destruction of the person being denounced, destruction
is intended literally. The transformation of identities is the destruction of one social object and the constitution of another.
The transformation does not involve the substitution of one
identity for another, with the terms of the old one loitering
about like the overlooked parts of a fresh assembly, any more
than the woman we see in the department store window that
turns out to be a dummy carries with it the possibilities of a

woman. It is not that the old object has been overhauled; rather it is replaced by another. One declares, *"Now,* it was otherwise in the first place."

The work of the denunciation effects the recasting of the objective character of the perceived other: The other person becomes in the eyes of his condemners literally a different and *new* person. It is not that the new attributes are added to the old "nucleus." He is not changed, he is reconstituted. The former identity, at best, receives the accent of mere appearance. In the social calculus of reality representations and test, the former identity stands as accidental; the new identity is the "basic reality." What he is now is what, "after all," he was all along.[6]

The public denunciation effects such a transformation of essence by substituting another socially validated motivational scheme for that previously used to name and order the performances of the denounced. It is with reference to this substituted, socially validated motivational scheme as the essential grounds, i.e., the *first principles,* that his performances, past, present, and prospective, according to the witnesses, are to be properly and necessarily understood.[7] Through the interpretive work that respects this rule, the denounced person becomes in the eyes of the witnesses a different person.

II

How can one make a good denunciation?[8]

To be successful, the denunciation must redefine the situation of those that are witnesses to the denunciation work. The denouncer, the party to be denounced (let us call him the "perpetrator"), and the thing that is being blamed on the perpetrator (let us call it the "event") must be transformed as follows:[9]

1. Both event and perpetrator must be removed from the realm of their everyday character and be made to stand as "out of the ordinary."

2. Both event and perpetrator must be placed within a scheme of preferences that shows the following properties:

(a) The preferences must not be for event A over event B, but for event of *type* A over event of *type* B. The same typing must be accomplished for the perpetrator. Event and perpetrator must be defined as instances of a uniformity and must be treated as a uniformity throughout the work of the denunciation. The unique, never recurring character of the event or perpetrator should be lost. Similarly, any sense of accident, coincidence, indeterminism, chance, or momentary occurrence must not merely be minimized. Ideally, such measures should be inconceivable; at least they should be made false.

(b) The witnesses must appreciate the characteristics of the typed person and event by referring the type to a dialectical counterpart. Ideally, the witnesses should not be able to contemplate the features of the denounced person without reference to the counterconception, as the profanity of an occurrence or a desire or a character trait, for example, is clarified by the references it bears to its opposite, the sacred. The features of the mad-dog murderer reverse the features of the peaceful citizen. The confessions of the Red can be read to each as the meanings of patriotism. There are many contrasts available, and any aggregate of witnesses this side of a complete war of each against all will have a plethora of such schemata for effecting a "familiar," "natural," "proper" ordering of motives, qualities, and other events.

From such contrasts, the following is to be learned. If the denunciation is to take effect, the scheme must not be one in which the witness is allowed to elect the preferred. Rather, the alternatives must be such that the preferred is morally required. Matters must be so arranged that the validity of his choice, its justification, is maintained by the fact that he makes it.[10] The scheme of alternatives must be such as to place constraints upon his making a selection "for a purpose." Nor will the denunciation succeed if the witness is free to look beyond the fact that he makes the selection for evidence that the correct alternative has been chosen, as, for example, by the test of empirical consequences of the choice. The alternatives must be such that, in "choosing," he takes it for granted and beyond any motive for doubt that not choosing can mean only preference for its opposite.

3. The denouncer must so identify himself to the witnesses that during the denunciation they regard him not as a private but as a publicly known person. He must not portray himself as acting according to his personal, unique experiences. He must rather be regarded as acting in his capacity as a public figure, drawing upon communally entertained and verified experience. He must act as a bona fide participant in the tribal relationships to which the witnesses subscribe. What he says must not be regarded as true for him alone, not even in the sense that it can be regarded by denouncer and witnesses as matters upon which they can become agreed. In no case, except in a most ironical sense, can the convention of true-for-reasonable-men be invoked. What the denouncer says must be regarded by the witnesses as true on the grounds of a socially employed metaphysics whereby witnesses assume that witnesses and denouncer are alike in essence.[11]

4. The denouncer must make the dignity of the suprapersonal values of the tribe salient and accessible to view, and his denunciation must be delivered in their name.

5. The denouncer must arrange to be invested with the right to speak in the name of the ultimate values. The success of the denunciation will be undermined if, for his authority to denounce, the denouncer invokes the personal interests that he may have acquired by virtue of the wrong done to him or someone else. He must rather use the wrong he has suffered as a tribal member to invoke the authority to speak in the name of these ultimate values.

6. The denouncer must get himself so defined by the witnesses that they locate him as a supporter of these values.

7. Not only must the denouncer fix his distance from the person being denounced, but the witnesses must be made to experience their distance from him also.

8. Finally, the denounced person must be ritually separated from a place in the legitimate order, i.e., he must be defined as standing at a place opposed to it. He must be placed "outside," he must be made "strange."

These are the conditions that must be fulfilled for a successful denunciation. If they are absent, the denunciation will fail. Regardless of the situation when the denouncer enters, if he is to succeed in degrading the other man, it is necessary to introduce these features.[12]

Not all degradation ceremonies are carried on in accordance with publicly prescribed and publicly validated measures. Quarrels which seek the humiliation of the opponent through personal invective may achieve degrading on a limited scale. Comparatively few persons at a time enter into this form of communion, few benefit from it, and the fact of participation does not give the witness a definition of the other that is standardized beyond the particular group or scene of its occurrence.

The devices for effecting degradation vary in the feature and effectiveness according to the organization and operation of the system of action in which they occur. In our society the arena of degradation whose product, the redefined person, enjoys the widest transferability between groups has been rationalized, at least as to the institutional measures for carrying it out. The court and its officers have something like a fair monopoly over such ceremonies, and there they have become an occupational routine. This is to be contrasted with degradation undertaken as an immediate kinship and tribal obligation and carried out by those who, unlike our professional degraders in the law courts, acquire both right and obligation to engage in it through being themselves the injured parties or kin to the injured parties.

Factors conditioning the effectiveness of degradation tactics are provided in the organization and operation of the system of action within which the degradation occurs. For example, timing rules that provide for serial or reciprocal "conversations" would have much to do with the kinds of tactics that one might be best advised to use. The tactics advisable for an accused who can answer the charge as soon as it is made are in contrast with those recommended for one who had to wait out the denunciation before replying. Face-to-face contact is a different situation from that wherein the denunciation and reply are conducted by radio and newspaper. Whether the denunciation must be accomplished on a single occasion or is to be carried out over a sequence of "tries," factors like the territorial arrangements and movements of persons at the scene of the denunciation, the numbers of persons involved as accused, degraders, and witnesses, status claims of the contenders, prestige and power allocations among participants, all should influence the outcome.

In short, the factors that condition the success of the work of degradation are those that we point to when we conceive the actions of a number of persons as group-governed. Only some of the more obvious structural variables that may be expected to serve as predictors of the characteristics of denunciatory communicative tactics have been mentioned. They tell us not only how to construct an effective denunciation but also how to render denunciation useless.

## NOTES

SOURCE: *American Journal of Sociology*, LXI (1956), 420–24.
* Acknowledgment is gratefully made to Erving Goffman, National Institute of Mental Health, Bethesda, Maryland, and to Sheldon Messinger, Social Science Research Council predoctoral fellow, University of California, Los Angeles, for criticisms and editorial suggestions.
1. These terms are borrowed from Alfred Schutz, "Common Sense and Scientific Interpretation of Human Action," *Philosophy and Phenomenological Research*, XIV (September 1953).
2. Talcott Parsons and Edward Shils, "Values, Motives and Systems of Action," in Parsons and Shils, editors, *Toward a General Theory of Action* (Cambridge: Harvard University Press, 1951).
3. Cf. the writings of Kenneth Burke, particularly *Permanence and Change* (Los Altos, Calif.: Hermes Publications, 1954), and *A Grammar of Motives* (New York: Prentice-Hall, Inc., 1945).
4. Richard Hays Williams, "Scheler's Contributions to the Sociology of Affective Action, with Special Attention to the Problem of Shame," *Philosophy and Phenomenological Research*, II (March 1942).
5. The man at whose hands a neighbor suffered death becomes a "murderer." The person who passes on information to enemies is really, i.e., "in essence," "in the first place," "all along," "in the final analysis," "originally," an informer.
6. Two themes commonly stand out in the rhetoric of denunciation: (1) the irony between what the denounced appeared to be and what he is seen now really to be where the new motivational scheme is taken as the standard and (2) a re-examination and redefinition of origins of the denounced. For the sociological relevance of the relationship between concerns for essence and concerns for origins see particularly Kenneth Burke, *A Grammar of Motives, op. cit.*
7. While constructions like "substantially a something" or "essentially a something" have been banished from the domain of scientific dis-

course, such constructions have prominent and honored places in the theories of motives, persons, and conduct that are employed in handling the affairs of daily life. Reasons can be given to justify the hypothesis that such constructions may be lost to a group's "terminology of motives" only if the relevance of socially sanctioned theories to practical problems is suspended. This can occur where interpersonal relations are trivial (such as during play) or, more interestingly, under severe demoralization of a system of activities. In such organizational states the frequency of status degradation is low.

8. Because the paper is short, the risk must be run that, as a result of excluding certain considerations, the treated topics may appear exaggerated. It would be desirable, for example, to take account of the multitude of hedges that will be found against false denunciation; of the rights to denounce; of the differential apportionment of these rights, as well as the ways in which a claim, once staked out, may become a vested interest and may tie into the contests for economic and political advantage. Further, there are questions centering around the appropriate arenas of denunciation. For example, in our society the tribal council has fallen into secondary importance; among lay persons the denunciation has given way to the complaint to the authorities.

9. These are the effects that the communicative tactics of the denouncer must be designed to accomplish. Put otherwise, in so far as the denouncer's tactics accomplish the reordering of the definitions of the situation of the witnesses to the denunciatory performances, the denouncer will have succeeded in effecting the transformation of the public identity of his victim. The list of conditions of this degrading effect are the determinants of the effect. Viewed in the scheme of a project to be rationally pursued, they are the adequate means. One would have to choose one's tactics for their efficiency in accomplishing these effects.

10. Cf. Gregory Bateson and Jurgen Ruesch, *Communication: The Social Matrix of Psychiatry* (New York: W. W. Norton & Co., 1951), 212–27.

11. For bona fide members it is not that these are the grounds upon which we are agreed but upon which we are *alike*, consubstantial, in origin the same.

12. Neither of the problems of possible communicative tactics or organizational conditions of their effectiveness has been treated here in systematic fashion. However, the problem of communicative tactics in degradation ceremonies is set in the light of systematically related conceptions. These conceptions may be listed in the following statements:

(1) The definition of the situation of the witnesses (for ease of discourse we shall use the letter S) always bears a time qualification.

(2) The S at $t_2$ is a function of the S at $t_1$. This function is described as an operator that transforms the S at $t_1$.

(3) The operator is conceived as communicative work.

(4) For a successful denunciation, it is required that the S at $t_2$ show specific properties. These have been specified previously.

(5) The task of the denouncer is to alter the S's of the witnesses so that these S's will show the specified properties.

(6) The "rationality" of the denouncer's tactics, i.e., their adequacy as a means for effecting the set of transformations necessary for effecting the identity transformation, is decided by the rule that the organizational and operational properties of the communicative net (the social system) are determinative of the size of the discrepancy between an intended and an actual effect of the communicative work. Put otherwise, the question is not that of the temporal origin of the situation but always and only how it is altered over time. The view is recommended that the definition of the situation at time (2) is a function of the definition at time (1), where this function consists of the communicative work conceived as a set of operations whereby the altered situation at time (1) is the situation at time (2). In strategy terms the function consists of the program of procedures that a denouncer should follow to effect the change of state $S_{t_1}$ to $S_{t_2}$. In this paper $S_{t_1}$ is treated as an unspecified state.

# 5

## SOCIAL CONTROL IN
## THE PRISON*

### *Richard A. Cloward†*

This paper attempts to identify aspects of the relationship
between social control and deviant behavior in the prison, and
particularly to show that systems of social control often generate the very behavior they were intended to avert. Unless
otherwise indicated, such terms as deviant and nonconformist
refer to individuals whose behavior varies from *formal custodial norms.*

## INITIAL PRESSURES TOWARD DEVIANCE:
## STATUS DEGRADATION

From the prisoner's point of view the administration of
criminal justice may be understood as a series of "status degradation ceremonies," which begin at the time of contact with
the police and end with the expiration of one's sentence. These
ceremonies have important consequences for the emergence
of deviant behavior in the prison. Two aspects of the ceremonies are crucial. First, status degradation entails the ritual
destruction of the individual's identity. As Garfinkel observes,
the work of "denunciation effects the recasting of the objective
character of the perceived other person: The other person becomes in the eyes of his condemners literally a different and
*new* person. . . . He is not changed, he is reconstituted. . . .
In the social calculus of reality representations and test, the
former identity stands as accidental; the new identity is the

† Richard Cloward is Professor of Social Work at the New York
School of Social Work, Columbia University.

'basic reality.' What he is now is what, 'after all,' he was all along."[1] Second, the new identity assigned to the individual is always of a lower order in the social scheme; he is defined as having been all along *"in essence of a lower species."*[2]

In a stable society most institutions succeed in converting force into authority. People conform not so much because they must as because they feel they should; that is, most institutions successfully motivate individuals to want to do what they have to do. But this conversion does not take place in the penal environment. Prisoners are less likely to impute legitimacy to the bases of social control in the prison than is typical of persons in other spheres of the society. Having been denounced, degraded, segregated, and confined, many renounce the legitimacy of the invidious definitions to which they are subjected, and thus further pressure toward deviance is created. This socially induced strain toward deviance, above all else, sets the stage for a major problem of social control in the prison.

The acute sense of status degradation that prisoners experience generates powerful pressures to evolve means of restoring status. Principal among the mechanisms that emerge is an inmate culture—a system of social relationships governed by norms that are largely at odds with those espoused by the officials and the conventional society. In other words, prisoners are led to seek from within their own numbers what the outside world so fully withholds: prestige. But a lofty state for some presupposes that the many in lowly states will accord legitimacy to these invidious distinctions; if eminence is to be enjoyed by some, then deference and homage must be secured from the lesser ranks. But deference is not so easily secured, especially in the prison. If, as Veblen said, prestige is always in short supply, it is the more so in the prison because so many are deprived of it. Consequently, these disenchanted individuals are forced into bitterly competitive relationships through which the essential superiority of one or another criminal status over other criminal statuses is asserted. Thus it is hardly surprising to find that the upper echelons of the inmate world come to be occupied by those whose past behavior best symbolizes that which society rejects and who have most fully repudiated institutional norms. For those who succeed in asserting the superiority of their particular criminal status, a sense of worth and dignity is the reward. According to McCorkle and Korn, "Observation suggests that the major problems with which the inmate social system attempts to cope center about the theme of social rejection. In many ways, the inmate social system may be viewed as providing a way of life which enables the inmate to avoid the devastating psychological effects of internalizing and converting social rejection into self-rejection. In effect, it permits the inmate to reject his rejectors."[3]

## FORMAL MECHANISMS OF SOCIAL CONTROL

With the emergence of an inmate system dominated by antisocial norms, the prison comes to be composed of two powerful groups, each of which seeks to secure its interests at the expense of the other. For the custodian, control is the central interest; for the inmate, escape from material and social deprivation. We are here concerned in part with the means by which these conflicting interests are resolved.

The custodian has at his disposal a variety of devices by which he aims to contain the threat posed by the organized inmate system. These devices involve both coercion and inducement, force and incentive. Some of them are relatively ineffective; others, while seemingly effective, are actually a source of further pressure toward deviant behavior.

Force assumes two forms in the prison community: physical violence and segregation. But the use of force is not absolute for, as we shall note, it is limited in a number of ways which hamper efforts to maintain control of the inmate population.

Under the impetus of nineteenth-century penal reform, the use of physical violence has been more or less eliminated as a legitimate technique of social control. Except in cases of riot, assault, escape, and similar crises, the custodian may not (legally, at least) take the life of or otherwise do bodily injury to the prisoner.

Segregation, as a technique of social control employed in human groups, may take at least two forms: expulsion from the group, and relegation to some special status within it. For several reasons neither of these devices is employed successfully in the contemporary prison.

In most organizations the problem of deviance can be partially solved by expulsion, as in an enterprise that utilizes the technique of firing. But this device can hardly be used by the prison custodian. Prisoners have been exiled from the larger society, and their early return to it (through parole or some other form of conditional release) presumably depends on a good record in confinement. If the individual fails to make an adequate adjustment to confinement, accumulated good conduct time may be withdrawn or parole may be denied. Furthermore, if he exhibits extreme deviance (such as assaulting a guard), his confinement may be lengthened by an additional sentence. In other words, the more disruptive the individual's behavior, the longer he is likely to remain within the organization. The custodian must therefore come to terms with him and devise solutions to the control problem within the organization itself. A limited form of expulsion is sometimes employed in penal systems that contain a number of institutions characterized by differences in degree of security (e.g., minimum-, medium-, and maximum-security prisons). An obstreperous individual in a minimum-security institution may be transferred to one of medium or maximum security. When transfer is employed as a control mechanism, however, one institution's solution simply becomes another's dilemma. The deviant cannot be expelled from the system as a whole; somewhere, someone must come to terms with him. Furthermore, there is far less use of the transfer mechanism than might be supposed. "Downgrading" an individual to an institution of greater security is sometimes defined as an administrative "confession of failure." Without inquiring into the organizational sources of this definition, the point is that constant pressure is exerted in penal systems to keep the individual at "the first point of contact"—to solve the problem of control within the institution to which he is initially assigned.

For extreme deviance, solitary confinement is the major formal mechanism of control that is available. Most modern prisons in the United States, however, being constructed on a more or less congregate architectural principle (i.e., barracks and dormitories or open faced, multiperson cells), have limited facilities for solitary confinement. Although these can be used to house nonconformists, some have to be reserved for inmates who exhibit psychotic behavior, and still others, for short-term punishment. There are usually statutory limitations on the length of time that a prisoner can be confined in solitary. For all these reasons there is a tendency to use solitary facilities sparingly and only in cases of extreme deviance. Segregation within the group therefore is not a particularly effective mechanism of social control.[4]

Since what the prison finds itself unable to compel must be induced, mechanisms are employed in modern penology to generate voluntary conformity and to maintain that docility among inmates that force alone cannot secure. In the absence of absolute force, the prisoner must be led to share in the process of social control. Systems of incentives are the devices by which the custodian seeks to elicit voluntary conformity. Modern prisons are characterized by two systems of formal incentives: Those that provide for early release, such as parole and time off for good conduct; and those that make life within walls somewhat more bearable, such as gradations in custody and privilege.

As mechanisms of social control, incentives are used to reduce or eliminate interaction among inmates. In penal life the bulk of proscribed behavior, such as smuggling contraband, is carried on by groups rather than by isolated individuals. Furthermore, the custodian is haunted by the specter of riot, revolt, or mutiny: because such disturbances represent a collective response, interpersonal relations of prisoners (however harmless they may appear superficially) are defined by the custodian as the combustible materials out of which crises spontaneously arise. Direct efforts to suppress the emergence of groups—such as periodic rotation of job assignments, routine shuffling of cellmates, interprison transfers, systems of informers, and the like—are ineffective. It is precisely because the custodian is unable to control inmates by *force* that the emphasis on *voluntary isolation* has come into being. Most of the resources available to the custodian are mobilized to enforce a definition of conformist behavior that above all else enjoins avoidance of interpersonal relations. In an institution studied recently, for example, a typical orientation lecture by the supervisor of prisoners began, *"Men, this institution is packed with guard-house lawyers"*; went on to note that *"You'll get nothing from the other prisoners but trouble"*; and ended with the exhortation, *"Do your own time!"* These same themes were detected in interviews with the more conforming inmates: *"You have to watch out for these other inmates.* They're always messing around and getting into trouble. *If you get mixed up with them you'll get in trouble too.* The best way is to keep to yourself. *I just go my own way."* In other words, "keeping out of trouble" was defined as "keeping away from other inmates"; the two phrases may be interchanged without doing appreciable violence to the meaning of either. And the warning implicit in official statements was inescapable: formal rewards (parole, time off for good conduct, etc.) would presumably be granted only to those who "go their own way," i.e., to those who assiduously abstain from participating in primary group activities.

Custodial exhortations to "go it alone" are one facet of a systematic attempt to restrain solidary relations among prisoners by reducing the frequency and saliency of their interaction. By definition, the model prisoner is the isolated prisoner;[5] but this has not always been true in American penology. The tendency to employ incentives to reduce interaction among inmates arose as other control mechanisms, such as prolonged solitary confinement, were progressively eliminated as standard prison practices. Understanding of the control problems posed for the present-day custodian may be aided, therefore, through review of the historical *relationship between communication and incentives*.

In the congregate system characteristic of early American penology,[6] there were no barriers to communication. Prisoners were confined in common areas with no regard whatever for variations in age, sex, criminal history, or mental status. Shocked by the promiscuity, violence, and organized deviant behavior so prevalent in congregate prisons, reformers moved to institute a *"separate* system." In 1791 at the Walnut Street Prison in Philadelphia—said to be the first penitentiary in the history of man—a small cell house, containing a total of sixteen cells, was erected in the yard. Although the main building remained a congregate prison until it was razed in 1835,[7] in the small building felons were segregated in solitary cells, largely without work, organized recreation, or human interaction. The underlying notion was that men were capable of positive change if conditions favorable to rehabilitation could be created. Most important was means of preventing the contamination of prisoners through social interaction, particularly of the younger and inexperienced prisoner by the older and hardened criminal. In addition, it was expected that a religious conversion would occur during the years of enforced meditation and result in the individual's reformation. In 1798 the Walnut Street Prison cell house was described in these words: "No communication whatever between the prisoners in the different cells can be effected, the walls being so thick as to render the loudest voice perfectly unintelligible."[8]

From these origins the famous Pennsylvania system of penology evolved. Western Penitentiary, at Pittsburgh, and Eastern Penitentiary, at Philadelphia, which were opened in 1826 and 1829 respectively, were founded on the principle of separation. But the very condition of enforced and prolonged isolation led ultimately to the repudiation of the *separate* system as a satisfactory mode of prison life, for it soon became evident that solitary confinement, while effectively reducing inmate interaction, interfered with other objectives. Notable among these was the requirement of hard labor. The separation of prisoners in small cells was incompatible with the development of efficient prison industries, and this led to considerable criticism. Furthermore, the appalling psychological consequences of prolonged solitary confinement generated public dissatisfaction with this feature. Consequently, in this country the Pennsylvania system never gained wide acceptance, although it was adopted as a model for the construction of many European prisons.[9]

In the United States the *congregate but silent,* or Auburn, system came to be the accepted form. This represented a compromise between the separate and congregate systems, for it combined the presumed virtues of solitary confinement during evening hours with the efficiency of communal dining, working, and recreation. The first such prison was occupied in 1821 in Auburn, New York. It contained industrial shops, dining halls, and large recreation yards in addition to individual cells. But whenever and wherever prisoners assembled, strict silence was enforced. A number of procedures were devised to prevent communication in any form: in dining halls, for example, prisoners were seated with their backs toward the center so that each looked only at the backs of others; in movement, the "lock-step" formation was exclusively employed. "Conversation or even simulated communication between the convicts became the epitome of willful behavior and called for summary punishment."[10] Hence these and similar devices, which are remembered as symbols of the now famous "silent system," may be understood as instruments used to suppress interaction among prisoners.

Successive reforms in American penology have all but removed obstacles to diffuse interaction among inmates. The trend in modern penology is toward "cottage," "barracks," and "dormitory" communities. In effect, a historic circle has closed, for in the span of a century the congregate architectural form has been restored to its former position of eminence. Out of this situation comes the contemporary dilemma of social control, for the removal of traditional barriers to communication among inmates opened the way to the emergence of organized deviant groups.

Parallel with the historic revision of prison architecture, a second change in prison life, i.e., the introduction of the use of incentives, was taking place. The basis for introducing incentives was laid early in the nineteenth century. In the words of Maconochie, an English penologist and the originator of the "mark system," a prisoner's liberation should "depend on the subsequent conduct and character evinced by him, rather than on the quality of his original offence."[11] In the United States the philosophy underlying the use of incentives was summarized by Wines and Dwight in a report in 1867 to the legislature of New York: rehabilitation may best be achieved "by placing the prisoner's fate, as far as possible, in his own hands, by enabling him, through industry and good conduct, to raise himself, step by step, to a position of less restraint."[12] This emphasis on flexible rather than rigid sentences has been embodied in three major forms: good time laws, parole, and the indeterminate sentence. The philosophy underlying the movement to institute incentives thus involved a humanitarian interest in penal discipline by inducement rather than coercion.

While the return to congregate architectural forms created conditions favorable to the emergence of organized deviant behavior, the development of incentives offered the custodian a new weapon with which to combat it. Because the custodian has few other instruments of control at his command, he must now define self-imposed isolation as a condition of access to formal rewards. Thus incentives have come to be used to reinforce the extreme custodial emphasis on a role model that entails "going it alone," "doing your own time," and "staying away from the other men." In other words, this use of incentives is an attempt to maintain a functional equivalent of the historic separate and silent systems under modern conditions of relatively free interaction among prisoners.

## INCENTIVES AS SELF-DEFEATING MECHANISMS OF SOCIAL CONTROL

We have tried to illustrate the paramount importance of incentives to rehabilitation and social reintegration in the pattern of penal control primarily because we view these mechanisms as essentially self-defeating. It will be suggested that systems of incentives, although intended to secure conformity, constitute one of the major sources of deviant behavior in the prison. This paradox ensues precisely because many prisoners "take seriously" the admonition to strive for the goals that are held to be available to them: the more fully men internalize an emphasis on these goals, the greater the eventual strain toward deviance. The difficulty arises, as we shall indicate presently, because *the goals to which prisoners are enjoined to aspire are largely unavailable to them.*

## The Goals: Rehabilitation and Social Reintegration

The notions of rehabilitation and social reintegration have always appeared to some extent in the philosophy of American penology, and among other things were a primary influence in the emergence of the penitentiary itself. Although the introduction of various incentives (e.g., the "mark system") was initially justified on the ground that they would be more effective than force in penal discipline, this emphasis was coupled with the further notion that the essential purpose of imprisonment should be reformation. The early use of incentives thus was an effort to secure penal discipline by institutionalizing routes back to the conventional society (e.g., by means of parole) for the well-motivated and deserving.

The development of this philosophy is credited in part to the work of the Quakers, through the Pennsylvania Prison Society, which was formed on May 8, 1787, as The Philadelphia Society for Alleviating the Miseries of Public Prisons. Propagating the doctrine of rehabilitation was among its foremost aims, as its constitution reveals:

When we consider that the obligations of benevolence, which are founded on the precepts and example of the Author of Christianity, are not cancelled by the follies or crimes of our fellow creatures, and when we reflect upon the miseries . . . [of incarceration] it becomes us to extend out compassion to that part of mankind, who are the subjects of these miseries. By the aids of humanity, their undue and illegal sufferings may be prevented . . . and such degrees and modes of punishment be discovered and suggested, as may, instead of continuing habits of vice, *become the means of restoring our fellow creatures to virtue and happiness.*[13]

This philosophy of penology, whose cardinal tenet remains the preparation of the individual for a socially acceptable role upon release from confinement, was explicitly expressed in the famous Declaration of Principles issued by the American Prison Association in 1870. According to Article II of this Declaration, "The treatment of criminals by society is for the protection of society. But since such treatment is directed to the criminal rather than to the crime, *its great object should be his moral regeneration. Hence the supreme aim of prison discipline is the reformation of criminals,* not the infliction of vindictive suffering."[14] This rehabilitative philosophy, whose sources were religious and humanitarian, has recently been buttressed by the rapid diffusion of principles of mental hygiene throughout our culture. The criminal or prisoner, far from being defined as an appropriate object for punishment, is now defined by the penologist as an appropriate object for treatment.

Central to the rehabilitative philosophy is the notion that the prisoner cannot be forced to assume a new identity or to undergo moral regeneration, for the application of negative sanctions will only embitter him the more. Rather, the prisoner should be led to co-operate in his own rehabilitation by virtue of a penal system that offers hope for a new way of life,[15] and that enables him to achieve that way of life.[16] Furthermore, his aspirations together with each forward step along the rehabilitative path must be reinforced by the conferral of a "well-devised and skillfully applied system of rewards for good conduct, industry and attention to learning."[17] In short, those conditions were to be institutionalized, which would ensure lofty aspirations and ways of achieving them as well.

Under the impetus of this philosophy, the modern prison has come to be characterized by all manner of structural mechanisms that presumably facilitate rehabilitation: religious guidance and confession, which have lately been supplanted in part by psychological guidance; vocational guidance and training; organized recreation and other constructive leisure-time activities. These devices are used to orient the prisoner toward socially desirable goals and to provide him with the values, knowledge, and skills required if he is to succeed in

making the treacherous passage from his degraded status
to a higher one.

## Access to Goals: A Problem of Definition

Given this philosophy of individual rehabilitation and social
reintegration, why are prisons characterized internally by so
intense a pressure toward deviant behavior? And why do rates
of recidivism remain so high? It is not because prisoners spurn
socially desirable goals, for quite the reverse is generally true;
most prisoners seek passage from their degraded status to a
socially acceptable one. The answer to these puzzling questions is to be found in the observation, if only implicit, of
the nineteenth-century penal reformers that, once the prisoner has been led to seek socially approved goals ("having
raised him up"), it is then necessary to provide socially approved access to the goals ("the further duty to aid in holding
him up").[18] But here we have the basic dilemma of the
prison: No matter how lofty the goals to which the prisoner aspires and no matter how successfully he acquires the
values, knowledge, and skills he needs to make the transition
to higher status, *the prison cannot make available legitimate
means of access to the goals he has been led to seek;* for his
public identity remains unchanged, even though he may have
undergone a "moral regeneration." The society in which he
seeks to become reintegrated continues to reject him ("once
a con, always a con") and thus perpetuates his inferior status.
Thus the society itself bars access by legitimate means to the
socially approved goals the prisoner has been led to covet.

The way in which the released prisoner is defined constitutes the central problem in parole programs. The process of
reintegration begins with the decision to give the prisoner early
release. This decision signifies that he has acquired the values
and skills prerequisite to successful social reintegration. Yet
conditional release before the expiration of sentence hardly
signifies a readiness on the part of the larger society to permit
the prisoner's reintegration. On the contrary, the invidious
definition that preceded confinement persists despite positive
changes in the prisoner's value orientation and social skills

which may have developed during confinement. The subsequent difficulties faced by parolees need hardly be documented here, for they constitute a central theme in every serious analysis of the administration of criminal justice: upon release, the parolee generally finds that employment opportunities are closed to him, and that interpersonal relations are strained. As social rejection is fully experienced, there ensues that familiar process in which the cumulatively embittered and frustrated individual "returns to crime" in order to escape material and social deprivation.

The high proportion of recidivists found in most penal populations complicates the problem further, for these individuals —most of whom are persuaded that "you can't make it legitimately on the outside"—constitute a potent socializing agent, whose influence eliminates the legitimacy of institutional norms for many first offenders. It is against this socializing force that the custodian mobilizes. In orientation processes he leads incoming prisoners to refer not so much to those who háve failed in the past as to those who have "made it." But the weight of time and numbers (if not of evidence) gives the advantage to the recidivist's portrayal of opportunities, and thus many first offenders are led to perceive that legitimate routes to success goals are closed. Under these conditions intense pressures toward deviance arise within the prison.[19]

From the preceding presentation of a basis for understanding the relationship between social control and deviant behavior in the prison, it should be evident that the position of the contemporary custodian is virtually intolerable. On the one hand, he is responsible for the control and management of large numbers of prisoners, but he has been required by successive reforms to relinquish traditional methods of control. Those now at his disposal are not only inadequate but, it is suggested, in some cases actually contribute to the emergence of deviant behavior within the prison. On the other hand, he is held accountable for the outcome of the prison experience—for the high rates of recidivism which plague correctional administration—but again he has not been provided with means that are adequate for rehabilitative purposes. The custodian cannot alter public definitions of the released prisoner, and it is the postrelease period that is crucial in the rehabilitative process. The custodian, in short, is expected to achieve two major goals, but adequate means to neither have been made available to him. Progressive reforms in penology have only made his dilemma more acute.

The irony of this situation is that the principal method of control now at the disposal of the custodian appears to be self-defeating—to have the unintended consequence of aggravating rather than resolving the problem of managing prisoners. Our hypothesis is that deviance arises in the prison largely in response to discrepancies between aspirations for rehabilitation and expectations of achievement.[20]

## EQUILIBRIUM IN THE PRISON: A HYPOTHESIS

Although the bulk of inmate behavior is characterized by passivity and docility, by defeatism and resignation, there are some prisoners who refuse or are unable to lower their aspirations and to accept their degraded position. Disillusioned and frustrated, they seek means of escaping degradation. They tend to repudiate the invidious definitions imposed on them, to resist the demeaning experiences that are commonplace in confinement, and to reassert their dignity and integrity in the face of debasement. These prisoners pose a major problem for the custodian. To check their defiant, rebellious tendencies, new mechanisms of control are required. The remainder of this paper is concerned with how an equilibrium is produced in this situation.

The fact is that prisons are relatively stable. Even prison riots may not properly be called rebellious movements, for they are essentially conservative rather than revolutionary. Furthermore, the inmate elite—men who have secured a measure of relief from degradation—are not oriented toward revolt: quite the contrary, they espouse a most conservative ideology, stressing maintenance of the *status quo*. It is this adaptive orientation on the part of dissident inmates that accounts for penal stability. Yet it is by no means clear why the dissident ultimately adapt to the existing social structure

instead of striking out against it. What countervailing mechanisms are used to convert rebellious tendencies into adaptive
ones?

We offer the hypothesis that pressures toward disruptive behavior are countered and channelized into adaptive patterns
by providing access to higher status by *illegitimate means.*[21]
In other words, we suggest that the official system accom-
modates to the inmate system in ways that have the consequence of creating *illegitimate opportunity structures.* We
suggest, further, that certain prisoners, as they become upwardly mobile in these structures, tend to become progressively conservative. This ideological conversion takes place
because these individuals develop a vested interest in maintaining the higher positions they have gained. Seeking to entrench their relative advantage over other inmates, they are
anxious to suppress any behavior that might disturb the present arrangements.

The behavior we are describing entails efforts to attain
success goals by illegitimate means. This form of behavior
often arises in other situations when men persist in aspiring
to higher status in circumstances that preclude success by
legitimate means.[22] Adaptations of this kind may vary in two
respects: in terms of the ends sought, such as wealth, power,
or status; and in terms of the means employed, such as force
and violence, or manipulation and fraud. This is not to say
that such behavior ever entails a single end, or that the means
used are ever of a single kind. Nevertheless, dominant emphases may often be detected. Hence it is possible to classify
forms of deviant behavior in terms of both the ends to which
men are oriented and the means they utilize.

Analyses of prison life have identified several different patterns of behavior of the kind that we are describing: (1)
the *merchant* or *peddler* role; (2) the *politician* or *big-shot*
role; and (3) the *real man* or *right guy* role.[23] The *merchant*
seeks access to and control over the distribution of goods
and services; the ends to which he is oriented are material
in nature. He is held in contempt by most of his fellows for
his "self-seeking attitudes," for his predatory, exploitative,
and fraudulent conduct. The *politician* is a figure of power,

commanding a superior position because he manipulates the transmission of information between the official and inmate systems. He obtains access to the control of information by conniving with officials, or by obtaining employment in a location that is strategic because information is available. Although he is feared and shunned, men submit to him because he can reward and punish by giving or withholding vital information. The *right guy,* renowned for his unerring loyalty to the inmate code whatever the personal sacrifice or show of official force, holds a position of immense honor and esteem; he is the charismatic leader of the inmate system. He gains prestige among his fellows largely because he is able to elicit a deferential response from the authorities: because he is capable of mobilizing and employing violence to achieve higher status, they defer to him in order to avert disruptive actions. The occupants of these several roles constitute the elite in respect to material possessions, power, and honor in the prison community. Though differing in specific goals and means, each role may be understood as a form of behavior in which general success goals are sought by illegitimate means.[24]

Although there is general agreement in the literature on the portrayal of these inmate roles, there have been few attempts to identify their sources, to assess their social functions, or to analyze their interrelations. Furthermore, there has been a pronounced tendency to discuss these roles as if they were independent of the official system, unconditioned and uninfluenced by it. In our view, however, the official system plays a vital part in *regulating* the types of inmate roles that emerge, the social functions they serve, and the relationships between them. We turn therefore to consideration of the way in which processes of social accommodation make available illegitimate avenues to goals.

## Structural Accommodation and Deviant Roles

Vast differentials in power are often said to characterize the official and inmate systems; in the former there is said to be a monopoly of power and in the latter, a poverty of power.

Actually, however, official mechanisms of social control are limited, as by scarce facilities for solitary confinement. Limitations on the exercise of power mean that devices must be evolved to secure the voluntary allegiance of inmates. Systems of incentives are one device, but, as we have indicated, limited access to formal rewards tends to produce rather than avert deviance. Limitations on power in the one system therefore compel adaptive or reciprocal adjustments between the two systems. In effect, concessions must be made by the officials to the inmates.

Tolerance of deviance is in some measure a functional requirement of all groups, but especially of large complex structures (such as prisons) because they are composed of so many and heterogeneous elements. Beyond this, a particular structure may exhibit attributes that compel great tolerance of deviance.[25] The inadequacy of means of control coupled with intense pressure toward deviance necessitates the maximum tolerance of deviance in prisons. In the final analysis, stability depends on reciprocal adjustments between the formal and inmate systems, for as prisoners often observe, "Sure, we have to get along with the screws [guards], but they have to get along with us, too."

The focal point of reciprocal adjustment lies, more often than not, with the lower echelon guards. Situated precariously between two powerful groups—superiors and inmates—guards experience the greatest pressure to accede to inmate demands in the interest of maintaining order. The formal means of control at their disposal are not only limited, but various pressures are exerted on them to avoid using what means they have. A guard who faithfully "wrote up" every inmate apprehended in a breach of discipline would soon be confronted by his superiors; if every guard reported every offense, the institution would wallow in the elaborate processes of adjudication and disposition. The question why the guard was unable to control inmates without continually invoking official disciplinary procedures would be raised. Officially, guards are enjoined to report rather than to conceal or to overlook deviant behavior of inmates; but the novice soon learns the informal rule that you "con them, chastise them, coerce them, *but never charge them.*" And throughout all this, the guard would probably detect the inference that he lacked the "forceful" or "commanding" personality required to "lead" men. Criticism of the institutional structure is deflected, and the guard's personality is questioned instead.

As a consequence of limitations on the use of formal mechanisms of control, guards typically resort to various informal patterns of social accommodation. Three major types of structural accommodation to the inmate system can be detected. The first, material accommodation, provides differential access by deviant means to material goods and services; this process paves the way for the *merchant* or *peddler*. The second, power accommodation, provides differential access by deviant means to information and custodial personnel; this prepares the ground for the *fixer* or *politician*. The third, status accommodation, provides differential access to status by deviant means; this results in the emergence of the *real man* or *right guy*. In other words, these patterns of accommodation generate deviant opportunity structures in which prisoners compete for material wealth, power, or status. These possibilities for upward mobility constitute the basic force regulating aggressive, disruptive behavior.

**Material Accommodation and the "Merchant."** Passivity can be secured in part through patterns of material accommodation because inmates, being severely deprived, seek scarce goods and services. To the extent that the custodian controls access to these goods, he is in a strategic position to "bargain" with persons who might otherwise threaten the stability of the system. Differential access to goods and services permits a role adaptation in which the occupant is set against both worlds, inmate and official. This role is governed by a strategy of exploitation, by tactics of force and fraud, coercion and connivance. The *merchant* or *peddler* manipulates and coerces both inmates and officials. By whatever devices available, he tries to overcome the material deprivations of confinement at the expense of others.

The activities of *merchants* vary widely. Some operate gambling games, often "fixed." They manufacture and distribute

pornographic literature, smuggle contraband (food, ciga-
rettes), commit acts of larceny, and the like. Ingenious individuals are even able to manufacture intoxicating liquors on
occasion:

Well, they caught up with me finally. (What happened?) The
Security Officer found some "jack" in the messhall, so they
put four of us on refrigeration [i.e., solitary confinement].
(How was it possible for you to make the stuff?) Well, you
got to make arrangements with the mess sergeant. He gets
the ingredients, and then we're in business. (What was his
percentage?) Well, it's sort of hard to explain. It's one of
those "you do this for me and I'll do this for you" sort of
things. (What do you mean?) Well, look at it this way. The
sergeant has to feed 1,500 men. It don't look good if he goofs.
He wants the job done right. Now we're the ones who do
the work, the cooking and all of that. So the sergeant, he says,
"Okay, you can make a little drink. But see to it that you
get that food on the lines, or the deal's off." (And what did
you do with the "jack"?) Sold it, most of it. There's plenty
of guys that would kick over big for a little drink.[26]

As this excerpt reveals, the activities of the *merchant* bring
him into contact with custodial officials who provide goods or
otherwise co-operate in these proscribed ventures, and with
inmates among whom goods can be marketed. He exploits the
custodial interest in control and the interest of inmates in
escape from material deprivation:

One solution for the deprivations posed by imprisonment lies
in the exploitation of fellow captives by means of manipulation and conniving. Sharp dealings in the exchange of goods
stolen from the supplies of the mess hall, workshops, and
maintenance details; trickery and fraud in gambling; syco-
phancy to secure one's ends; never "giving" but always "sell-
ing"; hoodwinking officials to effect the transfer of another
inmate either to eliminate an unwelcome competitor or to
make a position available for a confederate—all are forms of
a manipulative mode of adjustment to the frustrations of
prison life whereby escape from frustration is bought at the
expense of other prisoners.[27]

*Power Accommodation and the "Politician."* The prison *politicians*, sometimes known as *front-office men* or *big shots*, are generally located in jobs that provide intimate access to files, officials, and other sources of information and services. They may be typists, file clerks, or even janitors. With information obtained in their occupations, they are often able to predict when and where force will fall. Similarly, they form relationships with key custodial personnel and through them are often able to "put in the fix" for an inmate "client." The "fix" can involve a job change or a cell change, as well as special privileges:

> (How did you manage to get your new job in the library?) Well, it wasn't too hard. I knew a guy who worked down in the supply building. It just happens that the Supply Officer is also President of the Classification Board, so I fixed it with this inmate to put in a good word for me with the Supply Officer before the Board met. And that's all there was to it. (Why did your friend do that for you?) Friend, hell. I just said I knew him, but he ain't no friend. (And what did it cost you?) I don't know yet. But you can be sure he'll want a pay-off, and it won't be light.[28]

The *politician* controls the transmission of much information between the systems, as is shown in the following excerpt from an interview with a prisoner:

*Interviewer:* I notice that you finally got that job as chief clerk in the company. You've been working on that for some time, haven't you?

*Prisoner:* Yeah, I got it, and it sure took some doing. But it's worth it. You can make that kind of a job pay off.

*Interviewer:* How do you mean "pay off"?

*Prisoner:* Well, you get a lot of information about things on that job. You see papers, you hear guards talk, you overhear telephone conversations. Sometimes, if something big is cooking, the sergeant passes the word to me. And then I decide who to pass it on to. Like I said, you just know things that other guys don't know, and that means you got an edge on them.

*Interviewer:* You mean by "edge" that you can sort of have things your way with the other inmates?

*Prisoner:* Yeah, sort of like that. You don't have to take no crap off anybody. If a guy gets wise, you can fix him good.

*Interviewer:* How would you go about "fixing" him?

*Prisoner:* It's easy enough. Suppose I hear there's going to be a shakedown. So I pass the word, but not to this guy. He don't know it's coming, so he gets caught hands down with a bunch of crap in his locker. Maybe he gets restricted, or a couple of days in the "hole."

*Interviewer:* How did you manage to get this job?

*Prisoner:* Angles, angles.

*Interviewer:* Give me an example.

*Prisoner:* Well, it's mostly a matter of handling the company sergeant. I been working on him for a long time, and he finally paid off. It's a matter of knowing what a guy wants.

*Interviewer:* And what did the sergeant want that you could supply him with?

*Prisoner:* Information. Like I said, everybody wants information.

*Interviewer:* In the sergeant's case, you mean information about other prisoners.

*Prisoner:* Yeah, something like that. Just a word now and then about a little something that's going on that he don't know about. That's about all it takes.

*Interviewer:* How do the other prisoners feel about that?

*Prisoner:* What does it matter? What they don't know won't hurt them.

*Interviewer:* And what about you? Does it hurt you?

*Prisoner:* Listen, buddy, this ain't no dude ranch. Doing time is no picnic. It's every man for himself. You got to work the angles to survive. If you don't put the finger on a man, he'll put the finger on you. I don't rat out on just any old guy . . . only the ones that got it coming.[29]

As this excerpt suggests, the role of the *politician* arises in response to basic problems of control. Custodial officials are forced to enter into accommodative relationships in order to obtain needed information about deviant activities. Hence a mediating role is created in which the occupant acts as a transmitter of information between the two systems. Power attaches to this role, for by selectively controlling the transmission of information the occupant can reward and punish custodian and inmate alike.[30]

**Status Accommodation and the "Right Guy."** Perhaps the most significant accommodation, and admittedly the most subtle, is in the honorific sphere. Although all prisoners occupy the same objective status, they are differentially defined by officials in accordance with the potential control problems represented. The tendency of the official system to discriminate among various types of role adjustments and to distribute status accordingly is a most important form of accommodation.

Of all facets of the inmate code, none is more crucial than the concept of "rightness."[31] To be "right" carries the highest prestige in the inmate community and commands no little respect from the official community as well. "Rightness" implies bravery, fearlessness, loyalty to peers, avoidance of exploitation, adamant refusal to concede the superiority of the official value system, and repudiation of the notion that the inmate is of a lower order. It consists principally in the reassertion of one's basic integrity, dignity, and worth in an essentially degrading situation, and the exhibition of these personal qualities regardless of any show of force by the official system. Any tendency to weaken in the face of punishment is viewed as an admission of the superiority of official values, and against such admission the inmate system mobilizes. The concept of "rightness" arises, in short, in direct response to the most painful deprivations of confinement: of honor, status, prestige. By this third type of deviant behavior prisoners seek one of the highest social goals—esteem.

Processes of status accommodation are set in motion when a prisoner insists on expressing his sense of personal integrity by defying the officials. Having engaged in an act of conspicuous defiance, he is redefined by both peers and officials. Conspicuous defiance symbolizes allegiance to the inmate value system and warns the officials that a special control problem is about to arise. It is precisely in the handling of this problem that the futility of official force is exposed. The harsher the punishment, the greater the esteem elicited from other inmates.

Because resolutely defiant inmates cannot be contained by formal mechanisms of control, deference has to be given to them. The official system is compelled to tolerate these prisoners in order to minimize their potential for disruptive behavior:

*Prisoner:* . . . so, like I was saying, the guards know when to let well enough alone.

*Interviewer:* You mean it's okay to put the heat on some guys but not on others?

*Prisoner:* Exactly. The guard has to learn who is who. Now, some guys you can rough up, and nobody will care, like the cheese-eaters and squares. But there's other guys you better not put your hands on.

*Interviewer:* But if a guy gets tough, can't the guard slap him in the hole?

*Prisoner:* Listen, there aren't that many cells in the hole. *You can't force these guys . . . you gotta go along with them.* If you don't frig around with them, they won't frig around with you.

*Interviewer:* You mean there's a kind of truce between some inmates and the guards?

*Prisoner:* Exactly.

*Interviewer:* And who are these guys?

*Prisoner:* Well, they go by different names—"jivey," "straight," "right," and things like that. *But it all comes down to one thing. They take no crap off anybody, especially the guards.*[32]

This excerpt suggests that guards deal with rebellious prisoners by deferring to them. Why does official deference yield inmate passivity?

As noted earlier, the highest value of the inmate system centers in the reassertion of individual integrity. Yet how is one to demonstrate independence of the formal system? In part this can be done by overt defiance, by flaunting the rules. However, this is not a very stable mode of adaptation, for aggressive acts evoke aggressive reactions. *A far more desirable way is to force the officials to concede the integrity of one's value position,* and certain inmates orient themselves to precisely this end. They seek a truce with the officials, in which independence of official values can be exhibited with impunity. It is not enough simply to be left alone: the conformist is ignored by the officials, but this is because of *conspicuous conformity* to their values, and for this he is accorded low status in the inmate system. The *right guy,* however, seems to be left alone in spite of *conspicuous deviance* from official values, and this mark of "untouchability" results in high status among his peers. Furthermore, by demonstrating that the official system can be forced to capitulate without continually resorting to violence, he mobilizes sentiment in support of order and docility.[33]

**Structural Accommodation and Social Control.** The way in which patterns of accommodation solve problems of control in the prison may now be specified. Accommodation involves reciprocal expectations and obligations. If either party to the arrangement fails to fulfill his part of the bargain, the relationship is likely to deteriorate and break down. Each exercises power over the other. The guard may punish the inmate leader who fails to meet his obligations, by threatening to withdraw from the relationship and to form a liaison with another inmate. The inmate leader may punish the guard who fails similarly, by mobilizing other prisoners to embarrass him, if not to cast doubt on his ability to carry out his job. Each is captive and captor of the other.

The suggestion that structural accommodation results in stability has two implications: (1) that the custodian somehow intervenes in the process by which inmates obtain elite positions; (2) that upwardly mobile inmates tend to develop a conservative ideology. In other words, accommodative processes result in the development and diffusion of inmate norms that sanction passivity and docility.

**Control of Inmate Succession.** Succession to elite positions does not occur independently of the official system, but rather is conditioned in crucial ways by features of the prison structure. We suggest that accommodative patterns, while involving administrative concessions, nevertheless permit the custodian to influence inmate succession to elite positions.

Because accommodation between guards and inmates is widespread, it is often viewed as the scourge of the prison.[34] From an administrative viewpoint it is useful to refer to the process of accommodation as "corrupt," for it is one of the primary problems in penal management. From a structural viewpoint, however, this connotation may divert attention from the fact that, corrupt or not, the process by which the guard is forced to share power with inmates resolves an otherwise profound problem of control. Furthermore, use of the term "corrupt" should not be construed to mean that the guard relinquishes all semblance of control over inmates or that he is wholly in their power. He is a victim of pressures that compel him to accede to various inmate demands, and to this extent he is a captive of the inmate system, but he is not shorn of power. He resorts to another form of power which, although not always officially sanctioned, is effective—the power to influence inmate succession.

The ability of the guard to intervene in this way stems from two sources. First, the contender for an elite role, if he is to succeed, must elicit a special response from custodial personnel. In the case of the *merchant,* this response takes the form of a willingness, however reluctant, to enter into collusive arrangements of various kinds, including outright participation in contraband operations. Prisoners who are unable to secure such co-operation have little chance of succeeding in this particular role. Similarly, the *right guy* role arises because custodial personnel show a readiness, however reluctant, to confer status selectively on inmates who cannot be controlled by any other method short of force.

Second, although the guard must capitulate to the inmate system, he can exercise some choice as to whom he will capitulate to because there is always a surplus of contenders for elite positions. *The guard, in other words, regulates access to success goals by illegitimate means.* This is reminiscent of Whyte's remark that one function of the police in lower-class neighborhoods is to regulate, rather than to suppress, the rackets. Being unable to contain deviance, police officials accommodate. Yet the accommodation in which they engage enables them to gain a measure of control over illegal activities, for the success of a particular racketeer depends ultimately on the degree of police co-operation and protection (e.g., obtaining advance notice of raids, etc.) which he secures.[35] Similarly, the custodial official exercises a measure of control over deviant behavior in the prison because those who occupy elite roles are dependent on him for similar accommodations, whether honorific, material, or in the sphere of power.

Thus the custodial official brings order to what would otherwise be a chaotic successional process among inmates. Left to their own devices, inmates would doubtless engage in an unending struggle for access to elite roles, a struggle which is frequently characterized by violence even now. This does not mean that the guard has the power to elevate any inmate to an elite position, however. For the *right guy* role, for example, many inmates would be ineligible because they do not exhibit the criteria of "rightness" defined by the inmate code, and hence would not be accorded deference by the inmate population. But the guard does make the final selection among those who qualify for such deference. Succession, in other words, is conditioned by both the formal and inmate systems.

**Conservative Ideology of the Inmate Elite.** Which prisoners who seek elite positions are finally selected? What criteria differentiate successes and failures, those who are to become upwardly mobile and those who are to be relegated to inferior positions? Since we are principally concerned here with tracing the sources and consequences of various patterns of social control, we will not attempt a full answer to these questions but will examine the core criterion of selection: the ideology of the upwardly mobile. Inmate leaders develop two orientations toward other inmates, one tending to limit the use of illegitimate means, and the other tending to limit aggressive, disruptive behavior in the prison population as a whole.

Having succeeded in the struggle for higher status, inmate leaders must protect and consolidate their positions. Because of bitter competition, their supremacy in the inmate organization is inevitably challenged. Upwardly oriented contenders for elite positions continually exert pressure on guards to ne-

gotiate with them, either instead of or in addition to the existing elite. The latter must evolve defenses against these en-
croachments from below. And these defenses, to the extent
that they are effective, limit the emergence of an additional
deviant behavior.

Of the various devices worked out in the inmate society to
preserve leadership positions, none is so important as the control of communication between inmate and custodian. If access to elite positions depends on liaison with strategic custodial officials, then effective control of interaction between them
and potential successors to such positions may prevent the
possibility of displacement from below. Hence, the elite seek
to monopolize processes of communication, thereby counter-
ing efforts by other inmates to establish relations across caste
lines. It is a fact of no little significance that one of the most
universal of inmate norms is summarized in the imperative,
*Never talk to a screw.* The prisoner who violates this norm
is variously labeled a *rat, cheese-eater, squealer,* and the like.
Having once been so defined, the individual is subjected to the
most severe sanctions.

In the literature of penology, the prohibition against communication with custodial officials is generally interpreted as a
mechanism by which the inmate organization seeks to protect
itself against administrative interference—to prevent the authorities from detecting deviant activities. For example, an
individual who inadvertently or otherwise reveals a few bits
of information about the workings of a contraband ring may
upset an intricate network of relationships which has been
painstakingly developed over a long period. There can be no
doubt that the prohibition against cross-caste communication
contributes to the maintenance and protection of deviant activities. The more inmates are able to avoid surveillance by
the authorities, the more they may engage in proscribed
activities.

However, the prohibition against cross-caste communication has another social function of major importance: the protection of inmate leaders against displacement. The successful
*politician,* for example, is not subject to this normative prohibition, but is free to communicate with custodial officials on

many occasions. The justification offered for these contacts is, of course, that their purpose is to further the inmates' interests. Inmates as a whole recognize that this communication is necessary if the formal system is to be manipulated in their behalf. It is less widely recognized that curtailment of their interaction with officials has the consequence of entrenching the elite.[36]

By controlling communication across caste lines, inmate leaders limit the effectiveness of challenges to their positions. If contact with custodial officials is initiated by anticipatory successors, they are quickly defined by other inmates, and especially by the elite, as *rats*. Their activities will be questioned because they do not occupy positions in the inmate structure that justify frequent contacts with custodial officials. At the very minimum, these activities will be viewed as disruptive, and in all likelihood the perpetrators will be suspected of acting in their own interest rather than on behalf of the interests of all. Limits on cross-caste communication thus preserve and perpetuate the status of the inmate elite. And what is functional for the elite is in this case equally functional for the formal system: because pressures toward the use of illegitimate avenues to goals are effectively checked by inmates themselves, this aspect of the control problem is solved for the custodian.[37]

The inmate elite are also anxious to suppress any form of behavior among other inmates that would disrupt prison routines. This orientation develops because the inmate who wishes to retain his advantageous position finds it in his interest to aid in securing custodial objectives. If he cannot effectively counteract disruptive behavior among his peers, the officials may try to depose him and to elevate potentially more influential leaders.

An incident that occurred during my recent research illustrates the role of the elite as agents of social control. One morning a monthly issue of the prison magazine was being readied for distribution, and several hundred copies were soon delivered to strategic points throughout the penal community. In midafternoon an urgent order was telephoned from the office of the supervisor of prisoners to custodial personnel throughout the system: every copy of the magazine was to be confiscated immediately. Despite efforts to prevent disclosure of the reasons for this unusual order, pertinent information was rapidly uncovered and disseminated via the prison grapevine: "Hell, some guy used the Latin word 'niger' in a crossword puzzle and now the whole place is shook up. You'd think we were going to have a race riot over something like that." As a matter of fact, that is precisely what the authorities feared. Every effort was made to preclude the possibility that the otherwise innocent use of this word might precipitate a race riot. The unintended consequence of these "precautionary" measures was, of course, to inform the entire inmate population of the incident and more especially of the way it had been interpreted by the authorities: "They [the other prisoners] all know about it now. If them officers hadn't said anything about it, nobody would have thought about it. But now everyone's talking and the guys are smuggling copies around." The general reaction among prisoners—Negro and white alike —was one of obvious indignation: "How stupid can these officers get? Who gives a damn about a crossword puzzle? Hell, all it means is 'black'. Some guys might get hot under the collar, but they'll cool off . . . and if they don't . . . well, then they get quieted down whether they want to or not."

Through interviews being conducted at the time, it soon became clear that most prisoners were quite anxious to prevent a riot or anything resembling it. This is not to suggest that prisoners of different races enjoyed harmonious relationships, for quite the reverse was often true. But irrespective of general animosities, they generally desired "a quiet joint": "Brother that's all we need, a race riot. Those guards would be all over us. I tell you, the way they [the custodial officials] handled this thing, they darn near did have a riot on their hands." Prisoners were apprehensive not only about disruptive activities of their peers, but also about official behavior that tended to threaten existing arrangements.

Throughout this period of tension, the inmate elite were not idle. According to prisoners who were interviewed at the time, the elite played a vital role in averting a possible riot by "cooling off" impulsive persons who were all too ready to seize on the incident and to create an open conflict:

> It was touch and go for a while there, but the agitators finally quieted down. (You mean they just stopped agitating on their own?) No, the agitators didn't stop by themselves. They were given a little assist, if you know what I mean. (No, I'm not sure that I do. What do you mean?) Well, I mean that the big boys gave them a little nudge, cooled them off, you might say. (What do you mean, the big boys?) I mean the top guys, the right guys. They don't like things to be disturbed and messed up, so they move in any time anything starts to happen and put the damper on it. (How do these guys go about quieting things down?) Oh, they do a number of things. Maybe they'll just kind of circulate around the barracks and talk to people and tell them that this kind of thing will only lead to a lot of trouble for the inmates.[38]

These excerpts indicate that formal and inmate norms "work together" in strategic areas. Deviant behavior in the prison is above all else directed toward *circumventing the rules while leaving them intact*. The authorities view assault on a member of the custodial force as morally improper and prejudicial to discipline. Prisoners, on the other hand, do not generally view assault as morally improper and usually care nothing for discipline. Their behavior derives from a value orientation that stresses calculations of personal advantage, efficiency, or rationality. The inmate who assaults a guard is "fighting the system in the wrong way" and also making it difficult for everyone else. In the same fashion soldiers in combat may "keep going" not because they believe desertion from the front lines is morally reprehensible, but because they do not want "to let the other men down." In either case, the results are identical. This finding led the authors of *The American Soldier* to conclude: "One important general function of the existence of formal sanctions was . . . that when imposed they called into automatic operation informal sanctions, both social and internalized. The existence of these informal sanctions gave the formal sanction much of its force."[39] However, one distinction should be made here. Various materials in

*The American Soldier* imply that primary group norms tended to reinforce a whole range of official values. This contrasts markedly with the penal situation where many official values are repudiated. But with respect to the supreme custodial value —order and stability—there can be little doubt that *at least* this single value is shared by organized deviant groups in the inmate population.

The inmate elite occupy integrating roles. They stand between the inmate system and the formal system, bridging them and binding them together. They mediate and modify the diverse pressures emanating from each system. They bring order to an otherwise strifeful situation. Such functions may be performed because the occupants of elite positions, while "set against" the official value system, nevertheless avoid unnecessary conflict with it. Without these roles, the prison would be characterized by constant internecine warfare between the official and inmate systems, for control and dominance. Hence the inmate elite—because they emphasize accommodation and passivity—are strategic agents of social control. Without their intervention the custodian would have to resort to other and unsavory devices of control; or he might be forced to relinquish control, other than at the walls, to the more aggressive elements in the inmate population. Thus these roles may be viewed as functional for both the official and inmate systems. By exerting pressure on each system, the occupants of these roles secure compromises in the demands of each, and by serving the interests of both systems, they contribute to stability in both. We are led to the conclusion that the inmate elite constitute the single most important source of social control in the prison.[40]

# NOTES

Source: *Theoretical Studies In Social Organization of the Prison*, (New York: Social Science Research Council, Pamphlet #15, 1960), 20–48.
* This paper is part of a larger report based on research conducted recently in a large, permanent Army prison in an eastern state: Richard A. Cloward, "Social Control and Anomie: A Study of a Prison Community," unpublished Ph.D. dissertation, Columbia Uni-

versity (1959). All the data used in this paper are taken from my dissertation.

1. Harold Garfinkel, "Conditions of Successful Degradation Ceremonies," *American Journal of Sociology,* 61 (March 1956), 420–24.
2. *Ibid.,* 421.
3. Lloyd W. McCorkle and Richard Korn, "Resocialization Within Walls," *The Annals* 293 (May 1954), 88.
4. It should be noted that systems of "custody grading" have some effect on the control of prisoners. Most penal institutions are characterized by a system of internal stratification—of custody grades, such as maximum, medium, minimum, and "trustee" or "local parolee." In general, the lowest grade requires that the individual be placed in solitary confinement, and the highest allows him considerable freedom of movement. A most important feature of these internal systems of stratification is that they interfere with social cohesion among inmates. This comes about in at least two ways: (1) Individuals who are motivated to seek higher custody status are under pressure to become isolated because of the prevailing definition of conformity. Upward-oriented individuals are motivated to avoid entangling alliances with their fellows lest they jeopardize the chances of achieving a high position. (2) Those who have achieved higher status become all the more wary of entangling alliances in order to avoid being downgraded in custody. In short, one function of these systems of stratification is to sort inmates into various geographical and socially distinct strata; this reduces interaction and splits the strength of inmate organization.
5. The emphasis on voluntary isolation is not peculiar to the prison, for equivalent pressures are often detected in other systems, such as business and industry.
6. For a general history of American penology, see Harry E. Barnes and Negley K. Teeters, *New Horizons in Criminology* (New York: Prentice-Hall, 1943).
7. Cf. Negley K. Teeters, *The Cradle of the Penitentiary: The Walnut Street Jail at Philadelphia, 1773–1835* (sponsored by the Pennsylvania Prison Society, 1955); Thorsten Sellin, "Philadelphia Prisons of the Eighteenth Century," *Transactions of the American Philosophical Society,* 43 (March 1953), 326–30.
8. Quoted by Barnes and Teeters, *op. cit.,* 493, from the *Philadelphia Monthly Magazine* (February 1798), 100.
9. Barnes and Teeters, *op. cit.,* 540.
10. *Ibid.,* 523.
11. A. Maconochie, *Norfolk Island* (London: John Ollivier, 1848), 3. See also his *The Mark System of Prison Discipline* (London: Mitchell and Son, 1857).
12. F. H. Wines, *Punishment and Reformation* (New York: Thomas Y. Crowell & Co., 1895), 196.
13. Italics ours. For a history of this organization see Negley K. Teeters, *They Were in Prison* (Philadelphia: John C. Winston Co., 1937).
14. Transactions of the National Conference on Penitentiary and Reformatory Discipline at Cincinnati, 1870 (1871), as Revised and Reaffirmed in the *Proceedings of the 60th Annual Congress of the American Prison Association, Louisville, Kentucky, 1930,* 249; italics ours.

15. "Since hope is a more potent agent than fear, *it should be made an ever present force in the minds of prisoners.*" *Ibid.*, Article IV, Declaration of Principles; italics ours.

16. ". . . he must be put into circumstances where he will be able, through his own exertions, to continually better his own condition." *Ibid.*, Article V.

17. *Ibid.*, Article IV.

18. *Ibid.*, Article XXII.

19. One possible implication of this analysis is that pressures toward deviant behavior within the prison might be greatly ameliorated if more attention were given to the problem of creating opportunities for the prisoner to make a successful adjustment following release. Sometimes a prisoner who would otherwise be released on parole is held in confinement simply because he cannot secure in advance a guarantee of employment. The impact of such situations on other prisoners is intense and leads many to withdraw sentiments supporting the legitimacy of custodial norms and goals. Relatively too much attention, in my opinion, is being focused on problems of internal prison management and not nearly enough on the situation after release. As long as prisoners believe that life following release holds little for them, pressures toward deviant behavior in the prison will persist, and recidivist rates will remain high.

20. For a basic exposition of the way in which a marked discrepancy between "culturally prescribed aspirations and socially structured means for realizing them" leads to deviant behavior, see Robert K. Merton, *Social Theory and Social Structure* (Glencoe: Free Press, 1957), 131–60.

21. See Richard A. Cloward, "Illegitimate Means, Anomie, and Deviant Behavior," *American Sociological Review*, 24 (April 1959), 164–76.

22. See Merton, *op. cit.*, especially 141–49.

23. Cf. Gresham M. Sykes and Sheldon Messinger, "The Inmate Social System," *Theoretical Studies in Social Organization of the Prison*, (New York: Social Science Research Council, 1960), 10–11. For one of the first efforts to identify inmate role patterns, see Hans Riemer, "Socialization in the Prison Community," *Proceedings of the American Prison Association, 1937*, 151–55: for the most recent description, Gresham M. Sykes, *The Society of Captives: A Study of a Maximum Security Prison* (Princeton: Princeton University Press, 1958); Norman S. Hayner and Ellis Ash, "The Prisoner Community as a Social Group," *American Sociological Review*, 4 (June 1939), 362–69; and "The Prison as a Community," *ibid.*, 5 (August 1940), 577–83; Clarence Schrag, "Leadership Among Prison Inmates," *ibid.*, 19 (February 1954), 37–42; McCorkle and Korn, *op. cit.*, 88–98.

24. A fourth important role has been noted in the literature, though much less frequently and less clearly. This is a category of behavior exhibited by prisoners who are variously labeled as *heroes, martyrs,* or *screwballs.* These are described as being oriented toward "notoriety," and as declaring their "independence of official sanction by aggression and rebellion." This role has not yet become the focus of systematic analysis. It is not a stable role, but remains latent much of the time because so many forces combine to repress it. Furthermore, the *hero* emerges clearly only during periods of instability—notably during riots, strikes, and other mass demonstra-

tions. And when this role does become manifest, because of its bizarre character it is usually viewed as a form of psychological deviance such as that subsumed under the classification "psychopathic personality." Hence its fundamental sociological significance has rarely been detected. This role is analyzed in Cloward, "Social Control and Anomie," *op. cit.*, Chapter IX. See also Frank E. Hartung and Maurice Floch, "A Social-Psychological Analysis of Prison Riots: An Hypothesis," *Journal of Criminal Law, Criminology and Police Science,* 47 (May–June 1956), 51–57.

25. For a discussion of the relationship between group size and tolerance of deviance, see *The Sociology of Georg Simmel,* Trans., ed. by Kurt H. Wolff (Glencoe: Free Press, 1950), 88 ff.
26. See note 1.
27. Gresham M. Sykes, "Men, Merchants, and Toughs: A Study of Reactions to Imprisonment," *Social Problems* 4 (October 1956), 132–33.
28. See note 1.
29. See note 1.
30. The relationship between power and communication has been analyzed by Richard McCleery, "Power, Communications and the Social Order: A Study of Prison Government," unpublished Ph.D. dissertation, University of North Carolina, 1956; see also Richard McCleery, "Communication Patterns as Bases of Systems of Authority and Power." *Theoretical Studies . . .*
31. Gresham M. Sykes and Sheldon L. Messinger, *op. cit.*
32. See note 1.
33. This suggests a hypothesis regarding the sources of prison riots, namely, that they arise when patterns of official accommodation are disrupted. The sequence may be suggested as follows: a state of equilibrium exists in which various patterns of accommodation are operative; these patterns are disturbed, e.g., by a change in administration or in policy; in the process of relocating power and status, widespread tensions are generated among the inmates; these tensions pyramid until at last a riot is precipitated. The riot is conservative rather than revolutionary; through riots inmates seek to restore the *status quo ante,* i.e., by intimidation and force to restore the antecedent patterns of official accommodation.
34. For one recent analysis of accommodation, see Gresham M. Sykes, "The Corruption of Authority and Rehabilitation," *Social Forces,* 34 (March 1956), 257–62.
35. William F. Whyte, *Street Corner Society: The Social Structure of an Italian Slum,* enlarged ed. (Chicago: University of Chicago Press, 1955), 138.
36. There are discernible differences in the frequency and diffuseness of communication between custodial personnel and the occupants of various inmate roles. It seems clear that *politicians* and *merchants* must continuously interact with their captors; but *right guys* are apparently defined as such precisely because they eschew such interaction. Further evidence is needed to specify these differentials.
37. It should be noted that such limitations on access to illegitimate means generate pressure for another kind of nonconformity, namely, rebellion. Some prisoners, having perceived that access to the conventional opportunity structure is limited, seek to become upwardly mobile within the various deviant opportunity structures, *only to*

*fail again.* On the basis of various data reported in my dissertation (cf. note 1), it appears that individuals who are exposed to "double failure" are much more likely than others to exhibit the overt, aggressive tendencies characteristic of the *hero* or *martyr* role. Extremely aggressive behavior in the prison may thus have its sources in limitations on opportunity in *both* the conventional and deviant spheres.

38. See note 1.
39. Samuel A. Stouffer and others, *The American Soldier: Combat and Its Aftermath, Studies in Social Psychology in World War II*, 2 (Princeton: Princeton University Press, 1949), 114.
40. The point that the inmate elite are agents of social control was made by Hans Riemer two decades ago, *op. cit.*, 151–55. He states that the elite "impose stringent control upon the definitions of proper behavior from other convicts" and in this way secure a modicum of stability. The same point has been made in many later works. However, it is not enough to assert that the elite are a stabilizing influence. One must account for the emergence of their conservative orientation.

# 6

## CORRECTIONAL ADMINISTRATION AND POLITICAL CHANGE*

### Richard McCleery†

This paper will examine a series of events in the administrative history of a correctional agency, and the impact of constitutional change on that agency, as a basis for speaking to the general question posed to participants in this program—"The intellectual significance of administrative experience." In order to avoid the patent impossibility of that charge in its totality, it is necessary to reduce that task by definition and elimination. Risking the loss of implications that might seem vital from another point of view, the definitional fiat of the present paper is this: significance does not lie in the raw material of experience in any case, it lies in the processes of analysis which relate events to some more general, intellectual construct. That is to say, in criticism of a considerable amount of descriptive research, that one does not know what the significance of a case *is* until he knows what it is a case *of*.

Some may properly question the accuracy and completeness of the present paper, for it involves inherently personal elements of selection, but the events themselves are largely matters of public record. The significance of the events turns on the legitimately controversial question of whether certain conflicts reported below should be interpreted as a case of official incompetence, personality conflict, administrative reorganization, or the politics of statehood. In brief, the present analysis rests on an assumption that significance lies in the richness of hypotheses rather than in the wealth of experience.

A second approach to narrowing the present task is to ex-

† Richard McCleery is Director of Curriculum at Kauai Community College, Kauai, Hawaii.

amine and eliminate alternative lines of analysis which might be pursued under the present general assignment. In the course of this examination, fundamental differences among alternative lines of analysis may be clarified. The line of reasoning employed in analysis of a given situation may be extended logically in either of two directions: toward practical administrative recommendations or toward general intellectual significance. Our assignment is the latter, but, by noting the bitterness and conflict so often generated by "practical" recommendations, we may be warned of potential controversies inherent in extending analysis to high levels of abstraction. Perhaps this effort to find significance in our assumptions, rather than in experience, may generate an electric but cleansing academic storm.

A possible approach to the assigned task might be to take the type of analysis implied by the title, "What I have learned about human nature in twenty years of prison work." The potentially rich option of that approach is rejected here because it is not yet supported by an adequate foundation of reflective thought, not because of the contempt it would generate in this company. Certain things should be noted in this connection, however. First, that is the type of analysis often advanced by men with a wealth of administrative experience. Second, such analyses are often treated by the company of scholars with summary contempt—a contempt matched only by the practitioner's response to research of a type implied by such titles as "The relationship of certain personnel techniques to administrative efficiency." There are crucial differences and, perhaps, different values in the two lines of approach.

It is of interest that the reflections of an administrative graybeard on "human nature" are closer to the abandoned, classical heritage of political theory than the calculations of his academic counterpart. Much of classical political thought addressed itself to a search for axiomatic propositions about human behavior. The obvious futility of that search appears only in the effort to cast such propositions in unconditional, universal terms. An essential characteristic of scientific, as opposed to metaphysical, propositions is that they are conditional. Thus Galileo's proposition about falling objects holds only in the unfamiliar condition of a perfect vacuum, and Hobbes' assertions about human nature specify the unfamiliar conditions of that "state of nature" to which they are limited in his analysis. There are times when the patterns of prison life occur in a near vacuum of civilizing traditions and internalized social controls. As the conditions of life approach those prescribed for Hobbes' state of nature, research evidence and the common-sense wisdom of administrative experience combine to support a number of Hobbesian observations about the behavior of men so situated.

We cannot anticipate what condition of human behavior may eventually be taken by political theory as the intellectual equivalent of Galileo's condition of a perfect vacuum for the statement of uniformities. Behavior under conditions of "perfect" panic, perfect rationality, perfect custody, or perfect love might serve equally well as an axiomatic base for analysis of behavior in experienced situations. We may suggest, however, that a final break-through to a science of politics awaits some such conditional propositions. Therein lies a potential significance for what is learned about human nature from twenty years of work under prison conditions, or, for that matter, of work in any standardized, institutional setting. Seen in the light of Rousseau's political theory, significant meaning may be found in the common-sense saying of the traditional prison yard, "You don't have to be a son-of-a-bitch to take a job here; you will make it in six months anyway." Is there as much general significance in typical pieces of contemporary, technical research? Is there any answer to the charge of the experienced official against the academic consultant that, for all his degrees, titles, and statistics, he knows nothing about the prison, the state of the prison, or the prison state?

The conflict between practitioners and academics on concrete practice, so vividly expressed in regard to prison management, exposes the fundamental difference between alternative lines of analysis. The academic consultant sees significance in and bases recommendations on the functional interrelationship of positions at a given point of time. This is the only type of significance developed in most analyses and, indeed, the only type possible in most consulting practices or single-shot research studies. Stripped of their protective jargon, the concrete implications of such an analysis are similar to and little better than the suppressed criticisms of raw recruits. They identify internal contradictions in the logic of events at a moment in time or dysfunctions with regard to the agency's purpose as legally defined. But the operating values in the logic of agency action are never precisely those that are legally defined. Except where senior officials are suitably mystified by the cult of science or coerced by the sanctions of superior authority, they resist the recommendations of such an approach with bitter dedication.

The essential conservativism of senior officials rests on a Burkean perception of the prison as an institution with a past, a present, and a future. It stands on a sense of the functional relationship of states of affairs at different points of time, a feeling for the tensions which enter into maintenance of a moving equilibrium, and the valid insight that any substantial change portends problems of order for the future. When the experienced official is unable to ignore the proposals of the research consultant, he is normally able to negate their force by compromising modifications elsewhere in the administrative system. The administrative resistance which a consultant is often inclined to attribute to stubborn ignorance or perversity is often the product of a more broadly based, if less articulate, theory of the system than his own.

If the general assignment of this program is translated into a search for the implications of administrative experience for a general social science, a relevant criterion becomes that of the capacity of any line of analysis to generate valid predictions. From that standpoint, the ability of the practitioner with his time perspective to anticipate problems implicit in change seems to exceed that of the research consultant with his structural approach. It is this gift which so often permits the senior administrator or politician to frustrate or exploit the predictable recommendations of a consultant to predetermined policy ends. The repeated exploitation of "experts" for politically predetermined ends in the story to follow comes as a painful shock to the ideal of a neutral, scientific competence. An arguable conclusion of this paper is that a structural analysis of an institution at one point in time, uninformed by a theory of institutional change, has only as much general intellectual significance as it has practical consequences.

Having considered various approaches to the search for significance above, the analysis of the case to follow will focus in some measure on three hypotheses which have been advanced in the effort to discover significance in administrative experience:

1. One hypothesis regards the administrative agency as an institutionalized, problem-solving system. Assuming that administration is an effort to control some set of events in order to secure certain desired consequences; action, when based on valid assumptions, should be instrumental to the ends desired. Hence, administrative experience should provide a test of the validity of assumptions being acted on in regulating any state of affairs. For example, the assumption that increased communication between two agency units will enhance co-ordination of their roles with regard to a prescribed end should be subject to empirical verification.

2. A second proposed hypothesis assumes that the design of a regulating agency is related to the nature of the phenomenon being regulated. Hence, an evaluation of administrative experience should provide a means for generating and testing hypotheses about the nature of any set of events being regulated. Applied to the specific context of correctional administration, this hypothesis might imply a capacity to use experience as a basis for distinguishing "incorrigible" and reformable inmates or identifying the characteristics of the incorrigible.

3. A third hypothesis, one guiding much of the formal research on which this paper is based, is of a different character. It regards the correctional agency as an institution and a social system with energies and characteristics of its own, not as a problem-solving system operating at the behest of the state. Hence, for such purposes as the study of relationships between communications and authority, the prison may be considered as a society in microcosm and a source of insights into the nature of power structures in other settings.

The data on which the present analysis is based are drawn from observations, correspondence, conversations, public records, and intermittent periods of intensive study over a period of fifteen years. This extended period of observation is anchored at such points as two years of participant observation of Oahu Prison in 1945–47 and a year of concentrated research on its institutional culture and history in 1954–55. Of equal import to the analysis, however, is a carefully designed research study never executed at all. Earlier study had traced a disruptive process of administrative change to a point in 1955 at which authority had been re-established in a stable pattern extending throughout the structure of the prison community. In 1960, however, that pattern of authority collapsed in an explosive riot, and a study was formulated to explore the deterioration and failure of that system of social control.[1] Execution of that research, desperately sought by the senior, career officials of the prison system, was forbidden by the cabinet official and the governor. All research access to the prison and parole systems was prohibited.

If administrative experience has intellectual implications, it has emotional implications as well. The prohibition of what seemed to be an intellectually significant line of inquiry transformed the author from a detached observer of obscure interactions into an outraged if unwilling participant in a rising political storm. It transformed the research from a manageable, technical study of social process within the prison to an unmanageable inquiry into the complex political context of prison management and into the administrative logic of the decision to deny research. Reconstruction of the pattern of events within the prison in its crisis year of 1960 rests on little more than public testimony, institutional records, and the evidence of forty personal interviews at all administrative levels from the governor to parolees.

Analysis of the larger political context of prison management is a different matter. The hundred or more informants contacted with their varying perceptions of the case do not begin to represent a sample of the facets of the situation. The relevant data are, at once, too extensive and too private to permit even an effort at exhaustive accumulation. Hence, the search for a significant interpretation must take the form of exploring alternative theories in the hope of finding one consistent with a sequence of major events that are matters of public record. The fact of the author's emotional involvement with this case is undeniably evident in the pain and pace of writing these pages. The extent to which that involvement distorts, rather than motivates, the search for significance is a question and a caution submitted to the reader.

The set and sequence of events on which this analysis will focus can be outlined briefly here. A somewhat more extended treatment of background material will follow.

1. In January 1960, the Hawaii Prison System was transferred into a cabinet level Department of Social Services as part of a general reorganization of the executive branch following statehood. The first Departmental directive issued required that all information and press releases were to be sent over the director's desk.

2. Within three months, an employees' union emerged around internal, personnel problems in the prison as a major factor in its administrative situation.

3. This was followed immediately by a brief, sit-down strike by inmates for which no general set of grievances was ever advanced. The strike and a series of escapes extending back to the previous year became the occasion of a press campaign of protest against the prison management.

4. The late spring and early summer were marked by increasing intervention and a public overruling of career prison officials on administrative matters by the director of the department.

5. In July, the career officials drafted an administrative memorandum, later to become a matter of public controversy, to the director, citing instances of cabinet level interference in management and stating that these were bringing matters in the prison to a dangerously explosive state.

6. Immediately after that note, a violent and destructive riot—the first in forty years—erupted in Oahu Prison, and the National Guard was called out to restore order.

7. Shortly thereafter, a highly publicized but professionally unknown "consultant" was employed by the director, without consulting career officials, to study conditions in the prison.

The work of that consultant, assisted by investigators from the Attorney General's office, was issued to the press as a harsh, across-the-board denunciation of the prison staff.

8. Meanwhile, the aborted project for research on the collapse of authority within the prison was drafted on the mainland, cleared with top prison officials, financed by a research grant and, finally, prohibited by the cabinet official.

9. On the release of the consultant's report, the lay Parole Board, an administrative device designed to prevent political invasion of its domain, issued a public attack on the cabinet official for interference in parole and prison management, a defense of the prison staff and program, and a charge of "dictatorship and rising lust for power." This attack made public mention for the first time of the memorandum of July, warning of impending trouble in the prison.

10. After several action-packed days, top officials of the prison system joined members of the Parole Board in open rebellion against the director, charging, among varied particulars, the use of "third degree" methods in seventeen hours of intense, administrative pressure aimed at gaining a repudiation of the July memo. The outraged warden published his earlier memo in full and demanded an impartial study of the prison.

11. An interim committee of the House of Representatives, controlled by the Democrats, scheduled hearings on the matter, but the governor returned from a mainland trip in time to impose a temporary truce on the battle in his administration. By prohibiting all executive officials from testifying to the legislative committee, and by making promises of internal reform which are remembered differently by all conflicting parties, the governor let the air out of the scheduled hearings and regained an initiative to impose his own solution on the problem. The committee heard testimony from the acting chairman of the Parole Board who resigned in order to state his charges, but the issues were never joined and initiatives vanished by an Attorney General's ruling that called its legality into question.

Each of the above events except the second, the rise of the union, was reported in increasingly dramatic, front-page headlines, generating spasms of disorganized public agitation and protest as factors in the logic of further decision-making.

In time the exercise palled on the public, and a further hearing in the next legislative session proved inconclusive. As the waves of public excitement slowly subsided from the explosion, the principal actors left the stage. The advice of the first consultant was adopted after three months with the dismissal of the deputy warden, the superintendent of Oahu Prison. Then, on the basis of recommendations advanced by a second consultant to the cabinet official, the warden was reduced in rank, by-passed in the chain of command, and, eventually, dismissed. Finally, as in the story of the gingham dog and the calico cat, the director was removed by the governor "with regret" on the grounds of a report submitted by a third expert of his own.

Thus the battle ended with no apparent victor left on the field, but the implications of the conflict remain at all levels of the process of government. The balance between custodial and rehabilitative values in prison management, the balance between political and professional roles in administration, and the balance between executive and representative powers in government have been shaped by the conflict around these events. The manner of its resolution has provided precedents for the emerging constitution of the future.

At any point of time in this period, and at any level of the administrative hierarchy, it would have been valid for research to report that authority was at a point of collapse, efficiency was minimal, morale was in a crisis condition, and rebellion was brewing. Further, it would be natural, at least, to fix responsibility for those conditions in legally accountable officials. That, however, is to attribute more force to acts of individual will than formal grants of authority can convey. A more adequate interpretation and significant understanding of these events may be provided by considering them in the perspective of time and in terms of the internal momentum of institutional behavior. Surely this series of events confronts an academic theory of social control with a challenge and an opportunity, for each of the events noted constituted a crisis in the system of government. The background of these crises is sketched below in the organic constitution of the past.

## CONSTITUTIONAL CHANGE IN THE PRISON SYSTEM

In 1946, a new warden of the Hawaii Prison System inherited a prison government dominated by punitive concepts of reform and a purely custodial orientation. Its already obsolete physical plant was, even then, inadequate to the problem of security; and much of the process of social control had been delegated by a corruption of authority not uncommon in institutions of that type. Limited custodial forces and weak security equipment repressed serious disorder by enlisting tough and prison-wise senior inmates in the maintenance of a mutually tolerable *status quo,* gaining such assistance in exchange for privileges and informal authority.

Despite the myths and appearances of equality then, the resulting organization of the inmate community was a steeply graduated hierarchy of power and privilege, dominated by adjusted and confirmed old convicts. One inmate leader of the prison yard in 1946 banked an income of $8000 on the prison's official books entirely from earnings within the institution and was later convicted of income-tax evasion on that amount. That constitution of prison government produced a climate of repression and exploitation analogous to the culture of an extremely authoritarian state and hostile to the logic of moral rehabilitation, but it had obvious advantages and dominant roles for some elements of the prison community. These real advantages of the old system give a continuing appeal to the idea of a return to the "good old days" whenever problems emerge in an effort to operate the prison on different principles.

The new warden and the top-level staff which he recruited to the prison were unfamiliar with and shocked by the detailed processes of its government. Indeed, one of its working principles was that much of the operating detail of the old system should not be known to top officials—a principle familiar on other governmental levels. However, this new and largely inexperienced staff brought habits and expectations to the government of the prison which had devastating consequences for its traditional processes of control.

One of the first major acts of the warden, following futile efforts to be informed of practices within the institution, was to commission a study of the prison. (Perhaps a sign of vitality in any institution is a capacity to identify and resolve problems on the lowest operating level.) Although the report was used in the most generous manner possible, it led to the resignations of several custodial officers on grounds of long continued practices which, while functional in the context, were clearly illegal. The illegality of these shakedowns and sales of privileges was beyond doubt, but they had continued so long as to seem normal, and the dismissals remained a long-standing basis of discontent in the custodial ranks.

The suppression of these corrupt practices removed several crucial incentives from the processes of control. That, in turn, increased the burden on the punitive portion of the control system—the portion which consisted of repression, arbitrary force, and fear. However, at that juncture, the inexperienced staff formed a disciplinary committee to increase the quality of fairness and judicial concern for the rights of individuals in the process of punishment. This change decreased the arbitrary aspects of control through force—the "reign of terror" quality of previous sanctions which had made the security of the institution the highest law. Whatever their moral merits, the removal of corruption and the reduction of arbitrariness as methods of control had disturbing consequences. Institutional records show evidence of a widespread disorganization in the inmate community following a loss of status on the part of its old-convict leaders. Increases in the guard force and its training and strengthening of the physical plant were not sufficient to offset a wave of escape, violence, and internal tension at that time. Only the insulation from popular protest provided by territorial government and the grace period in which new officials are allowed to blame their mistakes on their predecessors permitted the survival of the reform group in the prison.

The impact of these early changes, by itself, illustrates certain conclusions which seem to have general import. *First,* the organizational structure of the institution is a complex of human energies and traditional roles in delicate balance, and ill-considered efforts to tamper with that balance are apt to release explosive results. *Second,* even in the authoritarian regime of the traditional prison—perhaps, especially there—a large part of the processes of social control were informal and internalized in the inmate body. The bulk of those coercing definitions which governed inmate behavior were communicated through their own peers and fears. Hence, the *third* conclusion is that control over inmates lies less in the steel and concrete in which their energy is confined than in the direction which is given to that energy. If that is true of inmates, it is even more true of employees and the limited force of administrative sanctions. During the past fifteen years, there have been three waves of tension, violence, and escape at Oahu Prison; and these bear almost no relation to the number of guns, guards, or security facilities available there.

**A New Direction:**   The early period of change and its consequences fixed conclusions of a different type in the minds of the now more experienced prison officials. Since corruption and terror seemed to be inevitable components of the old, authoritarian regime, they resolved that its punitive concepts had to be replaced with an entirely new philosophy and constitution of prison management. By 1950, the core of that philosophy had emerged from the values of the professional staff, and the direction of prison government began to take a revolutionary turn in contrast to the earlier phase of reform.

An attempt to summarize that revolution tends to deteriorate into cliches: rehabilitation instead of repression, leadership in place of dictatorship. It involved an effort to create an atmosphere within the institution which corresponded as far as possible with elements of the free society, and it encouraged the practice of responsible citizenship in place of the authoritarian submission which had prevailed. It included an effort to enlist the initiative and will of the inmates in the task of creating a healthy institution, in contrast with the repression of their initiative before. Finally, it involved the provision of institutional means to those ends which were quite out of character with the ways of life in the old prison.

The political circumstances of an appointive governor in the territory provided the conditions for such an administrative revolution. In the absence of an elective contest for the governor's post, there was little need to mobilize the resources of bureaucracy for political ends and the party in control of the executive branch had relatively little stake in the internal operations of the agency. Although the appointive governors in the past have been responsive to major political and economic forces in the territory, the absence of direct political responsibility permitted the executive to act as a buffer between bureaucrats and the mass public. Thus in the absence of political channels for transmission of unsophisticated popular protests or motives for mobilizing those, experimentation in prison government by career officials was possible to an unusual degree. The old Department of Institutions, an agency incorporating diverse functions, placed responsibility and permitted freedom for the governing of its several divisions in the professional division heads. This permitted officials to execute a thoroughgoing revolution in prison management from 1949 to 1953 with enough sensitivity to the social consequences to moderate the shock of sudden change. In addition, this condition of a comparative political vacuum served to allow the conduct of intensive research and study of the prison community as a relatively self-contained interactional system or society in microcosm.

Although the Inmate Council and its committees, the industrial and education programs, and other devices for appealing to the initiative of the inmates in redirecting their lives had a dramatic, cumulative impact on the prison community, it was a false assumption of the program and research on it that the resulting social reorganization would be immediate and direct. In fact, change was mediated through a redefinition of social roles far more complex than expected, and a new order emerged only after a period of prolonged and intense social disorganization. As the differences between the old punitive and the new treatment-oriented direction went to all aspects of prison life, they sharply altered the role and status of elements in prison society and produced bitter periods of tension and conflict.

From a purely legal standpoint, the revolution in the prison would seem to have been completed when the professional staff published a new policy manual as the constitution of prison government. In fact, however, the revolution had barely begun. The direction of energies within the prison community was still governed in large part by habit and the roles which had been communicated in the past, and the patterns of communication through which controlling definitions were transmitted remained a monopoly of custodial officers and senior inmates. The incentives and a wider range of activity which came with new programs were employed by the custodial force to gain conformity and exploited by old inmates to restore their status in place of the privileges lost with the passing of corruption. The means by which the "word" was communicated to the inmate body insured that the word would remain what it had been in the past: "Do your own time and never talk to a screw."

A matter of pride in the old inmate community was its ability to resolve its own internal conflicts in its own ways. There was substantial truth in the inmate claim, "The cons run the joint." However, the cons ran it in a way consistent with the dominant custodial values of peace and order. The hatred and contempt for "rats" which was shared by the guard force and inmate society rested on a valid sense of the fact that open communication constituted a serious threat to the traditional social order of the institution. As long as the extended freedom of movement and contact provided by new programs were exploited to reinforce the traditional order of the institution, escape and internal conflict remained minimal. Official sanctions, while harsh and arbitrary in the old prison, had been relatively infrequent as the inmates retained initial responsibility for internal social control. While that old order prevailed, the security record of the prison in 1951 and 1952 was the finest established in many years, and the incorrigible unit remained closed for an extended period. The group of men released in 1953, however, made the poorest record of parole success of any group released in many years. As long as new activities were exploited for status by hardened, prison-wise old cons, they accomplished nothing of their intended rehabilitative purpose. In that period of internal peace and good will, it was only the treatment staff and its newly created programs in the industrial area that were moving in a new direction.

Arbitrariness in the management of the old prison had given experienced inmates an advantage in their ability to predict and explain the events of that hostile and mysterious environment. Using a "devil theory" to explain every unfortunate event as the work of "rats," old cons, like a primitive priesthood, based much of their status on an ability to provide coherent and psychologically satisfying explanations of official action. By focusing the characteristic hatreds and hostilities of the inmates on nonconforming individuals, these leaders were equipped with a powerful instrument of social control. The reduction of arbitrariness and secrecy in management and an enlargement of the range of functions and contacts open to inmates undercut the old leaders and permitted a new leadership to emerge which violated the traditional expectations of inmate culture.

Gradually, the newly created patterns of prison life began to have an effect. The attitudes of fairness and frankness maintained by the staff, the more judicial disciplinary procedures, and the provision of means for co-operative activity gave rise to a more open and complex pattern of life in inmate society. Those patterns and the lines of communication implicit in them began to focus in the treatment unit and to by-pass the monopoly of communication once enjoyed by the custodial force. Treatment officials grasped the initiative at the staff level in the definition of policy and assumed an increasing responsibility for the manipulation of incentives, using these to reward self-improvement rather than simply adjustment in the prison. A counterelite to custodial officers at the official level and to inmate leaders in the yard began to emerge.

**The Crisis Barrier:** By 1953, inmate society was being led in two contradictory directions by competing forces within both staff and inmate groups, and the era of good will was replaced by one of confusion and violence. On the guard force, the oldest employees continued in the traditional direction out

of a studied ignorance of new policy directives, from the in-
ertia of intrenched habit and with a moral conviction that the
new ways of dealing with criminals were improper and
dysfunctional for the prison's legitimate ends. They were
joined in these positions by senior inmates whose overt contacts with the old guard indicated how the old myths of the
inmate culture had been tarnished. As the professional staff,
plus a growing number of inmates, moved in the direction
outlined by new policy, each day widened a split, weakened
communication of controlling definitions, and intensified a
competition for authority until authority failed entirely. Although the leadership of both factions at all levels seems to
have been responsible and sincere, the conflict, counter-
charges, and simple failure to be authoritative in the face of
uncertainty cost each leadership control over irresponsible
subordinates. A few custodial officers engaged in overt sabo-
tage of the new program, and bands of reckless young inmates went out of control as they saw chances to take advantage of divisions of authority with exploitation and violence.

The resulting period of internal violence and escape (escape is often a response to intolerable conditions) demonstrated that the inmate community had lost its capacity to
resolve conflicts internally with its own resources. An inability
of management to cope with the crisis through standard security measures indicates a similar weakness in the administration. Every failure of security equipped an honestly disgruntled
guard force with charges against the professional staff and
increased its belief in the virtues of the "good old days."
Finally convinced that there was no way to gain their point
within the administrative processes of the prison system, now
dominated by the professional orientation of the treatment
staff, the "old guard" sought external support from political
forces and found this from groups legitimately concerned with
the security situation as well as from others seeking an issue
to exploit. A legislative hearing in 1953 aired the complaints
of disgruntled guards and inmates and, by giving authoritative
expression to those views, brought the condition of the prison
to a state of utter turmoil. (While the present paper is not
prepared to speak to this point with confidence, it is suggested

that prison life in those circumstances approximates Hobbes' state of nature and permits empirical verification of certain of his propositions. It may be hypothesized that the prison riot and, perhaps, a considerable amount of mob behavior reflects a quest for certainty and a demand for some controlling definition of a confused situation. It may be less a rebellion against authority than a demand for it.)

The challenge to the complex structure of authority within the prison left formal sanctions meaningless and required that conflicts be resolved by force at all levels. As legislative hearings continued, tensions increased until rival factions within the prison yard armed themselves for mob action. At one point, the staff was forced to mount a machine gun on the cell block roof to forestall an impending riot. With the collapse of those social controls inherent in habit, traditional role definitions and social structure, control of the prison was reduced to a dependence on naked force and physical equipment which is never enough.

This challenge to the administration, however, required the staff and the warden to take a high degree of initiative in the face of anarchy. It forced them to express and communicate the direction of the prison in terms so clear as to remove confusion for both the legislative and the inmate body. It forced the staff to define and reinforce its role in the prison community in a way which established its leadership and mobilized inmate commitment to the new goals. In the course of those activities, the staff established communication patterns in the institution which had a continuing force in transmitting definitions of the situation. While complex and multipurposed, a crucial aspect of those communication patterns lay in the fact that they served to identify problems early and to raise them quickly to a level for authoritative resolution. Without the support of such communication patterns, the nominal authority of position was meaningless.

By the time the legislative committee had considered the evidence, endorsed the new direction of the prison, and rejected the claims for the old, the crisis of social control had been met internally and the prison was moving coherently on its new course. In the two years that followed, escape and

serious internal disorder declined again to negligible proportions and a perceptibly different social order emerged.

A number of mainland prisons attempted a transition to
the treatment emphasis in the years after World War II, but
a "crisis barrier" normally stopped those transitions short of
effectiveness. Over fifty major riots swept mainland institutions in the period from 1950 to 1953, and the most common result was to generate political protest, reverse the transition in an emphasis on greater physical "security," and return
to the safe, traditional, custodial system. "Rehabilitation" in
many of those institutions was reduced to a morale-building
function or to a sign on a door for public relations purposes.
The inmates who enjoyed the greatest stake in the old prison
had a capacity to ensure the continuance of the traditional
system by creating disturbances in the face of change and
generating demands for a return to the custodial emphasis.
By successfully passing through its period of crisis without a
destructive riot and by successfully resisting ill-articulated demands for reaction, Oahu Prison became one of the few such
institutions in America to make its revolution, for a time, a
meaningful and accomplished fact.

Study of the crisis within the prison generates conclusions
which go beyond prison to social institutions of other types.
*First,* the direction of human energies involves more than
the giving of formal orders and commands; it involves the
whole complex of processes by which roles are defined and
definitions are communicated within the group. *Second,* because the giving of direction is so deeply interwoven with the
whole system of social control, any effective change in the
direction of an agency has seriously disorganizing consequences. *Third,* when patterns of communication fail to cor-
respond to the structure of authority, a group is unable to
resolve its problems internally and conditions of conflict
emerge. It is natural for elements defeated in such conflicts
to seek aid outside the system, and only the morale reflected
in a binding institutional code prohibits such recourse in normal conditions. If external political forces are sought out by
discontented elements within the prison, and such forces take
the initiative from its officials in resolving internal problems,

the institutional structure of authority breaks down. Because the prison contains elements anxious to exploit any weakness of authority, it is vital that prison officials retain the initiative in resolving internal conflicts.

When a year of intensive research was focused on Oahu Prison in 1954 and 1955, its management, its security record, and its climate for rehabilitation were exceptionally sound. There were problems, for a prison is essentially a wall built around problems, but the disaffected elements which remained at all levels seemed resigned to the main emphasis of the institution and had ceased to play a dominant role in its social life. The prison at that time was subject to congratulation by many observers on a number of its records and qualities, but two distinguishing characteristics stood out on examination.

1. In contrast with normal attitudes of extreme defensiveness in prison officials, the Oahu Prison staff maintained an exceptional ability to recognize problems, to accept a joint responsibility for those problems, and to concentrate its resources on their solution. The ability to accept and profit from criticism was illustrated by a regular use of research and professional assistance.

2. In even more striking contrast with similar institutions elsewhere, the prison had displaced the traditional dominance of inmate society by crime-hardened recidivists and achieved a social climate favorable to co-operation and a high level of treatment activity based on voluntary participation.

By the end of 1955, a combination of active official leadership and constructive social pressure within the institutional community permitted the closing of the incorrigible unit again and a general reduction in the use of severe sanctions to coerce discipline.

**The Recent Conflicts:** Despite the prohibition of direct observation in the prison, institutional records and the full co-operation of many persons connected with the institution permit the recent conflicts in the prison to be viewed in a broader context of time and social process. That analysis provides a base from which to examine several hypotheses advanced to account for conflicts ranging from the prison riot to the insubordination of the prison's top officials.

The first of these hypotheses, that advanced by the director's consultants, attributes the series of disturbances to the drastic incompetence of the prison's career officials. The officials were charged with willful neglect of dangerously inadequate security measures and derelictions ranging across the width of the organization chart. A considerable accumulation of evidence—the growing incorrigible population, labor problems, the inmate strike and riot, and the open break with the director—demonstrates the failure of the career officials to resolve their problems with their own administrative resources in that period. Security measures were inadequate to contain the rising tensions within the institution. The predictable reaction of temporary consultants was to place responsibility squarely on the prison officials. That is, it was to reject the officials and, in the language of our first, more general hypothesis, to reject the assumptions on which the officials acted in the administrative process. However, this explanation seems inadequate to observers and employees who have watched the prison's record of progress over the years and seen it successfully break through the crisis barrier of its own administrative revolution. Viewed in the larger perspective of time, it seems necessary to concede some loss in the capacity of the prison staff to see and resolve internal problems, but it is also necessary to note differences in the nature of the problems faced and the manner in which they were posed.

On the side of the prison's failing administrative capacity, it is evident that the momentum and initiative which carried the staff through its early crisis period had declined in a later stage of consolidation. A decline in the vigor of staff leadership tended to resign initiative for the definition of the situation to custodial personnel—less eloquent or dedicated advocates of the new regime at best. Every three years, a majority of the inmate population is replaced by normal turnover, and new arrivals reach the prison with traditional expectations of its governing principle. Hence, controlling definitions of the situation must be transmitted effectively and continuously, and this accounts for the normal abdication of that function to old convicts. In recent years in Oahu Prison, traditional definitions and a hard core of older inhabitants regained some of their lost influence while inmate leaders with a commitment to the rehabilitative ideal lost in status and in their capacity to resolve conflicts in their society. This marks a weakening of forceful, official leadership. Gradually increasing failures in security and more frequent appeals to repressive force by inmates and officials indicate that leadership was failing to reach an expanding part of the prison population. This evidence, as always, supplied arguments for those who continued to favor the traditional, punitive approach. But the staff, confident that its record was sound and its revolution essentially secure, failed to recognize many of its problems and met others with explanations rather than solutions.

In this connection, as well as in conjunction with explanations which account for the conflict in terms of personality clashes, the role of one individual must be noted. The man who rose through the treatment ranks to the post of superintendent of Oahu Prison by 1955 was, as a subordinate, the most effective advocate of communication patterns which identified and resolved the problems of the institution. In his role of superintendent, however, he gradually became less receptive to the transmission of problems from below, limited the access of subordinates to the warden, and permitted the atrophy of various channels of communication which had marked the administration in its most vigorous phase. It is clear that discontent generated by unresolved problems was accumulating in the prison prior to the act transferring it into the Department of Social Services. It is not clear that management failures account for the intensity of the problems which followed.

During this time, the achievement of statehood placed the problems of the prison in a vastly more mature and different political context. Many of these differences are illustrated by a contrast between the processing of problems in 1960 and the handling of those in the crisis conditions of 1953. The territorial era, in which career officials could control the manner in which problems were presented and the means of their solution, was gone. The politics of statehood supplemented internal channels of communication with outside groups ready to seize on discontent and exploit that for political purposes. One of the political consequences of statehood and the nature of the governing coalition which resulted when labor threw its support to the Republican governor was to permit a union to represent the grievances of custodial employees in the prison. Although established just prior to 1960 in the institution, the union had few members and less influence until the Prison System was transferred into the Department of Social Services. After that time, it became a vital, if little noticed, factor in the series of emerging conflicts.

The prison officials resisted this external processing of institutional problems through the union on principle even after reorganization went into effect. Their refusal to confront the fact of the union, and the fact that union members enjoyed an advantage over them in direct, personal access to the cabinet level, betrayed a certain wooden-headed intransigence on the part of otherwise competent officials in the face of a vastly changed administrative and political situation. A series of private interviews with union guards supplied the director with the bulk of those opinions, objections, and observations issued in the report of the consultant employed after the riot. In the public conflict which followed, that channel of communication kept the director informed of every move and tactic planned by the prison staff, and it constituted a central strand in the emerging pattern of power. One aspect of the significance of the union in the changed situation, in addition to its rapidly expanding membership roll, is suggested by the inmate sit-down strike, an unsophisticated borrowing of the union concept as a means of venting discontent. The strike illustrates the consequences of any intervention which may crystallize division in a prison staff.

An explanatory hypothesis frequently advanced for these conflicts at their outset was to call them temporary maladjustments occasioned by the readjustments required in the Reorganization Act. Because that explanation was issued by those who clearly desired to minimize the conflict, and because the situation deteriorated over so long a period, this hypothesis has gained little credence. Some evidence to the contrary may be implied from the fact that the prison officials involved in the conflict had served successfully under both Democratic and Republican governors before and had survived the transition from one to another. Another consideration is the fact that the reorganization mandated few specific changes and the director issued very few orders to implement it. By itself, the reorganization does not constitute a sufficient condition for the disturbances that followed. Although the movement of the Prison System into the department was a necessary condition for much of what followed, its effect must be interpreted in the larger context.

In light of unresolved and accumulating internal problems, the Reorganization Act had a potential for disorganization. Designed to effectuate a constitutional mandate for increased political accountability through executive control, the act generated doubts as to the responsibility of career officials. These doubts were in their own minds as well as in the minds of their subordinates. Because matters had not been going well in the prison, some staff members reacted to uncertainty by taking a narrow definition of their responsibility at a time when an aggressive assertion of responsibility was most needed. The director withheld approval of the policy and procedure manual of the prison which had been in force for years and refused to confirm existing arrangements pending further study. Thus, a spirit of uncertainty sapped the initiative of career officials at just the moment when the most vigorous action was required to make their authority effective. Under more favorable circumstances within the prison, its officials might have grasped an opportunity to enlarge their role by mobilizing professional and citizen support for their program. Instead they retreated to await an endorsement from above that never came.

Under those circumstances, the characteristic vigor of the director captured the initiative from the prison staff in a manner which had explosive consequences. It was this energy of the director and the fact that the conflict later deteriorated into a name-calling contest which gives rise to explanations of the entire series of conflicts as a clash of personalities. This hypothesis must be examined in detail.

Something of the character of the aging warden and his chief subordinates may be implied from the administrative history sketched above, for that group remained almost intact from 1950 on. Although physically small, the warden was a warm and forceful personality, generally respected in the institution and throughout the state. Over two-thirds of the prison's inmates presented a petition on his behalf when he was under attack, and his abrupt dismissal produced a spontaneous disturbance in the prison yard. A major premise of the warden's administrative philosophy was that of delegating responsibility and authority to create an institutional climate of co-operative problem-solving. Perhaps too much of that delegated responsibility and authority was assumed by the superintendent of Oahu Prison, a coldly efficient and dedicated man who became the primary object of attack by the director.

By far the most dramatic of the personalities was that of the director, a lady of amazing energy and personal force who had risen from humble origins to a dominant role in both the formal and the "kitchen" cabinets of the administration. Lacking a college or professional education, she had risen through party offices and had a demonstrated talent for political organization. Efforts to prevent her appointment as director of Social Services by inserting professional qualifications for that post in the Reorganization Act had been made by the Democrats in the House but rejected in the Republican-dominated Senate. Well back into the territorial era, she had advocated the necessity of supporting the oligarchical party with a popular base, and she had played a leading role in forging an alliance with organized labor that weighed heavily in the party's victory in the first gubernatorial election under statehood. Deeply identified with the lower classes and regarding herself as the spokesman for those classes and their welfare, the lady had uncontestable political claims to the post she received.

In her office, the director completely dominated her subordinates by physical vigor and force of character. The deputy director, an ex-newsman who had managed publicity for the governor's campaign, was reduced to a pale shadow of her personality. Her administrative character was marked by an acid contempt for pretensions of middle-class respectability, which she properly identified with the opposition party, and for empty and mealymouthed bureaucratic jargon. She was quick to use and proud to boast of direct lines of communication with welfare clients, working-class employees, parolees, prison inmates or their families, and the general public, but her flat refusal to be "trapped" in the stilted conventions of administrative discourse throttled communication with top-level career officials. Pre-empting all news releases from divisions of the department to her own office and constructing each story with a sensitive eye to its broader political implications, she cast the definitions of each agency's role in terms of the language and expectations of the mass public. These public definitions of the prison's role, circulated in the course of hostile press coverage of escapes, differed in tone and emphasis from the controlling definitions of the situation imposed within the institution by its professional staff. These alternative definitions, implying simplistic antitheses between the goals of security and rehabilitation among other things, provided standards for popular criticism of professional officials and bases on which to crystallize conflicts within the institution.

The problems of the institution were the problems of people. Simply by moving forcefully to resolve those problems while career officials waited in uncertainty, the director assumed the role of a partisan of discontented elements among the employees and was widely perceived within the institution as an advocate of all the values those elements expressed. Her active intervention in management details unwittingly encouraged every disgruntled faction to seek political relief. With the director's door and the public press open to hostile criticism of the prison officials, disaffected elements within the institution felt no necessity to use internal channels to communicate their complaints. Thus by-passed, the authority of the warden and the entire structure of formal and informal power which focused in him to transmit his definitions of the situation were visibly undermined. The thinly disguised spirit of insubordination expressed by guards who looked to the union and its contacts for relief was more visibly demonstrated by a number of inmates in the weeks prior to the riot.

Exhaustive efforts by all sides to find some preliminary conspiracy, some structure of leadership, or even plausible grievances behind the inmate riot have uniformly failed. Its instant stimulus was nothing more than a callous but petty order to confine a hysterical inmate issued by the superintendent, an event with a thousand inconsequential precedents in the administrative practice of the institution. But the hysteria of the single inmate became a mass phenomenon, a reckless, violent, destructive outburst involving over half the inmate body in arson and uproar. The outbreak was a senseless thing, not clearly directed at injury to the guards and involving not a single escape or apparent attempt at escape. One of the most difficult problems of interpretation, one that has generated conspiratorial theories of the event by both parties to later conflicts, was the failure of the guard force to put down the disturbance. It was not beyond the reasonable resources of a disciplined custodial force, and the failure of the guards to control the riot at its outset provided ammunition for later charges of incompetence and lack of preparation at all levels. The hypothesis of this paper, the explanation for the calling of the National Guard, is that the custodial force did not really try to quell the riot. It was as though they took the position that the superintendent, having started the trouble, could take care of it himself. The structure of effective authority over the guard force had collapsed as certainly as had the structure of authority over the inmates. That second failure can be seen as a consequence and a reflection of the first.

Although various efforts have been made for a variety of partisan reasons to interpret the riot as a calculated protest against prison conditions later judged inadequate, these seem to fail. It is interpreted here as the hysterical outburst of men who need some degree of security against a condition of anomie, against a condition in which they could not know who was in charge or where they stood, against a condition in which a controlling definition of the situation and the pattern for its transmission had failed. When that demand to know where authority lay was answered by the National

Guard, the answer clearly implied that it no longer lay with the career officials of the institution.

If an explanation of the over-all case in terms of personality clashes is to hold at all, it must hold only for the period after the riot, for no clear evidence of hostility or animosity can be found earlier. At this point, however, the director perceived the previously ignored administrative warning as, at least, a calculated trick by the career officials to fix on her the responsibility for their own incompetence. As the conflict broadened later to involve her political opponents, the director came to think of the riot as possibly started or magnified as part of a broadly based political conspiracy to discredit her. At the outset, however, her response was quick and direct in publishing an "expert" study, fixing all the blame and laying charges of gross incompetence on the career officials. This was both a necessary defense and a preface to the dismissal of the officials, but it served as the immediate basis of an extended series of detailed administrative orders from the director's office. Ostensibly designed to tighten institutional security, the list contained orders designed to neutralize the warden's role and consolidate operating authority in the director's office.

For the increasingly restless elements in the prison to see the officials overridden and given all the blame for recent disturbances was more of an invitation to anarchy than even a well-ordered prison can stand. Mounting tensions required a continuous maintenance of intense security precautions and produced an intolerable situation. The Parole Board opened an attack on the director in the press. This was followed by a weekend of intense pressure on the warden to repudiate his warning memorandum. At that point, the warden engaged in his rebellion with public charges and a flat refusal to accept certain of the orders issued. The revolt of the warden and his top subordinates was addressed to the governor as much as to the general public, for the warden had been unable to gain an audience with the governor throughout the previous month. It was a desperate attempt to recapture that initiative necessary to maintain his authority in the prison, but it was more than that and less at the same time. In many respects, it was as emotional, as unplanned, and as ineffective as the outburst of prison inmates. It was a demand to know where he stood and to receive some authoritative definition of the situation on which to act. Finally, like the revolt of the inmates and that of the guards in similar circumstances, it was an appeal from the administrative to the political sphere for support and for a solution of unresolved problems. Its result was the governor's "unqualified endorsement" of the cabinet official.

The resolution of the conflict was long and painfully delayed. The political position of the director at that time was such as to require her endorsement, but the widespread, if temporary and disorganized, public support for the warden was such as to make his dismissal then impossible. The warden, who thought of himself as the only defense of a professionally sound penology, refused to resign and abdicate his painfully constructed prison program to the director's charge. The governor's refusal to permit the officials to testify before the legislative committee constituted an assertion that the problems of the administration must be solved internally and without the aid of the political opposition. His refusal to permit independent investigation or research in the prison or the Department of Social Services is an extension of that stand. These acts, in themselves, did not resolve the conflicts or define the roles of career and political officials in terms which made resolution possible. The career officials were retained in office until the public temper permitted their dismissal, but they were effectively by-passed by the construction of formal lines of communication and command, concentrating or legitimizing the direct authority of the director's office over the prison system.

One cannot entirely dismiss an explanation in terms of the clash of personalities in this case, for the existence of persons with the courage and vigor to play their roles in the conflict was one of its necessary conditions. Testimony given then and later at the director's eventual dismissal indicates a number of instances in which professional career officials had been displaced, repressed or humiliated by the energy of the director without resort to public conflict. The particular case has involved the confrontation of one role played with dynamic, aggrandizing energy with a second played with stubborn dedication. The assumptions of this paper are that an adequate understanding of the case requires at least a brief and superficial look at the stage and the situation which brought these roles into conflict.

In stable situations, it is possible to understand the major dimensions of institutional behavior with little reference to personality and individual motivation. Persons are normally responding to the settled demands of the situation and playing roles clearly defined by the nature, customs, and purposes of the groups in which they act. People are almost universally behaving in ways that are expected of them, and even aggressive, irrational behavior can often be explained in terms of role conflicts or contradictory expectations. Individuals are vastly different in personal characteristics, but a complex social institution incorporates a variety of roles, and complex formal and informal processes of selection combine to fill such roles with persons whose talent and temperament equip them to play traditionally defined parts. From this point of view, authority is seen as inherent in the processes by which controlling definitions of the situation are transmitted as premises in the logic of individual behavior.

It is unusual when a situation permits a person with rare resources of energy to reshape human institutions with a personal stamp. More often, society seeks in vain for a prince who does not come. The habits of subordination disqualify most men for leadership long before seniority places them in a position of power, and responsiveness to narrowly defined requirements is a habit which normally restrains the conduct of leaders within comfortable bounds. There are, however, times when institutions are in a process of change, when roles become uncertain and expectations confused, and dynamic individuals carve out a place for themselves consistent with their cravings. The Caesar or the Lincoln writes a page in the history of their societies because new roles are required in a state of uncertain transition and they have the will to define these. There are times when it is valid to say, with Egypt's Nasser, that there is "a role in search of a hero."

The condition of individualism placing its stamp on institutions is a condition of change which brings traditional expectations into question. People must doubt the usefulness or propriety of conventionally given definitions. In such conditions, the advantage lies with an individual who is unfamiliar with or prepared to disregard the conventional expectations. This is a quality of ruthlessness, a willingness to proceed without concern for the outraged sensibilities of others by virtue of a clear perception of a goal unseen by others. The warden, coming new to an unsettled prison situation in 1946, was such a person within the narrow confines of its institutional society. The explanation proposed here is that the director of the Department of Social Services was such a person, defining her own role on the larger stage of a society in transition to statehood.

This paper assumes that the several conflicts reported are not separate and disconnected events. Taken separately, they may be explained in terms of personality, the strains of reorganization, or administrative incompetence at various levels. Taken as a series, however, the conflicts ranging from the riot to the aborted clash between executive and legislative powers are consequences of statehood and a fundamental change in the constitutional system of social control in Hawaii.

The coming of statehood brought new opportunities and responsibilities into the total process of government. The opportunity to elect a governor, in particular, created a necessity for mobilizing political resources into an organization able to contest that election successfully, an organization far more substantial and centralized than those required for legislative district elections in the past. As a political organization emerges with sufficient power to be effective, as it did, that power becomes a factor in the environment of both political and administrative behavior. Control of the organization becomes an object of ambition to factions within the party, and the struggle for control, in turn, requires some type of organizational base, an organized popular following, business or labor support, or a segment of the bureaucracy. As a significant concentration of power, such organizations are forces to be checked, balanced, and incorporated in the complex framework of social control. Newly independent states elsewhere have often failed to constrain political forces unleashed by independence.

As indicated throughout the analysis above, the term "constitution" as used here applies to more than the legal formula assigning roles to agencies in the governmental process. Hawaii's formal constitution is quite standard except in its establishment of an exceptionally strong and centralized executive branch. Indeed, the provisions for a strong executive seem to assume the counterbalancing dispersion of power among organized groups in the society which have given rise to such provisions elsewhere. In a mature, pluralistic, interest group society, the various programs and agencies of government align themselves with or tend to fall under the domination of organized elements with a special stake in their activities, and a strong executive serves as a counterweight against that dispersion of responsibility. The distinctive characteristics of Hawaii's constitution of the present are not in its legal document so much as in the relative absence of a structure to extend the distribution of power throughout the society. Under these circumstances, the effective constitution of power is one in which the formal organs of government are organized to exercise powers conferred on them, a political organization has emerged to capture those offices, but those developments far outpaced the organization of interested publics to play their political role effectively.

As the legal skeleton of Hawaii's constitution takes on flesh, blood, and character in the definition of multitudinous details of the governmental process, the party in control of the executive enjoys an exceptional opportunity at this time to impose its will in the resolution of each uncertainty and to shape in detail the constitution of the future. This makes a virtue of uncertainty. The more extensive the climate of doubt as to the location of responsibility, the wider becomes the range of discretion to be exercised by political officials in view of political consequences. This is a concept which can account for a number of factors in the conflict in and around the prison system.

In the older states, it is not unusual to find a political organization or "machine" alert to exploit welfare agencies and their clienteles for partisan purposes. Law enforcement agencies lend themselves especially to such exploitation as a consequence of their internal discipline and extreme control over dependent persons. Thus, there is nothing unusual in the appointment of a highly skilled, political organizer to head the Department of Social Services or in systematic efforts at the concentration of power at the cabinet level in that agency. The distinctive characteristic of the recent transitional situation lies in the absence of internal checks and restraints on that concentration of power. An unusual feature of the case, in the absence of a system of social groups poised to exercise influence, was the exceptional power enjoyed by the few groups—the union, the director and her associates, and, eventually, those organized against her—organized for political action.

The failure of interest groups to keep pace with the organization of governmental and political machinery at the state level and to assume the role of an intervening force in the structure of social control produced a transitional period of "mass politics." This is witnessed by the temporary dominance of a "politics of personality" and the imposition of "mass values" as the controlling definitions of the correctional system. It is evidenced in instances of coercive force employed at various levels in the governmental process—use of the National Guard in the prison, the alleged "third-degree" methods of administrative problem solving, and the well-remembered threat of the director to "smash and destroy forever the professional reputation" of this author if he pursued his inquiry. Was the present case a calculated political raid on law enforcement agencies in the struggle for political power? Note the later reopening and resolution on obviously political grounds of a long-settled, administrative decision on the location of a $15,000,000 new prison plant. Or was this series of conflicts only an incident in the emerging politics of statehood?

To return now to our more basic questions, what is the significance of administrative experience? On the evidence of the case reviewed, the answer would seem to be that significance depends on the interpretation given rather than the experience itself. A wealth of successful experience by the administrators of the prison described did little more than render them incompetent and helpless in the face of a changed situation. Their ethic of political neutrality led them to fumble away what, at one point, seemed an unbeatable political position from which to defend their role and reduced them to the position of dispensable eunuchs in the director's court. An unfailing political capacity to predict the conclusions of standard expertise in the present case permitted the regular employment of consulting research to perform the functions of "hatchet men" in the political process. Can academic analysis of administrative experience achieve results more significant than that? Three hypotheses have been advanced for analysis in terms of the present case.

1. The first hypothesis was that administrative experience should provide a test of the validity of assumptions being acted on in the regulation of any state of affairs.

One proposition flowing from this study is that assumptions which were highly effective for one state of affairs were associated with anarchy and disaster in another. Hence, if the hypothesis is to have meaning, the "state of affairs" must be read as the "affairs of the state." Thus defined, the term provides something less than a measurable referent for empirical analysis. Further, the present case indicates that the controlling premises of behavior in an institution are not those formally published but, rather, those effectively transmitted through a complex structure of authority, influence, and communication. Thus, the working assumptions of behavior vary through time, through different levels of the institutional hierarchy at a single time, and in the extent to which acceptance of a common, controlling definition of the situation prevails. Except in the most rare instances of harmonious unanimity, these assumptions defy discovery and specification as completely as does the state of affairs.

Another proposition of this study is that the capacity to give controlling definition to operating premises is intimately related to status and power. In any institutional setting where authority itself is a value, the capacity to define the premises of the behavior of others is an object of almost continuous conflict. It is the very essence of the "political." To consider the subhypothesis advanced in this connection, any assumption about administrative communications in a prison must be considered in terms of its implications for the communication of a con-

trolling definition of the situation. The fact that the effective
test of administrative assumptions is their political viability
and contribution to institutional survival colors the manner in
which they are defined at each level of the hierarchy. Hence,
the assumptions of an administrative agency are not of the
character of scientific hypotheses about natural events. They
are value assumptions by virtue of the fact that they are political assumptions and subject to the limitation of scientific
analysis as applied to propositions of that type. The first hypothesis is rejected.

2. The second hypothesis holds that analysis of administrative experience should provide a means for generating and
testing hypotheses about the nature of any set of events being
regulated. This was elaborated to suggest that penal administration might provide insights into the nature of criminals or
incorrigibles.

There is a quality of obviousness about that proposition
which must make it applicable to the management of inani-
mate materials. In theory, at least, the "success" of different
problem-solving systems that are employed should provide insights into the nature of the problem. Unfortunately for this
approach, the problem of social control is something that
characterizes the society, not the criminal. Administrative solutions to the problems of social control are complicated by the
fact that society becomes more outraged by a single prison
escape than by fifty parole failures. It is possible to parole the
incurable car thief but not the completely rehabilitated murderer, and the behavior of administrators, car thieves, and
murderers in prison is guided by some degree of recognition
of those premises. Administration must accommodate to the
characteristics of the society as well as to those of the offender.
That is the lesson learned by officials in the present case at
their cost.

The cycles of incorrigibility and internal violence have
waxed and waned in the prison studied with little reference to
its formal structure as a problem-solving system. The cycles
of violence have expanded at times beyond the capacity of the
administrative mechanism to contain them. Speaking in general, prison administrations have been far more influenced

and disrupted in recent years by changes in public expectations than by changes in inmates. This is true in spite of the classic apology for prison riots that holds, "We just are not getting the type of men we used to." The custodial institution is a social system in its own right. Any substantial change in the administrative system produces corresponding changes in the total institutional community and the roles which govern behavior there. It is futile to talk about alternative ways to govern the same inmate community. Governed differently, it becomes a different social system with different behavioral roles and different problems for its inhabitants and the society at large.

It must be emphasized that the prison is not administering criminals. It is administering society's sense of justice and executing a definition of right. Because the meaning of those terms is never clear and certain, it must emerge in the operating details of administration. The struggle to impose operating definitions of those terms or maintain the vital continuity of existing definitions makes administration a crucial part of a continuous political process and identifies the career administrator's vital stake in that process. For more than a generation, we have mouthed the truism that politics and administration are functionally inseparable, but its implications have not been adequately extended into analysis. One of its implications is that the administrative agency cannot be conceived of as a problem-solving machine at the service of some abstract state. On the contrary, the administrative system must be regarded as a part of the state, an extension of the state, a reflection of the state and a participant in the continuous process of giving definition to the law—to those propositions which enter as axioms into the logic of individual behavior. Thus, the second hypothesis must be rejected.

3. The third hypothesis considered the prison system as a society in microcosm and a source of insights into the nature of power structures in other settings.

On the basis of the case examined, it is suggested that the prison and administrative experience there can serve as a source of insights into certain problems. If it tells us little about the nature of criminality, it may suggest many things about the relationship of communication patterns to authority and power. Research in the prison in the present case has suggested constructs useful in the analysis of change in the state at large. There are times when it seems that the larger structures of power in society are reflected in the prison as though in a still pool. However, recent events betray the fact that our capacity to treat the institution as a society in microcosm was a temporary and transient circumstance. For a brief period of time in the territorial era, as a consequence of that political arrangement, it was possible to consider the prison as a self-contained pattern of interaction. With the politics of statehood, that opportunity was lost and the institution became a part of the larger political process. The third hypothesis holds, if at all, under exceptional conditions.

However, in both the state prison and the state at large, it seems that similar conditions produce similar consequences for individual behavior and the system of social control. Change or failure of a controlling definition of the situation—of a common sense of the constitutional order of life—produces anarchic consequences and provides a license for those with the will and the organizational resources to define the constitution of the future for themselves. In such conditions, force, aggressiveness, and fear replace habit and customary roles as the main resources of social control. The administrative life of those who fail to catch the tide of human affairs at those times promises to be poor, solitary, nasty, brutish, and short. If the scholar or the administrator is to know what the significance of such a case is, he must know what it is a case of.

## NOTES

* Prepared for delivery at the 1962 Annual Meeting of the American Political Science Association, Washington, D.C., Mayflower Hotel. September 5–8, 1962.
1. The earlier studies of the governing of men and comparative prison cultures were supported by a grant from the Doris Duke Foundation and by the Institute for Research in Social Science, at the University of North Carolina. Discussions of that work are available in a monograph, *Policy Change in Prison Management* (Government Research Bureau, Michigan State University, 1957) and in *The Prison: Studies*

*in Institutional Organization and Change,* Donald Cressey, Editor (Holt, Rinehart & Winston, 1961). The projected study of the collapse of authority patterns within the prison was supported by a grant from the Social Science Research Council. The council graciously permitted, though it did not intend, the use of that grant to examine the larger administrative-political context after the technical project was forbidden, and responsibility for the present analysis lies entirely on the author.

# 7

# SOCIALIZATION IN CORRECTIONAL COMMUNITIES*

*Stanton Wheeler*†

This paper grows out of a tradition of sociological investigation established some twenty years ago by Donald Clemmer.[1] One of the most important of the many contributions in Clemmer's *The Prison Community* was his analysis of the changes inmates undergo during periods of confinement—changes Clemmer signified by use of the concept of *prisonization*. The present paper reviews the processes Clemmer described, provides an empirical test of some of his propositions, and attempts to relate the analysis of socialization processes to other features of correctional communities.

## PRISONIZATION

Clemmer employed the concept of prisonization to describe the central impact of the prison on its inmates—the impact of an inmate society whose code, norms, dogma, and myth sustained a view of the prison and the outside world distinctly harmful to rehabilitation. The core of this view was indicated in an inmate code or system of norms requiring loyalty to other inmates and opposition to the prison staff, who served as representatives of a rejecting society beyond the walls. The consequences of exposure to the inmate society were summed up by the concept of prisonization, which Clemmer defined as "the taking on, in greater or lesser degree, of the folkways,

† Stanton Wheeler holds a joint appointment as professor in the Department of Sociology and in the School of Law at Yale University and is also affiliated with the Russell Sage Foundation, New York.

mores, customs and general culture of the penitentiary."[2]
Clemmer saw prisonization as a specific illustration of more
general processes of assimilation occurring wherever persons
are introduced to an unfamiliar culture. The net result of the
process was the internalization of a criminal outlook, leaving
the "prisonized" individual relatively immune to the influence
of a conventional value system. Both Clemmer and the inmates who served as his principal informants felt that the degree of prisonization was the most important factor affecting
adjustment after release from the institution.[3]

Clemmer noted that no inmate could remain completely
unprisonized. Merely being an incarcerated offender exposed
one to certain "universal features" of imprisonment. These
included acceptance of an inferior role and recognition that
nothing is owed the environment for the supplying of basic
needs. Beyond these features were other conditions that he
felt influenced both the speed and degree of prisonization.
Thus prisonization would be lowest for those inmates who have
had "positive" and "socialized" relationships during prepenal
life, those who continue their positive relationships with persons outside the walls, those whose short sentences subject
them to only brief exposure to the universal features of imprisonment, those who refuse or are unable to affiliate with
inmate primary groups, and those who by chance are placed
with other inmates not integrated into the inmate community.
Clemmer felt that the most crucial of these factors was the
degree of primary group affiliation.[4]

Though some twenty years have passed since Clemmer's
work was first published, his account remains the most
thorough and detailed description of the socialization process
in prisons. The viewpoint expressed by Clemmer is based on
a direct social learning theory highly similar to Sutherland's
theory of differential association. The variables affecting degree of prisonization reflect the same influences Sutherland
noted—the frequency, duration, priority, and intensity of contact with criminal patterns.[5] When the concept of prisonization has been discussed by sociologists, the comments are
similar to a chief criticism of Sutherland's theory. Thus Cohen
finds the theory of differential association incomplete because

it fails to illuminate the conditions determining the presence of the delinquent culture.[6] Sykes and Messinger find the theory of prisonization incomplete because it fails to account for the presence of the inmate culture.[7] The theory is found wanting because it accounts only for the process of cultural transmission and does not explain why the culture is "there" to be transmitted. It is criticized for being incomplete rather than false. But in addition to this omission and the need for more evidence concerning the process, there is a further problem in employing the concept of prisonization that requires clarification before Clemmer's proposition can be adequately tested. It concerns the temporal frame of reference within which socialization effects are studied.

The usual way of treating the time variable in studies of assimilation is to classify persons according to their length of exposure to the new social setting. This conception is usually employed in studies of prison adjustment, and was explicitly stated by Clemmer, who directed his attention to "the manner in which the attitudes of prisoners are modified as the men spend month after month in the penal milieu."[8] Throughout his work Clemmer concentrated on the process of induction into the community. He had little to say about changes that might occur as inmates neared the time for release. His proposition that prisonization is the most important determinant of parole adjustment is based on the assumption that processes observed during the early and middle phases of incarceration continue until the inmate is paroled.

It is easy to understand how this emphasis on the process of induction developed, for it grew out of the awareness that the prison is a community with its own norms and structure. The task of accounting for processes of assimilation into the community developed as a natural concern. In addition there were no well-developed notions of what Merton has called "anticipatory socialization," the preparatory responses that frequently precede an actual change in group membership, such as the movement from prison to the broader community. The result is that we know much more about processes of socialization into the community than we do about readaptation to the outside world. There is evidence, however, that from the inmate's perspective the length of time *remaining* to be served may be the most crucial temporal aspect. Many inmates can repeat the precise number of months, weeks, and days until their parole date arrives, whereas few are equally accurate in reporting the length of time they have served. The inmate language system contains terms such as being "short" and having "short-time-itis" that suggest the importance of the last few weeks in the institution, just as the term "fish" denotes the new inmate's status.

These observations merely illustrate that at any given point in time the temporal frame of reference of different types of inmates may have various psychological and social meanings. So long as we restrict our analysis to the length of time since entrance into the prison, we may miss important features of the inmate's response to the institution.[9]

In order to clarify the different temporal aspects of socialization in the prison, the data reported below are divided into two sections. The first uses a definition of time similar to that implied by Clemmer, and allows for the test of his hypotheses. The second classifies inmates according to phases of their institutional career, thus enabling us to observe changes that may occur as inmates are preparing for release from the institution.

## RESEARCH SETTING AND METHOD

The research was conducted in a Western state reformatory, one of two adult penal institutions in the state. It is a walled, close custody institution receiving inmates from sixteen to thirty years of age. The only felony offenders excluded by statute from sentence to the reformatory are those convicted of capital crimes. The physical plant is roughly typical of many Northern state institutions designed to handle young adults.

Samples of inmates were drawn from each of the housing units of the institution, using stratified random sampling procedures with a variable sampling rate designed to increase the number of inmates in the sample who were in the early and late stages of their incarceration. Of 259 men originally assigned to the sample, 95 per cent completed questionnaires and 92 per cent of the questionnaires were usable for research purposes. The only inmates excluded from the sample design were those screened by the clinical psychologist as psychotic or near psychotic, or too low in intelligence to understand and respond meaningfully to the questionnaire. The sample n is 237 from an inmate population of approximately 750.[10]

Hypothetical conflict situations were used to develop an index of conformity to staff role expectations. Several conflict situations were employed in the research. The ones selected for the index were those that (a) gave evidence of normative consensus on the part of custody and treatment staff members, and (b) showed variation in inmate response. Five items adequately met these criteria. The items, arranged in decreasing order of "conformity to staff" response, were as follows:

1. An inmate, Owens, is assigned to a work crew. Some other inmates criticize him because he does more work than anybody else on the crew. He works as hard as he can.

2. Inmate Martin goes before a committee that makes job assignments. He is given a choice between two jobs. One job would call for hard work, but it would give Martin training that might be useful to him on the outside. The other job would allow Martin to do easier time in the institution. But it provides no training for a job on the outside. Martin decides to take the easier job.

3. An inmate, without thinking, commits a minor rule infraction. He is given a "write-up" by a correctional officer who saw the violation. Later three other inmates are talking to each other about it. Two of them criticize the officer. The third inmate, Sykes, defends the officer, saying the officer was only doing his duty.

4. Inmates Smith and Long are very good friends. Smith has a five-dollar bill that was smuggled into the institution by a visitor. Smith tells Long he thinks the officers are suspicious, and asks Long to hide the money for him for a few days. Long takes the money and carefully hides it.

5. Inmates Brown and Henry are planning an escape. They

threaten inmate Smith with a beating unless he steals a crowbar for them from the tool shop where he works. He thinks they mean business. While he is trying to smuggle the crowbar into the cell house, he is caught by an officer, and Smith is charged with planning to escape. If he doesn't describe the whole situation, he may lose up to a year of good time. He can avoid it by blaming Brown and Henry.

Responses to the first four items were on a four-category approve-disapprove continuum. Response categories for the fifth item were:

What should inmate Smith do?

He should clear himself by telling about the escape plans of Brown and Henry.

He should keep quiet and take the punishment himself.

On each of the items at least 75 per cent of the custody and treatment staff members were in the modal response category: They approve the inmate's conduct in items one and three, disapprove on two and four, and feel that inmate Smith "should clear himself . . ." Sixty-seven per cent of the staff were in agreement on all five items, and 93 per cent were in agreement on at least four items. Thus for these items there is a relatively high degree of normative consensus among staff as to proper inmate behavior. Inmates are classified into three categories, according to the number of situations in which the inmate response is the same as that of the modal staff response. The high conformity group includes inmates whose own response agreed with the staff in at least four of the five situations, the medium conformists those who agreed in two or three situations and the low conformists those who agreed in none or in one situation. The relatively small number in the extreme nonconformity group has led to their inclusion with the medium conformists at several points in the analysis.[11]

This index of conformity to staff expectations obviously taps only a part of the phenomena referred to as prisonization by Clemmer and others. It does seem to get at a central core: the acceptance or rejection of norms and role definitions applied to inmates by the prison staff. As a crude check on the possibility that the index serves also as a more general reflection of the inmate's support for law abiding values, an additional item was included that refers to behavior in civilian roles. The item was adapted from the studies by Stouffer and Toby designed to measure universalism-particularism and reads as follows:[12]

> Barker is riding in a car driven by his close friend, Davis, and Davis hits a person crossing the street. Barker knows that his friend was going at least 40 miles an hour in a 25-mile-an-hour speed zone. There are no other witnesses. Davis's lawyer says that if Barker testifies under oath that the speed was only 25 miles an hour, it may save Davis from serious consequences.

What do you think Barker should do?

> He should testify that Davis was going 25 miles an hour.
> He should not testify that Davis was going 25 miles an hour.

When this item is used as a criterion in place of the conformity index, the direction of all the relationships reported below still holds, although the degree of relationship is somewhat reduced. Thus there is some evidence that the index used here, although limited in reference to the prison situation, may serve as a more general measure of the inmate's values.

The conflict situations were presented in a questionnaire that also contained a brief self-conception inventory, background items, and items relating to participation in various institution activities. Inmates responded to the questionnaire in groups of ten to twenty, and under conditions of anonymity. Every precaution was taken to ensure free, private responses. Although no formal validity checks could be made, there is indirect evidence of validity in the fact that the rank order of proportion high conformity response is what would be expected from knowledge of the administrative process by which inmates are assigned to housing units. Thus the smallest percentage of high conformity response is found in the segregation unit (14%), followed by the close custody unit (21%), medium custody unit (34%), honor farm and reception unit (44% and 47%), and the protection unit (83%), where inmates are held for their own protection from other inmates, chiefly because they are defined as "rats" who have violated inmate norms regarding informing on other inmates.

Our interest is in tracing changes over time in response to the correctional community, from data gathered at one point in time. Several conditions could invalidate the assumption that the observed differences are due to the time variable. These include change in characteristics of inmates, changes in characteristics of the institution, and selective parole procedures. There is no evidence that the first two conditions could have operated in any significant degree. There had been only slight changes in the characteristics of incoming inmates for several years preceding the study, and no major administrative changes in program had been introduced over the previous three-year period. The major potential bias concerns selective parole policies. Presumably, inmates who have served longer sentences are more serious offenders who may have been more opposed to the staff at time of entrance into the institution. The average length of sentence in this institution is slightly over three years. The typical inmate serves two-thirds of this sentence, and almost all inmates serve at least eighteen months. Selective factors may be operating beyond the two-year period but are unlikely to be present in significant degree prior to that time. Yet evidence reported below shows changes over time that operate before selective factors are introduced. Thus while panel data are obviously needed to verify the relationships reported here, there is reason to believe that valid inferences may be made about temporal shifts.[13]

The statistical significance of the relationships is assessed by chi square, employed as a one-tailed test when Clemmer's hypotheses are being tested, and in the normal manner when inmates are classified into phases of their institutional career.[14] The gamma coefficient described by Goodman and Kruskal is used as a measure of degree of relationship throughout the paper.[15] The small number of cases in some of the tables suggests that the results can best be evaluated in terms of size and consistency of relationships rather than the degree of statistical significance obtained in any one table.

## RESULTS: LENGTH OF TIME SERVED AND CONFORMITY TO STAFF EXPECTATIONS

When the usual method of treating the time variable is employed, the results give strong support to Clemmer's propositions regarding prisonization. Table 1 shows the relationship between length of time served and conformity to staff norms. As expressed in this table, the effect of increased length of exposure is to reduce the proportion of men who conform to the staff's expectations. Furthermore, when analysis is made separately for first-termers and recidivists, there is evidence of a relearning process among the recidivists. Although recidivists are more likely to be nonconformists than are the first-termers, the effect of time served on their nonconformity is about the same. Instead of entering the prison already prisonized, a reprisonization process appears to occur.

If the process of prisonization is operating effectively, we should be able to observe its effects over shorter time periods. And we would expect the effect to be present particularly for offenders serving their first term in an adult penal institution. In table 3, inmates are classified into as refined time categories as can be justified with a small number of cases. The results are presented for a period up to one year, for which

TABLE 1

LENGTH OF TIME SERVED AND CONFORMITY TO
STAFF RULE EXPECTATIONS

| Length of time served | Per Cent High Conformity | Per Cent Medium Conformity | Per Cent Low Conformity | Total | n |
|---|---|---|---|---|---|
| Less than 6 months | 47 | 44 | 09 | 100 | 77 |
| 6 months–2 years | 32 | 54 | 14 | 100 | 99 |
| Over 2 years | 16 | 61 | 24 | 100 | 38 |
| Total | .. | .. | .. | | 214 |

$x^2$ (4df) = 12.00 p < .01

$\gamma = -.35$

period we can be almost positive that selective factors are not operating. The results again confirm Clemmer's observations, and suggest the importance of the first few months in the socialization process.[16]

A central theme in Clemmer's analysis is that the degree of prisonization will vary according to the degree of involvement in the informal life of the inmate community. In the present research, two items were used to tap the extent of inmate involvement. One item reflects the extensiveness of involvement in terms of the number of close friendships established

TABLE 2

LENGTH OF TIME SERVED AND CONFORMITY TO STAFF ROLE EXPECTATIONS, FOR OFFENDERS DIFFERING IN PRIOR PENAL COMMITMENTS

| | PER CENT HIGH CONFORMITY | | | |
|---|---|---|---|---|
| | No Prior Adult | | Prior Adult | |
| Length of time served | Commitment | n | Commitment | n |
| Less than 6 months | 49 | 51 | 40 | 25 |
| 6 months–2 years | 31 | 64 | 33 | 33 |
| Over 2 years | 19 | 26 | 06 | 12 |
| Total | .. | 141 | .. | 70 |

$$x^2 (2df) = 7.56 \; p < .025 \qquad x^2 (2df) = 2.50 \; p > .10$$
$$\gamma = -.40 \qquad\qquad \gamma = -.38$$

TABLE 3

PERCENTAGE HIGH CONFORMITY FOR FIRST-TERMERS OVER THE FIRST 12 MONTHS OF INCARCERATION

| Length of time served | Per Cent High Conformity | n |
|---|---|---|
| Less than 3 weeks | 56 | 18 |
| 3 to 6 weeks | 48 | 21 |
| 6 weeks to 6 months | 42 | 12 |
| 6 months to 1 year | 28 | 25 |
| Total | .. | 76 |

$$x^2 (1df) = 2.05 \; p < .10$$
$$\gamma = -.37$$

with other inmates. A second item reflects the intensity of involvement by ascertaining the degree to which inmates spend their free time with other inmates or by themselves. The relationship of each of these indexes of involvement to conformity to staff expectations is presented in tables 4 and 5.[17]

The results indicated in both tables lend support to the proposition that both the speed and degree of prisonization are a function of informal inmate involvement. During the first

TABLE 4

LENGTH OF TIME SERVED AND CONFORMITY TO STAFF ROLE EXPECTATIONS, FOR INMATES DIFFERING IN EXTENSIVENESS OF PRIMARY GROUP CONTACTS

| | Per Cent High Conformity | | | |
| | High Group | | Low Group | |
| Length of time served | Contacts* | n | Contacts* | n |
| --- | --- | --- | --- | --- |
| Less than 6 months | 45 | 31 | 48 | 46 |
| 6 months–2 years | 20 | 44 | 42 | 55 |
| Over 2 years | 06 | 18 | 30 | 20 |
| Total | .. | 93 | .. | 121 |

$$x^2 \text{ (2df)} = 8.37 \text{ p} < .01 \quad x^2 \text{ (2df)} = 1.82 \text{ p} > .25$$
$$\gamma = -.62 \qquad\qquad \gamma = -.20$$

* See footnote 17 for item wording.

TABLE 5

LENGTH OF TIME SERVED AND CONFORMITY TO STAFF ROLE EXPECTATIONS, FOR INMATES DIFFERING IN INTENSITY OF INMATE CONTACTS

| | Per Cent High Conformity | | | |
| | High Group | | Low Group | |
| Length of time served | Intensity* | n | Intensity* | n |
| --- | --- | --- | --- | --- |
| Less than 6 months | 42 | 40 | 51 | 35 |
| 6 months–2 years | 21 | 61 | 49 | 39 |
| Over 2 years | 00 | 16 | 27 | 22 |
| Total | .. | 117 | .. | 96 |

$$x^2 \text{ (2df)} = 9.75 \text{ p} < .005 \quad x^2 \text{ (2df)} = 3.58 \text{ p} < .10$$
$$\gamma = -.63 \qquad\qquad \gamma = -.27$$

* See footnote 17 for item wording.

time period there is no significant relation between involvement and conformity to staff opinion. However, the percentage of high conformists drops rapidly for inmates who are highly involved. For those who have little contact with other inmates as assessed by our items, the process of prisonization appears to operate, but the major impact is delayed until after two years have been served, and even then does not operate to the same degree as for highly involved inmates.

While our data do not enable us to specify clearly the time relationship obtaining between involvement and conformity, it is instructive to examine the relationship as though the reverse time sequence were in operation—as though the sequence were from conformity to involvement. As table 6 shows, the proportion of high conformists who are also involved in intimate interaction with other inmates decreases through time, while there is an increase in social contacts among the nonconformists.

These results of course raise the question of the interplay between social involvement on the one hand, attitudes and values on the other. Rather than thinking of one of these variables as an effect of the other, a more appropriate model of their interaction in the prison community might stress the

TABLE 6
LENGTH OF TIME SERVED AND EXTENSIVENESS OF
PRIMARY GROUP CONTACTS, FOR INMATES
DIFFERING IN CONFORMITY TO
STAFF EXPECTATIONS

| | PER CENT HIGH EXTENSIVENESS | | | |
| | High | | Low | |
| Length of time served | Conformists | n | Conformists | n |
|---|---|---|---|---|
| Less than 6 months | 39 | 36 | 41 | 41 |
| 6 months–2 years | 28 | 32 | 52 | 67 |
| Over 2 years | 14 | 7 | 55 | 31 |
| Total | .. | 75 | .. | 139 |

$$x^2 \text{ (1df)} = 1.33 \; p > .10 \quad x^2 \text{ (1df)} = 1.17 \; p > .10$$
$$\gamma = .31 \qquad\qquad \gamma = .17$$

structural incompatability of being both highly involved with inmates and an attitudinal conformist to staff expectations. The dominant normative order among inmates (at least in terms of power and visibility if not numbers) is strongly opposed to that of the staff. The inmate who values friendship among his peers and also desires to conform to the staff's norms faces a vivid and real role conflict. The conflict is not apparent or perhaps is not felt so intensely during the earliest stages of confinement, but with increasing length of time in the prison the strain becomes more acute; inmates move to resolve the strain either by giving up or being excluded from primary ties, or by a shift in attitudes. In either case the result leads to a polarization of noninvolved conformists and involved non-conformists. One group of inmates becomes progressively prisonized, the other progressively isolated. And as the marginal frequencies of tables 4 and 6 suggest, the dominant tendency is to move in the direction of nonconformity rather than isolation.[18]

This interpretation of changes over time in the prison community awaits panel data for its validation. In addition, three further problems may be noted. First, there is the question of what tips the balance in individual cases of conflict between conformity and involvement. Undoubtedly a number of factors come into play. Some inmates may have a stronger need for group affiliations than others, a need which can be satisfied in the prison only by association with other offenders. Still others may possess traits or occupy positions in the prison community that are important to the inmate leadership, and may thus be under greater pressure to become implicated in the inmate system. Another influence is the degree of attachment to families and friends outside the institution, a factor noted by Clemmer but one which the present research does not adequately measure. Partial evidence on the importance of such ties is revealed in the higher rates of conformity to staff expectations for married men, and for those who report that family members "have confidence" in them.

Second, there is the question of how the processes noted above are linked to the informally defined social types and roles noted in many studies of prison social structure. Although the categories suggested by the dimensions of involvement and conformity are too simple and crude to catch up the subtle aspects of inmate roles, certain parallels are evident. For example, the involved nonconformists are roughly equivalent to the "right-guys" noted in Schrag's typology and to the role of "real man" described by Sykes.[19] Our data suggest that the movement of inmates over time is in the direction of the right guy role, with a much weaker tendency toward the isolated role of "Square John." The data also point to the large number of inmates who are nonconformists to the staff but who remain relatively unaffiliated with inmate primary groups. This group is probably quite heterogeneous, being composed in part of those variously labeled outlaws, toughs, ballbusters, etc., highly egocentric in orientation and free of commitment to either the staff or inmate systems, and in part of less striking figures who are unable to establish strong ties with other inmates, even though desirous of doing so. Many of this latter type may have experienced what Cloward refers to as the pattern of double-failure.[20] The size of this category of unaffiliated nonconformists raises some important questions about the operation of inmate society. On the one hand it suggests limits to the conception that the inmate system generates a high degree of cohesiveness among its members. At the same time it suggests that informal involvement in the system is by no means a necessary condition for the emergence of strong opposition to staff norms.

A third problem posed by the above data, as well as Clemmer's earlier analysis and the descriptions of social types in prisons, concerns the absence of social bonds among the conforming inmates. Neither in our data nor in the language system of the prison is there evidence of a category characterized both by conformity to the staff *and* by strong social bonds with other inmates. What is it about the structure of the correctional community that makes conformity possible, apparently, only at the cost of isolation? The question is too complex to receive detailed treatment here, involving as it does at least in part the question of the origin of the negative inmate culture in prisons. Once established, however, the culture exerts pressure on both the inmates and the staff which operates largely to suppress the formation of solidary ties among the conformists. Evidence from other parts of this study suggests that inmates perceive the opinions of others to be more opposed to the staff than they actually are.[21] The resulting pattern of pluralistic ignorance operates to restrain even the initial seeking out of like-minded individuals. The same pressures lead to the frequent warnings from staff members to stay out of involvements with other inmates, and "do your own time." Thus the conforming inmate may be restrained from establishing supportive ties with others by both the official and the inmate systems. If the withdrawal pattern characteristic of those who conform to the staff is not offset by strong ties to persons outside the institution, the effects of social isolation may be quite severe. For these inmates, the modern institution may accomplish by social and psychological pressure what the Pennsylvania system accomplished by its physical design, and perhaps with some of the same consequences.[22]

## RESULTS: INSTITUTIONAL CAREER PHASE AND CONFORMITY TO STAFF EXPECTATIONS

In the following analysis inmates are classified into three categories: (a) those who have served less than six months in the correctional community and are thus in an *early phase* of their commitment; (b) those who have less than six months remaining to serve—the *late phase* inmates; and (c) those who have served more than six months and have more than six months left to serve—the *middle phase* inmates. This procedure enables us to examine changes in response that may occur as inmates are preparing for return to the broader community.

The relationship between phase of institutional career and conformity to staff expectations is presented in table 7. Two trends are apparent. First there is a steady increase in the proportion of low conformity responses. Second, there is a U-shaped distribution of high conformity responses. The trends suggest that two processes may be in operation. One process is that of prisonization. A progressive opposition to staff norms is observed when inmates are classified either by length of time served or by institutional career phase.

TABLE 7

PHASE OF INSTITUTIONAL CAREER AND CONFORMITY TO STAFF ROLE EXPECTATIONS

| Institutional Career Phase | Per Cent High | Per Cent Medium | Per Cent Low | Total | n |
|---|---|---|---|---|---|
| Early phase | 47 | 44 | 09 | 100 | 77 |
| Middle phase | 21 | 65 | 14 | 100 | 94 |
| Late phase | 43 | 33 | 25 | 100 | 40 |
| Total | .. | .. | .. | | 211 |

$$x^2 \text{ (4df)} = 20.48 \text{ p} < .001$$
$$\gamma = -.21$$

The second process appears to be one of differential attachment to the values of the broader society. The U-shaped distribution of high-conformity responses suggests that inmates who recently have been in the broader community and inmates who are soon to return to that community are more frequently oriented in terms of conventional values. Inmates conform least to conventional standards during the middle phase of their institutional career. These inmates appear to shed the prison culture before they leave it, such that there are almost as many conforming inmates at time of release as at time of entrance into the system.[23]

Empirical verification of these two processes will require panel studies. If future research supports the findings reported here, other important questions would be raised. What types of inmates follow the pattern of prisonization vs. the pattern of reattachment to the extra-institutional world? Where are these types located within the prison social structure? What events or conditions lead to one process rather than the other?

Can institutional authorities exert control over the processes by policy decisions?

## TABLE 8
### PHASE OF INSTITUTIONAL CAREER AND CONFORMITY TO STAFF ROLE EXPECTATIONS, FOR INMATES DIFFERING IN EXTENSIVENESS OF PRIMARY GROUP CONTACTS

| | PER CENT HIGH CONFORMITY | | | |
| Institutional Career Phase | High Group Contacts | n | Low Group Contacts | n |
|---|---|---|---|---|
| Early  phase | 45 | 31 | 48 | 46 |
| Middle  phase | 12 | 50 | 30 | 47 |
| Late  phase | 33 | 12 | 48 | 27 |
| Total | .. | 93 | .. | 120 |

$$x^2 \text{ (2df)} = 11.38 \; p < .01 \qquad x^2 \text{ (2df)} = 4.06 \; p > .10$$
$$\gamma = -.38 \qquad\qquad\qquad \gamma = -.07$$

The resocialization effect is apparent among inmates who have established close friendships in the institution, as well as among those who have not. Table 8 shows that inmates who stay out of close friendship ties exhibit as great an attachment to law-abiding standards during the late phase as during the early phase. The process of resocialization is evident among highly involved inmates, but not to the same degree.[24] And as the marginal distributions indicate, the rate of group involvement is highest during the middle phase. When the rate of involvement is examined separately for high and low conformists, the high conformists show a decline at each stage and the low conformists a sharp rise during the middle phase with a decline as time for release approaches.

Further evidence regarding the process of resocialization appears when recidivists are compared with first-offenders. As presented in table 9, the pattern for recidivists is similar to that for first-termers. Both groups show the decline in conformity during the middle phase with a rise in conformity in the late phase. The recidivists begin at a lower point and end at a lower point, but the adaptive response pattern is still evident.

TABLE 9
PHASE OF INSTITUTIONAL CAREER AND CONFORMITY
TO STAFF ROLE EXPECTATIONS, FOR OFFENDERS
DIFFERING IN PRIOR PENAL COMMITMENTS

| Institutional Career Phase | PER CENT HIGH CONFORMITY | | | |
| | No Prior Adult Commitment | n | Prior Adult Commitment | n |
| --- | --- | --- | --- | --- |
| Early phase | 49 | 51 | 40 | 25 |
| Middle phase | 21 | 63 | 22 | 32 |
| Late phase | 44 | 27 | 33 | 12 |
| Total | .. | 141 | .. | 69 |

$$x^2 \,(2df) = 11.1 \quad p < .01 \qquad x^2 \,(2df) = 1.44 \; p > .30$$
$$\gamma = -.19 \qquad\qquad\qquad\qquad \gamma = -.19$$

The findings concerning career phase for first-termers and recidivists suggest some revision of our thinking regarding the impact of time. Instead of viewing successive institutional careers as the development of an increasingly negative pattern, the results would suggest that a cyclical pattern of adjustment may hold for a sizable number of inmates—a cycle which has its lowest point during the middle of a period of institutional confinement, and may have its high point at some period on parole. If observations could be made on parolees, it is possible that we could locate other points in the cycle. The results suggest a complex process of socialization and resocialization as offenders move into and out of the correctional community. The model is that of a cycle with a negative trend rather than a monotonically increasing commitment to a criminal value system.[25]

## DISCUSSION

The prisonization theory is strongly supported when inmates are classified according to the length of time they have served. When they are classified into phases of their institutional career, however, the prisonization theory is inadequate as a description of changes over time. While it accounts for the increase in extreme nonconformity, it fails to account for the U-shaped distribution of high conformity responses. Recent attempts to develop a theory accounting for the content of the inmate culture provide some understanding of the possible bases for these two types of change.

**The Inmate Culture.**   Two explanations have been offered to account for the content of the inmate culture, one focusing on the process of "negative selection," the other on problem-solving processes. The *negative selection* approach begins with the obvious fact that the single trait held in common by all inmates is participation in criminal activity. Their criminal acts indicate in varying degrees an opposition to conventional norms. It follows that the inmate culture should give expression to the values of those who are most committed to a criminal value system—the long-termers, those who have followed systematic criminal careers, etc. And if the culture is viewed as an outgrowth of the criminogenic character of inmates, it is reasonable to expect a reinforcement process operating throughout the duration of confinement. This is consistent with the image of correctional institutions as "crime schools" and with a theory that accounts for changes in response to the prison largely in terms of prisonization.

The alternative view stresses the problem-solving nature of subcultures, and interprets the content of the inmate culture as a response to the adjustment problems posed by imprisonment, with all its accompanying frustrations and deprivations. In his analysis of social types in a state penitentiary, Schrag noted the way in which these types are focused around the problems of loyalty relations, of "doing time," of sexual outlet, etc.—problems which are not a direct carry-over from the outside world.[26] In a more recent functional analysis of the inmate social system, Sykes and Messinger note five major deprivations or attacks on the inmate's self-conception, including the rejected status of being an inmate, the material and sexual deprivations of imprisonment, the constant social control exercised by the custodians, and the presence of other offenders. They conclude:[27]

> In short, imprisonment 'punishes' the offender in a variety
> of ways extending far beyond the simple fact of incarcera-

tion. However just or necessary such punishments may be, their importance for our present analysis lies in the fact that they form a set of harsh social conditions to which the population of prisoners must respond or *adapt itself*. The inmate feels that the deprivations and frustrations of prison life, with all their implications for the destruction of his self-esteem, somehow must be alleviated. It is, we suggest, as an answer to this need that the functional significance of the inmate code or system of values exhibited so frequently by men in prison can best be understood.

Elsewhere they note:[28]

> The maxims of the inmate code do not simply reflect the individual values of imprisoned criminals; rather, they represent a system of group norms that are directly related to mitigating the pains of imprisonment under a custodial regime having nearly total power.

If this interpretation is valid, we might expect that the culture would exert its major impact on inmates during the *middle* of their stay, at the point in time when they are farthest removed from the outside world. We might also expect that as time for release approaches, the problems deriving from imprisonment recede relative to prospective adjustment problems on parole. Such a shift in reference should give rise to a resocialization process beginning prior to release. And if the culture has this problem-solving character, then recidivists as well as first-termers should exhibit the U-shaped pattern of response.[29]

These observations merely indicate that the two trends suggested by the data are consistent with two different interpretations of the inmate culture. On both theoretical and empirical grounds, the adaptive pattern would seem to deserve more attention than it has received in discussions of socialization in the prison. But whether either or both of these types of response are dominant patterns of adjustment in the prison cannot be assessed with the cross-sectional design used in the present study. A panel study in which inmates were interviewed in the early, middle, and late phases of incarceration, and scored as conformist (+) or deviant (−) in their orientation to the staff and the outside world, would yield eight possible response patterns describing the inmate's movement through his institutional career. In addition to the prisonization and adaptation patterns (+ − − and + − +) there are patterns of stable conformity and stable deviance (+ + + and − − −), a delayed prisonization pattern (+ + −), patterns of rehabilitation or delayed rehabilitation (− + + and − − +), and a counteradaptive pattern (− + −) in which the inmate appears to move toward a conventional orientation during the middle of his stay only to return to the deviant response as he approaches parole. Anecdotal evidence and informal observation suggest that all of these patterns might be found, though the prisonization and adaptation patterns may be the most frequent of those in which change occurs. One suggestion emerging from our analysis of the adaptive pattern is that while changes from early to middle phase may reflect events within the institution, changes near release are largely a response to the external world. As correctional programs develop their emphases on liberal visiting, family counseling and prerelease programs, they may be able to strengthen tendencies toward a positive change in attitude during the late phases of imprisonment. In turn, current sociological accounts of the inmate culture and adjustment processes may have to be revised to deal more systematically with these external influences.

**Conditions affecting type of response.** When Clemmer wrote *The Prison Community,* it was perhaps reasonable to note under "conditions affecting degree of prisonization" only the personal characteristics of offenders. Prisons were pretty much alike, classification between institutions was weak, and the processes Clemmer noted could be assumed to be relatively constant across a range of institutions. Current correctional systems increasingly depart from this image, and it is likely that both type of clientele and institutional program exert an effect on socialization processes. For example, the fate of those who enter prison with an initially conformist orientation probably depends in large part on the balance between initial conformists and deviants: as the proportion of initial deviants increases, there is greater pressure on the conformists to move away from the pattern of stable conformity. This relationship in turn probably depends on the average age of offenders in the institution. Thus adult maximum security prisons tend to get a very large proportion of inmates who are deviant at time of entrance, but the advanced age of initial conformists may mean that they are less susceptible to influence from the inmate culture. Juvenile institutions are likely to receive a larger number of offenders whose frames of reference are not solidified, and who may thus be more susceptible to peer-group influence. A less "negative" inmate culture may still produce the prisonization response. These features of the inmate population probably interact with staff programs (including the attempts in some institutions to neutralize the inmate culture) to create further modifications in the socialization process in different institutions. The growing differentiation of correctional institutions reinforces the need for comparative analyses and serves as a reminder of the limits of generalization from studies of the type reported in this paper.

**Prison and Parole Adjustment.** The suggestion that the inmate's response to the prison is adaptive—that he becomes deprisonized as well as prisonized—raises the question of the impact of incarceration on parole conduct. Failure on parole is frequently viewed as the result of internalization of a criminal value system while in prison. But evidence of a cyclical type of adjustment suggests that the process is more complex than is implied in the prisonization scheme. The value system learned in prison may serve as a set of rationalizations activated only when the parolee faces what he defines as barriers to success on parole. Even though the inmate sheds the culture of the prison, it will have provided him with justifications for criminal behavior that may be invoked in the event of post-release adjustment difficulties. The prisonization effect may still be operating, though not in the simple and direct fashion implied by the "crime school" image. Its effect is probably modified in important ways by different types of parole settings.

There is a danger, however, of pressing the concept of prisonization too far as an explanation of the prison's impact on parole behavior. Another feature of imprisonment would appear to have an extremely potent influence. This is the impact on the offender's self-conception rather than upon his attitudes toward the outside world. Almost all accounts of correctional processes note what Ohlin has referred to as the "self defining character of the experiences to which the offender is exposed by correctional agencies."[30] In many instances, these effects appear to be highly related to the prisonization process. The offender learns to reject society and in doing so comes to accept a conception of himself as a criminal, with an elaborate set of supporting justifications. But much of the impact of imprisonment appears to lie along another dimension of self-image—the tendency for the offender to internalize the social rejection implicit in his status and suffer the pains of a lowered self-esteem and self-rejection. In the work of McCorkle and Korn and more recently in Sykes and Messinger, these potential attacks on the offender's self-image are taken as a crucial condition giving rise to the inmate value system. Self-esteem is restored by participation in a system that enables the offender to "reject his rejectors, rather than himself."[31] But if the inmate culture has the problem-solving function stressed in these accounts, and if many men show an adaptive response, it follows that the salience of the culture is reduced as men prepare to leave it. This reduction is probably "functional" in the sense that many of the problems of imprisonment do in fact decrease as the inmate nears release. This would seem to be true of most of the threats to self noted by Sykes and Messinger, including the extensive social control of the custodians, the constant presence of other inmates, and the material and sexual deprivations. However, the sense of rejection and degradation implicit in the offender's status does not necessarily decline with release, for the ex-con label still applies. The inmate who sheds the negative outlook required by the inmate system may inherit in its place the rejecting feelings the culture served largely to deny. In this sense the function of the inmate culture may be to *delay* the facing of problems imposed by a degraded social status, rather than to solve them.

This interpretation may help account for the profound states of anxiety and lack of confidence in themselves which even seemingly "tough" inmates frequently display prior to release.[32] As the inmate turns his attention from the inside to the free community, as he makes contacts with employers and relatives, the definition of his status provided by the inmate code loses much of its significance. But it is precisely at this point when the meaning of being an inmate, *as it is viewed by the outside world,* is most likely to have its impact. Some inmates find an atmosphere of acceptance and encouragement. Many others may find that certain jobs are not open to them, that there is some question as to how welcome they are in the community, that they are generally defined as "risks" and not accorded full status. They may return to associations with other ex-offenders not so much to continue a criminal career as to find a more supportive social setting, though further crimes may well grow out of such contacts.

If this interpretation is correct, many of the psychological pains of imprisonment are revealed most clearly at time of release rather than entry. It suggests a basis for a cyclical fluctuation of attitudes as the offender sheds the culture of the prison, experiences social rejection, finds support among other former inmates, returns to crime and to prison, reincorporates prison values, and so on. If true, it points to another possible reason for the organization of therapeutic efforts around the time of release, as well as to the limitations of such efforts unless they can bring about a change in the response to the offender on the part of those in his parole environment. And it suggests that sociological research should be as concerned with the process of re-entry into the community as it has been historically with the problem of assimilation in prison.[33]

One final problem may be noted. Prisons along with other types of "total institutions" are usually assumed to have deep and long-lasting effects on the values of their members. The assumption is natural, deriving as it does largely from the potential effect of twenty-four-hour living establishments that allow only psychological means of escape. The view is supported by a tendency to study the processes of *induction* into such institutions, where the initial effects stand out very clearly.[34] But in most such institutions, membership is temporary. Inmates leave as well as enter. If the institutions tend to develop subcultures specific to the problems imposed by their rather unique character, their members may be insulated from lasting socialization effects. In the case of prisons, this insulation provides a less negative picture of the effects of the institution than emerges from analysis of the inmate culture. In therapeutically oriented total institutions, the positive effects may be suppressed. We might expect this suppression of lasting effects to occur particularly in institutions where membership is involuntary. Another relevant condition may be a known and relatively brief duration of confinement.[35] Both of these conditions are present in reformatories.

# NOTES

SOURCE: *American Sociological Review*, XXVI (October 1961), 697–712.
* Expanded and revised version of a paper read at the meetings of the American Sociological Association, Chicago, 1959. The author is greatly indebted to Dr. Clarence Schrag, University of Washington, for aid and criticism in the formulation of the research, and to the inmates and staff of Western State Reformatory for their co-operation.
1. Donald Clemmer, *The Prison Community* (New York: Rinehart and Co., 1958, reissue of original 1940 edition).
2. *Ibid.,* 299.
3. *Ibid.,* 300–2; 312.
4. *Ibid.,* 312. Clemmer noted two other conditions that affect degree of prisonization: degree of "blind acceptance" of the dogmas and codes of the inmate population, and degree of participation in gambling and abnormal sex activity. Since these variables seem so closely tied to the concept of prisonization, they might be thought of as indicators of that concept rather than as conditions that affect it.
5. Edwin H. Sutherland and Donald R. Cressey, *Principles of Criminology*, revised edition (New York: J. B. Lippincott Co., 1955), 78–79.
6. Albert K. Cohen, *Delinquent Boys* (Glencoe: Free Press, 1955), 18–19.
7. Gresham M. Sykes and Sheldon L. Messinger, "The Inmate Social System," in Richard A. Cloward, Donald R. Cressey, George H. Grosser, Richard McCleery, Lloyd E. Ohlin, Gresham M. Sykes, and Sheldon Messinger, *Theoretical Studies in Social Organization of the Prison* (New York: Social Science Research Council, 1960), 11–13.
8. Clemmer, *op. cit.,* 294.
9. In addition to possible differences in response depending on whether the inmate has a time orientation to the past, the present, or the

future (or perhaps an orientation which encompasses all these by stressing the total expected duration of confinement), there is of course the important variable of indefiniteness of knowledge about the date of release. See Maurice L. Farber, "Suffering and Time Perspective of the Prisoner," *University of Iowa Studies in Child Welfare,* 20 (1944), 153–227. The indefiniteness is probably more important in other types of total institutions, especially concentration camps, tuberculosis sanatoria, and mental hospitals. In correctional institutions the sentence and release authorities tend to develop routinized forms of administering the indeterminate sentence laws, so that most offenders know quite early in their stay about how long they will have to serve.

10. The analysis below excludes from the protection and segregation units fourteen inmates for whom data were lacking on the time variable. Another eight inmates were excluded because of nonresponse to one of the five items in the conformity index. The resulting n is 214. Wherever the reported n's fall below that figure it is due to lack of complete information on one of the independent variables. Results from each sampling unit have been combined in the analysis but have not been weighted for differences in sampling rates. Such differences could affect the results only if $r_{ab}$ in sampling unit X differs from $r_{ab}$ in sampling unit Y. Snedecor's test for heterogeneity showed no significant differences for ten of the most important relationships in the study. Therefore the simplification achieved by unweighted combining would seem to be justifiable.

11. Staff responses were based on samples of 81 of 111 custody staff members, and 18 of 21 treatment staff members. For a fuller discussion of the methodology employed, see Stanton Wheeler, *Social Organization in a Correctional Community* (unpublished Ph.D. dissertation, University of Washington, 1958). More recent analysis of the index suggests that the items form a Guttman scale with reproducibility = .92, only moderately high for five items. Results reported below are based, however, on the Likert scoring system used earlier. Differences are very slight and do not affect the conclusions.

12. Samuel A. Stouffer and Jackson Toby, "Role Conflict and Personality," in Talcott Parsons and Edward A. Shils, editors, *Toward a General Theory of Action* (Cambridge: Harvard University Press, 1951), 483.

13. It is not at all certain that those who have served longer are necessarily the more criminally mature inmates. Many who receive long sentences are first offenders who have committed what the law judges to be the more serious offenses. This judgment bears no necessary relationship to the inmate's orientation to staff or to other inmates. For evidence on the complex relationship between length of time served and adjustment after release, see Donald L. Garrity, *The Effects of Length of Incarceration upon Parole Adjustment and Estimation of Optimum Sentence: Washington State Correctional Institutions* (unpublished Ph.D. dissertation, University of Washington, 1956).

14. The one-tailed chi square test may be ambiguous in tables with df greater than 1. Inspection of the tables presented below suggests that the one-tailed test in these cases is justified. Cf. the discussion be-

tween Grusky and Shaw, *American Journal of Sociology*, 65 (November 1959), 301–2.

15. Leo A. Goodman and William H. Kruskal, "Measures of Association for Cross-Classifications," *Journal of the American Statistical Association*, 49 (December 1954), 747–54. The "gamma" measure reflects the probability of like vs. unlike orders in the classification. It is a useful measure when one deals with ordered classes, and it avoids some of the problems of chi-square based measures. However, it has one property in common with most other measures of association for cross-classifications in that its value depends in part on the marginal distributions. This effect is relatively minor when the measure is used for comparisons within a given set of data provided the marginals on the independent variables are roughly similar across the tables. The effect of differing marginals should probably be controlled, however, in any comparison with data from a different sample. See the discussion on pages 745–47 of the Goodman and Kruskal paper.

16. Richard Cloward reports a similar finding based on research in a military prison. See Helen Witmer and Ruth Kotinsky, editors, *New Perspectives for Research on Juvenile Delinquency* (Washington, D.C.: U.S. Department of Health, Education and Welfare, Children's Bureau, 1956), 80–91.

17. The items used to measure extensiveness and intensity were:
    Have you developed any close friendships with other inmates since you have been in the reformatory?
    ...... Yes, several (more than 5)
    ...... Yes, a few (3 to 5)
    ...... Yes, one or two
    ...... No
    Think back over the past month in the reformatory. How would you say you spent most of your free time?
    ...... Mostly with a group of inmates who are together quite a lot
    ...... With one or two inmates
    ...... With several different inmates, but not in any one group
    ...... Mostly by myself
    In Tables 4 and 5, the top two categories are combined for high involvement, the bottom two for low involvement.

18. The strain may be similar to that noted in small group research, between the expressive and instrumental roles. Persons who initially play both the best-ideas and best-liked roles tend to drop the former role for the latter as interaction continues. Talcott Parsons, Robert F. Bales, and Edward A. Shils, *Working Papers in the Theory of Action* (Glencoe: Free Press, 1953), 150–61.

19. Gresham M. Sykes, *The Society of Captives* (Princeton: Princeton University Press, 1958), 84–108. Clarence C. Schrag, *Social Types in a Prison Community* (unpublished master's thesis, University of Washington, 1944).

20. Richard A. Cloward, "Illegitimate Means, Anomie, and Deviant Behavior," *American Sociological Review*, 24 (April 1959), 175.

21. "Role Conflict in Correctional Communities," in Donald R. Cressey, editor, *The Prison: Studies in Institutional Organization and Change* (New York: Holt, Rinehart & Winston Co., 1961).

22. The suggestion that prisonization and social isolation are alternative

forms of response to the prison, each posing different problems of adjustment upon release, does not preclude the possibility that inmates may adopt both forms of response at different stages in their incarceration. Again, panel studies are required to trace the interactions between these forms of response. For some suggestions of possible linkages between the two patterns, see Lloyd E. Ohlin, *Sociology and the Field of Corrections* (New York: Russell Sage Foundation, 1956), 37–40.

23. Another potential bias required analysis at this point. Inmates receiving the longest sentences are more likely to be included in the middle phase, while inmates receiving short sentences are overrepresented in the late phase. The differences between middle and late phase inmates could thus be due to selective factors.

The best available check on the existence of such a bias is to consider the responses of middle and late phase inmates separately in terms of total expected time to be served. If the result is due to selection, the differences between middle and late phases should disappear.

This procedure yielded the following results: For low total time inmates, the percentage high conformity was 28 per cent in the middle phase, 44 per cent in the late phase, for low conformity from 11 per cent to 25 per cent. For high total time inmates, the per cent high conformity moved from 21 per cent in the middle phase to 38 per cent in the late phase; for low conformity from 15 per cent to 25 per cent. Thus the relationships hold when total length of sentence is controlled. Use of other cutting points for total time served produced roughly similar results, though suggesting that resocialization operates more strongly for inmates with short sentences, much less strongly for inmates with long sentences.

24. One may question the use of gamma as a measure of association for U-shaped distributions such as those indicated in table 8, for (provided the marginals are balanced) the measure will give a value of zero for a perfectly U-shaped distribution, although obviously there is "a relationship." One might think of the measure in the present case as reflecting the "net effect" of imprisonment, in which case the measure appropriately gives a value of zero if changes between the early and middle phases are offset by changes between the middle and late phases. Table 8 also demonstrates the dependence of gamma on the marginal distribution. If our sample contained equal numbers of inmates in the early, middle, and last phases, the gamma for the relationship among the "high contacts" group would drop from −.38 to −.18, and for the "low contacts" group from −.07 to zero.

25. A pattern similar to that found here has been observed in a state penitentiary. See Peter Garabedian, *Western Penitentiary: A Study in Social Organization* (unpublished Ph.D. dissertation, University of Washington, 1959).

26. Clarence C. Schrag, *op. cit.* See also Gresham M. Sykes, *op. cit.*, 84–108.

27. Gresham M. Sykes and Sheldon L. Messinger, *op. cit.*, 15.

28. *Ibid.*, 19.

29. A third possible interpretation is that the U-shaped distribution would disappear if one could control adequately for a "social desirability" response set which may be more likely during the early and late stages of confinement. The conditions of administration of the re-

search were designed, of course, to reduce this possibility, but further controls are necessary before this interpretation can be ruled out. The increase in extreme nonconformity during the late stage shows that the effect is not a general one. Also, one would expect that if the effect is operating, it would be sustained at least until inmates had received their sentences, (sometime between the third and sixth months of incarceration). But the evidence from table 3 suggests that the decline in conformity operates before this major administrative decision is made.

30. Ohlin, *op. cit.,* 33.

31. Lloyd W. McCorkle and Richard Korn, "Resocialization Within Walls," *The Annals of the American Academy of Political and Social Science,* 293 (May 1954), 88–98.

32. Robert Lindner, *Stone Walls and Men* (New York: Odyssey Press, Inc., 1946), 422.

33. Prison officials have long been aware of the potential changes in offenders as they near release, and in some institutions special programs are devoted to "prerelease" training or therapy. Useful information on changes in adjustment associated with release is being developed by Daniel Glaser in his panel study of inmates in the federal prison system. (Editor's note: The report of the study has been since published in book form: Daniel Glaser, *The Effectiveness of a Prison and Parole System,* [Bobbs-Merrill, 1964].)

34. It appears that studies of mental hospitals as well as prisons have emphasized the induction process. For a perceptive account of induction phenomena in mental hospitals, see Erving Goffman, "The Moral Career of the Mental Patient," *Psychiatry,* 22 (May 1959), 123–42. For a suggestion that the effects of these processes in mental hospitals and other types of total institutions may well disappear with release, see Goffman, "On the Characteristics of Total Institutions," *Proceedings of the Symposium on Preventive and Social Psychiatry* (Walter Reed Army Institute of Research, Washington, D.C., April 1957), 35–36. (Editor's note: An expanded version of this paper appears as chapters 1 and 2 of Donald R. Cressey, editor, *The Prison: Studies in Institutional Organization and Change* [New York: Holt, Rinehart & Winston, 1961], 15–106.)

35. Some of the effects of involuntary membership have been outlined by Festinger, "An Analysis of Compliant Behavior," in Sherif and Wilson, editors, *Group Relations at the Crossroads* (New York: Harper and Brothers, 1953). See also John W. Thibaut and Harold H. Kelley, *The Social Psychology of Groups* (New York: John Wiley and Sons, Inc., 1959), 168–90. The concept of voluntary membership itself deserves further clarification. Membership in colleges and professional schools is usually regarded as voluntary, since the member chooses to apply. Since membership in such institutions is frequently the only means of achieving other desired ends (such as the legal right to teach, practice medicine, etc.), elements of involuntary membership are present. Membership may be something to be endured rather than enjoyed. Such settings may produce less over-all change in values than is usually supposed. Thus Becker and Geer found a U-shaped attitudinal shift in medical students similar in form to our findings for the reformatory. The idealism of entering students was corroded during the middle of their stay, under the pressure to get

the training and grades necessary for graduation, though it emerged again as they neared "release." See "The Fate of Idealism in Medical School," *American Sociological Review*, 23 (February 1958), 50–56. Newcomb's finding of a steadily increasing commitment to the institution's values at Bennington College may be attributed in part to the relatively earlier age at entrance, the spirit of newness, and the high prestige of the institution and its staff. As such it may not be typical of the pattern of value change to be found in many colleges or universities lacking these qualities. Theodore Newcomb, *Personality and Social Change* (New York: Dryden Press, 1943).

# 8

# EFFECTIVE INSTITUTIONS FOR JUVENILE DELINQUENTS: A RESEARCH STATEMENT

*Robert Vinter and Morris Janowitz†*

Until the recent past, many correctional institutions for juvenile and youthful offenders were characterized by harsh and punitive practices. "Hard core" delinquent youth were confined under conditions of repression and, occasionally, brutality.[1] Gradually these practices have given way with an increase of general humanitarian values and because of the efforts of dedicated career personnel. Today only isolated examples of institutions patterned after the adult prison are to be found. Custody and care of delinquent youth continue to be the goals of correctional agencies, but there are growing aspirations for remedial treatment. The public expects juvenile correctional institutions to serve a strategic role in changing the behavior of delinquents.[2]

Contrary to expectations, persistent problems have been encountered in attempting to move correctional institutions beyond mere custodialism. The introduction of mental health perspectives and of skilled personnel—psychiatrists, psychologists, social workers—has been the dominant trend. Despite strenuous efforts and real innovations, significant advances beyond custody have not been achieved.[3] This article sets forth a brief analysis of certain problems apparent in the development of more effective programs and describes a field research project aimed at exploration of these problems. The writers are co-directors of this research.[4]

Some of the problems in improving institutional effectiveness stem from three major misconceptions. First, the correctional agency cannot be expected, by itself, to resolve the

† Robert Vinter is an associate professor at the School of Social Work at the University of Michigan; Morris Janowitz is a professor in the Department of Sociology at the University of Chicago.

personal and social problems posed by delinquency. These problems must be resolved primarily through other community organizations. Juvenile correctional institutions, if they had effective remedial programs, would assist other groups and agencies to perform their preventive functions.

Second, the mental health approach tends to conceive of the delinquent as a person characterized primarily by emotional problems.[5] While this formulation is theoretically justified in the sense that all persons must learn to live with frustration, it is only partially accurate. As a basis for designing services and treatment practices, it must be substantially broadened in order to take into account the social dynamics of delinquency.

Third, many of the specific psychotherapeutic practices advocated by specialized personnel now employed in correctional institutions are both inadequate and insufficient. Efforts to modify juvenile correctional institutions from custodial to remedial agencies have been impeded. They will continue to be impeded if the method of operation is merely a projection of processes that ideally take place in the two-person psychotherapeutic system. In the most advanced residential centers, psychotherapeutic practices have been modified to conform to the nature of delinquency, on the one hand, and to the reality of institutional life, on the other. As a result, these residential centers do not practice conventional psychotherapy, but have evolved a therapeutic milieu in which rehabilitation takes place.[6] But the fragmentary and segmented therapeutic practices which characterize most innovations in juvenile institutions are believed to be inadequate and insufficient to attain remedial goals. It is illusory to proceed on the assumption that the "ideal" conditions which exist at a few residential settings can be achieved by most juvenile correctional institutions.

## PERFORMANCE CRITERIA FOR CORRECTIONAL INSTITUTIONS

An effective correctional institution has specific objectives both for the short-run confinement period and for the long-run period after release. These objectives must be based on adequate conceptions of delinquency. In actual practice juvenile delinquency is conceived of essentially as nonconformity with legal norms of the community. Youth are judged as delinquent and are committed to correctional institutions when it is impossible to maintain conformity in their behavior through conventional community groups and controls. Theoretically, their deviancy may be psychologically defined as inability to internalize and accept desirable social norms and values because of the failure of personal controls; or socially defined as the inability of community systems to enforce appropriate roles because of the failure of social controls.[7] Achievement of conformity is the primary goal of correctional services. Historically, correctional institutions have attempted to achieve conformity by repressive confinement, once believed to enhance personal controls. Repression does not produce conformity after release, however. There is no evidence to show that repressive measures induce positive personality change or conformity to legal norms. In fact, the experience of being dominated leads to covert rebellion within the institution and continued delinquent behavior after release.

The central problem is that the deviant person, socially or psychologically defined, cannot be expected to conform on the basis of mere submission in the open, individualistic, achievement-oriented society. He must develop positive skills and emotional controls which make it possible for him to master in some degree his social environment. Such mastery requires the securing of gratifications while behaving in socially acceptable ways.

Many institutional populations include large proportions of both "social" and "psychologically disturbed" delinquents. Social delinquents are persons with relatively adequate and undamaged personalities. Their deviancy usually originates in adherence to nonlegal values and norms, induced through membership in various subcultural groups (family, friendship, neighborhood) sharing such deviant values.[8] Disturbed delinquents are those with damaged or otherwise inadequate personalities. The source of their deviancy is usually inability to internalize social norms and to restrain impulsivity, or to achieve a viable state of emotional integration. Thereby the disturbed delinquent is unable to secure gratification in conventional ways.[9]

The proportion of these types among client populations is unknown. Reports from the field suggest an increase in the proportion of disturbed delinquents. There are, of course, still others among institutional populations who cannot be so characterized, e.g., the mentally retarded, neglected children, psychotics, and others. It is well recognized that such youth should not be in correctional institutions and cannot be effectively served by them.

The specific objectives of remedial institutions are to aid in the development of effective personal controls and to maintain successful social controls. Criteria for evaluating the performance of institutions must be consistent with the social and psychological dimensions of delinquent deviancy. For the social delinquent, this means development of new sets of values and norms which will permit him to function in the community. For the disturbed delinquent, it means the development of ego and superego controls which will permit him to restrain his impulsivity and achieve emotional gratification in the community.

## CRITIQUE OF PRESENT PROGRAMS

Most institutional programs for juvenile delinquents can be described as falling somewhere along a custodial-therapeutic continuum. Emphasis at one pole is on containing the delinquents and affording at least momentary relief and protection to their home communities. There is little attempt to change the clients, except as enforced obedience and confinement are assumed to inhibit further deviancy. At the other pole, emphasis is on achieving personality change through a variety of specific treatment services. The majority of institutional programs appear to fall between the polar extremes; they present varying degrees of both custody and treatment.

Increasing public concern with humanitarian values has reduced support for purely custodial goals. Institutions, particularly those for children and youth, are expected to serve their clients in some ways, as well as to segregate them from the local community. Therapeutic institutional programs are enjoying considerable vogue, partly in their mere contrast to custodial practices. However, as developed in most juvenile correctional institutions, these therapeutic programs are limited in their theoretical conceptions and in their resources. Psychotherapeutic services and techniques generally assume voluntarism in client participation. Yet there is nothing voluntary about the client's entrance into the institution and very little about his typical experiences and relationships within the program. An essential condition of therapeutic practice, therefore, is not fulfilled. The presumption of client homogeneity is another limitation of the therapeutic approach. Therapeutic services are seemingly based on the presumption that each client either has internal problems or has difficulty in relating to his social environment. For the social delinquent in particular, this presumption has doubtful validity; such clients usually manifest effective ego strength and are well oriented to their immediate social environment, although it may be a deviant subculture. Treatment approaches directed at similar emotional problems or seeking certain psychological responses (e.g., guilt, insight, communication skills) are, therefore, incongruent with actual client characteristics.

Therapeutic programs are also limited in their implementation. Social workers, clinical psychologists, psychiatrists, and special teachers are among the specialized personnel in correctional institutions. These professional workers have introduced a variety of specific practices and services such as refined diagnostic procedures, individual counseling, individual and group treatment, case study, and staff consultation. But with isolated exceptions of some small institutions,[10] such therapeutic services are segmented and partial. A major difficulty in implementing a therapeutically oriented program is the critical shortage of specialized personnel.[11] The shortage precludes programs requiring high staff-client ratios and intensive screening of all personnel.

The crucial limitation, however, stems from the origin of psychotherapeutic practices in the two-person system. Much interaction in the correctional institution involves larger social systems, for which projections cannot be made from clinical practice. Therefore, persistent problems are encountered in attempting to move institutional programs beyond the plateau of discrete and segmented therapeutic practices. The introduction of such practices not infrequently leads to new strains in the institution. These may result in an increase of custodial emphases in particular areas or even the conversion of therapeutic practices to the service of custodial ends.[12]

The approaches that have been reviewed are collectively referred to in this article as segmented therapeutic practices. They are so characterized because they are typically introduced piecemeal and neither guide the entire institutional program nor wholly infuse it. Remedial programs, in contrast, are conceived as meeting the requirements set forth. That is, they are based on adequate conceptions of delinquency, and they provide directions for institutional operation that are both comprehensive and realistic.

## COMPARATIVE RESEARCH

Implementation of remedial goals requires an understanding of the particular dilemmas that confront correctional institutions in this period of transition. The persistence of barriers to increased effectiveness and the difficulties encountered with the introduction of therapeutic practices merit special study. With these purposes in mind a comparative study has been undertaken of a sample of six correctional institutions serving juvenile delinquents and youthful offenders. The sample is designed to contrast institutions in terms of the type and extent of their therapeutic practices. During a three-year period it also will be possible to study changes occurring within these institutions. Specific observational and measurement procedures have been developed out of previous studies.[13] The research task is to formulate and test a conception of a comprehensive program that includes all of the subsystems in the institution and is, therefore, designed to maximize the remedial effectiveness of the total program.

In order to analyze the dilemmas of correctional institutions as they introduce segmental therapeutic programs, it is appropriate to consider such institutions as a special type of social system, namely as a bureaucratic or large-scale organization. While the theoretical analysis of organizational behavior is hardly as well developed as that of personality development, the essential foundations have been formulated. The guiding lines of a sociological perspective can be found in the writings of such persons as Max Weber, Talcott Parsons, Harold Lasswell, and Herbert Simon.[14] The bureaucratic organization is characterized by its premeditated effort to assemble personnel and resources in order to achieve specific goals. Among the questions that need to be asked in analyzing organizational behavior are: How do the goals of the organization fashion its internal workings? What is the basis of its authority system, and what types of sanctions is it able to exercise? What is the impact of informal social relations on the formal organizational structure? The sociological perspective stresses the need to understand organizational dynamics in terms of all the subsystems which operate within the correctional institution. This implies not merely the specialized therapeutic personnel but all of the groups that are part of the daily operations.

All organizations are confronted with dilemmas in the pursuit of their goals. The introduction of therapeutic programs into custodial institutions presents basic and pervasive conflicts. For the purposes of research, it is possible to think of five subsystems in the correctional institution. These are: client organization, staff-client relations, staff-staff relations, institution-local-community relations, and staff-parent-organization relations. The assumption is made that an effective remedial program requires an appropriate articulation of all of these. A set of illustrative hypotheses for each subsystem can be offered to explain organizational behavior as the institution moves from a custodial to a segmented therapeutic program. The hypotheses are of two types. In each case the first hypothesis (A) indicates the initial response in the organization as therapeutic programs are introduced. The second hypothesis (B) indicates the presumed secondary consequences on remedial effectiveness. The rationale for the hypotheses is set forth with some indication of available evidence. These hypotheses provide direction for a comparative study of juvenile correctional institutions.

## I. Client organization

(A) *The informal client leadership which develops with the introduction of segmented therapeutic practices is judged by the staff as being more co-operative, better adjusted to the institution, and more likely to conform after release than the informal leadership which develops under predominantly custodial practices.*

(B) *Accommodation between staff and clients must exist in all types of institutions. In the custodial system, co-operation between the staff and clients is limited and based on dissimilar goals, while the introduction of segmented therapeutic practices tends to produce more generalized co-operation, based on more similar goals.*

A client culture and informal leadership emerge within all institutional systems. Major functions of the client leaders are to present role models for other clients and to mediate between the clients and the staff. In custodial institutions co-operation is certain to be limited and to be directed toward dissimilar ends; client leaders support the institutional order since open conflict would jeopardize the status system which provides them with social and tangible rewards (e.g., contraband).[15] Covertly, however, they disseminate anti-institutional orientations and enforce an informal system opposed to remedial values.[16] The repressive practices of the custodial program reinforce and validate the client leaders' oppositional views.

The functions served by client leaders require that they possess relatively effective personalities with strong ego controls. They must be able to sustain relations with their peers, to organize covert client activities, and to restrain impulsivity so that they may maintain minimal co-operative contact with staff members.[17] Because of their personal effectiveness and their strategic roles, these informal leaders are of crucial importance in any attempt to influence the client population.

Except in crisis situations, highly disturbed individuals are unable to meet the demands posed for client leadership.

The problem is twofold: (1) to infuse the client system with a high level of commitment to legal values and norms and (2) to reinforce weak ego controls through the dynamics of the peer group. Both aims can be assisted by the informal leadership, since more positive emphases and benign practices in therapeutic programs usually result in greater harmony between staff and clients. Clients who become leaders or who are invested with leadership by the staff are viewed as co-operative, best-adjusted, and most likely to succeed upon return to their home communities. These leaders conform more closely to the remedial ideology of the institution than the rest of the clients or than client leaders in custodial programs. Infusion of a high level of therapeutic commitment can have the effect of producing an informal leadership cadre whose behavior is more likely to disseminate the staff ideology.[18] However, because of the partial and segmented nature of actual therapeutic practices, many other features of institutional life vitiate the positive influence of the leaders on clients. Desirable values and role models which may be presented by client leaders are insufficient to offset negative effects of institutional conditions not governed by treatment considerations. Under these circumstances, undesirable definitions and delinquent role models will persist and be reinforced among the clients.[19] Therefore, an increase in co-operation between client leaders and staff toward similar goals is an essential requirement for the remedial institution but hardly sufficient to guarantee an effective program. It is an object of the research to determine how much and what types of therapeutic efforts are necessary to infuse such a set of attitudes among the informal leaders.

## II. Staff-client relations

    *(A)* *While custodial programs maintain sharp cleavages between the staff and the clients, based on domination-submission, the introduction of segmented therapeutic practices results in staff-client relations based on a mixture of domination and persuasion.*

*(B)* *The shift in authority patterns with the introduction*
*of a segmented therapeutic program produces incon-*
*sistent and particularized organizational practices that*
*thwart the goals of the institution.*

The cleavage between staff and clients in the custodially
oriented institution is especially marked; it assumes the character of domination and submission. Co-operation and positive
involvement of the clients can generally be secured only by
means responsive to their interests. Incongruity between custodial aims and client interests necessitates domination by
staff. This customarily takes the form of repressive practices
which enforce client obedience and submission.[20] Such practices and staff-client relations reinforce delinquent values
among clients and prevent, or even reverse, the development
of ego controls.

The introduction of specific therapeutic practices usually
implies that clients are handled in a more permissive manner. There interests are respected, and emphasis is placed on
persuasion by staff and consent by clients. These more benign
relations may characterize both the specific therapeutic services (e.g., individual and group counseling sessions) and the
entire range of interaction between clients and staff members. The spread of such client-staff relations is limited for
most institutions, however, to those practices and personnel
clearly designated as therapeutic. Other areas of institutional
operation (e.g., work details) and other groups of personnel
(e.g., house parents) may not be similarly guided by therapeutic considerations and objectives. Major inconsistencies are
thus introduced into the institutional system, and clients are
treated differently depending on the situation and the personnel group.[21]

The remedial program requires that staff-client relations
maximize the development of ego controls and offer a coherent value system as an alternative to delinquent values. The
development of ego controls can be facilitated as clients are
helped to increase their mastery and to gain positive self-
images. These processes are induced by relations with adult
staff members which are consistent and responsive to client

interests. The necessity for adequate custody poses a major dilemma in achieving desirable staff-client relations, since it appears to dictate procedures which limit the bases for co-operation. Furthermore, maintenance of consistency and infusion of co-operation into all areas of staff-client relations may be especially problematic for larger institutions. These issues create particular difficulties in designing effective interpersonal relations for the correctional institution. To ensure an adequate solution, there must be an organizational format which permits a pattern of consistent and generalized relations between staff and clients. It is an object of the research to compare different organizational formats as they contribute to a solution of this dilemma.

### III. Staff-staff relations

(*A*) *The introduction of treatment personnel to develop a segmented therapeutic program produces an unstable bifurcation of the organization.*

(*B*) *This bifurcation results in both a thwarting of remedial goals and a conversion of therapeutic practices into support for custodial goals.*

Except in the case of the small, newly created, treatment-oriented institution, specialized therapeutic personnel have been gradually added to existing correctional staff. Resources available are insufficient to permit the wholesale replacement of staff with specialized personnel, and tenure staff must be retained. These latter are, primarily, persons responsible for custodial functions, group management, and organizational maintenance. Institutional purposes continue to include custody as a major goal; therapeutic personnel are the newcomers, and the treatment practices they initiate are typically superimposed on the basic program. Therapeutic personnel tend to differ in many respects from other staff: they have additional education and special training, they are affiliated with professional associations, and they are oriented toward professional rather than institutional careers.

Given these conditions, it is not difficult to comprehend the cleavages that characteristically develop between staff groups.

Professional workers maintain conceptions of appropriate goals for correctional institutions which differ from those of nonprofessional personnel and place greater emphasis on treatment than on custodial purposes. Because of their specialized training and distinctive goal conceptions, they are oriented toward introducing and engaging in new practices, and they propose different bases for decision-making.[22] The specific practices they introduce tend to be, therefore, disconnected from other aspects of the total program. For example, clinicians may try to refine the diagnostic and classification procedures, yet clients may continue to be assigned to the same general program and living arrangements which prevailed under earlier regimes. Or social workers and psychologists may institute individual and group treatment practices, while in most other respects the clients continue to experience custodially oriented conditions. It must be observed that the several professional groups have somewhat different commitments and approaches. Within a given institution, rivalry and competition stemming from these differences increase the problems. Cleavages among staff and segmentation of operating practices create a climate of inconsistency for clients and a struggle among staff groups for the co-operation of clients.

Not infrequently professional competencies are converted to serve custodial rather than therapeutic functions. Thus, diagnostic skills may be used to identify and segregate clients who are low custodial risks, or interpersonal influence skills may be used to produce client conformity to institutional norms. As long as a general strain toward custodialism continues to characterize these institutions, therapeutic personnel tend to withdraw and to show high rates of turnover.[23] The high mobility of professional personnel and their dissatisfaction when harnessed to custodial functions directly contribute to institutional instability. This thwarts the achievement of remedial goals, disrupts harmonious institutional functioning, and even threatens maintenance of custody when staff conflict is too great.

Inconsistency and hindrance can be expected when new practices are introduced into an operating system that remains

unchanged in most other respects. Conflict and rivalry can
be expected when new kinds of personnel are introduced into
a staff structure that retains former employees and leaves
their roles substantially unchanged. These newer personnel
and practices are expected to serve treatment purposes, yet
the relationship of treatment to custody is not, in most instances, examined or clarified. The compatibility and integration of treatment and custody must be enunciated by the top
institutional authorities as a basic operating premise. Internal
stresses and unanticipated patterns are certain to occur, partly
generated by the process of change, and partly arising from
differences in personnel perspectives. Such tension can be
utilized in resolving dilemmas if the goals are integrated and
strongly supported by administrative authority.[24] Yet nothing
less than a redesign of institutional operation will permit an
incorporation of therapeutic personnel which leads to co-
operation rather than conflict.[25] Approaches to modification
of operating patterns include maximizing contributions to
remedial goals by all staff echelons and divisions, rather than
circumscribing their activities. The solution to this dilemma
requires a centralization of decision-making over the goals
and broad policies of the organization, and a decentralization of implementation of day-to-day practices. An object of
the research is to determine the structure and the patterns of
communication which provide optimum balance between centralization and decentralization.

### IV. Institution-local-community relations

(A) *While custodial programs maintain essentially non-
permeable boundaries between the institution and the
community, the introduction of segmented therapeutic
practices results in greater range and frequency of contacts between the clients and the local community.*

(B) *Unless special efforts and mechanisms are developed, an increase in the range and frequency of client-
community contacts tends to mobilize critical resistance
in the local community, which thwarts the goals of the
institution.*

To protect communities, increase punishment, and create effective restraints, adult penal institutions developed "maximum security" arrangements. Many juvenile correctional institutions developed similar patterns. Location of sites, design of buildings, and security practices were all directed at severely limiting contact between clients and the local community. Custodially oriented institutions have perpetuated many of these patterns. Extreme segregation increases client degradation and crystallizes delinquent self-images. Because of these adverse effects, the introduction of therapeutic considerations has sought to increase clients' contacts with the local community. Such contacts take various forms: more frequent visits by relatives and friends, less restricted correspondence, short home visits, trips and outings for community events, and intramural services by local volunteers. Reduction of boundaries has also led to location of institutions nearer urban communities and to avoidance of walls and fences, with construction design resembling modern schools or even villages. Benefits are seen as community reinforcing of institutionally presented legal norms and values, extending the range of client experience and providing opportunities for the development of ego controls, and increasing incentives for positive client change. Such patterns also permit a more gradual transition from institutional to community life than is possible when clients are released from maximum security conditions.[26]

An increase in clients' contacts with the local community also results, however, in greater risks. More truancy is possible, and incidents occurring off the grounds cannot be readily anticipated or handled. These events are highly visible to the local community and are customarily criticized and opposed. Critical resistance increases in the local community, which retains expectations consonant with earlier institutional emphasis on secure custody. Thus, the unilateral introduction of therapeutic practices resulting in greater client contact with the community often mobilizes opposition to the institution. The problem is aggravated by an attenuation of controls within the institution: as a consequence of greater freedom and permissiveness throughout the program, more clients may truant or engage in behavior violating custodial norms. Such incidents generally become known to the local community, adding to its sense of jeopardy.[27] Ways must therefore be devised by which client contact with the community can be increased so as to facilitate remedial effects without, at the same time, jeopardizing institutional relations with its local community. It is the object of the research to evaluate existing efforts and to determine means of increasing the permeability of boundaries without increasing community resistance.

### V. Staff-parent-organization relations

(A) *As the institution moves from custody toward segmented therapeutic practices, the parent organization (e.g., state departments which control correctional institutions) tends to establish expectations for achievement beyond the capacities of the institution.*

(B) *Conflicting pressures on the parent organization, combined with its unrealistic expectations, create instability in institutional directors and their key personnel.*

Because most attention has been focused on therapeutic practices and specialized personnel, there is widespread hope that their introduction will be accompanied by a significant increase of treatment effectiveness. Parent organizations are especially likely to maintain such expectations. They are often responsible for many of the innovations associated with therapeutic programs, including the addition of professional staff. Moreover, there are substantial pressures operating on parent organizations to reinforce their desire for achievements beyond secure custody. An increase of humanitarian values among the general public, direct pressures by powerful interest groups (e.g., professional associations, welfare organizations), and legislative and community emphases on the solution of delinquency problems raise the level of the parent organization's expectations. The location of juvenile institutions under the jurisdiction of organizations which administer children's services means that they become subject to different and more remedial expectations of this larger field.

Concurrent with desire for increased rehabilitational effectiveness, however, the parent organization typically continues to demand adequate custodial achievement by the operating institution. Enhancement of treatment effects should not, in this view, be accomplished at the expense of security. The rate of runaways, outbreaks, and rebellious episodes permissible under a primarily custodial orientation does not change when the institution shifts to a treatment orientation. Indeed, with the development of a therapeutic program in the operating institution, the parent organization may even lower its tolerance of such episodes.

Such expectations by the parent organization ignore crucial problems in the movement toward treatment. For any agency undergoing change it is to be expected that, at least temporarily, special stresses and difficulties will arise. The parent organization can grant the institution little in the way of a moratorium to accomplish a major shift in its orientation; public criticism and pressure continue without regard to internal organizational transitions. As indicated previously, present knowledge and administrative skill seem unable to achieve an adequately integrated pursuit of the dual objectives of custody and treatment. Parent-organization requirements that the juvenile institution achieve both custody and treatment (but without specification of how this is to be done) may, therefore, be unrealistic. The perspective of this statement conceives that custody and treatment are potentially compatible; but this is not to say that institutional means for their integrated implementation are currently known, except as these are being explored for the very small institution.

Institutional executives under unrealistic expectations and conflicting demands communicate these pressures downward through the staff structure and contribute to already serious operating problems.[28] Personnel dissatisfaction and turnover, rivalry among staff group, and—among lower-echelon staff—a pervasive sense of futility and injustice are some of the internal consequences of an institution's troubled relations with its parent organization. Executives are therefore induced to isolate their staff members from adverse outside pressures. At one extreme they may concur with local communities' preferences for locating institutions away from population centers:

the citizens fear depredations by truant clients, while the executives fear the impact of citizen criticism on their personnel. At another extreme, executives may attempt to monopolize contact between the institutions and their parent organizations. In between these extremes are patterns of discouraging staff membership in many types of external associations, forbidding public statements by staff, or limiting contact by outsiders with the institution. Such procedures may temporarily reduce conflicting pressures on the institution and its operating staff. However, they do not create the conditions for a stable and viable relationship between the institution and its parent organization. An object of the research is to determine the devices by which directors are able to isolate their personnel from conflicting pressures from the outside and the means by which they are able to contain the consequences of disruptive contradictory pressures.

The research as outlined will seek solutions to these dilemmas through comparative and longitudinal study of existing institutional patterns, rather than through experimental programs. Although not an evaluation of existing therapeutic services, this study is designed to throw light on the organizational arrangements and processes necessary to incorporate skilled personnel into existing organizations. It is hoped that this research will contribute to an understanding of the organizational practices required to increase the effectiveness of juvenile correctional institutions.

## NOTES

SOURCE: *Social Service Review*, XXXIII (June 1959), 118–30.

1. Albert Deutsch, *Our Rejected Children* (Boston: Little, Brown & Co., 1950).
2. *Institutions Serving Delinquent Children: Guides and Goals* (Children's Bureau Publication No. 360, Washington, D.C.: Government Printing Office, 1954), 1–8; Herbert A. Bloch and Frank T. Flynn, *Delinquency: The Juvenile Offender in America Today* (New York: Random House, 1956), chapter XV.
3. Negley K. Teeters and John O. Reinemann, *The Challenge of Delinquency* (New York: Prentice-Hall, 1950), 451–81; F. Gordon Pleune, M.D., "Effects of State Training School Programs on Juvenile Delinquents," *Federal Probation*, XXI (March 1957), 24–33.

4. The research is supported by the National Institute of Mental Health, Public Health Service, under grant M-2104.
5. Kate Friedlander, *The Psychoanalytic Approach to Juvenile Delinquency: Theory, Case Studies, Treatment* (New York: International Universities Press, 1947).
6. Bruno Bettelheim and Emmy Sylvester, M.D., "A Therapeutic Milieu," *American Journal of Orthopsychiatry*, XVIII (January 1948), 191–206; Fritz Redl and David Wineman, *Controls from Within* (Glencoe, Ill.: Free Press, 1951).
7. Albert J. Reiss, Jr., "Delinquency as the Failure of Personal and Social Controls," *American Sociological Review*, XVI (April 1951), 196–207.
8. Albert K. Cohen, *Delinquent Boys: The Culture of the Gang* (Glencoe, Ill.: Free Press, 1955), esp. chapters IV and V.
9. Various terms are used to convey this distinction. Hewitt and Jenkins have distinguished three types: the "socialized delinquent," the delinquent characterized by "unsocialized aggressive behavior" (including the psychopath), and the delinquent characterized by "overinhibited behavior." Lester E. Hewitt and Richard L. Jenkins, M.D., *Fundamental Patterns of Maladjustment: The Dynamics of Their Origin* (Springfield, Ill.: monograph published by the State of Illinois, 1946). Jenkins has argued that most delinquency can be characterized as "adaptive" (e.g., the socialized delinquent) or "maladaptive" (e.g., the unsocialized delinquent). See Richard L. Jenkins, M.D., "Adaptive and Maladaptive Delinquency," *Nervous Child*, II (October 1955), 9–11. Cf. William and Joan McCord, *Psychopathy and Delinquency* (New York: Grune & Stratton, 1956).
10. August Aichorn, *Wayward Youth*, 8th ed. (New York: Viking Press, 1947); Bettelheim and Sylvester, *op. cit.*; Redl and Wineman, *op. cit.*; Lloyd W. McCorkle, Albert Elias, and F. Lovell Bixby, *The Highfields Story: An Experimental Treatment Project for Youthful Offenders* (New York: Henry Holt & Co., 1958).
11. *Training Personnel for Work with Juvenile Delinquents* (Children's Bureau Publication No. 348 Washington, D.C.: Government Printing Office, 1954), see esp. part I.
12. Robert D. Vinter and Roger M. Lind, *Staff Relationships and Attitudes in a Juvenile Correctional Institution* (Ann Arbor, Mich.: School of Social Work, University of Michigan, 1958); Harvey Powelson and Reinhard Bendix, "Psychiatry in Prison," *Psychiatry*, XIV (February 1951), 73–86; Gresham Sykes, "The Corruption of Authority and Rehabilitation," *Social Forces*, XXXIV (March 1956), 257–62.
13. Oscar Grusky, "Treatment Goals and Organizational Behavior" (Ph.D. dissertation, University of Michigan, 1957); Vinter and Lind, *op. cit.*
14. Max Weber, *The Theory of Social and Economic Organization*, trans. A. M. Henderson and Talcott Parsons, ed. Talcott Parsons (London: Oxford University Press, 1947); Talcott Parsons, *The Social System* (Glencoe, Ill.: Free Press, 1951); Harold D. Lasswell, *Politics: Who Gets What, When and How?* (New York: McGraw-Hill Book Co., 1936); Herbert A. Simon, *Administrative Behavior*, rev. ed. (New York: Macmillan Co., 1957).
15. Lloyd Ohlin and William Lawrence, "Role of Inmate System in In-

stitutional Treatment Process," *Proceedings of the National Association of Training Schools and Juvenile Agencies,* LIV (1958), 115–36.

16. Clarence Schrag, "Leadership among Prison Inmates," *American Sociological Review,* XIX (February 1954), 37–42.

17. Helen L. Jennings, *Leadership and Isolation,* 2nd. ed. (New York: Longmans, Green & Co., 1950), 148–50, 164–66; Grusky, *op. cit.*

18. McCorkel, Elias, and Bixby, *op. cit.;* Grusky, *op. cit.* Cf. Schrag, *op. cit.*

19. Donald R. Cressey, "Changing Criminals: The Application of the Theory of Differential Association," *American Journal of Sociology,* LXI (September 1955), 116–20.

20. N. A. Polansky, "The Prison as an Autocracy," *Journal of Criminal Law and Criminology,* XXXIII (May–June, 1942), 16–22.

21. Vinter and Lind, *op. cit.,* chapter VI; Cressey, *op. cit.;* George H. Grosser, "The Role of Informal Inmate Groups in Change of Values," *Children,* V (February 1958), 25–27.

22. George H. Weber, "Conflicts Between Professional and Non-Professional Personnel in Institutional Delinquency Treatment," *Journal of Criminal Law, Criminology, and Police Science,* XLVIII (June 1957), 26–43.

23. Cf. Lloyd E. Ohlin, Herman Piven, and Donnell M. Pappenfort, "Major Dilemmas of the Social Worker in Probation and Parole," *National Probation and Parole Journal,* II (July 1956), 211–26.

24. Elliot Studt and Bernard Russell, *Staff Training for Personnel in Institutions for Juvenile Delinquents* (Children's Bureau Publication No. 364, Washington, D.C.: Government Printing Office, 1958).

25. Lloyd E. Ohlin, "The Reduction of Role Conflict in Institutional Staff," *Children,* V (March–April, 1958), 65–69.

26. McCorkel, Elias, and Bixby, *op. cit.,* chapter II.

27. Vinter and Lind, *op. cit.,* 17–20.

28. For this perspective the writers are indebted to information gained through the Workshop on Staff Development for Administrators of Institutions for Juvenile Delinquents, sponsored by the Children's Bureau at Rutgers University, 1958.

# 9

# THE INMATE GROUP IN CUSTODIAL AND TREATMENT SETTINGS*

*David Street†*

Previous accounts of correctional institutions generally have portrayed these organizations as handicapped by the informal inmate system. This system, it has been said, invariably is built around norms and values of solidary opposition to the official system and to staff, and its objectives are to minimize interference and maximize accommodations from staff, to enhance inmates' access to both official and unofficial values, to exert vigorous control over communication between inmates and staff, and to sanction an ideal model of behavior in which the inmate becomes a master at "playing it cool." So far as this system succeeds, inmates released from the institution may leave more "prisonized" than rehabilitated. Such a description often has been treated as universally valid for adult institutions,[1] and the same account appears in generally accepted descriptions of juvenile institutions.[2]

Applicable as this image of the inmate system may be to many penal institutions, it has several deficiencies as a general description and analysis. First, most of the research on which it is based involves case studies and unsystematic observation and has lacked adequate methods to assess similarities and differences between organizations or even to make satisfactory estimates of any variability in inmate orientations within the single population studied. Yet, the notion that inmate attachment to oppositional groups and culture varies has been at least implicit in much of this research,[3] and it is clearly

† David Street is an assistant professor in the Department of Sociology at the University of Chicago.

explicit in recent systematic research such as the Wheeler and Garabedian studies of socialization in the prison.[4]

Second, the "solidary opposition" account fails to consider adequately the consequences for the inmate social system of changes in the larger organization, particularly the introduction of modern treatment ideology and technology.[5] Treatment programs, if they go beyond the simple insertion of psychotherapeutic counseling into the institutional program, require fundamental alterations in staff behavior toward inmates. The distinctive sociological character of the correctional institution and the deviant background predispositions of the inmates may indeed give rise to certain patterns of group development in all correctional organizations, but it is equally probable that variations in the institutional context generate changes in the inmate system.

Third, applied a priori to juvenile correctional institutions, the generally accepted account ignores important differences between these organizations and those for adults, including the relatively short stay and presumed lesser criminality of the juveniles and the possibility that many of the social forms that constitute severe deprivation and degradation in the adult correctional institution, where men are treated like children, may not be so degrading in the juvenile institution.

Finally, many researchers in the correctional field, lacking comparative methods, have been insufficiently sensitive to a significant theoretical question: under what organizational conditions do the members of an organization collectively become committed to or alienated from the official objectives of the organization?[6] By stressing the impact of deprivation and degradation on the inmates and the ways in which the inmates defend themselves, these researchers have developed a plausible hypothesis: that the inmate group serves the function of alleviating its members' deprivation and degradation.[7] Yet, they have failed to go further and inquire into the effects of varying levels of deprivation or analyze the conditions necessary to stimulate, permit, and sustain the successful use of such a group solution to the problems of deprivation.

In contrast, this paper will treat inmate group patterns as

problematic, bringing a comparative perspective to bear on data from several juvenile institutions. This analysis should have implications for the general proposition that the characteristics and functions of informal groups vary with the larger organizational context. Hypotheses linking the larger organization to the informal inmate system were developed by considering, first, the implications of variations in goal emphasis among juvenile institutions, and, second, the characteristics of the inmate group, conceived as a problem-solving system.

## GOALS AND INSTITUTIONS

Goals may usefully be regarded as the conception of the organization's tasks held by the members whose positions make their definitions of events authoritative. Their conception of task is expressed in their views of the organization's desired end product, the "materials" it must work with, the ideal and practical requirements of the task, and the organization's distinctive competencies for it. The goals imply and set limits upon the organizational technologies seen as appropriate. Thus, goals define as required, or preferred, alternative sets of social relations between staff and inmates.

Analysis of the goals of correctional institutions provides a basis for classifying these organizations along a rough custodial-treatment continuum. This classification reflects the relative emphasis on containing the inmates as against rehabilitating them. More analytically, the continuum incorporates two dimensions of the staff conception of the organization's task: the staff members' view of the actual rehabilitational potential of the inmates, and their concept of the "materials" they have to work with and the implicit "theory of human nature" they apply to these materials.[8] At the custodial extreme, major emphasis is placed on the need to protect the community by containing the inmates within the institution. The inmates are seen as simple, similar, and relatively unchangeable creatures who require simple, routine, conventional handling. To suc-

ceed here, the inmate must conform. At the treatment extreme, community and containment are comparatively unim-
portant, and stress is put on changing the inmate's attitudes
and values by increasing his insight or otherwise altering his
psychological condition. The inmate's social identity is viewed
as problematic, and the inmates are seen as relatively complex beings who need complex, individualized, flexible handling—an attitude that sometimes requires such departures
from conventional morality as tolerance of "acting out." To
succeed here, the inmate must indicate intrapsychic change.
These variations in organizational goals are accompanied by
variations in the distribution of power in the organization: as
institutions become more treatment-oriented, power to define
events flows into the hands of a highly educated and profes-
sionalized "clinic staff."

These characterizations of the custodial and treatment types
of institution are supported by a wide variety of data from
the institutions we studied. The institutions were selected non-
randomly to ensure variation in goals and other dimensions.
Each was studied intensively through observation, interviewing, analysis of documents and file data, and administration of
questionnaires to virtually all staff members and inmates.[9]
Two of the institutions stressed custody; the other two, treatment. Ranked from more custodial to more treatment-oriented
and identified by mnemonic labels, they were:

*Dick* (Discipline)—a large (200-250 inmates) public institution which had no treatment program, whose staff felt no
lack because of this, and which concentrated on custody, hard
work, and discipline.
    *Mixter* (Mixed Goals)—a very large (375-420 inmates)
public institution with poorly integrated "mixed goals" of
custody and treatment. Some treatment was attempted, but this
was segregated from the rest of the activities, and for most
boys the environment was characterized by surveillance, frequent use of negative sanctions, and other corollaries of an
emphasis on custody.
    *Milton* (Milieu Therapy)—a fairly large (160-190 inmates)
public institution using not only individual therapy but a range

of other treatment techniques. This institution resembled Mixter in its bifurcation between treatment and containment staffs and activities, but by and large the clinicians were in control, used treatment criteria, and influenced the nonprofessional staff to allow the inmates considerable freedom.

*Inland* (Individual Therapy)—a small (60-75 inmates) private "residential treatment center" in which the clinicians were virtually in complete control, allowing much freedom to the inmates while stressing the use of psychotherapeutic techniques in an attempt to bring about major personality change.

TABLE 1
INMATE-STAFF RATIOS AND CONTACTS

|  | CUSTODIAL | | TREATMENT | |
|---|---|---|---|---|
|  | *Dick* | *Mixter* | *Milton* | *Inland* |
| Inmate-Staff Ratio | 3.9 | 2.3 | 1.7 | 1.5 |
| Inmate-Social Service Staff Ratio | 125.0 | 45.9 | 22.2 | 15.0 |
| Frequency of Inmate-Social Service Contact[a] | .13 | .47 | .76 | .85 |

[a] Proportion of respondents to inmate questionnaire reporting two or more contacts with social service staff in the last month.

TABLE 2
PERSPECTIVES OF STAFF MEMBERS, BY INSTITUTION[a]

| *Percentages of Staff Who:* | CUSTODIAL | | TREATMENT | |
|---|---|---|---|---|
|  | *Dick* | *Mixter* | *Milton* | *Inland* |
| (1.) Perceive the executive's view of organizational purpose as bringing change in inmate attitudes, values, and insight. | 10 | 19 | 38 | 51 |
| (2.) Say they would approve of sacrificing custodial security in order to introduce a new treatment program. | 41 | 53 | 76 | 80 |
| (3.) Say you can change most inmates. | 56 | 39 | 72 | 78 |
| (4a.) Believe you can trust and | | | | |

## TABLE 2, *Continued*

| | | | | |
|---|---|---|---|---|
| have close relationships with delinquents (3-item scale). | 68 | 53 | 79 | 78 |
| (4b.) Think staff are expected to develop close relationships with inmates. | 19 | 23 | 46 | 54 |
| (4c.) Say understanding is important in working with delinquents (3-item scale). | 16 | 32 | 63 | 83 |
| (5a.) Think staff must keep order at all times. | 58 | 45 | 13 | 14 |
| (5b.) Believe delinquents need much discipline (5-item scale). | 76 | 67 | 34 | 15 |
| (5c.) Say they would invoke strong sanctions for a wide variety of inmate misbehaviors (5-item index). | 61 | 68 | 24 | 10 |
| (6a.) Believe the best way of an inmate to get along is "don't break any rules and keep out of trouble." | 58 | 46 | 8 | 3 |
| (6b.) Believe inmate must do what he is told and do it quickly. | 92 | 75 | 44 | 16 |
| (7.) Believe all inmates should get the same discipline for rule-breaking. | 85 | 50 | 30 | 30 |
| (8a.) Believe informal inmate groups always or usually have a bad influence. | 96 | 26 | 4 | 5 |
| (8b.) Believe inmates should keep to themselves. | 40 | 38 | 15 | 3 |
| Numbers of Respondents | (57–62) | (115–170) | (105–108) | (37–40) |

[a] Differences in proportions between staff of the two custodial and two treatment institutions are statistically significant at or beyond the .05 level on every item.

Limitations of space preclude full analysis and documentation of these differences between organizations, which in any case are presented elsewhere,[10] but some indication of their nature may be conveyed by data on staff-inmate ratios and contacts (table 1), and by data from the staff questionnaire (table 2). Higher ratios of staff, especially social services staff, to inmates, and higher inmate-social service contacts characterize the treatment institutions. The questionnaire results show that in the more treatment-oriented institutions staff members are more likely (1) to see the organization's goal as producing change in attitudes, values, and insights; (2) to value treatment programs more highly than custodial considerations; (3) to believe that inmates can be rehabilitated; and (4) to believe that adults can have trusting, close, and understanding relations with inmates, the development of such relationships being part of the staff's task. In contrast, staff members in the more custodial organizations are more likely (5) to stress order, discipline, and the use of powerful negative sanctions; (6) to insist on inmate conformity to institutional rules, including immediate response to staff members' demands; (7) to believe in universalistic application of rules; and (8) to have negative attitudes toward informal relations among the inmates, believing that the inmates should keep to themselves. Such attitudinal differences between institutions hold up among cottage parents and in other groups when the respondent's staff position and his education are controlled,[11] and, further, the implied differences in behavior toward the inmates are confirmed by observations made in the institutions of the use of physical punishment, for example. To see how these different institutional environments affect the inmates, let us consider the inmate social system.

## THE INMATE GROUP

Informal group structure grows out of primary relations among inmates in all institutions, and it can be assumed to have a significant role in socializing and relating the inmate to the institution, in defining informal norms of inmate behavior and approved sets of values and beliefs, and in defining and allocating valued objects (e.g., contraband) among the inmates. Given the inmate group as a system potentially oriented toward ameliorating its members' deprivation, two major environmental factors could condition its response: (1) variations in the balance of gratifications and deprivations, and (2) variations in the conditions under which the group must attempt to solve its problem—that is, in the patterns of control and authority that the staff exercise over inmate action and behavior.

**1. Variations in the balance of gratifications and deprivations.** By limiting the available supply of rewards and thus creating a high ratio of deprivation to gratification the institution sets the stage for the development of a system for obtaining and distributing scarce values, both licit (e.g., choice job assignments) and illicit (contraband). Development of such a system presupposes that some inmates have access to values in short supply, and that inmates are sufficiently interdependent to set up a system of allocation and stabilize it in role expectations. Continuing access to the valued objects, and various forms of mutual aid, requires a division of labor, which in turn is likely to produce a leadership structure reflecting differential power with regard to values within the system. Norms of reciprocity are likely to develop, to limit the advantages of those powerful enough to monopolize scarce values, but the latter nevertheless form a leadership cadre in which power is relatively highly centralized. To the extent that the system is deeply involved in the secretive and illicit transactions of contraband allocation, these leaders may have, at least covertly, very negative attitudes toward the staff and institution. Such leadership cadres might influence the group and make it more hostile to the official system than it otherwise would be.

**2. Variations in staff patterns of control and authority.** Rigid and categorical practices of control and authority are likely to facilitate the inmates' recognition of a common fate and their potentialities for collective problem-solving. Differences in authority, general status, age, and often social class, between staff and inmates, generally lead inmates to see each other as members of the same category in all institutions, but the authority structure and its impact vary among institutions.

Frequent scheduling of mass activities in the company of other inmates, group punishment, and administering physical punishment before groups of inmates enhance the probability that inmates identify strongly with one another against staff. When, in addition, staff maintain domineering authority relationships and considerable social distance, inmates further perceive themselves as members of a group opposed to staff, and divergent interests between these groups are more fully recognized.

Staff patterns of control and authority also limit inmate association and group elaboration. Thus at the same time that rigorous practice of control and authority stimulate recognition of a common problem and the use of group solutions, they also make such solutions more difficult to achieve. Although only extreme techniques, such as keeping the inmates locked in separate rooms, effectively prevent the emergence of social relations among the inmates,[12] rigorous control could severely limit and structure opportunities for interaction and group formation—particularly the formation of groups covering the entire institution. In this situation, group activities must be conducted on a covert level, involving norms of secrecy and mutual defense against the staff.

## HYPOTHESES

These two dimensions, gratification-deprivation and patterns of control and authority, link the institutional goals with the responses of the inmate group; both vary between the custodial and treatment settings. On the first of these dimensions, treatment institutions place much less emphasis on degradation ceremonies, the use of powerful sanctions, and denial of impulse gratification, and much greater emphasis on providing incentives, objectives, and experiences that the inmates consider desirable. On patterns of control and authority, treatment institutions place much less stress on surveillance, control over inmate association, restrictions of freedom, rigid conformity to rules, and domination and high social distance in authority relations. The simultaneous effects of these dimen-

sions on informal groups in each type of setting should be as
follows:

**The Custodial Setting.** Because of the high level of deprivation, the group is organized to allocate legitimate and illicit values and provide mutual aid. These functions reflect
and generate relatively negative and "prisonized" orientations
toward the institution and staff. Although staff control and authority practices increase the need for inmate group solutions,
they also handicap interaction and group formation, so that
integration and solidarity are relatively underdeveloped. The
leaders, highly involved in illicit and secret activities, tend to
have a negative orientation toward the institution.

**The Treatment Setting.** The inmate group is organized
more voluntaristically, around friendship patterns. Since the
level of deprivation is lower, mutual aid is less necessary, and
any ameliorative system tends to lose its market. The group is
involved in the allocation of values among its members, but
these are positive rewards, more consonant with staff definitions
of merit. Staff give much freer rein to inmate association, so
that primary group integration and norms of group solidarity
are at a higher level than in the custodial setting. This cohesiveness does not necessarily imply opposition to staff, however, for the inmate group emphasizes more positive norms
and perspectives and greater commitment to the institution and
staff. Leaders' orientation is also more positive.

Finally, the more positive character of staff behavior toward inmates and the positive orientation of the inmate group
generate more positive attitudes toward self among the inmates of treatment institutions than among those in custodial
organizations.

Data are not available to test all features of the foregoing
contrasts, but a reasonably satisfactory test can be made of the
following specific hypotheses:

1. In the custodial institutions, the dominant tone of the in-
    mate group will be that of opposition and negative, "pris-
    onized" norms and perspectives with regard to institu-
    tion, staff, and self; in the treatment institutions, positive,
    co-operative norms and perspectives will dominate.

2. Inmate groups in the custodial institutions will display somewhat lower levels of primary relations and weaker orientations of solidarity than will groups in the treatment institutions.

3. Relatively unco-operative and negative leaders will emerge in the inmate groups of the custodial institutions; relatively co-operative and positive leaders will emerge in the treatment institutions.

## FINDINGS

The hypotheses will be tested here by analyzing results of the inmate questionnaire. The inmates' responses, shown by institution in table 3, convey the dominant tone of inmate group norms and perspectives.[13]

TABLE 3
### INMATE PERSPECTIVES, BY INSTITUTION

| Percentage of Inmates Who: | CUSTODIAL | | TREATMENT | | Statistical Significance[a] |
|---|---|---|---|---|---|
| | Dick | Mixter | Milton | Inland | |
| Score high positive on summary index of perspectives on the institution and staff.[b] | 42 (209) | 44 (364) | 58 (155) | 85 (65) | p < .01 |
| Score high on co-operation with staff on summary index of "ratting."[c] | 54 (209) | 46 (364) | 49 (155) | 54 (65) | N.S. |
| Gave a "prisonized" response to question about the best way to get along.[d] | 74 (202) | 73 (348) | 55 (151) | 45 (60) | p < .01 |
| Gave a "prisonized" response to question | | | | | |

## TABLE 3, Continued

| | | | | | |
|---|---|---|---|---|---|
| about ways to receive a discharge or parole.[e] | 59 (187) | 47 (352) | 27 (140) | 13 (65) | p < .01 |
| Score positive on self-image index.[f] | 38 (188) | 42 (327) | 51 (143) | 79 (60) | p < .01 |

[a] Significance refers to the difference between the inmates of the two custodial institutions combined and those of the two treatment institutions.

[b] The specific items summarized by this index were (paraphrased): (1) Is this a place to help, send, or punish boys? (2) Rather be here or in some other institution? (3) Summary: Did you think this would be a good or bad place, and what do you think about it now? (4) Agree that the adults here don't really care what happens to us. (5) Agree that the adults here are pretty fair. (6) Agree that adults here can help me. (7) How much has your stay here helped you?

[c] The specific items summarized in this index followed a presentation of hypothetical situations, and were (paraphrased): (1) Should a boy warn an adult that boys plan to rough up his friend? (2) Should he warn an adult that inmates plan to beat up a staff member? (3) Would you tell an adult which boys were stealing from the kitchen, when group punishment was being used? (4) Would you try to talk a boy out of running?

[d] The question was "Regardless of what the adults here say, the best way to get along here is to . . ." ("stay out of the way of the adults but get away with what you can" and "don't break any rules and keep out of trouble" were classified as "prisonized" responses, and "show that you are really sorry for what you did" and "try to get an understanding of yourself," as "nonprisonized").

[e] The question was "*In your own words,* write in what you think a boy has to do to get a parole or discharge from here" (responses of conformity, avoidance of misbehavior, "doing time," and overt compliance were coded as "prisonized").

[f] Those classified as "positive" on the index of self-image said that they had been helped by their stay a great deal or quite a bit and that the way they have been helped was by having "learned something about myself and why I get into trouble," rather than having "learned my lesson."

Findings on all but one of these items support the hypotheses.[14] Inmates in the treatment-oriented institutions more often expressed positive attitudes toward the institution and staff, nonprisonized views of adaptation to the institution, and positive images of self-change. The exception is that on the index of "ratting to staff" no difference between custodial and treatment institutions appeared.

**Background Attributes and Length of Stay.** Question immediately arises as to whether these differences in perspectives

TABLE 4

PERCENTAGES OF INMATES POSITIVE ON INDEX OF
PERSPECTIVES ON INSTITUTION AND STAFF, BY
SELECTED BACKGROUND CHARACTERISTICS
AND INSTITUTION[a]

|  | CUSTODIAL | | TREATMENT | |
|  | Dick | Mixter | Milton | Inland |
|---|---|---|---|---|
| Seriousness of major offense[b] | | | | |
| Less serious | 38 | 52 | 57 | 82 |
|  | (66) | (75) | (67) | (45) |
| More serious | 42 | 43 | 60 | 90 |
|  | (140) | (286) | (84) | (20) |
| Number of offenses | | | | |
| Less than 3 | 42 | 52 | 51 | 87 |
|  | (161) | (40) | (43) | (54) |
| 3 or more | 40 | 43 | 60 | 73 |
|  | (48) | (307) | (112) | (11) |
| Number of times returned to this institution[c] | | | | |
| None | 44 | 47 | 62 | 84 |
|  | (156) | (283) | (135) | (63) |
| One or more | 31 | 38 | 29 | 100 |
|  | (52) | (78) | (17) | (2) |
| Previous institutionalization of any kind[d] | | | | |
| None | 42 | 48 | 61 | 94 |
|  | (191) | (295) | (118) | (16) |
| Some | 33 | 33 | 50 | 83 |
|  | (15) | (66) | (34) | (6) |
| Age | | | | |
| Under 16 | 34 | 50 | 56 | 85 |
|  | (94) | (204) | (121) | (41) |
| 16 and over | 47 | 40 | 62 | 83 |
|  | (114) | (160) | (34) | (24) |

## TABLE 4, Continued

| | | | | |
|---|---|---|---|---|
| **Race** | | | | |
| White | 43 | 47 | 62 | 82 |
| | (181) | (245) | (104) | (55) |
| Nonwhite | 24 | 40 | 48 | 100 |
| | (25) | (116) | (48) | (10) |
| **I.Q.[e]** | | | | |
| 90 and below | 30 | 45 | 58 | 80 |
| | (44) | (120) | (41) | (5) |
| 91 and above | 37 | 43 | 64 | 85 |
| | (38) | (203) | (56) | (55) |
| **Family situation** | | | | |
| Intact, no problems | 46 | 49 | 62 | 80 |
| | (95) | (204) | (42) | (39) |
| Not intact, or problems | 36 | 40 | 56 | 92 |
| | (111) | (157) | (108) | (26) |
| **Rural-urban origin[f]** | | | | |
| "Rural" | 41 | 50 | 55 | 100 |
| | (208) | (126) | (107) | (3) |
| "Urban" | . . . | 43 | 64 | 85 |
| | (0) | (235) | (45) | (60) |
| **Occupation of father or other head of household** | | | | |
| White collar | 22 | 71 | 63 | 78 |
| | (18) | (21) | (8) | (18) |
| Blue collar or not in labor force | 42 | 44 | 58 | 85 |
| | (179) | (330) | (141) | (34) |

[a] Data were obtained from institutional files. The index of perspectives on institution and staff is described in Table 3.

[b] The "more serious" category includes arson, forgery, sex offenses, breaking and entering and crimes of violence, but excludes truancy, "incorrigibility," "maladjustment," theft, and vandalism.

[c] The Milton figures underestimate the actual number of returnees to some unknown degree because ordinarily only those who are recommitted to the institution, after having been supervised for several months following release by another state agency, are entered in institutional records as returnees. Others, returned during the period of supervision, generally are not so classified.

[d] Information on the majority of cases at Inland was missed due to coding error.

[e] The majority of inmates at Dick were not tested.

[f] "Urban" inmates are from counties with at least one city of 90,000 or more; "rural" inmates come from counties that do not have such a city.

on the institution and staff, adaptation, and self might not reflect variations in inmates' predispositions rather than variations in the institutional setting. A careful analysis of the impact, by institution, of delinquency history, past institutional record, age, race, IQ, family situation, urban-rural background, and social class indicates a negative answer to this question.[15]

Table 4 shows that the direction of the effect of each of the background variables on perspectives varies from institution to institution, and that the custodial-treatment differences in perspective hold up when background attributes are controlled. In nearly every instance, the inmates of both treatment institutions were more likely to have positive perspectives on staff and institution than the inmates of either custodial institution. The three exceptions to this predicted pattern were: (1) among those with fewer offenses, Mixter inmates (51 per cent positive) did not differ from those in Milton (50 per cent positive); (2) disproportionately few (29 per cent) of the Milton inmates classified as returnees had positive perspectives; and (3) a disproportionately large number of positive responses came from Mixter inmates with white-collar backgrounds.

The first of these exceptions suggests that a portion of the relatively negative over-all response at Mixter may be a result of its heavy recruitment of inmates with many offenses. But this would not explain why those with three or more offenses are so negative compared with similar inmates at Milton and Inland. The second exception is probably a result of the fact that the Milton returnees, as indicated in the note to the table, are not directly comparable with the others, apparently constituting an especially "hard core." The last exception may simply reflect the small number of "white-collar" inmates at both Mixter and Milton. Altogether, these exceptions do not challenge the conclusion that these background attributes cannot explain the observed differences between types of institution.

Similarly, interinstitutional variations were not simply a reflection of the fact that the treatment institutions usually keep their inmates longer. Data on this point may also be used to assess the degree to which the prisonization model or one of its variants "fits" these institutions.[16] Figure 1, graphing positive perspectives on the institution and staff against length of stay, indicates that differences between types of institution cannot be accounted for by differences in average length of stay. Inmates of the treatment institutions are more likely to express positive perspectives at almost every point in time. Within the

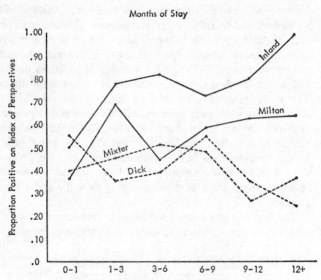

Months of Stay

Number of cases on which the proportions were computed:

| | 0-1 | 1-3 | 3-6 | 6-9 | 9-12 | 12+ |
|---|---|---|---|---|---|---|
| Inland | 2 | 9 | 17 | 15 | 5 | 15 |
| Milton | 11 | 29 | 29 | 22 | 30 | 28 |
| Mixter | 74 | 103 | 96 | 48 | 11 | 27 |
| Dick | 19 | 25 | 61 | 59 | 22 | 21 |

FIGURE 1. LENGTH OF STAY AND PERSPECTIVES ON INSTITUTION AND STAFF

custodial institutions, the over-all trend is for the proportion negative to increase with length of stay. Although this tendency toward increasing negativism in the custodial institutions is akin to what one would predict under the prisonization model, attitude changes in the treatment institutions are in the opposite, positive direction. In these institutions, the proportion expressing positive perspectives increases rapidly over time in the early months and, after a downturn, increases further in the later months.[17]

**Effects of Primary Group Integration on Perspectives.** Data on integration into inmate group provide a more adequate test of the hypothesis about the dominant tone of the inmate group if one assumes that when those who are better integrated express more positive perspectives, it is because their group exerts a positive influence, and when the better-integrated are more negative, it is because their group exerts a negative influence. Operationally, the better-integrated inmates are those who said they had two or more friends in the institution.[18]

The findings clearly indicate that positive attitudes are more closely associated with primary group integration in the treatment institutions than in the custodial institutions (table 5).

TABLE 5

INMATE PERSPECTIVES, BY INTEGRATION
INTO THE INMATE GROUP[a]

| *Percentages of Inmates Who:* | CUSTODIAL | | TREATMENT | |
|---|---|---|---|---|
| | *Dick* | *Mixter* | *Milton* | *Inland* |
| Score high positive on index of perspectives on institution and staff | | | | |
| Nonintegrated | 36 | 36 | 31 | 55 |
| | (62) | (115) | (26) | (11) |
| Integrated | 44 | 49 | 64 | 89 |
| | (146) | (247) | (126) | (52) |
| | p < .05 | | p < .01 | |
| | Q = .22 | | Q = .61 | |
| Score high co-operation on "ratting" index | | | | |
| Nonintegrated | 48 | 48 | 23 | 46 |
| | (62) | (115) | (26) | (11) |

TABLE 5, *Continued*

| Integrated | 56 | 44 | 55 | 56 |
|---|---|---|---|---|
|  | (146) | (247) | (126) | (52) |
|  | N.S. |  | p < .01 |  |
|  | Q = .01 |  | Q = .49 |  |

Give prisonized response on
　　question about best way
　　to get along

| Nonintegrated | 73 | 73 | 72 | 60 |
|---|---|---|---|---|
|  | (62) | (110) | (25) | (10) |
| Integrated | 76 | 74 | 51 | 44 |
|  | (139) | (238) | (123) | (48) |
|  | N.S. |  | p < .05 |  |
|  | Q = .04 |  | Q = −.39 |  |

Are positive on index of self-
　　image

| Nonintegrated | 31 | 37 | 35 | 44 |
|---|---|---|---|---|
|  | (52) | (101) | (23) | (9) |
| Integrated | 41 | 44 | 55 | 86 |
|  | (135) | (225) | (119) | (49) |
|  | N.S. |  | p < .01 |  |
|  | Q = .16 |  | Q = .50 |  |

[a] Kendall's Q is used to measure the association between integration and the score or response indicated.

Results on the four indices significantly related to integration consistently display the predicted pattern. Thus integration into the inmate group was more strongly associated with positive perspectives on the institution and staff in the treatment setting than in the custodial environment. Further, despite the fact that custodial and treatment settings did not differ with respect to scores on the "ratting" index (see table 3), integration and co-operation with staff are positively associated in the treatment but not in the custodial setting. (This finding principally reflects the strong positive association in Milton; in Inland and in both custodial institutions, it was relatively weak.) Finally, in the treatment institutions integration was inversely associated with the prisonized view of adaptation and positively related to a positive self-image, while in the custodial institutions there was little or no association with these indices.

An analysis of the joint impact of integration and length of stay on these attitudinal measures indicated that variations in length of stay did not account for these variations in the relation between integration and attitudes.

**Levels of Inmate Primary Relations and Solidarity.** A variety of findings consistently support the second hypothesis, that inmates in the treatment setting have more highly developed primary relations and stronger orientations of solidarity (table 6).[19] Inmates of the treatment institutions more frequently reported "hanging around" with other inmates, having several friends, and (reflecting the difference between Mixter and Milton) wanting to see other inmates again after release. In addition, the treatment inmates more frequently indicated a willingness to talk with other boys about a personal problem and more often rejected the view that you "have to be pretty careful what you say or do" around other inmates.

### TABLE 6
### INMATE SOCIAL RELATIONS, BY INSTITUTION

| Percentages of Inmates Who: | CUSTODIAL | | TREATMENT | | Statistical Significance[a] |
|---|---|---|---|---|---|
| | Dick | Mixter | Milton | Inland | |
| Hang around with three or more boys | 59 | 71 | 78 | 91 | p < .01 |
| Have three or more close friends (integration index) | 70 | 68 | 83 | 83 | p < .01 |
| Want to see all or most inmates again after release | 27 | 14 | 35 | 27 | p < .01 |
| Would talk to other inmates about a personal problem | 58 | 50 | 66 | 76 | p < .01 |
| Say you don't have to be careful around the other boys | 14 | 18 | 21 | 27 | p < .05 |

TABLE 6, *Continued*

Are high on index of
    solidary orienta-
      tion           27    28      31      55       p < .01
Numbers of
    Respondents   (202– (356–  (152–  (62–
                 208)  363)   155)   64)

   [a] Refers to differences between the custodial and treatment organizations.

Finally, scores on an index of solidarity orientation, here defined as emphasis on general loyalty to the group beyond primary ties with particular others, show a similar pattern. In the treatment settings, especially Inland, inmates were more likely to express such an orientation than were those in the custodial institutions. In neither setting was solidary orientation related to a statistically significant degree to perspectives toward the institution and staff or to scores on the "ratting" index.[20]

**Leadership.**   Data bearing on the third hypothesis, that the attitudes of inmate leaders would be relatively positive in the treatment setting and relatively negative in the custodial environment, also tend to follow the predicted pattern. Boys who were nominated four or more times as having the most "influence" in the institution were classified as leaders.[21] On three attitudinal indices, statistically significant differences between leaders and nonleaders were found in either the custodial or treatment setting (table 7). Leadership is more strongly associated with positive perspectives on staff and institution in the treatment environment than in the custodial setting, reflecting the strongly positive association at Milton. The same finding emerges on the self-image index—again the Milton leaders are highly positive. On the index of "ratting," leadership and co-operation with staff tend to be negatively associated in all institutions, but the association is stronger in the custodial than in the treatment institutions. Thus, findings on all three indices support the hypothesis that leaders have more positive perspectives in the treatment environment.

## TABLE 7
### LEADERSHIP AND PERSPECTIVES TOWARD THE INSTITUTION AND STAFF[a]

| Percentages of Inmates Who: | CUSTODIAL | | TREATMENT | |
|---|---|---|---|---|
| | Dick | Mixter | Milton | Inland |
| Are positive on index of perspectives toward the institution and staff | | | | |
| Nonleaders | 42 | 45 | 53 | 83 |
| | (177) | (318) | (130) | (48) |
| Leaders | 37 | 48 | 80 | 88 |
| | (32) | (46) | (25) | (17) |
| | N.S. | | p < .01 | |
| | Q = −.005 | | Q = .52 | |
| Are highly co-operative on index of "ratting" | | | | |
| Nonleaders | 56 | 47 | 51 | 56 |
| | (177) | (318) | (130) | (48) |
| Leaders | 38 | 37 | 44 | 47 |
| | (32) | (46) | (25) | (17) |
| | p < .01 | | N.S. | |
| | Q = −.26 | | Q = −.14 | |
| Are positive on index of self-image | | | | |
| Nonleaders | 39 | 41 | 47 | 75 |
| | (162) | (287) | (120) | (44) |
| Leaders | 32 | 53 | 74 | 87 |
| | (25) | (40) | (23) | (16) |
| | N.S. | | p < .01 | |
| | Q = .09 | | Q = .53 | |

[a] Q measures the association between leadership and the score or response indicated.

A separate analysis indicates that these differences among leaders characterize both "integrated" and "nonintegrated" leaders. And other data, on inmate perceptions of leadership in general, support the characterization of leaders in the treatment settings as having more positive attitudes.[22]

These and the other findings reported here indicate a difference between the two treatment institutions, Milton and Inland. On the one hand, data on inmate perspectives, effects of length of stay, and social relations clearly indicate that inmates have more positive attitudes and more highly developed primary relations at Inland. On the other hand, group involvement, as measured by integration and leadership, was more closely associated with positive perspectives at Milton than at Inland. Milton is a "milieu" institution; perhaps this finding reflects its conscious attempt to manipulate the inmate group.

**Data from Additional Institutions.** Data on inmate groups in three other institutions for juvenile offenders, studied less thoroughly than the four organizations just analyzed, shed additional light on the custodial-treatment differences I have reported. The first of these units, *Maxwell* (Maximum Security) was a geographically and administratively separate part of Mixter, established to handle the "most difficult" inmates of the parent institution shortly before the end of our field work. The other units, *Regis* (Religious) and *Bennett* (Benign), were small private institutions that were "open," sending their charges away from the institution every day for ordinary public or parochial schooling. In their goals and in the staff's behavior toward the inmates, these two open institutions seemed to fall between the custodial and treatment types; their goal might be characterized as "training." The inmate is viewed as changeable, but such simple techniques as altering skills and habits are considered appropriate. Within this training model, Regis stressed constant work and recreation activities along with indoctrination and enforcement of obedience and religiosity, while Bennett emphasized the creation of a homelike environment with staff serving as parental surrogates.

Results from these three units are represented by findings on the association between integration into the inmate group and responses to four attitudinal items (table 8). These data, together with those from the major institutions (table 5), show, first, that integration is negatively associated with positive perspectives on the institution and staff, co-operativeness with staff in "ratting," and self-image in Maxwell but not in the

TABLE 8

INMATE PERSPECTIVES, BY INTEGRATION INTO THE
INMATE GROUP, IN MAXIMUM SECURITY
AND OPEN UNITS[a]

| Percentages of Inmates Who: | MAXIMUM SECURITY | OPEN | |
|---|---|---|---|
| | Maxwell | Regis | Bennett |
| Score high positive on index of perspectives on institution and staff | | | |
| Nonintegrated | 64 | 84 | 36 |
| | (11) | (19) | (11) |
| Integrated | 54 | 63 | 91 |
| | (33) | (38) | (23) |
| | $Q=-.19$ | $Q=.17$ | |
| Score high co-operation on "ratting" index | | | |
| Nonintegrated | 45 | 47 | 27 |
| | (11) | (19) | (11) |
| Integrated | 21 | 32 | 35 |
| | (31) | (38) | (23) |
| | $Q=-.51$ | $Q=-.15$ | |
| Give prisonized response on question about best way to get along | | | |
| Nonintegrated | 60 | 72 | 60 |
| | (10) | (18) | (10) |
| Integrated | 73 | 71 | 45 |
| | (33) | (38) | (22) |
| | $Q=.28$ | $Q=-.14$ | |
| Are positive on index of self-image | | | |
| Nonintegrated | 56 | 40 | 33 |
| | (9) | (15) | (9) |
| Integrated | 60 | 58 | 71 |
| | (30) | (31) | (21) |
| | $Q=.09$ | $Q=.49$[b] | |

[a] Q measures the association between integration and the score or response indicated.

[b] Difference in proportions significant at the .05 level.

custodial or treatment institutions, and that a direct association between integration and "prisonized" response to the third item occurs only at Maxwell. Second, patterns in the two open institutions are generally inconsistent: Regis resembles Maxwell on the first two items, Bennett resembles the treatment institutions on all items, and in both institutions the association between integration and self-image is positive, as it is in the treatment institutions.

These findings and other results suggest that in Maxwell— which, with its stringent security regulations, resembles the traditional adult prison more than any of the other institutions —the "solidary opposition" model fits the inmate group reasonably well. Only in this institution was the relation between scoring high on the index of solidary orientations and strong opposition to staff on the "ratting" index statistically significant ($p < .05$ and $Q = .75$). Our data collection took place only three months after the unit was opened, however, and after several crises of organizational birth, when the inmates may have had a special *esprit de corps* because they were the first group considered incorrigible enough to be sent there. We have no evidence, therefore, that the "solidary opposition" model will continue to fit inmate groups in this type of setting.

Despite the fact that Regis and Bennett were open, allowing their inmates considerable freedom away from the institution, this milieu did not consistently generate as positive a response as did the closed treatment setting. On the other hand, the fact that on some dimensions, e.g., self-image, the association with integration is positive, and as strong as in Milton and Inland, suggests that a relatively benign, open environment might make it possible to achieve some of the benefits of treatment without the expense of a treatment program.

## DISCUSSION

These findings generally support hypotheses about differences between custodial and treatment settings with regard to inmate norms and perspectives, social relations, and leadership and therefore clearly challenge the general applicability of the "solidary opposition" model of the inmate group, at least to juvenile institutions. Variation in organizational goals gave rise to differences in inmate orientations and characteristics of the inmate group, and only in the limited data from a new maximum security unit was there any consistent indication that the "solidary opposition" model was appropriate. By treating the balance of gratification and deprivation and patterns of staff authority and control as variables affecting the inmates, I have replaced the assumption that inmates form solidary and oppositional problem-solving groups with the assumption that, under different conditions, different patterns of orientations, social relations, and leadership occur among the inmates. This more open perspective should be applicable to the study of adult institutions, too.

Although we were unable to obtain comparable data on recidivism for the various institutions, our findings indicate tentatively that both custodial and treatment organizations tend to accomplish their proximate goals. By stressing covert opposition and "playing it cool," the custodial inmate group encouraged behavior consistent with the custodial goals of containment and conformity. Thus, the level of "prisonized" orientations was higher among the custodial than among the treatment inmates. Similarly, the treatment inmate group seemed to produce in its members an orientation consistent with the goal of achieving change. Evaluating outcomes with reference to goals is more difficult in the treatment case, of course, for the nature of the most appropriate technology for rehabilitation is undiscovered. Under the current treatment technologies, however, a minimally positive orientation toward the agents of change, e.g., the counselors, is clearly a necessary precondition to successful rehabilitation. The inmate groups in the treatment settings more frequently encouraged a positive orientation, and less often encouraged the development of a negative self-image, apparently, than in the custodial institutions.

Finally, this research suggests that the study of correctional institutions would be substantially improved if researchers more frequently recognized the generality of the concept of social control and the variety of devices used to maintain control. All correctional organizations exercise a great deal of control over their inmate members, but while custodial organizations emphasize formal and severe sanctions directed at ordering and containing the inmates, treatment institutions are more likely to rely on informal, personal sanctions and incentives directed at behavior perceived as relevant to inmate change. The implementation of a treatment program in a previously custodial environment implies a shift not to less control, but rather to *different types of control* exercised on the bases of different criteria. As numerous writers have pointed out, humanitarian pressures have already limited severely the use of the most repressive (and perhaps most effective) custodial techniques in American juvenile institutions, even though most of them still are predominantly custodial. Under continuing humanitarian pressure, and faced with evidence that custodial techniques are incompatible with other organizational goals, these institutions are very likely to alter their patterns of authority and control in the coming decades. Researchers interested in the question of implementing successful rehabilitation programs in correctional settings might do well to consider and investigate more fully a variety of combinations of different social control and rehabilitation techniques. Perhaps the treatment model represented in this research is the only really viable model, or perhaps other models, e.g., some form of the "training" model, could combine order-keeping and rehabilitation successfully and in a manner more compatible with the budgets and present commitments of most institutions today.

## NOTES

SOURCE: *American Sociological Review,* 30 (February 1965), 40–55.
* An earlier version of this paper was read at the meetings of the Midwest Sociological Society, Milwaukee, Wisconsin, April 1963. This research was carried out in part under a predoctoral fellowship from the National Institute of Mental Health, Public Health Service, and was done in close association with a comprehensive study of juvenile correctional institutions directed by Robert D. Vinter and Morris Janowitz and supported by NIMH grant M-2104. Not only the data from this project but also the ideas and criticisms of the participants were of great help.

1. For example, Sykes and Messinger, reviewing over thirty-five studies of correctional organizations, conclude that "Despite the number and diversity of prison populations, observers of such groups have reported only one strikingly pervasive value system . . . [which] commonly takes the form of an explicit code. . . . The maxims are usually asserted with great vehemence . . . and violations call forth a diversity of sanctions ranging from ostracism to physical violence. . . . The chief tenets . . . [include] those maxims that caution: *Don't interfere with inmate interests,* which center of course in serving the least possible time and enjoying the greatest possible number of pleasures and privileges in prison. The most inflexible directive [is] *Never rat on a con.* . . . The prisoners must present a united front against their guards no matter how much this may cost in terms of personal sacrifice." Gresham M. Sykes and Sheldon L. Messinger, "The Inmate Social System," in Richard A. Cloward, *et al., Theoretical Studies in Social Organization of the Prison* (New York: Social Science Research Council, 1960), 5–8.

2. For example, Lloyd E. Ohlin and William C. Lawrence, "Social Interaction Among Clients as a Treatment Problem," *Social Work,* 4 (April 1959), 3–14. Similar treatments of the inmate group in juvenile correctional organization are found in Richard A. Cloward, "The Correctional Institution for Juveniles: A Discussion of Selected Problems" (paper read at the New York School of Social Work seminar on juvenile institutions, 1956); and George H. Grosser, "The Role of Informal Inmate Groups in Change of Values," *Children,* 5 (January–February 1958), 25–29. Other analyses suggesting that the inmate system in these institutions operates principally to oppose or circumvent the organization's aims include Howard Polsky's study of a cottage in a treatment institution, reported in "Changing Delinquent Subcultures: A Social Psychological Approach," *Social Work,* 4 (October 1959), 3–16, and *Cottage Six—The Social System of Delinquent Boys in Residential Treatment* (New York: Russell Sage Foundation, 1962); and Lloyd Ohlin's observations on a training school for girl delinquents, "Reduction of Role Conflict in Institutional Staff," *Children,* 5 (March–April 1958), 65–69.

3. Variation in inmate attitudes and behavior underlies the whole notion of prisonization. See Donald Clemmer, *The Prison Community* (New York: Rinehart, 1958), and the various studies of social types in the prison, for example, Clarence Schrag, "Social Types in a Prison Community" (unpublished M.A. thesis, University of Washington, 1944), and his "Leadership Among Prison Inmates," *American Sociological Review,* 19 (February 1954), 42, in which he writes of "a number of dissentient minorities [which] resist, at least to some extent, the dominant influence of the typical leader group."

4. Stanton Wheeler, "Socialization in Correctional Communities," *American Sociological Review,* 26 (October 1961), 697–712, and Peter G. Garabedian, "Social Roles and Processes of Socialization in the Prison Community," *Social Problems,* 11 (Fall 1963), 139–52, and "Legitimate and Illegitimate Alternatives in the Prison Community," *Sociological Inquiry,* 32 (Spring 1962), 172–84. See also the discussion of the inmate society as made up of three subcultures dependent on latent identities, in John Irwin and Donald R. Cressey, "Thieves, Convicts, and the Inmate Culture," *Social Problems,* 10

(Fall 1962), 142–55, along with the contributions by Wheeler, Schrag, and Donald L. Garrity to Donald Cressey (ed.), *The Prison: Studies in Institutional Organization and Change* (New York: Holt, Rinehart & Winston, 1961).

5. The major empirical works directly addressing the problems of the inmate group but taking exception to the general view of it are studies of treatment-oriented camps for young offenders by Oscar Grusky, "Organizational Goals and the Behavior of Informal Leaders," *American Journal of Sociology*, 65 (July 1959), 59–67, and Bernard Berk, "Informal Social Organization and Leadership Among Inmates in Treatment and Custodial Prisons" (unpublished Ph.D. dissertation, University of Michigan, 1961). Other writings deriving from the same study as the present report, and directly relevant to many parts of it, include Robert Vinter and Morris Janowitz, "Effective Institutions for Juvenile Offenders: A Research Statement," *Social Service Review*, 33 (June 1959), 118–31; Mayer Zald, "The Correctional Institution for Juvenile Offenders: An Analysis of Organization 'Character'," *Social Problems*, 8 (Summer 1960), 57–67, and "Comparative Analysis and Measurement of Organizational Goals: The Case of Correctional Institutions for Delinquents," *Sociological Quarterly*, 4 (1963), 206–30; Rosemary Conzemius Sarri, "Organizational Patterns and Client Perspectives in Juvenile Correctional Institutions" (unpublished Ph.D. dissertation, University of Michigan, 1962); *Juvenile Correctional Institutions Project, Research Report* (Ann Arbor: University of Michigan, 1961); and David Street, "Inmate Social Organization: A Comparative Study of Juvenile Correctional Institutions" (unpublished Ph.D. dissertation, University of Michigan, 1962).

6. After considerable study and discussion, informal groups have come to be viewed as neither wholly reflective of the larger structure nor wholly determinative of it; rather, the role of these groups in the attainment of organizational ends varies according to the organizational context. Students of industrial plants generally have stressed the negative impact of informal groups on productivity (for example, see the classic discussions of informal relations and structures in F. J. Roethlisberger and W. J. Dickson, *Management and the Worker* [Cambridge: Harvard University Press, 1941], and Orvis Collins, Melville Dalton, and Donald Wray, "Restrictions on Output and Social Cleavage in Industry," *Applied Anthropology*, 5 [1949], 1–14), while sociologists who have studied military organization have traced the positive functions of such groups: Samuel A. Stouffer, *et al.*, *The American Soldier* (Princeton: Princeton University Press, 1949), vol. II., 130–49; Edward A. Shils, "Primary Groups in the American Army," in Robert K. Merton and Paul F. Lazarsfeld (eds.), *Continuities in Social Research: Studies in the Scope and Method of "The American Soldier"* (Glencoe, Ill.: Free Press, 1950), 19–22; and Edward A. Shils and Morris Janowitz, "Cohesion and Disintegration of the Wehrmacht in World War II," *Public Opinion Quarterly*, 12 (1948), 280–315. For a recent conception of this problem in general terms, see Amitai Etzioni, *A Comparative Analysis of Complex Organizations* (New York: Free Press of Glencoe, 1961).

7. The inmate system is seen as providing new, deviant standards that allow the inmates to assuage guilt by "rejecting their rejectors"

(Lloyd W. McCorkle and Richard Korn, "Resocialization Within Walls," *The Annals*, 293 [May 1954], 88–98), to achieve compensatory status and to benefit from contraband and illegitimate activities (Ohlin and Lawrence, *op. cit.*), and to defend against aggression and exploitation by other inmates (Sykes and Messinger, *op. cit.*). The latter authors, even though they seem to assume that the inmate group is inevitably cohesive and opposed to official goals, also suggest that the extent of deprivation and degradation might predict the inmate group's response (p. 19).

8. On the theory of human nature, see Erving Goffman, "On the Characteristics of Total Institutions: Staff-Inmate Relations," in Cressey, *op. cit.*, 78.

9. Here I shall report findings principally on the four "closed" institutions studied intensively in the juvenile corrections project. Near the end of this paper I shall refer to findings on three additional institutions, not as directly comparable for the problems discussed here. For details of questionnaire administration and other research techniques, see Street, *op. cit.*, 198–202.

10. See especially Juvenile Correctional Institutions Project, *op. cit.*

11. *Ibid.*, chapters 7 and 9.

12. Even this technique is not necessarily effective. See Richard McCleery's account of an adult maximum security unit, "Authoritarianism and the Belief Systems of Incorrigibles," in Donald Cressey (ed.), *The Prison: Studies in Institutional Organization and Change, op. cit.*, 260–306.

13. Indices were derived partly from the results of a factor analysis of inmate responses. For details of this analysis and of the construction of indices, see Street, *op. cit.*, 213–24.

14. I have used statistical tests of difference between groups of respondents heuristically, to help decide whether to deny predicted differences between the custodial and treatment types of organization. Although the nonrandom selection of institutions, the clustering of all respondents in four organizations, and the sampling of entire institutional populations make use of the word "test" in its strict sense illegitimate, no more appropriate bases for decision-making are available. Note, too, that because the tests (as well as the measures of association presented below) combine the data for each of the pairs of institutions, to highlight the differences between the custodial and treatment types, the results may obscure differences within pairs. Important within-type variation will be discussed in the text.

15. Street, *op. cit.*, 75–83.

16. Clemmer, *op. cit.*, Wheeler, "Socialization . . . ," *op. cit.*, and Garabedian "Social Roles . . . ," *op. cit.*

17. Institutional records show that average stay before release is: Dick, 10 to 11 months; Mixter, 7.5 months; Milton, 15 months; and Inland, 11.5 months, with an average of 18 months for those who complete the institution's program.

18. The question was: "How about *close* friends? Some boys have close friendships with other boys here and some boys don't. How many of the other boys here are close friends of yours?" We assumed that a respondent who reported one or no friends was not really integrated into the group, having at best only a single "buddy." While this definition of integration is subject to questions regarding the probable

reporting error and the relation of this "primary relations" interpretation to other meanings of the concept, it provides an empirically profitable starting point for analyzing the consequences of integration.

19. The specific questions asked were: (1) "Do you usually hang around here with several guys, a few, mostly with one boy, or with none?" (2) The integration question (see note 18); (3) "How many of the boys you have met here would you like to see again after you get out?" (4) "Suppose you had been feeling sad for several days and are very upset about a personal problem. Are there any *boys* here you would go to and talk with about the things that made you sad?" (5) "Some boys say that you have to be pretty careful about what you say or do around the other boys here, or else they may give you a rough time. What do you think about this?" (6) Summary of responses to "How much of the time do you think most of the boys here really stick together, and are loyal to each other?" And "Regardless of how much the boys actually do stick together now, how much do you think they *should* stick together?" Respondents who answered both questions positively were scored high on the solidarity orientations index.

20. That these differences in social relations actually follow from organizational control practices is suggested by responses to a question asking for agreement or disagreement with the statement that "You have to be careful about the boys you get friendly with around here. To stay out of trouble with the adults, you have to keep to yourself." Considerably higher proportions of inmates rejected this statement in the treatment setting (79 per cent in Inland and 52 per cent in Milton) than in the custodial institutions (30 per cent in both Mixter and Dick).

21. The specific question was "What three boys are best at getting other boys to do what they want them to do—that is, which three have the most influence among the boys? Think of the boys that you know in your cottage, in school, and in the work program or recreation."

22. Street, *op. cit.*, 116–18.

# 10

## THE CORRECTIONAL INSTITUTION FOR JUVENILE OFFENDERS: AN ANALYSIS OF ORGANIZATIONAL "CHARACTER"*

*Mayer N. Zald†*

### INTRODUCTION

During the last decade the sociological study of large organizations has emphasized the limitations of Weber's ideal-type of bureaucracy as a model of organizational behavior. Moving away from a focus on bureaucracy and its pathologies, organizational research has begun to examine the variety of factors that affect and limit different types of organizations. The purpose of this paper is to describe the juvenile correctional institution as one type of large-scale social organization.[1]

First of all, institutions for delinquents share with other organizations, such as hospitals, certain attributes usually associated with communities. Secondly, they belong to a class of large-scale social organizations that have multiple goals, and thus have functional problems like these organizations. Thirdly, correctional institutions are of interest because of their critical role in our society's attempt to minimize antisocial behavior.

In this paper the major patterns of similarity and dissimilarity between correctional institutions and other types of organizations will be delineated and explained. Further, some of the dimensions along which correctional institutions vary among themselves will be indicated. A "character analysis" of these organizations, as systems of action, may make it possible (a) to summarize and integrate a scattered body of knowledge; (b) to specify areas where research is needed;

† Mayer Zald is an associate professor in the Department of Sociology at Vanderbilt University.

and (c) to set forth some concepts and dimensions that may be useful in such research.

The concept of organizational "character," most fully developed by Philip Selznick,[2] stresses interdependencies, commitments, fixed limitations and capacities of different types of organizations. Using the concept of organizational "character" the present analysis aims at a middle range level of theoretical abstraction.[3]

To describe the "character" of correctional institutions, we will discuss their goals, their relationships to the larger community, and, finally, their internal structures.[4]

## THE GOALS OF CORRECTIONAL INSTITUTIONS

Like universities, mental hospitals, and some other large-scale social organizations, correctional institutions can be said to have multiple goals. Their prime functions are to incarcerate —that is, establish custody over—the offender *and* to rehabilitate the delinquent. These goals may be incompatible because maximization of one may lead to inadequate fulfillment of the other. Business firms, in contrast, typically have one primary goal and several secondary goals or "functions" that are usually evaluated in relation to the primary goal.

It is often said that mental hospitals and, to a lesser extent, prisons are moving from an emphasis on incarceration and punishment to an emphasis on treatment and rehabilitation. Institutions for delinquents have had a goal of rehabilitation from the beginning. Bowler and Bloodgood[5] point out that the first Houses of Refuge in Boston, New York, and Philadelphia were quite clear in their emphasis upon rehabilitation as the primary goal of the organization. The earliest state institutions combined emphasis on rehabilitation with a covert goal of custody. Advocates of military training, of farming, of vocational programs all visualized their programs as rehabilitative. Society has become more humanitarian and less repressive in its concepts of social control. As social welfare, mental hygiene, and social science concepts have spread, the general public and the expanding mental health professions have pressed for the implementation of treatment goals, even though the details of treatment techniques have in themselves been subject to considerable debate among contending professional groups.

In many states physical punishment and repressive controls have been legally denied the juvenile institution, and rehabilitative goals have been formally established. Yet it is rarely the case that correctional institutions can also abandon custodial goals. A variety of legal statutes govern the admission and retention of the offender by the institution, and assignment of the delinquent is often intended to protect the community. Rehabilitative goals have not been substituted for custodial goals in most cases; rather they have been added to organizational goals. It is possible, therefore, to place a given institution on a continuum whose poles are defined by goal ratios in which custody or rehabilitation predominate. Most institutions may be characterized by the degree of dominance of one goal over the other. However, knowledge of the goal ratio alone is insufficient for understanding the structures of the institutions. Institutions with similar goal ratios may stress differing means. Thus one treatment-oriented institution may stress the casework relationship as the primary means, while another might stress the utilization of the milieu. One custodial institution might stress negative sanctions for running away while another might not allow opportunities for escape.

All of the diverse functions associated with these two goals are not inherently in conflict. A custodially oriented institution, for example, could use techniques usually associated with treatment to achieve discipline and control.[6] Conversely, custodial control may be a prerequisite in some cases for effective rehabilitation. In certain situations custodial needs and therapeutic needs might dictate similar policies or decisions. But it is also true that they might dictate divergent solutions. If the multiple goals of the organization have not been clearly delineated and their relationship defined, the potentiality of organizational conflict is raised. That is, consensual validation of the norms and rules and of their relative importance will be absent.

In a formal sense an organization may be said to have split

or multiple goals when the goal-setting agents—those who charter the organization and to whom the highest organizational authorities are responsible—conceive of the organization as having multiple purposes or functions. However, the actual degree of dominance of one goal over another is not wholly determined by the chartering agents. Even if they were to specify quite precisely the relative emphasis upon goals that were to be expected, the organization might not be able to realize this goal ratio. Depending upon its resources, structure, personnel, and clientele, the institution might be more or less successful in attaining its goals. Moreover, in many cases there may be a large degree of indeterminancy in the charter. Internal and external pressure groups may argue for one or another interpretation of the goals at various times and for policies which support their interpretations.[7] The existence of the two major goals of custody and rehabilitation heightens the possibility of conflicting occupational role groups and the development of conflicting policies. The manner in which multiple goals affect the relation of the institution to the larger society and how they affect the structure and effectiveness of the organization will be discussed in later sections.

## THE ORGANIZATION AND
## THE EXTERNAL ENVIRONMENT

The relation of an organization to its environment may profitably be discussed in terms of (1) external factors that affect the input of facilities and legitimation, (2) the process of evaluation of the output of the organization, and (3) factors that affect the demographic characteristics of staff and clientele.

**Sources of Legitimation and Facilities.**  Resource inputs to an organization are of several different kinds and effect the autonomy or independence of an organization. The designation of organizations as autonomous is largely a matter of degree. Any organization exists in a matrix of intricate relations with the larger society and must meet certain standards in order to exist. One organization may be said to be more autonomous than another to the extent that it has greater control over its environment, has more freedom in determining its own goals, judging its own effectiveness, and perpetuating its own personnel. An organization may have a narrowly limited area of operation and yet be largely autonomous in its operation. The converse may also be true. A correctional institution organized under a department of corrections is ordinarily less autonomous than is an institution less directly related to a department of government. The more a private institution depends on a limited number of sources for facilities, the more its autonomy is limited.

Public institutions receive facilities—money and capital investment—from legislative and judicial units of government or their administrative agents, while private institutions are primarily dependent upon charitable organizations or fundraising drives. Both public and private institutions receive legitimation from the state and from professional and lay associations. As sources of facilities, legislatures operate primarily with reference to two criteria: the tenor of the times and the pressure of the budget. The variability of both of these factors is conducive to organizational instability.

Facilities for public institutions are often channeled through a state agency responsible for all organizations of a similar type. Operating through a state department has both advantages and disadvantages for an organization. On the one hand it allows all of the correctional institutions to be treated as a single power unit rather than as fragmented institutions. It is a further advantage to give the job of organizational defense into a separate department of government with prestige and a staff of civil servants. However, this arrangement necessitates meeting standards set by an external agency directly responsible for the institution's continual effectiveness. Since the agency is more likely to accept rehabilitative goals, it is not in direct contact with the clients, is more often in contact with standard-setting national welfare agencies, such as the Children's Bureau, we would expect the operating organizations to develop defensive patterns of relating to the parent agency. This should be especially true of the more custodially oriented organizations.

There is little research in this area. The literature on public administration treats of somewhat similar situations in its discussion of central office-field office relations, but there are no systematic studies of the relationship of correctional institutions to their administrative departments.

Private institutions, although relatively more autonomous in establishing organizational policy and acquiring personnel, have the complex problem of ensuring the receipt of facilities through fund-raising associations and foundations.

Etzioni[8] has recently traced the implications, for both society and organizations, of receiving financial support from a source different from the payment of clients for services received. Almost all public and many private organizations fall into this category. As compared with business organizations, such organizations should have problems in harmonizing the possibly conflicting interests of clients and sponsors. First, there is not a necessary relationship between the quality of service rendered to clients and the input of resources. Secondly, clients sent to these organizations are usually involuntary participants.

**Evaluation of Output.** It is obvious that any large-scale organization must satisfy the needs of others in the society by its output if it is to continue in existence. Organizational stability is dependent upon how successful it is in fulfilling its custodial and rehabilitative tasks with the allotted resources. Unlike a private business, which may go into bankruptcy if it fails to offer a satisfactory product, correctional institutions monopolistically meet a continuing need of our society. Thus, lack of organizational success in satisfying this need is more likely to lead to a turnover of executive personnel.

The output of the correctional organization is evaluated by the agencies directly in contact with it, and, more diffusely, by the general public. The broader public usually becomes involved in the organization only when: (1) the organization does not maintain control over those committed to it, as reflected in riots or escapes; (2) some level of care dictated by the standards of the times is not maintained; (3) public norms of humanitarian treatment are violated. Public officials, professional associations, and crusading journalists may bring pressure to bear when the second and third conditions occur as judged by professional criteria. Ohlin and Pappenfort have pointed out that there are many possible incidents which could be used to threaten organizational stability. Only a few of these are actually turned into crises, sometimes by external organizations or associations.[9]

The rehabilitative output of the organization can be judged in terms of several criteria. It can be judged by evaluating the recidivism rate of released clients, by evaluating the "personality" changes occurring while in the institution, or by evaluating the degree to which the organization meets standards (empirical or theoretical) which are supposed to ensure success. At best, however, rehabilitation seems to "pay off" to the society at large only in the long run. However, when there are either runaways or other "incidents" the larger public is quick to apply pressure. Since control and rehabilitation are not always compatible and since rehabilitation is a vague and difficult to establish criterion, a continuous pressure for emphasizing control instead of rehabilitation is implied, if an institution is to be free of demands for reorganization.

In addition to official agencies directly related to the institution, various professional associations influence operations by establishing standards for their members and for organizations utilizing the members' services. Social work, psychiatric, correctional, medical, and educational associations all formulate standards which can be utilized in defense of their functions, and which are related to their "professional images." Sociologists have, unfortunately, rarely studied the relationships *between* organizations. As Levine, White, and Pierson note, sociologists make many assumptions about the interaction of organizations, but few study it directly.[10] Ohlin's paper, "Interest Group Conflict and Correctional Objectives," is one of the few exceptions to this generalization.[11]

An institution may attempt to create sources of support by co-opting elements of the local community.[12] Co-optation may involve the formation of citizens' advisory committees or the encouragement of volunteer activities for the institution. Such devices, while helping to create a stable relationship with the community, may also lead to lessened organizational autonomy, problems of internal co-ordination, and others.

**Demographic Characteristics of Staff and Clients.** The external environment affects not only the type and amount of resources allocated to the institution but also affects its personnel and clientele. The state of the local labor market may markedly affect the character of institutional personnel. For instance, a college community can provide staff at the lower levels quite different from an industrial community in terms of their orientation toward juvenile offenders. This does not imply that college students *per se* are more desirable as rehabilitative employees. Rather, a college community provides a large number of potential employees whose ideologies may be more compatible with the rehabilitative philosophy, but whose student status precludes high salary demands. However, use of college students leads to high turnover and other instabilities.[18] Further, the opportunity for various types of activities, for both clients and staff, will vary from community 'to community. The size of the local community may also determine the off-the-job social relations of the staff. The isolation of some institutions increases the dependence of the staff upon each other for social activity, heightening the communal aspects of the institution.

The characteristics of the clients are to an even greater extent affected by the environment of the institution. Clients are provided the organization by the courts. Operating under mandates from the legal system, the courts must determine who among their clientele are to be sent to correctional institutions and how the clients are to be treated. This complex decision involves a variety of factors, such as the available capacity of institutions in the area, the nature of the offense, and the available ways of dealing with the offender. The nature of this decision may be systematic apart from the requirements for admission formally set by an institution. For example, offenders may be sent to the institution in the absence of a reasonable alternative and not with the intention of thereby protecting society or rehabilitating delinquents. If this were a constant practice, it would affect organizational operation at several points including, among others, its discharge policy and process, its training program, its distribution of facilities, and the nature of its clientele. Some of these problems have been dealt with in social work research concerning the intake and referral systems of agencies. However, this research tends to be administrative rather than sociological.

The type of community from which the delinquent comes may also influence his values and orientations. The physical isolation of the correctional institution also contributes to the degree of deprivation that the delinquent feels; e.g., he may be deprived of contacts with family and peers.

Client characteristics together with the input of facilities largely determine the degree to which various organizational goals can be pursued. If, as workers in the field claim,[14] delinquents have become more aggressive, brutal, and acting-out in their antisocial acts, more organizational activity may have to be devoted to meeting custodial requirements in order to placate the surrounding community.

## THE INTERNAL SYSTEM

Within an institution power and resources are distributed to maintain stability and attain goals. However, depending upon the distribution of power and the ideology of key personnel goals may be redefined and reshaped to differing specifications than those held by the governing board of the institution. The translation of goals into organizational practice can be shown by discussing three sets of interpersonal relationships; (1) staff relationships with other staff, (2) staff relationships with clients, and (3) client relationships with clients.

Staff-staff relations. The formal table of organization of the correctional institution defines the positions and the authority relations among positions that are supposed to characterize the institution. At a minimum, the table indicates a superintendent and an assistant superintendent; teachers, a nurse; a business and maintenance staff; and a staff variously called cottage parents, attendants, or supervisors. Even the most custodial institution for delinquents must have teachers, for in most states the law requires that children under sixteen years of age go to school. As institutions adopt contemporary modes of differentiating and treating delinquents, psychologists, psychiatrists, and social workers are added to the staff. The formal organization is not synonymous with the actual organization, nor is it complete. Any discussion of the internal structure of a correctional institution must include an analysis of the informal structure of the staff—as well as the social organization of the clientele. McCleery,[15] John and Elaine Cummings,[16] and Novick[17] have shown that even on the formal level, however, the correctional institutions with different goal orientations will differ sharply in their authority structures; decentralization of power tending to be greater in rehabilitative institutions.

The existence in the organization of more than one goal raises the probability of role behavior having to meet diverse criteria. It allows conflict to develop between position occupants whose individual tasks are associated with the divergent goals. Thus, cottage parents and counselors whose performances largely are judged, respectively, in terms of their contributions to custodial and rehabilitative goals and whose perspectives are largely shaped by these goals, will often find themselves in conflict.[18] "Interest groups" may form in any organization. But the value of their effects on the organization can usually be determined by reference to the dominant goal. In correctional institutions a group may develop an ideology, defenses, and norms which further its goal and its power and prestige at the expense of another group's goals and power.[19]

Correctional institutions with marked custodial orientations are characterized by the relatively high actual power of the cottage parent and custodial staff, while institutions with predominantly rehabilitative orientations raise the power level of rehabilitative positions, defining custodial roles in relation to the rehabilitative function and lowering the power of the cottage staff. In many cases, where the definition of goals is in flux and unstable, intergroup conflict may be chronic or the external and internal necessities of control will emphasize custodial goals by default. For example, eligibility for discharge, in theory a rehabilitative decision, may be manipulated by the custodial staff as a control sanction.

Even if intergroup conflict is minimal, conflicting role expectations of the administration may lead to intrarole conflict. Thus the cottage counselors at one of the schools described in the MacIver report on institutions for delinquents seem to be subject to extreme role strain.[20] Cressey[21] and Grusky[22] have described such conflicts in a prison setting and in the setting of a minimum security camp. In less custodial institutions the cottage parent is generally asked to maintain control but is not, from his point of view, given the sanctions to do his job right.

Since correctional institutions are often in an unstable relation to their environment, superintendents typically find a good deal of their time taken up with organizational defense; that is, with protecting the organization and maximizing the receipt of facilities and legitimation.[23] The superintendent may be led to abrogate his authority to personnel that ensure organizational stability. The combination of chronic pressure to economize, the inherent difficulty of evaluating the efficacy of rehabilitative policy, and the need to maintain organizational stability and control create recurring pressures that minimize the rehabilitative orientation. However, there is evidence that various organizations of personnel and policy are compatible with a given budget, and, furthermore, that adequate funds do not ensure rehabilitative organization.[24]

A typical bifurcation occurs along professional-nonprofessional lines. Part of the staff is highly educated, trained, middle class, and professionally oriented, while another part tends to be poorly trained, have little education, and is of lower class origin. Status distinctions may lead to restricted communication between groups, turning each into a closed social unit similar to the status-linked groupings in hospitals.

Adult members of lower status groups have difficulty gaining access to higher status groups. In contrast, many organizations provide defined channels of mobility by which members can rise in the organization. Blocked upward mobility increases the individual's dependence on his own status group for support and solidifies the group as a unit for social control. This tends to raise the power of key custodial personnel through their ability to reward or punish individuals dependent on them. Thus effective institutionalization of rehabilitative policy is further blocked. Barriers to communication and interaction are probably lowest between the maintenance staff and the custodial staff, allowing informal patterns of co-operation to develop. Some institutions have developed committee mechanisms to help bridge this gap.[25]

**Staff-client relations.** As compared with most organizations in our society, staff-client relationships differ significantly in the juvenile correctional institution. Basic to this difference are four characteristics: (1) clientele and staff form a community; (2) the clients typically are drawn from a low social class and are social deviants; (3) staff are in a clearly superordinate position in relation to clients; and (4) adult and adolescent cultures are markedly divergent in our society. The fact that the staff associate almost continuously with the clients means that relationships tend to diffuseness, particularism, and affectivity; staff may easily develop warm relationships with some boys and none at all with others. This is in contrast with most bureaucratic organizations in which the relationships with clients tend toward specificity, universalism, and affective neutrality. In most correctional institutions the cottage personnel tend to interact on a more intimate, diffuse, and personalized basis with the delinquents than do the rehabilitative, professional staff. The professional staff tend to interact on a segmented and specific basis with the clients.[26] Thus, in many ways, lower level staff have more chance to establish warm, supportive relationships than anyone else, which according to current theory, are necessary for changing identifications and values. Yet, the demands of the role of the cottage parent and his own attitudes may only reinforce the boys' estrangement from society. Cottage staff find themselves confronted with the problem of managing from fifteen to seventy boys. They must accomplish routine housekeeping, keep order, and prevent escapes. Unlike prisons, juvenile institutions usually do not even provide a wall to contain the delinquents. Few sanctions are available to the cottage staff; they have little training, often get little positive support from the professionals or the administration, and are most readily evaluated in terms of the visible criteria of control and cleanliness.

The correctional institution must maintain discipline and minimize violence in a population that has demonstrated its own lack of personal controls. The difficulty of maintaining control will vary with the age, sex, and traits of the delinquents that the institution serves. Since rewards may be largely controlled by staff, they have the opportunity to develop a variety of reward structures to achieve ends. However, the reward structure is a reflection not only of the ends sought but also of staff perspectives on what means will achieve these ends. This entails a view of the nature of the clientele and how they will respond (an implicit learning and behavior theory).

As stated by Gilbert and Levinson,[27] the custodial orientation gives rise to an ideology that focuses upon the inherent nature of the client's difficulty and his lack of maleability. The ideology stresses rigid distinctions between types of people and the use of authoritarian techniques of interpersonal control. In contrast, the ideology of rehabilitation and therapy focuses on the sociopsychological causes of deviancy, on maleability, and on permissiveness in interpersonal relations.

The utilization of sanction structures and interpersonal relationships congruent with these ideologies may have great effect upon client attitudes and upon client informal organization.[28] Client attitudes may be hostile to the organization, or docile but distant, or co-operative and cynical, or co-operative and personally involved in the institution's program. An instructive comparison of attitudes can be made from the description of attitudes reported by Clemmer[29] and McCorkle, Elias, and Bixby.[30] Our knowledge in this area has been gained predominantly with prison populations. We would expect antisocial and antiorganizational attitudes to be less crystallized for juvenile offenders than for adult criminals. Therefore, the institution should be able to have a greater effect upon the former.

Staff-client relations in an institution with custodial goals tend to be more restrictive than in a rehabilitative institution. They are more "rule-oriented" and work to maintain social distance between staff and client. In ideal form they serve to maintain an objective fairness. At worst, favoritism and individual bargaining take place.[31]

**Client-client relations.** Rehabilitation implies a substitution of positive social values for antisocial values. Yet it has long been said that the major product of penal institutions is the teaching of criminal values. If it is assumed that the juvenile delinquent is more amenable to change than the adult offender and is less committed to antisocial patterns, then the values esteemed by the client informal organization may be crucial in negating or supporting delinquent behavior patterns.

The incoming delinquent is completely dependent upon other offenders and upon staff for all social gratifications and deprivations, and for many definitions of cognitive reality. Thus, other clients serve as a major socialization agent to organizational practices and perspectives. As in any social system, clients rank actors and behave toward them in terms of a set of relevant criteria. The new client must, if he or she is to gain status and its rewards, adequately meet these criteria.

To a certain extent status criteria are imported into the organization. Instrumental and socioemotional leadership have a degree of similarity in both delinquent and nondelinquent peer groups. Sophistication, athletic ability, personal appearance, strength, personality characteristics are all brought with the boy into the organization. However, the criteria that may be most affected by institutional practices are also those that are most relevant to rehabilitative goals. For instance, client organization may stress "con" values—the unfairness of society and staff, and the necessity of proving one's worth by antisocial behavior; or it may stress the necessity of facing reality, being fair, and proving one's worth by socially approved means.

Like the mental hospital which must accommodate the hospital to the patient, correctional institutions with rehabilitative aims cannot merely force the offender to accommodate to it. They require voluntaristic participation and identification. We would expect client organization to favor attitudes that support goals of rehabilitation the more the clients perceive the staff as working for the interests of the clients.[32] When there is not this perception, overt compliance may take place, but covertly rehabilitative goals are sabotaged. Professional staff working in predominantly custodial institutions have often found themselves being "used" by the other staff and by the clients.

Some kind of *modus vivendi* must be reached between client leadership and staff in any institution if perpetual crisis is to be avoided. Staff in an institution have something to bargain with. They can "sell" prerogatives, positions, and psychological rewards. And what they "sell" influences not only the ranking criteria but also the structure of client organization. Structures can be found ranging from those that are hierarchically organized around the control of violence and communication to those that are less rigid and decentralized.[33] The multiple goals of most institutions affect client structure by: (1) introducing inconsistencies into the relationships between staff and clients; (2) allowing clients to play off one staff group against the other; and (3) by presenting client organization with an unstable situation. The existence of conflicting staff groups contributes to the breakdown of a rigid client structure by giving access to facilities to clients who are not among the more influential of the clients, thus breaching the monolithic client system of more custodial institutions or prisons.

The ability of the institution to affect client organization is also dependent upon the personality structure of the offender. Reiss's investigations would imply that the "Relatively Integrated" delinquent should be more adaptive than either the "Defective Super-Ego" or the "Weak Ego" offender.[34] Since the delinquent subculture supports the values of the peer group, the problem of the correctional institution is to structure the situation so that the antisocial values of the primary group are replaced by more positive ones.[35] Rehabilitation of the "Defective Super-Ego" and the "Weak Ego" offender may well require both extinction of delinquent values and development of socially approved values by therapeutic techniques.

## CONCLUSIONS

We have attempted to delineate the character of correctional institutions for delinquents. Reflecting a growing body
of literature, the analysis has stressed the fact, that, like other
large-scale organizations, these dependent institutions are involved in a web of relationships with the external environment.

Strategically, the analysis has proceeded from the characteristics of the goals and the external environment to the
structured relationships of the staff and their effects upon client
behavior. Some of the characteristics which are most striking
about correctional institutions are (a) the critical climate of
opinion in which they operate; (b) the fact that they are
resource-deprived institutions; (c) the abstract quality of rehabilitative goals and the difficulty of proving one technique
to be more successful than another; (d) the multiplicity of
functions assigned the institutions; and finally (e) the fact that
these are "total institutions."

Correctional institutions will vary along many of the dimensions discussed. For example, we should not expect all local communities to have equal tolerance of escapees. The size
of the community, its history, and other factors will condition its reaction to the institution. Similarly we should not
expect all guards or cottage parents to develop ideologies congruent with the goals of the organization. Future research must
be directed at ascertaining the conditions under which the
phenomena herein described occur.

## NOTES

SOURCE: *Social Problems,* VIII (Summer 1960), 57–67.
* This paper was written as part of an ongoing project supported by re-
    search grant M-2104, from the National Institute of Mental Health,
    Public Health Service. Morris Janowitz and Robert Vinter, directors
    of the project at the University of Michigan, have greatly aided the
    author by their critical comments on earlier drafts of the paper.
    The conceptual framework of the project is included here. The gen-

eral hypotheses which the project attempts to test are stated in a previous publication by Robert D. Vinter and Morris Janowitz, "Effective Institutions for Juvenile Delinquents: A Research Statement," *Social Service Review*, 33 (June 1959), 118–31.

1. The terms large-scale organization and organization are used interchangeably in this paper.

2. Philip Selznick, *Leadership and Administration: A Sociological Interpretation* (Evanston: Row Peterson, 1957).

3. Frances Scott has recently discussed mental hospitals and prisons within a Parsonian framework: "Action Theory and Research in Social Organization," *American Journal of Sociology*, 64 (January 1959), 386–96. The analysis presented here will be less inclusive.

4. On occasion this analysis uses studies of mental hospitals as well as prisons. Paucity of organizational research on juvenile correctional institutions, as well as similarities among these organizations, justifies this extension. Pertinent recent studies include, for prisons: Richard H. McCleery, *Policy Change in Prison Management* (Lansing: Governmental Research Bureau, Michigan State University, 1957), and "Communications Patterns as Bases of Systems of Authority and Power," in Richard A. Cloward, *et al., Theoretical Studies in Social Organization of the Prison* (New York: Social Science Research Council, 1960), 49–77; Gresham Sykes, *The Society of Captives: A Study of a Maximum Security Prison* (Princeton: Princeton University Press, 1958). For mental hospitals: Ivan Belknap, *Human Problems of a State Mental Hospital* (New York: McGraw-Hill, 1956); William Caudill, *The Psychiatric Hospital as a Small Society* (Cambridge: Harvard University Press, 1958); Alfred H. Stanton and Morris Schwartz, *The Mental Hospital* (Glencoe: Free Press, 1957); Milton Greenblatt, Daniel G. Levinson, and Richard Williams, editors, *The Patient and the Mental Hospital* (Glencoe: Free Press, 1957).

5. Alida C. Bowler and Ruth S. Bloodgood, *Institutional Treatment of Delinquent Boys, Part I. Treatment Programs of Five State Institutions* (Washington: Children's Bureau Publication No. 228, 1935), 9.

6. Robert D. Vinter and Roger Lind, *Staff Relationships and Attitudes in a Juvenile Correctional Institution* (Ann Arbor: School of Social Work, 1958); Harvey Powelson and Reinhard Bendix, "Psychiatry in Prisons," *Psychiatry*, 14 (February 1951), 73–86.

7. Donald R. Cressey, "The Nature and Effectiveness of Correctional Techniques," *Law and Contemporary Problems*, 23 (autumn 1958), 754–71.

8. Amitai Etzioni, "Administration and the Consumer," *Administrative Science Quarterly*, 3 (September 1958), 251–64.

9. Lloyd E. Ohlin and Donnell Pappenfort, "Crisis, Succession and Organization Change" (mimeographed paper, 1956).

10. Sol Levine, Paul E. White, and Carol L. Pierson, "Interaction Among Organizations" (paper delivered at the 1959 meetings of the American Sociological Society).

11. Lloyd E. Ohlin, "Interest Group Conflict and Correctional Objectives" (paper prepared for the Ad Hoc Committee on Correctional Organization of the SSRC, April 1957).

12. Philip Selznick, *TVA and the Grass Roots* (Berkeley: University of California Press, 1949).

13. Robert M. MacIver, director, "Three Residential Treatment Centers,"

*Interim Report No. IX of the Juvenile Delinquency Evaluation Project of the City of New York* (March 1958), 23.

14. "Juvenile Delinquency," *Interim Report of the Committee on the Judiciary, U.S. Senate* (Washington: Government Printing Office, 1954), 34.

15. McCleery, *Policy Change . . . , op. cit.,* and "Communication Patterns . . . ," *op. cit.*

16. Greenblatt, Levinson, and Williams, editors, *op. cit.,* 50–72.

17. A. G. Novick, "Training School Organization for Treatment," *The Proceedings of the National Association of Training Schools and Juvenile Agencies,* 54 (Chicago, 1958), 72–80.

18. George H. Weber, "Conflicts Between Professional and Non-Professional Personnel in Institutional Delinquency Treatment," *Journal of Criminal Law, Criminology and Police Science,* 48 (June 1957), 26–43.

19. Belknap, *op. cit.,* 123–44; Powelson and Bendix, *op. cit.;* Vinter and Lind, *op. cit.*

20. McCleery, *Policy Change . . . , op. cit.,* 23.

21. Donald R. Cressey, "Contradictory Directives in Complex Organization: The Case of the Prison," *Administrative Science Quarterly,* 4 (June 1959), 1–19.

22. Oscar Grusky, "Treatment Goals and Organizational Behavior: A Study of an Experimental Prison Camp" (unpublished Ph.D. dissertation, University of Michigan, 1957).

23. Vinter and Lind, *op. cit.*

24. Lloyd E. Ohlin, "The Reduction of Role Conflict in Institutional Staff," *Children,* 5 (March–April 1958), 65–69.

25. Leita P. Craig, "Reaching Delinquents Through Cottage Committees," *Children,* 6 (July–August 1959), 129–34; Novick, *op. cit.*

26. Grusky, *op. cit.*

27. Greenblatt, Levinson, and Williams, editors, *op. cit.,* 20–36.

28. Grusky, *op. cit.;* Clarence Schrag, "Leadership Among Prison Inmates," *American Sociological Review,* 19 (February 1954), 37–42.

29. Donald Clemmer, *The Prison Community* (Boston: Christopher, 1940), 152.

30. Lloyd W. McCorkle, Albert Elias, and F. Lovell Bixby, *The Highfields Story* (New York: Henry Holt, 1958), 109–57.

31. Gresham M. Sykes, "The Corruption of Authority and Rehabilitation," *Social Forces,* 34 (March 1956), 257–62.

32. In many ways delinquents stand in a relation to the organization similar to the primary members of military or industrial organizations. Their identification with the organization seems to be a crucial determinant of their organizational behavior.

33. McCleery, *Policy Change . . . , op. cit.;* H. Ashley Weeks and Oscar W. Ritchie, *An Evaluation of the Services of the State of Ohio to Its Delinquent Children and Youth* (Columbus: Bureau of Educational Research, Ohio State University, 1956).

34. Albert Reiss, "Social Correlates of Psychological Types of Delinquency," *American Sociological Review,* 17 (December 1952), 710–18; and "Delinquency as the Failure of Personal and Social Control," *op. cit.,* 16 (April 1951), 196–207.

35. Donald R. Cressey, "Contradictory Theories in Correctional Group Theory Programs," *Federal Probation,* 18 (June 1954), 20–25.

# 11

## ACTION THEORY AND RESEARCH IN SOCIAL ORGANIZATION*

*Frances Gillespie Scott†*

The general theory of action as put forth in the writings of Talcott Parsons and his associates[1] and in two recent articles by Parsons[2] provides a theoretical framework for research on social organization which offers an alternative to *ad hoc* studies. Of theoretical and methodological importance is its conception of the organization as a social system in its own right, related in stated ways to other social systems, all operating within the society, which in its turn is seen as the most inclusive system.

An organization is defined as "a social system which is organized for the attainment of a particular type of goal; the attainment of that goal is at the same time the performance of a type of function on behalf of a more inclusive system, the society."[3] The society, acting on the basis of its values, evaluates, ranks, and rewards an organization according to the latter's contribution to the society's functioning. The result is the differential distribution of power to organizations performing different functions.[4] Continued access to and exercise of power are, to be sure, directly related to the organization's ability to operate successfully, that is, to its continuing performance of socially valued functions. It would follow that, if the functions are highly valued and so the prestige of the organization is high, the requisite power will be allocated sooner or later, and, if the functions are obsolete, unnecessary, or ill-performed, the organization will either acquire new ones or cease to exist. An analysis of the allocation of power

† Frances Scott is an associate professor in the Department of Sociology at the University of Oregon.

and its exercise is crucial to an analysis of the structure and function of the organization.[5]

**Organizational types.** On the most general level organizations may be classified according to the *primacy* of the type of function as assessed by the society. It is with reference to the function in the *society* as a system that we now view organizations. Parsons' conception of the four basic problems of any action system is of central interest.[6] An "action system" is composed of a number of units (which are, observably, role behaviors in a *social* system); this action system is confronted with a series of basic problems which must be solved if it is to continue operating as a system. These are: (1) *adaptive problems,* the adapting of behavior to the physical and social environment of the system and the manipulation of objects, including persons, so as to make for more favorable relations; (2) *gratificatory problems,* activity connected with the attainment and enjoyment of the goals of the system; (3) *integrative problems,* activity directed to the "adjustment" of the relations of system members to each other; and (4) *pattern-maintenance problems,* activity directed toward the maintenance of the identity of the system as a system, renewal and reaffirmation of its own values and existence.

In a social system some of the members have primarily adaptive roles, some primarily integrative, and so on. The system is conceived as directing attention, by virtue of the interaction of its members among themselves or with members of other systems, to first one and then another problem. Normally, the direction of activity or movement is from the solution of pattern-maintenance problems to either the solution of adaptive or integrative problems and thence to the solution of goal-attainment problems. A "phase" of a social system is considered as the interval of time when one of the four is being given primacy.[7]

This paradigm is, first of all, applied to the society as a social system to determine the predominant system problem of the society at any given time toward the solution of which a given organization is functioning and thus the type of goal of the organization. An indication of the power allocated to it is given by the type of function, or goal, and by its relationships to other organizations. The paradigm is also applied to the organization itself as a social system with problems of its own system maintenance. Indeed, the paradigm is applicable not only on these two levels of analysis but further in investigating smaller divisions of the organization, such as departments, as social systems in their own right, thus establishing for each role the primacy of the problem of the organizational system toward which behavior in the role is directed.[8]

In relationships between a system and its component subsystems, the subsystems perform functions that are primarily, but not exclusively, directed to one or another of the system problems. For example, the economy as a subsystem of society functions to produce goods valued by the society; these goods may be used to solve the adaptive system problem of the larger society by "adding value" to the society's ability to control and manipulate its environment. The functions of any subsystem may contribute to the solution of more than one system problem, just as any given action of a role incumbent within the subsystem may contribute to the solution of more than one problem for the subsystem. However, the relative primacy of the function for solution of one of the four system problems of the larger system is the basis for classification of the organization.

**Methodological usefulness of organizational types.** While it may be extremely enlightening to contrast the internal structure of organizations which perform different and perhaps differentially evaluated functions for the society, and hence belong to different primary types on the most general level, it is methodologically important to compare the structure of organizations which function with respect to the same problems of the society, in order to derive generalizations valid for this type. When such preliminary work has been accomplished, comparisons of organizations belonging to different primary types would provide generalizations valid for all organizations, as well as statements of special variables which affect the organizational structure and the interaction processes in organizations performing different and differently valued functions. If this work were undertaken systematically with the theory of action as the explicit theoretical frame of reference, prediction in terms of action theory would then be possible.

The empirical work on bureaucracy, industrial organizations, and the social organization of various specialized institutions such as mental hospitals yields hypotheses which can be stated in systematic terms and which future studies can utilize and attempt to test. We shall examine investigations of mental hospitals and penal institutions, classified as integrative organizations which operate to solve integrative problems for the society.

Similar theoretical formulations and research hypotheses can eventually be constructed for organizations having different functions, for example, churches and schools as pattern-maintenance organizations, business and manufacturing organizations as functioning to solve adaptive problems, and some governmental agencies and fiduciary firms as oriented to goal attainment. Systematic relationships thus established can lead to valid generalizations about social organizations.

## RELATIONS OF INTEGRATIVE ORGANIZATIONS TO SOCIETY

Although there are other organizations which perform integrative functions, mental hospitals and penal institutions have been chosen for two principal reasons. First, there apparently has been no systematic linking of studies of these organizations, although the fruitfulness of such a comparison has been suggested by several writers. This may be due to a division of labor whereby social psychologists study mental hospitals and criminologists study penal institutions in an attempt to solve practical problems which have been considered entirely different. Second, as yet there have been few published structural studies of either of these, especially of prisons.[9] Their philosophies of administration and their public expectations are undergoing considerable change at present; hence they offer opportunities for experimental studies in the processes of organizational change and accompanying structural transformations.

In the activity of these organizations directed to solution of society's integrative problem, the emphasis is upon identifying and determining the relationships between and among the units in such a way that the system is enabled to maintain itself. A distinction is made between members and nonmembers on the basis of their particular relationship to the system, and the release of emotionally toned activity toward them is permitted. However, the system's interest in the individual member is not in terms of his specific performances in a given role but in his diffuse quality as system member. He must demonstrate that he shares the same values, that he has the same expectations, that he "likes the same things," as the other members, or at least that he is trying to come to this state of affairs. The integrative organization functions to see to it that members of society *do* in fact manifest the same values and expectations within allowable limits and, if they do not, to win them over or to expel them. Classified with mental hospitals and prisons as integrative are organizations concerned with "the adjustment of conflicts and the direction of motivation to the fulfillment of institutionalized expectations."[10] Interest groups, the courts, the legal profession, and jails, parole agencies, reformatories, and general hospitals also belong in this category. The last are included because the ill person is considered as temporarily relieved of his social responsibilities but is expected to help cure himself as soon as possible so he may return to the full status of societal member.[11]

Both the criminal and the madman are viewed as nonsystem members in all respects. The madman is committed to a mental hospital and the criminal is sentenced to prison without their consent and against their will.

**The goals of integrative organizations.** The primary goal of these organizations is protection of society from former members who have been designated as feared and dangerous by the courts. In varying degrees punishment is also an aim. However, a relatively new course of action has been gaining acceptance, that is, "treatment" or resocialization. It was extended first to madmen, who were redefined as mentally ill; eventually, it was applied to the criminal, who in many circles is also considered either as mentally ill or as socially maladjusted and in need of treatment rather than punishment. There has been a shift from the protective closing of ranks as a technique of integration to the re-forming, in a literal sense, of the offending member and then readmitting him to the system. The re-forming has become a new goal of these organizations.

**Relations to other organizations in society.** The complications which arise from the often coexisting goals of protecting society by safe custody and of resocialization are reflected in the relationships of the organizations to others as diverse as state legislatures, newspapers, courts, research agencies, professional associations, and private philanthropic and "social action" interest groups. Frequently, appropriations of public money for the operation of the mental hospital or prison are foci of contention with these outside groups.[12] These power relationships between and among organizations affect the attainment of goals and can and do result in their redefinition.

Power is allocated by society to organizations in a proportion roughly correlative to the importance of their functions. The one considered most important in American society today is the solution of the adaptive problem (e.g., economic production, technical competence), although this may be in the process of change.[13] Probably next is pattern maintenance (e.g., science, education), on the one hand, and the maintaining of personal motivation on the other (e.g., family, personal health). Integrative problems come third. This consideration, when combined with the fact that state mental hospitals and penal institutions are thought of as nonprofit organizations and yet must recruit personnel in a competitive labor market, leads to difficulties in financing and staffing.

That budgeting for both organizations is usually done by state legislatures[14] distinguishes organizations such as prisons and mental hospitals from the privately financed or general hospital. Public schools, highway construction and maintenance, military and defense activities, of course, compete with integrative organizations for tax appropriations, possibly at the expense of mental hospitals and prisons. Such deprivation of financial resources has apparently led, in part, to the production by inmates (prisoners or patients) of goods and services necessary to their own maintenance, so that the "output" of the organization is used as human resources for the upkeep of the organization. The system necessity for this particular kind of work has important implications for internal structure.

Several considerations enter into the problem of personnel recruitment: the existence of a free labor market, the inability to pay a fair wage, and the generally low prestige of workers who perform personal services, unless they are professionals. The professional personnel—physicians, nurses, psychiatrists, psychologists, sociologists—create further problems of recruitment; such persons have professional standards and ethics which are often violated in the day-to-day operation of large-scale mental hospitals and prisons. They often have professional standards of success which have little or nothing to do with their formal position in the organization but are related to the outside. However, many mental hospitals and prisons have been able to provide intern or in-service training. Thus a relatively constant stream of medical interns, junior psychiatrists and psychologists, student psychiatric social workers and nurses, and prospective parole and probation officers pours in and out; few of them remain.

Furthermore, mental hospitals have historically been administered by medical doctors, on the commonly held assumption that physical and mental diseases are closely related; penal institutions have been administered by untrained political appointees, on the assumption that little professional skill is necessary to keep men safely confined. Neither organization has had trained administrators; the experience neither of a doctor nor of a politician necessarily equips one to attain the two goals of the organizations simultaneously; yet, if these organizations do not enjoy a traditional method of recruitment which guarantees effective personnel, it is because society has not granted the requisite power.

State mental hospitals and prisons usually have little to say about the assignment of inmates, which further distinguishes them from other organizations performing similar integrative functions. For example, private hospitals may require that patients be cared for by specified physicians and so on; "interest groups" have varying conditions of membership; private psychiatric hospitals almost always select patients on financial and sometimes symptomatic grounds. In private general or psychiatric hospitals, as contrasted with state mental hospitals or prisons, we should expect to find different points of strain which would to a large degree stem from their very different relationships to the larger society and other organizations with respect to financing and admittance of patients.

**Problems created by the value system of society.** The value system of society must be taken into account when considering exchange across the boundaries of the organizational system with other units of society, for example, the occupations as exemplified by specific employers; here the social worker in the mental hospital and the guidance or welfare officer in the prison (who may also be a social worker) play crucial roles.

One job of the social worker is to see to it that the society, or at least the local community, accepts the "cured" inmate as a system member. This usually means that the prospective "readmitted" member must accept society's values in making his own living and in his behavior in general. Society is reluctant to take back those it has defined as nonmembers, especially since diffuse, affectively toned actions have been taken against them. On the individual level we might profitably analyze this reluctance as guilt or fear; in the social system it involves receiving a member who is thought likely to disrupt the system. This consideration, combined with the inability of experts to effect reliable cure or resocialization in any given case, makes the problem of exchange across the boundaries of the organizations as systems unlike the problems of exchange, for example, of pattern-maintenance organizations, like universities, which also "produce" socialized and trained human beings. The larger social system does not *want* the products of the mental hospital or the prison. But the social worker or, to some extent, the administrator is expected to find a market for these products. Here the social worker is faced with revising the value system of society, a difficult and sometimes impossible task. When it can be accomplished locally, the problems of exchange are solved;[15] otherwise, frustration results both for the organization and for the social worker, whose loyalty to the organization may be jeopardized.[16]

Certain aspects of the operation of prisons, and to some extent of mental hospitals, have traditionally put strains upon the loyalty of employees, in addition to those strains brought about by low-prestige, low-salaried employment. Few are motivated by personal or professional ethics to remain in positions simply to help other people when better-paying positions carrying higher prestige are available. Added to this is the frequent requirement that employees live in the institution or be on call at all hours or the further restrictions on personal life which conflict with society's conception of a contract of employment as based principally upon technical or productive efficiency and not upon one's way of life.

That change is taking place in the value system of the society with respect to integrative organizations is evident from public concern with "cure," therapy, rehabilitation, resocialization, or whatever name is given to the process by which outcaste members are expected to be transformed into responsible persons who can be reincorporated into the societal system. It is this very concern which presents dilemmas and misunderstandings within the internal system of the mental hospital and the prison, for the staff of these organizations are also members of the larger society.

## STRUCTURAL PROBLEMS IN INTEGRATIVE ORGANIZATIONS

The operative code of an organization, its mechanisms of achieving its goals, is a problem of internal structure; it is this area which has been the focus of most empirical studies. Strains arise not only from power relations with other subsystems, from conflicts and changes in social values, but also from the structure of the organization itself. We shall examine some of these strains, especially as they become manifest through the role of the attendant in the mental hospital and the guard in the prison and of the professional "treatment" officers of both organizations, always assuming that both or-

ganizations explicitly hold to the equally valued goals of custody and of resocialization and that the relative emphasis given
either goal varies considerably from one concrete organization
to the next.

Mechanisms of goal attainment may be seen in the structure
of authority through which processes having to do with policy
decisions, allocative decisions, and integration of the organization take place. If the only goal of the prison, for example,
were custody and/or punishment, a rigidly hierarchical structure, resembling as closely as possible the prototype of the
military organization, would be ideal. In fact, prisons have
traditionally been organized along much these lines. In such an
organization the inmate population is to be "kept in its place,"
quiet and confined. There is little need for communication
from guards to warden, for decisions are made by the warden
and transmitted downward. The prison is run "by the book,"
and rules for the behavior of inmates, as well as guards, theoretically are universally applied and swiftly enforced. There is
likely some division of labor, for example, a recognition of the
"business" part of the prison, the "medical," and the "custody"
divisions. Policy and allocative decisions, however, place the
emphasis upon the custodial division and assign it primacy not
only with respect to facilities and personnel but with respect
to implementation of its goal—secure confinement.[17] The
structure of mental hospitals has been of this nature, with
separation of the custodial from the medical-psychiatric functions and emphasis upon the goals of the former, owing to
whatever exigencies of operation. Although the goal of the
mental hospital has from the beginning been resocialization or
cure to a greater extent than has that of the prison, in actual
fact the two organizations have traditionally achieved virtually
the same goal, namely, custody.

**Goal implementation and the "inmate subsystem."** We
have outlined above the conception of an action system, the
maintenance of which requires the solution of the four system
problems of adaption, goal attainment, integration, and pattern maintenance. Our postulate is that solution of the integrative problem of the organizational system of the mental
hospital or prison and the structural problems connected with

it require primacy in order that the goal of resocialization be carried out successfully.

Here we must consider not only the subsystem within the organization, such as the "professional subsystem" composed of physicians, psychiatric "experts," social workers, and nurses, and the "attendant subsystems" in the mental hospital, and their organizational parallels in prisons, but the very important fact that goal implementation for the organization is predicated upon the existence of an "inmate subsystem," with which the whole of the organizational staff must come to terms.[18] This inmate subsystem is both raw material and product to the staff. However, resocialization requires it to be intimately associated with the staff subsystems, to adopt their values and goals, and to help with their goal implementation. Hence the staff system must, as a functional prerequisite to goal attainment, integrate the inmate system into its own system. This is a more formal way of stating what has been attempted in organizations where "twenty-four-hour therapy," the "therapeutic community," and "total push" emphasis has been introduced. It is, on the organizational level, what is implied by Sutherland's "differential association" theory.[19]

The traditional conception of therapy is individualistic: the doctor and patient form a microscopic social system wherein the rules of the game of the outside world are suspended. This is a one-to-one relationship; it is time-consuming, requires highly skilled professional services, and in the present shortage of professional personnel is obviously unattainable in state mental hospitals and penal institutions. In the latter, indeed, it is doubtful whether such therapy can ever be completely successful because of the workings of the inmate system. However, systematic theoretical consideration provides us with a key; resocialization can be realized by "integrative therapy." By this, we do not mean group therapy as practiced by one psychiatrist and a group of patients but a common effort by the entire staff of the mental hospital or prison to integrate individuals and groups belonging to the inmate system into its own social system; only when this has been done can the resocialization goal be accomplished. This requires a reorientation of the values of the employees, and especially of nonprofessional staff, so that they accept, as system members, persons stigmatized by social expulsion. And it requires supreme integrative efforts within the organization to keep the system together in the face of these unusual requirements. The very structure of both mental hospitals and prisons has resulted in the most strenuous requirements being placed upon those persons least likely to be able to accept and deal with them from the standpoint either of training or of professional ethics, namely, the attendant and the guard. Upon them, too, fall custodial and housekeeping duties; they are responsible for preventing escapes, for preventing inmates from injuring each other, and for seeing that the wards are clean.

The consequences of incomplete integrative processes, both on the level of the integration of inmate with guard subsystems and of the integration of guard with professional subsystems, can hinder goal attainment. In a prison which recently became treatment-oriented, the professional staff mistrust the ability of the guards to accept the deviations of prisoners (i.e., to accept them as members of the guards' own system) and hence withhold information which would be important to the guard in dealing with the inmate, except from some guards who are considered more responsible. There is incomplete integration of the professional subsystem with the guard subsystem, as well as lack of integration of the guard subsystem with the inmate subsystem. The result has been a testing and challenging of the skill, authority, and knowledge of the professionals by the guards, which sometimes is observed by inmates, before whom the professional cannot easily defend himself, with ensuing defeat and degradation of the professional. The extent to which fear of the inmates, either as a group or as individuals, prevents integration of the attendant-guard system and the inmate system is indeterminate; the discussion of fear of inmates is taboo, at least in prisons. This is an aspect of the integrative process which warrants further research.

Interesting parallels may be seen in the use made of the inmate system in the mental hospital and in the prison. For example, both systems give rise to a classification of inmates which is not in accordance with the professional classification but is custodial. In mental hospitals patients are classified by attendants as "privileged patients, limited privilege patients, and patients without privileges." In prisons, the guards classify prisoners as "minimum, medium, or maximum security risks." Every new patient or prisoner must undergo classification; his actions for the first few days or weeks of his confinement play a large part in establishing his category, and assignment ultimately affects his chances for treatment, for work and recreation—indeed, for his entire experience there. The classification is essentially the basis of a status hierarchy, made mandatory by the demands placed upon the attendant-guard for custody and for housekeeping. The attendant must rely upon some of the patients not only to keep the wards clean and tidy but to control other patients; the guard in a parallel manner must rely upon some of the prisoners. The effect of the structure of informal authority is to emphasize custody or housekeeping at the expense of resocialization. Even more subversive results arise: patients in actual fact are put in the position of controlling the chances of other patients for treatment and privileges. There are indications that prisoners control the accumulation of "good time" by other prisoners through the ability to "frame," "mess up," or "bring heat to" a fellow prisoner, leading to punishment, solitary confinement, and loss of parole chances. The privileged inmates are those most useful to the attendant-guard system and, to some extent, those most nearly integrated with it. But, instead of this leading to prompt readmission into society when the inmate is cured, it may lead to the inmate's being kept on to do custodial work and housekeeping, especially in mental hospitals.

The integrative situation in prisons is different in at least one important respect: the relative strength, hostility, and rationality of the inmate subsystem. Each new prisoner not only must be subjected to classification by the guards but also must come to terms with the inmate subsystem and be assigned a status there. The values of the "prisoner's code" are inimical to those of the guard; hence the problem of integration becomes even more difficult of solution and crucial to resocialization. McCorkle suggests that the chief value in the inmate system is the possession and exercise of coercive power, a condition which disorganizes the system, where, indeed, many

controls are not internal but are supplied by the external coercion of the guard's system.[20] However, this shaky inmate
system is not further undermined and exploited for resocialization purposes because the guards need it to keep order in the
prison. Moreover, the custodial officer is likely to look upon
the psychiatrist or other treatment officer as obstructing discipline, while the latter regards the former as obstructing treatment. This is, in fact, precisely what is occurring, because of
the lack of system integration of the two arms of the organization's staff.

We can now see why a change from custodial to "therapeutic" structure may result in prison riots. If the administration permits the allocative and integrative decisions necessary
to implementing resocialization, this means a change in the
established relationship between the guard's system and the
inmate system and a breakdown of the inmate system as an
effective means of coercing inmates and guards. The old relationship in which the guard had to grant privileges to powerful inmates in order to perform his own custodial and housekeeping duties gives way to a situation where the need for and
preferred response to treatment determines the relationship
between guard and prisoner and between guard and professional as well. Resocialization is given equal or preferential
value with custody, and a concomitant breakdown of the old
basis of guard-inmate interaction results.[21]

The result of the interrelationships between the attendant-
guard subsystem and the relative paucity of professional personnel and the prestige and authority differentials between
them and the attendant-guard subsystem is a blocking and/or
distortion of communication precisely at the point crucial to
goal attainment. The attendant-guard is given authority for
custody but not at all or only indirectly for resocialization. Yet
he is expected to promote resocialization, although he neither
knows how nor has he been assigned clear-cut authority to do
so. Nevertheless, attendants feel that they know what is good
for the patient and what his capacities with respect to resocialization are; guards feel that they know what the prisoner is
"really" like and what steps must be taken to control him—
because they are, in fact, the persons nearest him for the long-

est periods of time and because they are, in fact, in the position to implement or ignore directives.

In actual practice the professional who most highly values resocialization and is most capable of implementing it is separated from the inmate not only by the attendant-guard system but also by his administrative functions, such as supervision of personnel, record-keeping, and so on. What little time he has left for direct therapeutic work is likely to be confined to the few inmates who are already in a favorable position vis-à-vis the attendant-guard system; and these are not necessarily the inmates who can benefit most from therapy or who need it most in the light of the goals of the organization. This problem is particularly crucial in mental hospitals, where "back-ward" patients tend to accumulate over the years. In prisons, under the present system of sentencing for a minimum number of years, successful cure often could not hasten release. Whether the inmate subsystem can, under these conditions, ever contribute positively to resocialization is problematic. Certainly, it would have to be closely integrated with the attendant-guard system, and the attendant-guard system, in turn, would have to be closely integrated with the professional system.

The structure of an organization which gives primacy to integrative problems, under conditions where integration involves the dual problems of integration of an uninterested or hostile subsystem and of system members themselves, must of necessity be decentralized with respect to allocative decisions, in so far as is possible within the limits of its total resources and facilities. In the mental hospital the attendant must be able to requisition whatever supplies he needs on the ward without bureaucratic delays and inconveniences; he must be able to ask for and receive additional personnel during critical periods when such personnel might very well enable members of the attendant system to interact more frequently and intimately with the members of the inmate system and hence prevent overt outbreaks.[22] It is the attendant who is most likely to be able to anticipate the day-to-day needs, both physical and emotional, of the ward.

But this does not mean that decentralized decision-making must necessarily lead to unclearness and confusion of the lines of authority. The decision to assign allocative decisions to the attendant is itself a policy decision and can be made only when both the attendant-guard and the professional subsystems are agreeable to relinquishing some of their former authority. Such agreement is closely linked with decisions related to integration of the organization; if allocative decisions are to be decentralized to facilitate goal implementation, the professional and the attendant-guard subsystem must be in agreement, and the attendant-guard must be so integrated into the professional system as to be motivated toward implementing the resocialization of the inmate. It is known that attendants and guards have a conception of mental illness and of crime different from that of the professional staff. Furthermore, it does not seem possible to set forth specific "rules of treatment." The professional must work through the attendant-guard subsystem to reach the inmate system, which is the object of resocialization; apparently, the only way is through a conscious decision to concentrate upon integration of the attendant system with the professional system on one level and, through it, integration of the inmate system with the attendant system, as the means of goal attainment.

**Structural restrictions unfavorable to goal implementation.** It is suggested that indeterminate sentences, the length of which would be determined by professionals such as psychiatrists, psychiatric social workers, or sociologists, based upon the inmates' progress toward resocialization or incorporation of conventional social values, would overcome some of the hindrances to therapy of fixed sentences. On the one hand, this involves the relationship of the prison as an organization to the courts; we would have here the commutation of legitimately imposed sentences by an unauthorized organization; profound changes must take place in values to legitimize such procedure. An important practical obstacle, at the moment, is the inability of social scientists to measure such variables as degree of resocialization or of incorporation of values. On the other hand, even with indeterminate sentences, the "prisoner's code" will not permit special privilege based on treatment criteria, for it is extremely difficult, as we have seen, to state just what are the rules for treatment because of their individualistic nature. Release would be considered by other inmates as special privilege, with resulting disturbances and further alienation from the guard subsystem. Theoretically, effective integration could overcome these disturbances; empirically, since such procedures have never been tried, the result is problematic.

## NOTES

Source: *American Journal of Sociology*, LXIV (January 1959), 386–95.
\* Expansion of a paper read to the American Sociological Society, Seattle, August, 1958.

1. Talcott Parsons, *The Social System* (Glencoe: Free Press, 1951); Talcott Parsons and Edward A. Shils (eds.), *Toward a General Theory of Action* (Cambridge, Mass.: Harvard University Press, 1952); Talcott Parsons, Robert F. Bales, and Edward A. Shils, *Working Papers in the Theory of Action* (Glencoe: Free Press, 1953).
2. Talcott Parsons, "Suggestions for a Sociological Approach to the Theory of Organizations—I and II," *Administrative Science Quarterly*, I (June and September 1956), 63–85 and 225–39.
3. *Ibid.*, 238.
4. See Talcott Parsons, "A Revised Analytic Approach to the Theory of Social Stratification," in Reinhard Bendix and S. M. Lipset (eds.), *Class, Status and Power* (Glencoe: Free Press, 1953), 92–128.
5. For a more detailed discussion see *ibid.*; also Parsons *et al.*, *Working Papers*, esp. chapter V.
6. See Parsons *et al.*, *Working Papers*, esp. 179–90.
7. *Ibid.*, chapters III and V.
8. The application of the paradigm on different levels of analysis is suggested by Parsons, "A Revised Analytic Approach to the Theory of Social Stratification," *op. cit.*, esp. 108–11.
9. A notable exception is Donald Clemmer, *The Prison Community* (Boston: Christopher, 1940). Several studies by other American social scientists are nearing completion.
10. Parsons, "Suggestions for a Sociological Approach to the Theory of Organization," *op. cit.*, 229.
11. Parsons, *The Social System*, chapter X, "The Case of Modern Medical Practice," esp. 439–47.
12. See Lloyd E. Ohlin, "Interest Group Conflict and Correctional Change," unpublished paper read before the Social Science Research Council Conference Group on Research in Social Organization of Correctional Agencies, April 1957.
13. Parsons, "A Revised Analytic Approach to the Theory of Social Stratification," *op. cit.*, 106.
14. See Ivan Belknap, *Human Problems of a State Mental Hospital* (New York: McGraw-Hill Book Co., 1956), 31–36; M. Greenblatt, R. H. York, and E. L. Brown, *From Custodial to Therapeutic Patient Care in Mental Hospitals* (New York: Russell Sage Foundation, 1955), 38–39; Clemmer, *op. cit.*, 274.

15. See Maxwell Jones, *The Therapeutic Community* (New York: Basic Books, 1953).
16. L. E. Ohlin, Herman Piven, and D. M. Pappenfort, "Major Dilemmas of the Social Worker in Probation and Parole," *National Probation and Parole Association Journal,* II (July 1956), 211–25.
17. For a discussion of the difficulties this causes for the professional subsystem see Harvey Powelson and Reinhard Bendix, "Psychiatry in Prison," *Psychiatry,* XIV (February 1951), 73–86.
18. For a discussion of the "inmate system" in prisons see Lloyd W. McCorkle and Richard Korn, "Resocialization Within Walls," *Annals of the American Academy of Political and Social Science,* CCXCIII (May 1954), 88–98; McCleery, *op. cit.*
19. Donald R. Cressey, "Changing Criminals: The Application of the Theory of Differential Association," *American Journal of Sociology,* LXI (September 1955), 116–20.
20. McCorkle and Korn, *op. cit.,* 90.
21. See Greenblatt *et al., op. cit.,* chapter XV, 295–321.
22. That such additional personnel can be effective in preventing ward disturbances and that attendants can sense when such disturbances are about to erupt is shown by A. H. Stanton and M. S. Schwartz, *The Mental Hospital* (New York: Basic Books, 1954), 394–400.

# THE THERAPEUTIC FUNCTION
## OF PRISONS

# INTRODUCTION

In their recent book, *Organization for Treatment*, Street, Vinter, and Perrow characterize "people-changing" organizations as those which "work not only with or through people but also *on* them."[1] Examples of such organizations range from the school, church, family, and other developmental institutions, which stress *socialization*, to the prison, mental hospital, military training camp, and other total institutions, which stress *resocialization* or *redevelopment*. The characterization is particularly apt to the discussions contained in the next seven selections. If the prison is to fulfill its integrative function to larger society, it must be in fact a "people-changing" organization. The issue of priority of tasks about which one hears so much—the protection of society versus the treatment offenders—evades a basic reality. The only means by which society can achieve its desired protection is a resocialization of the deviant which leads to his reintegration into society. Mere incarceration and even the most brutal psychophysical punishment, short of execution, can provide only a short-term protection at best and may in the long run actually compound the danger from which society seeks some relief.

In most jurisdictions of the United States, the correctional institution has moved, however slightly, beyond the rat-infested dungeon and ingenious forms of corporal punishment which have been the "negative" deviant's historical legacy. Yet acceptance and implementation of the resocialization function is still highly tentative. To a degree, this is due to resistances by "old line" personnel who ritualistically perpetuate traditional methods. The author of one of the following selections points out that corrections has yet to incorporate all the postulates which were enunciated in the Declaration of Principles at Cincinnati during the autumn of 1870 (and which were taken in large measure from the works of Alexander Maconochie, according to Justice John Barry[2]). But the reluctance to accept and implement the resocialization function also follows from the inability of the human behavior sciences to offer efficient, reliable tactics and strategies of change. One must bear in mind that sociology, a major intellectual parent of criminology and corrections in this country, has given change, as opposed to constancy, the lesser share of its attention.

Since the late 1940's, a body of theory with some promise of application to the correctional task has emerged: group dynamics theory. In selection 12, Cartwright outlines the group dynamics approach and synthesizes eight basic principles of the group-oriented change process. The major premise of this approach is that human behavior, criminal or other, is a function of group relations. Consequently, any program designed to rectify unacceptable deviance displayed by the individual must attempt to alter the individual's group relations.

A classic in its field, Cartwright's article has served as a springboard for numerous analyses and experimental applications, not only in corrections but also in education, business and industrial management, and ethnic relations.[3] One such study is selection 13, by Cressey, in which Sutherland's theory of differential association is fused to the group dynamics framework. Cressey contends that the implications of the differential association theory for the diagnosis and treatment of criminals are consistent with the principle of changing individual behavior by changing group properties. The product of the fusion, he argues, can be effectively utilized in correctional work.

Grosser's article, which developed from an advanced seminar on authoritative settings held at Columbia University in 1956, moves the discussion of group dynamics to a practical evaluation of the part played by informal inmate group structures during attempts to alter the group members' value patterns. These informal structures which emerge in institutional populations, and which are reflected by what is commonly termed the "inmate code" or "subculture," are intensely potent. If properly understood and utilized, they can become powerful forces toward desired change; if ignored or under-estimated, they can be powerful obstacles which no amount of executive decree or other formal administrative procedure can penetrate. In short, these informal group structures must be considered part of the institution's structural reality, or they can nullify even the best efforts of superior personnel. In selection 14, Grosser examines these potentially constructive influences and suggests some techniques for harnessing them to the correctional task.

Finally, in selection 15, Hall, Williams, and Tomaino analyze the alternative strategies of change employed by correctional workers and relate these strategies to the prevailing theories of change offered by the behavioral sciences. The authors base their analysis on a model that was developed from extensive research into patterns of managerial behavior and organizational change in business and industry. But, they contend, the model constitutes a more nearly universal contribution as "a descriptive and diagnostic tool for the systematic analysis of goal-oriented behaviors." As a demonstration of this expanded utility, the authors identify six different strategies of change and assess the significance of each to the corrections profession.

As the first four selections within this section imply, corrections has long operated without an adequate theory of action. If a crude analogy can be permitted, the current dilemma facing correctional agents reminds one of the healer who sets out to "cure" a population afflicted by some age-old disease, but without knowledge of human anatomy and physiology and without any understanding of the epidemiology of the affliction. If corrections is to serve "people-changing" functions relative to its clientele and integrative functions relative to the larger society, certainly it must command a unified theory of treatment which incorporates reliable diagnostic tools. All of this, of course, presupposes some understanding of the "epidemiology of the affliction."

Gibbons suggests in selection 16 that, even though we are far from a reasonably complete knowledge of deviant behavior, we do know a little more about it than is sometimes imagined, at least enough to initiate the development of a "comprehensive conceptualization of treatment based upon a set of empirically grounded diagnostic types." To this end, he proposes an exploratory diagnostic model of nine "adult-offender types" and relates to each his estimation of the most appropriate dimension of treatment from those currently available. While Gibbons' typological model shows improvements over many previous offerings, it too suffers from reliance upon the legal denotations of criminal acts, which tend to be rather artificial and may or may not possess any direct connection with the more basic dynamics of human behavior.

Continuing the discussion of deficiencies in the theory of correctional action, Cressey's second contribution to "The Therapeutic Function of Prisons" critically analyzes the various treatment practices now in use and concludes that few of them are grounded in legitimate theory. Even those which exhibit some acceptable relation to theory have not been sufficiently verified as either effective or ineffective in achieving change in the offender. Of particular interest is Cressey's incisive discussion of a major obstacle to meaningful program evaluation—the "vocabulary of adjustment." This vocabulary enables a person to "prove" that any research into the effectiveness of a favored technique or program is inconclusive. Corrections is not alone in its use of such a rationalizing vocabulary, but it does seem to stand slightly apart from other professions if one considers the extent and intensity of the usage. Personnel who have made investments—intellectual or otherwise—in the correction of criminal behavior often try to justify "whatever it is they are doing as corrective." This has resulted in the inclusion of everything from brass-polishing to road-construction to garden-tending in our *repertoire* of "treatment" techniques.

In the concluding selection, Schnur analyzes the role of research in corrections—what it can and cannot be expected to accomplish. As the author points out, serious misunderstandings concerning the capabilities of research have led to skepticism and hostility on the part of correctional workers (and at the same time, to some of the most insipid activity passing as scientific investigation). Research scientists can advise correctional workers, but it is not they who must make the final decisions concerning correctional policy. Research can predict probable consequences, but words such as "certain" and "never" are quite foreign to it. It can illuminate possible solutions, but it cannot ensure successes. It can lead to "favorable" *and* "unfavorable" information, but it cannot protect either—and especially the latter—from the censor of vested interests.

Schnur notes that "perhaps what is needed as much as research of the field variety is an investigation and analysis of the research that has been done." The meager results would indeed be embarrassing in view of the haphazard manner in which much of correctional research is conducted. But one deficiency which Schnur fails to mention—correction's isolation—should be even more embarrassing. For not only is it isolated (maybe decreasingly so) from other disciplines in this country, it is almost totally unaware of developments in other countries, particularly those of Europe.

Before concluding these introductory remarks, it would be appropriate to note the existence of a major question of ethics relevant to the correctional task, a question which has received occasional attention but not the close and continuous scrutiny it demands. It is the fundamental problem of means in relation to ends or goals. Once effective techniques of inducing change in a person's behavior are discovered, will they be used regardless of their nature? In view of the frantic concern with "skyrocketing crime rates"[4] and the vulnerable position of the prison inmate, there is a distinct possibility corrections will become so end-oriented that any workable method, which under other circumstances would be considered inhumane, will be employed. The tendency toward this orientation is already discernible.

## NOTES

1. David Street, Robert D. Vinter, and Charles Perrow, *Organization for Treatment: A Comparative Study of Institutions for Delinquents* (New York: Free Press, 1966), 3 ff.
2. Cited by Harry Elmer Barnes and Negley K. Teeters, *New Horizons in Criminology*, 3rd edition (Englewood Cliffs: Prentice-Hall, 1959), 425, note 8.

3. A recent example in corrections would be the Provo Experiment in Utah. See LaMar T. Empey and Jerome Rabow, "The Provo Experiment in Delinquency Rehabilitation," *American Sociological Review*, XXVI (October 1961), 679–95; and, Whitney H. Gordon, "Communist Rectification Programs and Delinquency Rehabilitation Programs: A Parallel?" and "Reply to Whitney H. Gordon," *op. cit.*, XXVII (April 1962), 256–58.

4. For a good analysis of the faulty methodology which interprets present crime rates as "skyrocketing," see David M. H. Richmond, "On the Alleged Increases in U.S. Criminality: A Critical Method for Evaluation of Crime Statistics," *Dialogue*, (March 1967), 8–20.

# 12

## ACHIEVING CHANGE IN PEOPLE: SOME APPLICATIONS OF GROUP DYNAMICS THEORY*

*Dorwin Cartwright†*

I

We hear all around us today the assertion that the problems of the twentieth century are problems of human relations. The survival of civilization, it is said, will depend upon man's ability to create social inventions capable of harnessing, for society's constructive use, the vast physical energies now at man's disposal. Or, to put the matter more simply, we must learn how to change the way in which people behave toward one another. In broad outline, the specifications for a good society are clear, but a serious technical problem remains: How can we change people so that they neither restrict the freedom nor limit the potentialities for growth of others; so that they accept and respect people of different religion, nationality, color, or political opinion; so that nations can exist in a world without war, and so that the fruits of our technological advances can bring economic well-being and freedom from disease to all the people of the world? Although few people would disagree with these objectives when stated abstractly, when we become more specific, differences of opinion quickly arise. How is change to be produced? Who is to do it? Who is to be changed? These questions permit no ready answers.

Before we consider in detail these questions of social technology, let us clear away some semantic obstacles. The word "change" produces emotional reactions. It is not a neutral

---

† Dorwin Cartwright is a professor and Director of the Research Center for Group Dynamics at the University of Michigan.

word. To many people it is threatening. It conjures up visions of a revolutionary, a dissatisfied idealist, a troublemaker, a malcontent. Nicer words referring to the process of changing people are education, training, orientation, guidance, indoctrination, therapy. We are more ready to have others "educate" us than to have them "change" us. We, ourselves, feel less guilty in "training" others than in "changing" them. Why this emotional response? What makes the two kinds of words have such different meanings? I believe that a large part of the difference lies in the fact that the safer words (like education or therapy) carry the inplicit assurance that the only changes produced will be good ones, acceptable within a currently held value system. The cold, unmodified word "change," on the contrary, promises no respect for values; it might even tamper with values themselves. Perhaps for this very reason it will foster straight thinking if we use the word "change" and thus force ourselves to struggle directly and self-consciously with the problems of value that are involved. Words like education, training, or therapy, by the very fact that they are not so disturbing, may close our eyes to the fact that they too inevitably involve values.

Another advantage of using the word "change" rather than other related words is that it does not restrict our thinking to a limited set of aspects of people that are legitimate targets of change. Anyone familiar with the history of education knows that there has been endless controversy over what it is about people that "education" properly attempts to modify. Some educators have viewed education simply as imparting knowledge, others mainly as providing skills for doing things, still others as producing healthy "attitudes," and some have aspired to instill a way of life. Or if we choose to use a word like "therapy," we can hardly claim that we refer to a more clearly defined realm of change. Furthermore, one can become inextricably entangled in distinctions and vested interests by attempting to distinguish sharply between, let us say, the domain of education and that of therapy. If we are to try to take a broader view and to develop some basic principles that promise to apply to all types of modifications in people, we had better use a word like "change" to keep our thinking general enough.

The proposal that social technology may be employed to solve the problems of society suggests that social science may be applied in ways not different from those used in the physical sciences. Does social science, in fact, have any practically useful knowledge which may be brought to bear significantly on society's most urgent problems? What scientifically based principles are there for guiding programs of social change: In this paper we shall restrict our considerations to certain parts of a relatively new branch of social science known as "group dynamics." We shall examine some of the implications for social action which stem from research in this field of scientific investigation.

What is "group dynamics"? Perhaps it will be most useful to start by looking at the derivation of the word "dynamics." It comes from a Greek work meaning force. In careful usage of the phrase, "group dynamics" refers to the forces operating in groups. The investigation of group dynamics, then, consists of a study of these forces: What gives rise to them, what conditions modify them, what consequences they have, etc. The practical application of group dynamics (or the technology of group dynamics) consists of the utilization of knowledge about these forces for the achievement of some purpose. In keeping with this definition, then, it is clear that group dynamics, as a realm of investigation, is not particularly novel, nor is it the exclusive property of any person or institution. It goes back at least to the outstanding work of men like Simmel, Freud, and Cooley.

Although interest in groups has a long and respectable history, the past fifteen years have witnessed a new flowering of activity in this field. Today, research centers in several countries are carrying out substantial programs of research designed to reveal the nature of groups and of their functioning. The phrase "group dynamics" has come into common usage during this time, and intense efforts have been devoted to the development of the field, both as a branch of social science and as a form of social technology.

In this development the name of Kurt Lewin has been outstanding. As a consequence of his work in the field of individual psychology and from his analysis of the nature of the pressing problems of the contemporary world, Lewin became convinced of society's urgent need for a *scientific approach* to the understanding of the dynamics of groups. In 1945 he established the Research Center for Group Dynamics to meet this need. Since that date the center has been devoting its efforts to improving our scientific understanding of groups through laboratory experimentation, field studies, and the use of techniques of action research. It has also attempted in various ways to help get the findings of social science more widely used by social management. Much of what I have to say in this paper is drawn from the experiences of this center in its brief existence of a little more than five years.[1]

## II

For various reasons we have found that much of our work has been devoted to an attempt to gain a better understanding of the ways in which people change their behavior or resist efforts by others to have them do so. Whether we set for ourselves the practical goal of improving behavior or whether we take on the intellectual task of understanding why people do what they do, we have to investigate processes of communication, influence, social pressure—in short, problems of change.

In this work we have encountered great frustration. The problems have been most difficult to solve. Looking back over our experience, I have become convinced that no small part of the trouble has resulted from an irresistible tendency to conceive of our problems in terms of the individual. We live in an individualistic culture. We value the individual highly, and rightly so. But I am inclined to believe that our political and social concern for the individual has narrowed our thinking as social scientists so much that we have not been able to state our research problems properly. Perhaps we have taken the individual as the unit of observation and study when some larger unit would have been more appropriate. Let us look at a few examples.

Consider first some matters having to do with the mental health of an individual. We can all agree, I believe, that an important mark of a healthy personality is that the individual's self-esteem has not been undermined. But on what does self-esteem depend? From research on this problem we have discovered that, among other things, repeated experiences of failure or traumatic failures on matters of central importance serve to undermine one's self-esteem. We also know that whether a person experiences success or failure as a result of some undertaking depends upon the level of aspiration which he has set for himself. Now, if we try to discover how the level of aspiration gets set, we are immediately involved in the person's relationships to groups. The groups to which he belongs set standards for his behavior which he must accept if he is to remain in the group. If his capacities do not allow him to reach these standards, he experiences failure, he withdraws or is rejected by the group, and his self-esteem suffers a shock.

Suppose, then, that we accept a task of therapy, of rebuilding his self-esteem. It would appear plausible from our analysis of the problem that we should attempt to work with variables of the same sort that produced the difficulty, that is to work with him either in the groups to which he now belongs or to introduce him into new groups which are selected for the purpose and to work upon his relationships to groups as such. From the point of view of preventive mental health, we might even attempt to train the groups in our communities— classes in schools, work groups in business, families, unions, religious and cultural groups—to make use of practices better designed to protect the self-esteem of their members.

Consider a second example. A teacher finds that in her class she has a number of troublemakers, full of aggression. She wants to know why these children are so aggressive and what can be done about it. A foreman in a factory has the same kind of problem with some of his workers. He wants the same kind of help. The solution most tempting to both the teacher and the foreman often is to transfer the worst troublemakers to someone else or, if facilities are available, to refer them for counseling. But is the problem really of such a nature that it can be solved by removing the troublemaker from the situation or by working on his individual motivations and emotional life? What leads does research give us? The evidence indicates, of course, that there are many causes of aggressiveness in people, but one aspect of the problem has become increasingly clear in recent years. If we observe carefully the amount of aggressive behavior and the number of troublemakers to be found in a large collection of groups, we find that these characteristics can vary tremendously from group to group even when the different groups are composed essentially of the same kinds of people. In the now classic experiments of Lewin, Lippitt, and White on the effects of different styles of leadership, it was found that the same group of children displayed markedly different levels of aggressive behavior when under different styles of leadership.[2] Moreover, when individual children were transferred from one group to another, their levels of aggressiveness shifted to conform to the atmosphere of the new group. Efforts to account for one child's aggressiveness under one style of leadership merely in terms of his personality traits could hardly succeed under these conditions. This is not to say that a person's behavior is entirely to be accounted for by the atmosphere and structure of the immediate group, but it is remarkable to what an extent a strong, cohesive group can control aspects of a member's behavior traditionally thought to be expressive of enduring personality traits. Recognition of this fact rephrases the problem of how to change such behavior. It directs us to a study of the sources of the influences of the group on its members.

Let us take an example from a different field. What can we learn from efforts to change people by mass media and mass persuasion? In those rare instances when educators, propagandists, advertisers, and others who want to influence large numbers of people have bothered to make an objective evaluation of the enduring changes produced by their efforts, they have been able to demonstrate only the most negligible effects.[3] The inefficiency of attempts to influence the public by mass media would be scandalous if there were agreement that it was important or even desirable to have such influences strongly exerted. In fact, it is no exaggeration to say that all of the research and experience of generations have not improved the efficiency of lectures or other means of mass influence to any noticeable degree. Something must be wrong with our theories of learning, motivation, and social psychology.

Within very recent years some research data have been accumulating which may give us a clue to the solution of our problem. In one series of experiments directed by Lewin, it was found that a method of group decision, in which the group as a whole made a decision to have its members change their behavior, was from two to ten times as effective in producing actual change as was a lecture presenting exhortation to change.[4] We have yet to learn precisely what produces these differences of effectiveness, but it is clear that by introducing group forces into the situation a whole new level of influence has been achieved.

The experience has been essentially the same when people have attempted to increase the productivity of individuals in work settings. Traditional conceptions of how to increase the output of workers have stressed the individual: select the right man for the job; simplify the job for him; train him in the skills required; motivate him by economic incentives; make it clear to whom he reports; keep the lines of authority and responsibility simple and straight. But even when all these conditions are fully met we are finding that productivity is far below full potential. There is even good reason to conclude that this individualistic conception of the determinants of productivity actually fosters negative consequences. The individual, now isolated and subjected to the demands of the organization through the commands of his boss, finds that he must create with his fellow employees informal groups, not shown on any table of organization, in order to protect himself from arbitrary control of his life, from the boredom produced by the endless repetition of mechanically sanitary and routine operations, and from the impoverishment of his emotional and social life brought about by the frustration of his basic needs for social interaction, participation, and acceptance in a stable group. Recent experiments have demonstrated clearly that the productivity of work groups can be greatly increased by methods of work organization and supervision which give more responsibility to work groups, which allow for fuller participation in important decisions, and which make stable groups the firm basis for support of the individual's social needs.[5] I am convinced that future research will also demonstrate that people working under such conditions become more mature and creative individuals in their homes, in community life, and as citizens.

As a final example, let us examine the experience of efforts to train people in workshops, institutes, and special training courses. Such efforts are common in various areas of social welfare, intergroup relations, political affairs, industry, and adult education generally. It is an unfortunate fact that objective evaluation of the effects of such training efforts has only rarely been undertaken, but there is evidence for those who will look that the actual change in behavior produced is most disappointing. A workshop not infrequently develops keen interest among the participants, high morale and enthusiasm, and a firm resolve on the part of many to apply all the wonderful insights back home. But what happens back home? The trainee discovers that his colleagues don't share his enthusiasm. He learns that the task of changing others' expectations and ways of doing things is discouragingly difficult. He senses, perhaps not very clearly, that it would make all the difference in the world if only there were a few other people sharing his enthusiasm and insights with whom he could plan activities, evaluate consequences of efforts, and from whom he could gain emotional and motivational support. The approach to training which conceives of its task as being merely that of changing the individual probably produces frustration, demoralization, and disillusionment in as large a measure as it accomplishes more positive results.

A few years ago the Research Center for Group Dynamics undertook to shed light on this problem by investigating the operation of a workshop for training leaders in intercultural relations.[6] In a project, directed by Lippitt, we set out to compare systematically the different effects of the workshop upon trainees who came as isolated individuals in contrast to those who came as teams. Since one of the problems in the field of intercultural relations is that of getting people of good will to be more active in community efforts to improve inter-group relations, one goal of the training workshop was to increase the activity of the trainees in such community affairs. We found that before the workshop there was no difference in the activity level of the people who were to be trained as isolates and of those who were to be trained as teams. Six months after the workshop, however, those who had been trained as isolates were only slightly more active than before the workshop, whereas those who had been members of strong training teams were now much more active. We do not have clear evidence on the point, but we would be quite certain that the maintenance of heightened activity over a long period of time would also be much better for members of teams. For the isolates the effect of the workshop had the characteristic of a "shot in the arm," while for the team member it produced a more enduring change because the team provided continuous support and reinforcement for its members.

III

What conclusions may we draw from these examples? What principles of achieving change in people can we see emerging? To begin with the most general proposition, we may state that the behavior, attitudes, beliefs, and values of the individual are all firmly grounded in the groups to which he belongs. How aggressive or co-operative a person is, how much self-respect and self-confidence he has, how energetic and productive his work is, what he aspires to, what he believes to be true and good, whom he loves or hates, and what beliefs and prejudices he holds—all these characteristics are highly determined by the individual's group memberships. In a real sense, they are properties of groups and of the relationships between people. Whether they change or resist change will, therefore, be greatly influenced by the nature of these groups. Attempts to change them must be concerned with the dynamics of groups.

In examining more specifically how groups enter into the process of change, we find it useful to view groups in at least three different ways. In the first view, the group is seen as a source of influence over its members. Efforts to change behavior can be supported or blocked by pressures on members stemming from the group. To make constructive use of these pressures the group must be used *as a medium of change*. In the second view, the group itself becomes the *target of change*. In order to change the behavior of individuals it may be necessary to change the standards of the group, its style of leadership, its emotional atmosphere, or its stratification into cliques and hierarchies. Even though the goal may be to change the behavior of *individuals,* the target of change becomes the group. In the third view, it is recognized that many changes of behavior can be brought about only by the organized efforts of groups *as agents of change*. A committee to combat intolerance, a labor union, an employers' association, a citizens' group to increase the pay of teachers— any action group will be more or less effective depending upon the way it is organized, the satisfactions it provides to its members, the degree to which its goals are clear, and a host of other properties of the group.

An adequate social technology of change, then, requires at the very least a scientific understanding of groups viewed in each of these ways. We shall consider here only the first two aspects of the problem: the group as a medium of change and as a target of change.

## THE GROUP AS A MEDIUM OF CHANGE

**Principle No. 1.** *If the group is to be used effectively as a medium of change, those people who are to be changed and those who are to exert influence for change must have a strong sense of belonging to the same group.*

Kurt Lewin described this principle well: "The normal gap between teacher and student, doctor and patient, social worker and public, can . . . be a real obstacle to acceptance of the advocated conduct." In other words, in spite of whatever status differences there might be between them, the teacher and the student have to feel as members of one group in matters involving their sense of values. The chances for re-education seem to be increased whenever a strong we-feeling is created.[7] Recent experiments by Preston and Heintz have demonstrated greater changes of opinions among members of discussion groups operating with participatory leadership than among those with supervisory leadership.[8] The implications of this principle for classroom teaching are far-reaching. The same may be said of supervision in the factory, army, or hospital.

**Principle No. 2.** *The more attractive the group is to its members the greater is the influence that the group can exert on its members.*

This principle has been extensively documented by Festinger and his co-workers.[9] They have been able to show in a variety of settings that in more cohesive groups there is a greater readiness of members to attempt to influence others, a greater readiness to be influenced by others, and stronger pressures toward conformity when conformity is a relevant matter for the group. Important for the practitioner wanting to make use of this principle is, of course, the question of how to increase the attractiveness of groups. This is a question with many answers. Suffice it to say that a group is more attractive the more it satisfies the needs of its members. We have been able to demonstrate experimentally an increase in group cohesiveness by increasing the liking of members for each other as persons, by increasing the perceived importance of the group goal, and by increasing the prestige of the group among other groups. Experienced group workers could add many other ways to this list.

**Principle No. 3.** *In attempts to change attitudes, values, or behavior, the more relevant they are to the basis of attraction to the group, the greater will be the influence that the group can exert upon them.*

I believe this principle gives a clue to some otherwise puzzling phenomena. How does it happen that a group, like a labor union, seems to be able to exert such strong discipline over its members in some matters (let us say in dealings with management), while it seems unable to exert nearly the same influence in other matters (let us say in political action)? If we examine why it is that members are attracted to the group, I believe we will find that a particular reason for belonging seems more related to some of the group's activities than to others. If a man joins a union mainly to keep his job and to improve his working conditions, he may be largely uninfluenced by the union's attempt to modify his attitudes toward national and international affairs. Groups differ tremendously in the range of matters that are relevant to them and hence over which they have influence. Much of the inefficiency of adult education could be reduced if more attention were paid to the need that influence attempts be appropriate to the groups in which they are made.

**Principle No. 4.** *The greater the prestige of a group member in the eyes of the other members, the greater the influence he can exert.*

Polansky, Lippitt, and Redl have demonstrated this principle with great care and methodological ingenuity in a series of studies in children's summer camps.[10] From a practical point of view it must be emphasized that the things giving prestige to a member may not be those characteristics most prized by the official management of the group. The most prestige-carrying member of a Sunday-school class may not possess the characteristics most similar to those of the minister of the church. The teacher's pet may be a poor source of influence within a class. This principle is the basis for the common observation that the official leader and the actual leader of a group are often not the same individual.

**Principle No. 5.** *Efforts to change individuals or subparts of a group which, if successful, would have the result of making them deviate from the norms of the group will encounter strong resistance.*

During the past few years a great deal of evidence has been accumulated showing the tremendous pressures which groups can exert upon members to conform to the group's norms. The price of deviation in most groups is rejection or even expulsion. If the member really wants to belong and be accepted, he cannot withstand this type of pressure. It is for this reason that efforts to change people by taking them from the group and giving them special training so often have disappointing results. This principle also accounts for the finding that people thus trained sometimes display increased tension, aggressiveness toward the group, or a tendency to form cults or cliques with others who have shared their training.

These five principles concerning the group as a medium of change would appear to have readiest application to groups created for the purpose of producing changes in people. They provide certain specifications for building effective training or therapy groups. They also point, however, to a difficulty in producing change in people in that they show how resistant an individual is to changing in any way contrary to group pressures and expectations. In order to achieve many kinds of changes in people, therefore, it is necessary to deal with the group as a target of change.

## THE GROUP AS A TARGET OF CHANGE

**Principle No. 6.** *Strong pressure for changes in the group can be established by creating a shared perception by members of the need for change, thus making the source of pressure for change lie within the group.*

Marrow and French report a dramatic case study which illustrates this principle quite well.[11] A manufacturing concern had a policy against hiring women over thirty because it was believed that they were slower, more difficult to train, and more likely to be absent. The staff psychologist was able to present to management evidence that this belief was clearly unwarranted at least within their own company. The psychologist's facts, however, were rejected and ignored as a basis for action because they violated accepted beliefs. It was

claimed that they went against the direct experience of the
foremen. Then the psychologist hit upon a plan for achieving
change which differed drastically from the usual one of argument, persuasion, and pressure. He proposed that management
conduct its own analysis of the situation. With his help
management collected all the facts which they believed were
relevant to the problem. When the results were in, they were
now their own facts rather than those of some "outside" expert.
Policy was immediately changed without further resistance.
The important point here is that facts are not enough. The
facts must be the accepted property of the group if they are
to become an effective basis for change. There seems to be
all the difference in the world in changes actually carried out
between those cases in which a consulting firm is hired to do
a study and present a report and those in which technical experts are asked to collaborate with the group in doing its own
study.

**Principle No. 7.** *Information relating to the need for
change, plans for change, and consequences of change must
be shared by all relevant people in the group.*

Another way of stating this principle is to say that change
of a group ordinarily requires the opening of communication
channels. Newcomb has shown how one of the first consequences of mistrust and hostility is the avoidance of communicating openly and freely about the things producing the
tension.[12] If you look closely at a pathological group (that
is, one that has trouble making decisions or effecting co-
ordinated efforts of its members), you will certainly find
strong restraints in that group against communicating vital information among its members. Until these restraints are removed there can be little hope for any real and lasting changes
in the group's functioning. In passing it should be pointed out
that the removal of barriers to communication will ordinarily
be accompanied by a sudden increase in the communication
of hostility. The group may appear to be falling apart, and
it will certainly be a painful experience to many of the members. This pain and the fear that things are getting out of
hand often stop the process of change once begun.

**Principle No. 8.** *Changes in one part of a group produce strain in other related parts which can be reduced only by eliminating the change or by bringing about readjustments in the related parts.*

It is a common practice to undertake improvements in group functioning by providing training programs for certain classes of people in the organization. A training program for foremen, for nurses, for teachers, or for group workers is established. If the content of the training is relevant for organizational change, it must of necessity deal with the relationships these people have with other subgroups. If nurses in a hospital change their behavior significantly, it will affect their relations both with the patients and with the doctors. It is unrealistic to assume that both these groups will remain indifferent to any significant changes in this respect. In hierarchical structures this process is most clear. Lippitt has proposed on the basis of research and experience that in such organizations attempts at change should always involve three levels, one being the major target of change and the other two being the one above and the one below.

IV

These eight principles represent a few of the basic propositions emerging from research in group dynamics. Since research is constantly going on and since it is the very nature of research to revise and reformulate our conceptions, we may be sure that these principles will have to be modified and improved as time goes by. In the meantime they may serve as guides in our endeavors to develop a scientifically based technology of social management.

In social technology, just as in physical technology, invention plays a crucial role. In both fields progress consists of the creation of new mechanisms for the accomplishment of certain goals. In both fields inventions arise in response to practical needs and are to be evaluated by how effectively they satisfy these needs. The relation of invention to scientific development is indirect but important. Inventions cannot proceed too far ahead of basic scientific development, nor should they be allowed to fall too far behind. They will be more effective the more they make good use of known principles of science, and they often make new developments in science possible. On the other hand, they are in no sense logical derivations from scientific principles.

I have taken this brief excursion into the theory of invention in order to make a final point. To many people "group dynamics" is known only for the social inventions which have developed in recent years in work with groups. Group dynamics is often thought of as certain techniques to be used with groups. Role playing, buzz groups, process observers, postmeeting reaction sheets, and feedback of group observations are devices popularly associated with the phrase "group dynamics." I trust that I have been able to show that group dynamics is more than a collection of gadgets. It certainly aspires to be a science as well as a technology.

This is not to underplay the importance of these inventions or of the function of inventing. As inventions they are all mechanisms designed to help accomplish important goals. How effective they are will depend upon how skillfully they are used and how appropriate they are to the purposes to which they are put. Careful evaluative research must be the ultimate judge of their usefulness in comparison with alternative inventions. I believe that the principles enumerated in this paper indicate some of the specifications that social inventions in this field must meet.

## NOTES

SOURCE: *Human Relations,* IV (1951), 381–92.
* This paper is based on a lecture delivered at Wayne University, Detroit, in the Leo M. Franklin Lecture Series, 1950–51.
1. Dorwin Cartwright, *The Research Center for Group Dynamics: A Report of Five Years' Activities and a View of Future Needs* (Ann Arbor: Institute for Social Research, 1950).
2. K. Lewin, R. Lippitt, and R. K. White, "Patterns of Aggressive Behavior in Experimentally Created 'Social Climates,'" *Journal of Social Psychology,* X (1939), 271–99.
3. Dorwin Cartwright, "Some Principles of Mass Persuasion: Selected

Findings of Research on the Sale of United States War Bonds," *Human Relations,* II (1949), 253–67.

4. K. Lewin, *Field Theory in Social Science* (New York: Harper & Brothers, 1951), 229–36.

5. L. Coch and J. R. P. French, Jr., "Overcoming Resistance to Change," *Human Relations,* I (1948), 512–32.

6. R. Lippitt, *Training in Community Relations* (New York: Harper & Brothers, 1949).

7. K. Lewin, *Resolving Social Conflicts* (New York: Harper & Brothers, 1948), 67.

8. M. G. Preston and R. K. Heintz, "Effects of Participatory vs. Supervisory Leadership on Group Judgment," *Journal of Abnormal and Social Psychology,* XLIV (1949), 345–55.

9. L. Festinger, *et al., Theory and Experiment in Social Communication: Collected Papers* (Ann Arbor: Institute for Social Research, 1950).

10. N. Polansky, R. Lippitt, and F. Redl, "An Investigation of Behavioral Contagion in Groups," *Human Relations,* III (1950), 319–48.

11. A. J. Marrow and J. R. P. French, Jr., "Changing a Stereotype in Industry," *Journal of Social Issues,* I (1945), 33–37.

12. T. M. Newcomb, "Autistic Hostility and Social Reality," *Human Relations,* I (1947), 69–86.

# 13

## CHANGING CRIMINALS:
## THE APPLICATION OF THE THEORY OF
## DIFFERENTIAL ASSOCIATION

### *Donald R. Cressey†*

Sociological theories and hypotheses have had great influence on development of general correctional policies, such as probation and parole, but they have been used only intermittently and haphazardly in reforming individual criminals. Since sociology is essentially a research discipline, sociologist-criminologists have devoted most of their time and energy to understanding and explaining crime, leaving to psychiatrists and others the problem of reforming criminals. Even the sociologists employed in correctional work have ordinarily committed themselves to nonsociological theories and techniques of reformation, leading the authors of one popular criminology textbook to ask just what correctional sociologists can accomplish which cannot be accomplished by other professional workers.[1]

Perhaps the major impediment to the application of sociological theories lies not in the nature of the theories themselves but, instead, in the futile attempt to adapt them to clinical use. Strictly speaking, the now popular policy of "individualized treatment" for delinquents and criminals does not commit one to any specific theory of criminality or any specific theory of reformation, but, rather, to the proposition that the conditions considered as causing an individual to behave criminally will be taken into account in the effort to change him. An attempt is made to diagnose the cause of the criminality and to base the techniques of reform upon the diagnosis. Analogy with

† Donald Cressey is Dean of the College of Letters and Science at the University of California at Santa Barbara.

the *method* of clinical medicine (diagnosis, prescription, and therapy) is obvious. However, by far the most popular interpretation of the policy of individualization is that the *theories,* as well as the methods, of clinical medicine must be used in diagnosing and changing criminals. The emphasis on this clinical principle has impeded the application of sociological theories and, it may be conjectured, success in correctional work.

The adherents of the clinical principle consider criminality to be an individual defect or disorder or a symptom of either, and the criminal as one unable to canalize or sublimate his "primitive," antisocial impulses or tendencies,[2] who may be expressing symbolically in criminal behavior some unconscious urge or wish arising from an early traumatic emotional experience,[3] or as a person suffering from some other kind of defective trait or condition.

In all cases the implication is that the individual disorder, like a biological disorder, should be treated on a clinical basis. An extreme position is that criminality actually is a biological disorder, to be treated by modification of the physiology or anatomy of the individual. However, the more popular notion is that criminality is analogous to an infectious disease like syphilis—while group contacts of various kinds are necessary to the disorder, the disorder can be treated in a clinic, without reference to the persons from whom it was acquired.

Sociologists and social psychologists have provided an alternative principle on which to base the diagnosis and treatment of criminals, namely, that the behavior, attitudes, beliefs, and values which a person exhibits are not only the *products* of group contacts but also the *properties* of groups. If the behavior of an individual is an intrinsic part of groups to which he belongs, attempts to change the behavior must be directed at groups.[4] While this principle is generally accepted by sociologists, there has been no consistent or organized effort by sociologist-criminologists to base techniques or principles of treatment on it. Traditionally, we have emphasized that sociologists can make unique contributions to *clinical* diagnoses, and we have advocated the development of a "clinical sociology" which would enable us to improve these diagnoses.[5] But here we reach an impasse: if a case of criminality is attributed to the individual's group relations, there is little that can be done *in the clinic* to modify the diagnosed cause of the criminality. Moreover, extra-clinical work with criminals and delinquents ordinarily has merely extended the clinical principle to the offender's community and has largely ignored the group-relations principle. For example, in the "group work" of correctional agencies the emphasis usually is upon the role of the group merely in satisfying the needs of an individual. Thus the criminal is induced to join an "interest-activity" group, such as a hiking club, on the assumption that membership in the group somehow will enable him to overcome the defects or tendencies considered conducive to his delinquency.[6] Similarly, in correctional group therapy the emphasis is almost always on the use of a group to enable the individual to rid himself of undesirable psychological disorders, not criminality.[7] Even in group-work programs directed at entire groups, such as delinquent gangs, emphasis usually is on new and different formal group activities rather than on new group attitudes and values.

The differential association theory of criminal behavior presents implications for diagnosis and treatment consistent with the group-relations principle for changing behavior and could be advantageously utilized in correctional work. According to it, persons become criminals principally because they have been relatively isolated from groups whose behavior patterns (including attitudes, motives, and rationalizations) are anticriminal, or because their residence, employment, social position, native capacities, or something else has brought them into relatively frequent association with the behavior patterns of criminal groups.[8] A diagnosis of criminality based on this theory would be directed at analysis of the criminal's attitudes, motives, and rationalizations regarding criminality and would recognize that those characteristics depend upon the groups to which the criminal belongs. Then, if criminals are to be changed, either they must become members of anticriminal groups, or their present procriminal group relations must be changed.[9]

The following set of interrelated principles, adapted in part from a more general statement by Dorwin Cartwright,[10] is intended as a guide to specific application of the differential association theory to correctional work. It is tentative and directs attention to areas where research and experimentation should prove fruitful. Two underlying assumptions are that small groups existing for the specific purpose of reforming criminals can be set up by correctional workers and that criminals can be induced to join them. The first five principles deal with the use of anticriminal groups as *media* of change, and the last principle emphasizes, further, the possibility of a criminal group's becoming the *target* of change.

1. If criminals are to be changed, they must be assimilated into groups which emphasize values conducive to law-abiding behavior and, concurrently, alienated from groups emphasizing values conducive to criminality. Since our experience has been that the majority of criminals experience great difficulty in securing intimate contacts in ordinary groups, special groups whose major common goal is the reformation of criminals must be created. This general principle, emphasized by Sutherland, has been recognized and used by Gersten, apparently with some success, in connection with a group therapy program in the New York Training School for Boys.[11]

2. The more relevant the common purpose of the group to the reformation of criminals, the greater will be its influence on the criminal members' attitudes and values. Just as a labor union exerts strong influence over its members' attitudes toward management but less influence on their attitudes toward say, Negroes, so a group organized for recreational or welfare purposes will have less success in influencing criminalistic attitudes and values than will one whose explicit purpose is to change criminals. Interesting recreational activities, employment possibilities, and material assistance may serve effectively to attract criminals away from procriminal groups temporarily and may give the group some control over the criminals. But merely inducing a criminal to join a group to satisfy his personal needs is not enough. Probably the failure to recognize this, more than anything else, was responsible for the failure of the efforts at rehabilitation of the Cambridge-Somerville Youth Study workers.[12]

3. The more cohesive the group, the greater the members'

readiness to influence others and the more relevant the problem of conformity to group norms. The criminals who are to be reformed and the persons expected to effect the change must, then, have a strong sense of belonging to one group: between them there must be a genuine "we" feeling. The reformers, consequently, should not be identifiable as correctional workers, probation or parole officers, or social workers. This principle has been extensively documented by Festinger and his co-workers.[13]

4. Both reformers and those to be reformed must achieve status within the group by exhibition of "proreform" or anticriminal values and behavior patterns. As a novitiate, the one to be reformed is likely to assign status according to social position outside the group, and part of the reformation process consists of influencing him both to assign and to achieve status on the basis of behavior patterns relevant to reformation. If he should assign status solely on the basis of social position in the community, he is likely to be influenced only slightly by the group. Even if he becomes better adjusted, socially and psychologically, by association with members having high status in the community, he is a therapeutic parasite and not actually a member until he accepts the group's own system for assigning status.

5. The most effective mechanism for exerting group pressure on members will be found in groups so organized that criminals are induced to join with noncriminals for the purpose of changing other criminals. A group in which criminal A joins with some noncriminals to change criminal B is probably most effective in changing criminal A, not B; in order to change criminal B, criminal A must necessarily share the values of the anticriminal members.

This process may be called "retroflexive reformation"; in attempting to reform others, the criminal almost automatically accepts the relevant common purpose of the group, identifies himself closely with other persons engaging in reformation, and assigns status on the basis of anticriminal behavior. He becomes a genuine member of this group, and at the same time he is alienated from his previous procriminal groups. This principle is used successfully by Alcoholics Anonymous to "cure" alcoholism; it has been applied to the treatment of psychotics by McCann and Almada; and its usefulness in criminology has been demonstrated by Knopka.[14] Ex-convicts have been used in the Chicago Area Projects, which, generally, are organized in accordance with this principle, but its effect on the ex-convicts, either in their roles as reformers or as objects of reform, appears not to have been evaluated.

6. When an entire group is the target of change, as in a prison or among delinquent gangs, strong pressure for change can be achieved by convincing the members of the need for a change, thus making the group itself the source of pressure for change. Rather than inducing criminals to become members of pre-established anticriminal groups, the problem here is to change antireform and procriminal subcultures, so that group leaders evolve from among those who show the most marked hospitality to anticriminal values, attitudes, and behavior. Neither mere lectures, sermons, or exhortations by correctional workers nor mere redirection of the activities of a group nor individual psychotherapy, academic education, vocational training, or counseling will necessarily change a group's culture. If the subculture is not changed, the person to be reformed is likely to exhibit two sets of attitudes and behaviors, one characteristic of the agency or person trying to change him, the other of the subculture.[15] Changes in the subculture probably can best be instigated by eliciting the co-operation of the type of criminal who, in prison, is considered a "right guy."[16] This principle has been demonstrated in a recent experiment with hospitalized drug addicts, whose essentially antireform culture was changed, under the guise of group therapy, to a proreform culture.[17] To some extent, the principle was used in the experimental system of prison administration developed by Gill in the Massachusetts State Prison Colony.[18]

# NOTES

SOURCE: *American Journal of Sociology*, LXI (September, 1955), 116–20.
1. Harry Elmer Barnes and Negley K. Teeters, *New Horizons in Criminology* (New York: Prentice-Hall, 1951), 644.
2. Sheldon and Eleanor T. Glueck, *Delinquents in the Making* (New

York: Harper & Brothers, 1952), 162–63; see also Ruth Jacobs Levy, *Reductions in Recidivism through Therapy* (New York: Seltzer, 1941), 16, 28.

3. Edwin J. Lukas, "Crime Prevention: A Confusion in Goal," in Paul W. Tappan (ed.), *Contemporary Correction* (New York: McGraw-Hill Book Co., 1951), 397–409.

4. Cf. Dorwin Cartwright, "Achieving Change in People: Some Applications of Group Dynamics Theory," *Human Relations,* IV (1951), 381–92.

5. See Louis Wirth, "Clinical Sociology," *American Journal of Sociology,* XXVII (July 1931), 49–66; and Saul D. Alinsky, "A Sociological Technique in Clinical Criminology," *Proceedings of the American Prison Association,* LXIV (1934), 167–78.

6. See the discussion by Robert G. Hinckley and Lydia Hermann, *Group Treatment in Psychotherapy* (Minneapolis: University of Minnesota Press, 1951), 8–11.

7. See Donald R. Cressey, "Contradictory Theories in Correctional Group Therapy Programs," *Federal Probation,* XVIII (June 1954), 20–26.

8. Edwin H. Sutherland, *Principles of Criminology* (New York: J. B. Lippincott Co., 1947), 6–9, 595, 616–17.

9. Cf. Donald R. Taft, "The Group and Community Organization Approach to Prison Administration," *Proceedings of the American Prison Association,* LXXII (1942), 275–84; and George B. Vold, "Discussion of *Guided Group Interaction in Correctional Work* by F. Lovell Bixby and Lloyd W. McCorkle," *American Sociological Review,* XVI (August 1951), 460–61.

10. *Op. cit.*

11. Sutherland, *op. cit.,* 451; Charles Gersten, "An Experimental Evaluation of Group Therapy with Juvenile Delinquents," *International Journal of Group Psychotherapy,* I (November 1951), 311–18.

12. See Margaret G. Reilly and Robert A. Young, "Agency-initiated Treatment of a Potentially Delinquent Boy," *American Journal of Orthopsychiatry,* XVI (October 1946), 697–706; Edwin Powers, "An Experiment in Prevention of Delinquency," *Annals of the American Academy of Political and Social Science,* CCLXI (January 1949), 77–88; Edwin Powers and Helen L. Witmer, *An Experiment in Prevention of Delinquency—the Cambridge-Somerville Youth Study* (New York: Columbia University Press, 1951).

13. Leon Festinger *et al., Theory and Experiment in Social Communication: Collected Papers* (Ann Arbor: Institute for Social Research, 1951).

14. Robert Freed Bales, "Types of Social Structure as Factors in 'Cures' for Alcohol Addiction," *Applied Anthropology,* I (April–June 1942), 1–13; Willis H. McCann and Albert A. Almada, "Round-Table Psychotherapy: A Technique in Group Psychotherapy," *Journal of Consulting Psychology,* XIV (December 1950), 421–35; Gisela Knopka, "The Group Worker's Role in an Institution for Juvenile Delinquents," *Federal Probation,* XV (June 1951), 15–23.

15. See Edwin A. Fleishman, "A Study in the Leadership Role of the Foreman in an Industrial Situation" (Columbus: Personnel Research Board, Ohio State University, 1951) (mimeographed).

16. See Hans Riemer, "Socialization in the Prison Community," *Pro-

*ceedings of the American Prison Association,* LXVII (1937), 151–55.
17. James J. Thorpe and Bernard Smith, "Phases in Group Development in Treatment of Drug Addicts," *International Journal of Group Psychotherapy,* III (January 1953), 66–78.
18. Howard B. Gill, "The Norfolk Prison Colony of Massachusetts," *Journal of Criminal Law and Criminology,* XXII (September 1937), 389–95; see also Eric K. Clarke, "Group Therapy in Rehabilitation," *Federal Probation,* XVI (December 1952), 28–32.

# 14

## THE ROLE OF INFORMAL INMATE GROUPS IN CHANGE OF VALUES

*George H. Grosser†*

The group nature of much delinquency is an important point from which to examine the treatment process in training schools for delinquent youth. It reminds us that the behavior of individuals is strongly influenced by their group membership and by the interplay of the various groups to which they belong.

Such a paucity of research data is available from the field of corrections that what I have to say can be presented only as suggestive of researchable hypotheses. My theoretical propositions are drawn largely from experiments carried on in the fields of industrial relations, group dynamics, and small-group research, rather than from the field of corrections.

An individual's adherence to social norms is determined not only by the initial internalization of values but also by interaction with other individuals adhering to the same values. The group, in other words, has a definite effect on the persistence or change of norms which complements the psychodynamic forces working within the individual.

In a training school for juvenile offenders, most of the residents are adolescents. While they are there because of having violated the law, they nevertheless share a large part of the values of society or at least of society's subcultures. Their delinquent behavior encompasses only a small range of their total behavior. The training school exercises a custodial and reformative function and, regardless of its philosophy, pro-

† George Grosser is an associate professor in the Department of Psychiatry at the Tufts University School of Medicine.

vides an authoritarian setting. That is, the administration does not exist by or depend on the consent of the residents and is the sole determinant of policy for the institution.

Within the training school an interaction of two groups, the administration and the inmates, is constantly taking place. Between these groups is a line of cleavage defined by a differentiation in status, which is reinforced by the difference in status between delinquents and representatives of the law outside the institution. The integration within one social system of two such different groups, as in an institution, contains many facets not found elsewhere in a democracy:

1. The inmates and the administration are so separate in status that rising from the lower to the higher is an impossibility.

2. While the administration has a specific task orientation, the inmate population does not share this or have any specific task orientation of its own. Predominantly membership- or group-oriented, the inmate population has no group goal which the young people recognize as valid and achievable through their own co-ordinated efforts. Moreover, both administration and inmate population maintain networks of informal organization among their memberships.[1]

This informal group structure arises out of needs generated within the institution and within the subcultures from which the young people have come. It is based on:

1. Adolescent needs for peer-group relationships, generated by the conflicts that adolescent status in our society produces.

2. The normal tendency for people spending extensive amounts of time together to cluster into informal groups on the basis of affective ties.

3. The need of persons in the same boat for support from one another. In this sense, the inmate social system has many of the aspects of a minority group under stress.

4. The adolescent need for friends of one's own sex in a culture in which heterosexual relations in childhood and adolescence are generally frowned upon.[2]

## The Role of Informal Groups

The informal groups tend to maintain their identity, their norms, and their cohesiveness, for, since they serve the needs already mentioned, their persistence is consciously and unconsciously striven for by the membership. Some of their mechanisms for survival explicitly threaten or violate discipline in the institution; others do not and therefore are often considered not particularly noteworthy. On the whole, however, the self-maintenance of the group is synonymous with the maintenance of the value system of its members. This fact tends to defeat the reformative aims of the institution. This is so even when the groups conform in large measure to the demands of the institution.

Among the mechanisms of group control which these informal groups share with other groups under stress are:

1. Recruitment and screening of membership and transmission of the institutional lore to the newcomer.
2. The development of social norms and rituals—characteristic institutional slang, ritual forms of interaction, the sharing of secrets with respect to illicit activities, and the establishment of a definite hierarchy of leaders and followers.
3. The application of sanctions to violators of the group code, ranging from gossip and ostracism to outright violence.
4. The development of loyalty and group ties.
5. The constant reinforcement of the separateness of the group through an attempt to create an orthodoxy of beliefs. This is done by informal communication, the spreading of news through the grapevine, and biased interpretation of the administration's policy, especially where it concerns the fate of particular group members.

## Obstacles to Change

As indicated, the informal groupings in training schools for juvenile delinquents not only fulfill many of the inmates' basic needs but tend to become self-perpetuating with the development of mechanisms of group control and group maintenance. They militate against change in the delinquent's value system and against true rehabilitation of those individuals who throughout their stay remain attached to this type of social organization. In the absence of reliable research data, the author, from personal experience in training schools, would estimate this group as comprising from 30 to 50 per cent of the inmate population.

While the obstacles to change differ from person to person, depending upon past experience and character formation, these informal groups in general present conditions which are often hampering to the best efforts of individual therapy. Psychological and sociological research has shown that the stabler the frame of reference of an individual the more resistant is he likely to be to a contradictory frame of reference, and that the stability of a frame of reference depends not so much on the individual's own experience and reality testing as it does on group consensus and reinforcement.[3] This reinforcement of an existing frame of reference makes it extremely difficult for an individual to change even when he has considerable ambivalence in his feelings toward his group. The group always has mechanisms for displacing intragroup hostility onto outsiders.

It is, then, not surprising that so many failures occur among training-school alumni. To blame this on the environment to which the delinquent is sent after release is begging the question, for he will select those associations which are congenial to his character and values. It is likely that in many cases the individual, unchanged by his training-school experience, seeks out a delinquent environment upon release.

### The Task of Change

The accumulating evidence that persistence and change of norms are not solely a factor of the individual's own personality structure, but also depend on successive group affiliations and on the resolution of conflicting loyalties in these affiliations is of crucial significance for training schools. What seems to work so effectively in the maintenance of antisocial values could, if the theoretical assumptions are sound, also work in the opposite direction. Evidence that the group can effectively change the individual's value system has been produced by a variety of social-psychological experiments in laboratories and a number of studies in actual life situations.[4] The common element in all these studies is that the individual's frame of reference, attitudes, and value system experience a change under group influence if the individual desires acceptance in the group with which he has been brought into contact. Most delinquents who enter training schools want to be accepted by their fellow inmates.

Therefore, if we wish the young person upon his release from the training school to become integrated into a peer group that pursues constructive aims and does not violate the law, we must somehow prepare him in the training school for such group affiliation. A mere environmental change, such as a foster home, will not be sufficient if the individual emerges from the training school unchanged.

Bringing about change, therefore, would require producing within the institution an informal peer group which is not focused on hostility to the administration and to law-abiding society and to let such a group influence the newcomer. How is such a group to be molded? Can psychotherapy, for instance, achieve this goal?

## Psychotherapeutic Methods

Traditional individual therapy is essentially a dyadic relationship. As such, it rests on the transference of the patient's affectional feelings and excludes other from this relationship. The incentive to change which comes from the patient's relationship to the therapist is purely individual. Therefore, as far as a group is concerned it constitutes a divisive element. It arouses jealousy and antagonism, suspicion and mistrust.

There is considerable evidence in the literature on institutions that the informal social group distrusts and resents individual therapy and that this resentment is in direct proportion to the strength of the group's hostility toward the administration and of the need for social cohesion aroused by its members' defensiveness. The effect of intensive individual psychotherapy is to separate the patient from the informal group, since a motivation stronger than group influence has set in and the identification with the therapist replaces identification with group members and leaders. Such a relationship seems to be achieved more successfully with individuals whose group loyalty to the informal inmate organization is not particularly strong to begin with, and who, because of specific neurotic problems, have always moved on the fringes of the informal group. With those group members who maintain a very strong loyalty to their informal peer group, individual therapy is very often, though by no means always, ineffective.

In general, individual therapy tends to weaken the informal organization and atomize its membership. Since it cannot be effectively provided to all, partly because it promises no success in some cases, partly for economic reasons, it cannot be expected to change group values.

As limitations of individual therapy have become recognized, group therapy has been called upon to fill in the gaps. However, it too has its limitations.

The beneficial effects of group therapy on withdrawn individuals, some types of alcoholics, and other isolates, have raised expectations for this type of treatment which, in the case of juvenile delinquents, have not as yet been fulfilled. The most important misconception of the applicability of certain forms of group therapy seems to lie in the failure to understand that in the case of many a delinquent the need is neither to foster his integration into his peer group nor to help him overcome a sense of isolation. Indeed, the average individual in a state training school, whatever his personality difficulties, shares a value system and a considerable degree of intimacy with like-minded individuals. It is, perhaps, precisely for the sake of this sharing that he has entered into delinquent activity. Therefore, the traditional form of group psychotherapy, which is supposed to effect reorientation of an individual to his society, misses the mark, creates a conflict between the members of the informal social group, and tends to isolate the patient rather than help him integrate into nondelinquent society.

A more hopeful version of the process, called guided group interaction, has been tried out by McCorkle, Bixby, and others.[5] Its aims and mode of attack seem more likely to satisfy the conditions necessary for changing group, and hence individual, values. How effective it can be is not as yet clearly apparent, but very likely with a group of selected individuals, on a very small scale, as in the current Highfields project, it can succeed. At Highfields, an experimental institution in New Jersey, the individuals are there for such a short time that they hardly have time to become strongly attached to an informal group structure. While this experiment may ultimately be of use, the method is not practicable within the framework of most training schools as set up now.

While efforts at both individual and group psychotherapy can be useful within institutions, their effectiveness is limited by the institutional setting and the varieties of individual personalities it includes.

### Carriers of Change

Historical and experimental evidence amassed during the past few years points to the potentialities of the social group as an effector of change in values. Evidence from industrial relations, the armed forces, religious sects, and small-group research indicates a way to the development of hypotheses suitable for testing in correctional settings. The following are only a few of the propositions that seem particularly relevant:

1. Changes in the attitudes and values of group members are directly related to the needs that can thereby be fulfilled. Therefore, if recognized needs can be envisaged as better met by a change in group goals or values, the group is likely to change.
2. Such changes are the more effective the more the members have participated in formulating and discussing them.
3. Value changes in organized groups are more effective if the group is definitely task-oriented and if clear-cut communication and understanding exist concerning the goal to be reached and the means whereby it is to be reached.
4. Change in values of group members is positively correlated with a lack of competitiveness and conflict within the group.

5. Change is related to the degree in which each individual sees that his effort is needed for the achievement of the common goal or the maintenance of his standing within the group.

6. Changes of attitudes and values are more likely to occur through group goals set through the group's own motivation rather than imposed from outside the group, and are less likely to occur through goals dictated by an outgroup with which the ingroup is in conflict.

### Steps Toward Change

Among the suggestions for training schools that can be derived from these propositions are the following:

1. Ways might be explored for making the institutional population's informal organization, as well as the individual, more task-oriented. In other words, attempts might be made to discover what other goals, especially group goals, aside from the goal of release from the institution, can be explicitly fostered and achieved by the population of the training school. This is an exceedingly complicated problem but one well deserving of exploration, for the aimlessness of life in many an institution contributes many undesirable features to the informal social organization.

The possibilities of task orientation are not exhausted by industrial work or work in the ordinary sense of the word. These possibilities include well-defined group goals and an array of means to their achievement. General goals enunciated by the administration as, "We are here to learn to live together," or, "We should learn to get along with our fellow man," are not task-oriented in the sense referred to here. Parenthetically, task orientation among adolescent groups in general is a pressing need in present-day society and if made part of a delinquency prevention program might well have strong beneficial effects.

2. Since the breaking up of informal organization is difficult to achieve, and even when achieved may not be very beneficial because of the resulting individual isola-

tion, means might be explored for lessening the social distance between the administration and the informal social groupings.

If the adolescent in a training school is eventually to live as a part of law-abiding society, he must be able to see himself in a role accepted by law-abiding society. The greater the distance between administration and institutional population the less likely are the young people's groups to change in a desirable direction.

The process of reducing social distance between administration and institutional population is not as difficult in respect to adolescents as to adults. Even the delinquent adolescent leans toward accepting the leadership and ascendancy of older persons because he has his dependency needs and because general cultural patterns tend in this direction. For the administration to share experiences with the informal organization and to recognize its position may be one way of lessening social distance.

3. Reward systems might be developed for group rather than individual performance. Group incentive will become easier to stimulate as a more task-oriented group life is developed in institutions. The present system of individual rewards tends to foster isolation and to leave the more antagonistic group members untouched.

4. Use of the existing group leadership to foster change within the group might also he explored. Leaders are generally considered troublesome because the direction in which they assert their leadership more often than not runs counter to the aims of the administration. However, just as informal groups are part and parcel of any large-scale organization, so are informal group leaders. Since they play an important part in maintaining group cohesiveness and fostering group identification, they can be key figures in an attempt to utilize the group for effecting change of individual values.

5. Finally, since many group members might be amenable to therapy, informal groups might be made the units of therapy rather than artificially formed groups based on individual selection. While Slavson and others have suggested that the usual type of group therapy is counter-

indicated for certain types of character disorders,[6] a more directive form, such as guided group interaction, utilizing the informal grouping might be helpful in changing group goals. This could be followed up by a more traditional type of therapy, group or individual, for some persons.

### In Summary

It seems, then, that the informal groups which emerge in a training-school population might be made to serve important retraining functions if properly utilized. This suggestion is based on the observations that much delinquent behavior is group behavior and that the social group is a crucial agent in the maintenance or change of the value systems of its constituent members. A better understanding of the group dynamics within a training school may serve to make it a more effective agency in the retraining of juvenile offenders.

## NOTES

SOURCE: *Children*, V (January–February 1958), 25–29.

1. Donald Clemmer, *The Prison Community* (Boston: Christopher, 1940); Norman S. Hayner and Ellis Ash, "The Prison as a Community," *American Sociological Review* (June 1939), 362–69.
2. Edith Buxbaum, "Transference and Group Formation in Children and Adolescents," in *Psychoanalytic Study of the Child, vol. I* (New York: International Universities Press, Inc., 1945).
3. Muzafer Sherif, *The Psychology of Social Norms* (New York: Harper and Bros., 1936); Solomon E. Asch, "Effects of Group Pressure upon the Modification and Distortion of Judgments," in D. Cartwright and A. Zander, editors, *Group Dynamics: Research and Theory* (Evanston, Ill.: Row, Peterson and Co., 1935); Theodore M. Newcomb, "Attitude Development as a Function of Reference Groups: The Bennington Study," in Guy E. Swanson, Theodore M. Newcomb, and E. L. Hartley, editors, *Readings of Social Psychology* (New York: Henry Holt and Co., 1952).
4. Kurt Lewin, "Group Decision and Social Change," in Swanson, Newcomb, and Hartley, editors, *op. cit.;* Samuel A. Stouffer, *et al., The American Soldier, vol. II* (Princeton: Princeton University Press, 1949).
5. F. Lovell Bixby and Lloyd W. McCorkle, "Guided Group Interaction in Correctional Work," *American Sociological Review* (August 1951), 455–59.
6. S. R. Slavson, *The Practice of Group Therapy* (New York: International Universities Press, 1947).

# 15

## THE CHALLENGE OF CORRECTIONAL CHANGE:
## THE INTERFACE OF
## CONFORMITY AND COMMITMENT

*Jay Hall, Martha Williams, and Louis Tomaino*†

The field of corrections seems to be caught up in a peculiar paradox. At long last, it is beginning to receive the kind of public support and attention that it has needed. State and federal legislatures are beginning to appropriate more funds for improved correctional systems. Community organizations are becoming active in programs of rehabilitation, and research projects of correctional significance are popping up all over the country. In the mdist of all this, however, the correctional worker has been lost in the shuffle. Indeed, in many respects he is as isolated from the mainstream of society as are the individuals with whom he must work; as a consequence, he finds it increasingly difficult to maintain his identity. Aside from the impact of this on the individual worker, such a blurring of identity has sweeping implications for the professional image of the whole correctional field. Thus, the paradox is that the field of corrections is beginning to come into its own as an important social force while, at the same time, the correctional worker is sinking into the morass of professional ambiguity.

An interesting facet of this paradox is the fact that much more has been written about the offender and how he should be handled than about the correctional worker who must do the work or, for that matter, about the work itself. The upshot

† Jay Hall is a visiting professor of management in the College of Business Administration at the University of Texas; Martha Williams is an associate professor in the School of Social Work at the University of Texas; Louis Tomaino is an associate professor at the Wharton School of Social Work, San Antonio, Texas.

of this is that the field of corrections is characterized by a "practice without theory" approach to its task; the only attention paid to the individual worker is in the form of prescribing the kind of person he *should be*, rather than a formulation of the task-relevant skills which should make him professionally unique. So it is that in some quarters the correctional worker must be a "discreet person of good moral character," while in others he must categorically be a "trained social worker," and in some others he must be "any person of good character who has earned a college degree and can give proof of having supervised the work of at least three other people for not less than two years." On the basis of these criteria one is still left with the question, "Who is the correctional worker and what does he do?" It would seem that until this question is answered little real progress will be made in either the theories of corrections or the training of correctional personnel. Moreover, such an answer will not be forthcoming until the objectives of correctional agencies have been clarified to the point of allowing some measure of success and failure in the attainment of objectives.

## THE DILEMMA OF THE CORRECTIONAL WORKER

If we can accept the suggestion of social scientists that one's identity is, to a great extent, dependent upon the role he performs in society and that this role, in turn, is defined for him in terms of the objectives of his culture, then the dilemma of the correctional worker may be brought into sharper focus. The objectives of the correctional culture are to protect the public and rehabilitate the offender, and herein lies much of the dilemma which confronts the correctional worker. While it follows at a common sense level that successful rehabilitation of offenders would at one and the same time result in a protection of the public, there are basic procedural and timing discrepancies between the two facets which frequently create ambiguity and frustration on the part of the worker. The problem lies not so much in the statement of objectives *per se*, therefore, as it does in the individual correctional worker's *perception* of those objectives.

"Protection of the public" is a crisis-oriented objective and, as such, it addresses itself to swift and definitive action. "Rehabilitation of the offender," on the other hand, would seem to speak to a more fundamental type of action which is less observable and anything but swift. Thus, the correctional worker is urged to move quickly and decisively in one instance and to be tolerant, insightful, and helpful in another. No real guidelines for priority are given in the statement of objectives, and the worker is left to his own devices in translating the objectives into action. It is at this point that the identity of the individual worker, if not that of the profession, begins to slip away; for taking objectives as the source of role definition, the conditions have been created for role conflict. Put another way, this says that the correctional worker may feel that he must serve two masters; each with different demands.

As Sarbin[1] has pointed out, to be caught up in a conflict of roles situation can be particularly punishing and demoralizing. For many correctional workers, the role conflict which results from the perceived discrepancy between the protection and rehabilitation components of correctional objectives has proved to be virtually immobilizing and the tendency has become one of dichotomizing the goals so that they might be dealt with as two separate issues. This separation of issues, as a reaction to the ambiguity and frustration generated by the total objective, has utility for simplifying the task of the correctional worker and reduces it to a level of abstraction with which he can comfortably cope. Such a dichotomy may not create the conditions for an effective program of corrections, however, for typically the worker does not stop with a mere partitioning of goals, but tends to lose sight of one or the other facets of his objective and comes to identify with but a single aspect of the correctional process. In its least extreme form, this tendency is reflected in a "Render unto Caesar that which is Caesar's and unto God that which is His" approach to protection and rehabilitation; in its more extreme forms, however, it results in some workers' describing their work as "law enforcement," while others view themselves as "helping persons" concerned with treatment issues. Needless to say, the goals of "law enforcers" are not the same as those of "helping persons," nor are the strategies they are likely to employ. As a result, the corrections profession itself is divided along protection-rehabilitation lines and theorists are still trying to resolve questions posed by John Augustus and Major Savage one hundred years ago. So it is that we are still asking who the correctional worker is and what he does.

## THE CORRECTIONAL WORKER AS AN AGENT OF CHANGE

It begins to appear that a different perspective toward the work of corrections is needed, and the objectives of corrections may provide the context for this perspective, just as they did for the dilemmas cited above. Implicit in the charges of protection and rehabilitation is a more fundamental consideration than either of these taken separately, and this is the mission *change*. The task of the correctional worker, when stripped to its most essential elements and presented in its most incisive form, is one of *changing* individuals from offender to nonoffender status, with the result that the public will then be protected and the offender can be considered to be rehabilitated. Indeed, those who describe the work of corrections as "law enforcement" or "treatment" are not speaking to the goals of corrections at all; they are really revealing their own assumptions about how change can be brought about. Thus, by adopting a *change* perspective to the correctional task and by redefining the correctional worker as an agent of change, it may become possible to gain insight into why various workers see their work as they do and to actually evaluate their assumptions systematically within the context of change theory. At the same time, because there is an abundance of theory and research regarding the induction of change, such a perspective may allow an influx of new theories and criteria for effective corrections and, thereby, lead to a clarification of the professional image of correctional workers.

Therefore, let us consider the correctional worker in a new light; namely as society's professional agent of change. Simultaneously, let us begin to assess more systematically some of the assumptions and their consequent strategies which have prevailed in the field of corrections with an eye toward testing their efficacy for the successful induction of change.

## THE CHANGE GRID: A MODEL OF CHANGE AGENT STRATEGIES

Corrections has long been characterized by an eclectic approach to its task, and this is good so long as objectives are clearly defined. In looking at the process of change, a new source of theory becomes available, and this is applied social psychology as it has been used in management training.

### The Managerial Grid Concept

Robert Blake and Jane Mouton, two pioneering behavioral scientists engaged in the study of management and organizational change, have recently synthesized the results of years of theory and experience into a conceptual model of managerial behavior called the *Managerial Grid*.[2] This model, based as it is on complex theory and empirical research, has proved to be a powerful instrument for creating insight into the managerial process and for the development of new management techniques. In addition to its use in management, however, the Blake and Mouton grid technique constitutes a more universal contribution in that it provides a descriptive and diagnostic tool for the systematic analysis of goal-oriented behaviors in terms of (1) the dichotomized needs or concerns which motivate an individual and (2) the personal assumptions or "theories" the individual has about the relationship between these concerns and their relevance for deciding on the relative importance of each.

Correctional objectives call attention to two such concerns within a change context and we have already seen that people manifest assumptions about their relative importance. Therefore, it would seem that the grid technique of analysis might have much to say for the task of correctional change and the strategies various correctional workers employ as agents of change. Let us proceed, then, to draw upon existing theory and research in the area of change and, out of this, to construct a Change Grid which will allow an assessment of individual change agent strategies and their significance for the corrections profession.

## Identifying the Basic Dimensions of the Change Grid

The concerns of the correctional worker provide the basic dimensions of the Change Grid. As they stem directly from the objectives of corrections, these might be called a concern for protection of the public, on one hand, and a concern for rehabilitation of the offender, on the other. Within a more general change context, however, these reflect concerns for (1) conformity on the part of the changee and (2) acceptance of or commitment to the program of change on the part of the changee.[3] Thus, we will take as the basic dimensions of the Change Grid the individual change agent's *concern for conformity* and *concern for commitment*. Research in the induction of change, while not focusing directly on these two areas of concern to agents of change, has indicated that the degree to which an agent is concerned for either dimension is closely related to the effectiveness and duration of his change strategies.[4]

## Orienting and Scaling the Change Grid Dimensions

The concern for conformity and the concern for commitment are conceived in the grid format as being independent of each other. That is, a concern for one is not theoretically contingent upon a concern for the other. Whatever relationship may be found to exist—be it positive, negative, or zero—is imposed by the individual change agent; in its pure form, however, the grid is based on independent concerns. In view of this the two dimensions may be thought of as being oriented at right angles to each other as shown in the chart 1. In it, the horizontal axis of the Change Grid represents the *concern for changee conformity* experienced by agents of change. The vertical axis represents the *concern for changee commitment* which a change agent is likely to have in working with a changee.

Since we are also interested in the degree to which a particular change agent is concerned about these basic dimensions, it is necessary to provide a measurement of "degree of concern." Therefore, each axis has been scaled from 1 to 9 (as was the case with Blake's and Mouton's grid) in order to reflect the degree to which a person is concerned for either conformity or commitment. For purposes of our discussion, the value 1 denotes a minimal "concern for" while the value 9 denotes a maximal "concern for." Thus, by placing the two concerns at right angles to each other and by scaling the degree of concern represented, the change strategies of individual change agents can be evaluated from the standpoint of the *relationship* which they perceive between concerns for conformity and concerns for commitment.

## Conflict Assumptions of Change

Three approaches to achieving change in others rest on the assumption that the concern for conformity and the concern for commitment are in basic conflict with each other and, therefore, mutually exclusive. The person who embraces this assumption and perceives the two concerns as immutably separate finds himself in a self-imposed force-choice situation in which he must choose one or the other, but never both, as his particular focus of concern. The change agent assumptions and strategies which result from this perception are (reading grid fashion, right and up) the 9/1 Change via Compliance approach, the 1/9 Client-centered Change approach, and the 1/1 Custodial Change approach. Each of these is found in corrections and, it should be mentioned at the outset, each approach can result in change.

**The 9/1 position—Change via Compliance.** The lower

THE CHANGE GRID
Individual Strategies of Change

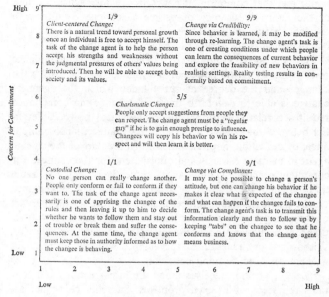

*Concern for Conformity*

CHART 1

right-hand corner of the grid represents that change strategy which is characterized by a maximal concern for conformity and minimal concern for commitment. This strategy is based on the assumption that the majority of people whose behavior has been deemed in need of change will actually change only if what is required of them is clearly spelled out and consistent enforcement of these requirements is ensured. The importance of the changee's commitment to these requirements is either minimized or denied entirely. Two somewhat different assumptions contribute to this strategy. Some change agents feel, on one hand, that if changes in behavior can be induced under conditions allowing little deviation from specified requirements, commitment will occur in time on the basis of the *fait accompli* effect. This assumption is particularly apparent in "legalized" change. Other agents, on the other hand, feel that commitment concerns are impractical in view of the natural resistance of people to change coupled with the fact that these people are primarily committed to the behavior which is the target of change in the first place.

The success of programs of change based on compliance rests primarily in the power of the influencing agent over the changee and the degree of surveillance which the agent of change is able to devote to the case. Change via compliance requires a relatively formal and well-defined power differential between the change agent and the changee, since compliance, by definition, implies an ability on the part of the change agent to mediate rewards and punishment for the changee for compliance and noncompliance, respectively. At the same time, change via compliance requires maximum surveillance on the part of the change agent, since conformity on the part of the changee occurs on the basis of power differences rather than on the basis of commitment to the conforming behavior. Withdrawal or reduction of surveillance will usually result in a decrease in conforming behavior.

The 9/1 position receives much use in corrections and contains the seeds of its own problems. Surveillance is increasingly difficult to maintain due to large case loads and ever-rising offense rates. There is also some question as to who can perform surveillance more effectively—the policeman or the correctional worker. Some jurisdictions compel the worker to assume a dual stance of policeman-change agent which reinforces the 9/1 approach. It also follows that the power ingredient in 9/1 takes on an added dimension as required by the police role, thereby limiting the change planning of the agent.

**The 1/9 position—Client-centered Change.** The "client-centered" strategy of change, as represented in the upper left-hand corner of the grid, reflects the assumption that people are basically motivated by growth needs and will gravitate toward the social values representative of the mature person once they have been freed to do so. This strategy focuses on the commitment of the individual, since growth requires freedom of choice of the type which is apt to result in high commitment. It rejects the concern for conformity since implicit in such a concern is a host of subjective values and judgments regarding "correct" behavior. These are seen as antithetical to the free choice situation. Thus, client-centered change is designed to help the individual accept his own shortcomings, as a means of finding himself in his society and accepting others as well. As such, it tends to focus on the "there-and-then" determinants of present behavior.

Change under client-centered conditions requires a minimal power differential between change agent and changee, with minimal surveillance. What power difference there is is likely to be tipped in favor of the changee. It is necessary under this strategy that the changee feel that he is master of his own fate and capable of making his own decisions without the restricting demands of the change agent being emphasized as under other strategies. The agent of change, in effect, reduces his own power in the change situation in order to force the burden of change onto the shoulders of the changee and avoids influencing either the occurrence or direction of change beyond the point of "freeing" the changee to grow. Trust and appreciation are central to this relationship and concerns for conformity are seen as mutually exclusive of such considerations.

This is the kind of change which has permeated the traditional social work change strategies. Such approaches tend to form a "free floating" change tactic which has difficulty integrating with the structured corrections milieu. This factor helps explain partially the conflicts which correctional social workers have experienced in the authoritarian setting.

**The 1/1 position—Custodial Change.** Custodial change, as depicted in the lower left-hand corner of the grid, is based on the premise that individuals are basically autogenous and, therefore, change or fail to change as a result of their own desires. Custodial change strategies are not change strategies at all in the strictest sense of the word, but reflect the change agent's unique perception of his own role rather than a concern with inducing change. It may well be that custodial change represents the resolution of conflicts and frustrations which many change agents experience in the face of pressures to effect change, on one hand, and resistance to change attempts, on the other. The result is an increasing conviction that individual propensities for maladaptive behaviors are in direct conflict with external attempts to effect more adaptive behavior. Individual behavior—whatever its dynamics—is viewed as too deeply ingrained to change substantially, and what changes do occur are seen as more a product of changee desires than change agent strategies.

Therefore, the role of the change agent under custodial change is reinterpreted to reflect the more mechanical aspects of the task; namely, providing the appraisal of limitations, consequences of failure to conform, and evaluation of adjustment. The custodial change agent focuses more on accurate documentation and reporting than on plans for change and operates more as a detached observer of progress than as an initiator of action. Personal power is rechanneled toward these pursuits and may be seen by the changee as implying a *laissez-faire* condition. Surveillance is usually of the mechanical nature, relying on formally scheduled contacts rather than on the informal types which characterize both 9/1 and 1/9 strategies.

The 1/1 approach has long been a thorn in the side of correctional administrators because of its unimaginative "mechanical" approach to human dilemmas. It is important to realize, however, that this approach to change tends to result from the conditions of the agency *per se,* rather than from any inherent trait of the change agent. For example, change agents who are predisposed toward 1/9 strategies may well revert to a custodial approach should they find themselves in an essentially 9/1 agency, and vice versa. Similarly, heavily bureaucratic practices on the part of agencies promote 1/1-ism by holding to within-rank promotions and administrative appointments which perpetuate the "party line."

### Reciprocal Assumptions of Change

While the three change strategies discussed so far represent conflict or suppression orientations to the concerns for conformity and commitment, there are others which are based on the assumption of a reciprocal relationship between concerns. These strategies reflect a recognition of the fact that both concerns are the legitimate domain of the correctional agent of change; but they subscribe to the notion that conformity and commitment concerns exist in a reciprocal relationship such that the degree to which the change agent is concerned about one determines automatically the degree to which he can be concerned about the other. Thus, the implicit assumption is that it is necessary to be concerned about both conformity and commitment, but that one must strike a "mechanical balance" between the two in order to do this. Two commonly used strategies fall under this assumption.

**The 9/1 to 1/9 Paternalism Pendulum.** Blake and Mouton identified the existence of a "wide arc pendulum" phenomenon in management which they felt lay at the roots of paternalistic practices. Similarly, a pendulum approach to change seems to be employed by many correctional change agents. The paternalism pendulum approach stems from a recognition of the need for both conformity and commitment in achieving change, and seeks to deal with the two concerns separately because of their assumed reciprocity. The paternalistic change agent pursues a 9/1 compliance-oriented course in matters pertaining to changee behavior and a 1/9 client-centered course in issues not directly related to the plan of change. By virtue of requiring strict compliance to the plan for change, on the one hand, and by offering help and support in non-change areas, on the other, the change agent is likely to be seen as paternalistic. That is, he may fall into the role of a father figure who metes out both punishments and rewards and thereby increases his control over the changee. Implicit in this approach is the notion that continued compliance may result in increased rewards in areas not germane to behavior change *per se*. As such, this approach reflects an attempt to show concern about the feelings of the changee while at the same time exacting model behavior. The changee, in turn, may be confused and frustrated by the lack of consistency which such a strategy interjects into the change process.

**The 5/5 Position—Charismatic Change.** In the center of the Change Grid is found the 5/5, or charismatic change, strategy. This approach to change also proceeds on the assumption that, while concerns for conformity and commitment are both necessary and realistic, they exist as reciprocals; i.e., it is possible to be concerned for both, but the more concern one has for one the less he can have for the other. Basically, the charismatic change agent is more concerned with conformity, and in this respect his strategy may be thought of as a distorted 9/1 approach. At the same time, however, he is eager to gain enough commitment to the conforming behavior to ensure its continued use. (It might be noted that this is the first instance in which this concern for change duration has entered into a change strategy.)

Since the 5/5 change agent can appreciate the resistance changees might feel toward adopting certain required behaviors, he attempts to gain commitment to *himself* as an agent who behaves in the prescribed manner, rather than to the behavior *per se*. Accordingly, he feels that it is important for the change agent to understand the problems of the changee while at the same time being mindful of the requirements for more adaptive behavior. The 5/5 change agent relies heavily on social power and his own attractiveness in dealing with changees, and may well work hard to be seen as "a regular guy." By gaining the respect and admiration of changees, the charismatic change agent feels that he can also win co-operation by virtue of the fact that those who respect him will desire his respect in turn and will conform in order to gain it. Needless to say, this is a unique approach to effecting change and requires a unique person for its employment. The success of such a strategy rests on the ability of the change agent to maintain the balance of social power via his own attractiveness in the situation. Because of this, both the direction and duration of change become tenuous and subject to numerous distracting influences. Moreover, change achieved on the basis of the somewhat manipulative charismatic approach is analogous to "cure by transfer" and, consequently, tends to endure only so long as the change agent is both attractive and near at hand. Because of its "personalized" quality, it requires frequent informal contacts between the change agent and changee as a means of reinforcing the importance of the relationship.

## SUMMARY

By orienting the concern for conformity and the concern for commitment dimensions at right angles to each other, it has been possible to delineate several strategies of change which are commonly encountered when individuals attempt to influence others. The individual strategies of change which have been touched on thus far reflect a strong orientation toward the incompatibility of *concerns for conformity* and *concerns for commitment*. It may be this orientation which is responsible for the general lack of a systematic approach which currently characterizes corrections and the professional ambiguity discussed earlier.

## AN INTEGRATION OF THE CONCERNS FOR CONFORMITY AND COMMITMENT

Realistically, if a change strategy is to be effective, the change agent *must* be concerned with a behavioral shift in a given direction, i.e., conformity. Contrary to many of the assumptions underlying other strategies, it is not necessarily judgmental to expect individuals to employ certain kinds of behavior. Rather, personal experience—without regard for personal values and labels—indicates fairly consistently that some behaviors result in constructive, mature relationships with one's environment, while others result in destructive and debilitating relationships. These consequences are less a product of one's value-ladened interpretation of another's behavior than they are of reality-based fact. At the same time, it seems apparent on the basis of research in the social sciences that for change to endure (as well as to occur in its strictest sense) some degree of commitment to that change is necessary on the part of *both* changees and agents of change. The fact that many people see these two concerns as conflicting may merely reflect their lack of the theoretical orientation or the skills whereby the two concerns can be made to converge in a single strategy.

A quite different strategy is represented in an assumption

based on research in the behavioral sciences which indicates that where there is a high level of participation and involvement in goal-setting activities there is an equally high degree of commitment and conformity to the behaviors deemed necessary for goal attainment.[5] This is the assumption underlying the remaining anchor position on the grid.

**The 9/9 position—Change via Credibility.**   This strategy is based on the assumption that for change to be undertaken by a changee the reasons for it must be understood and credible and the behaviors required must be agreed upon by all parties to the process. In effect, this assumption focuses on the setting and testing of goals initially as in the selective and individualized use of probation or parole conditions, and then on the invention and selection of those behaviors most likely to result in goal attainment. The role of the agent of change becomes one of an *interventionist* rather than that of sanctioner or supporter. His task under the 9/9 strategy becomes one of establishing the credibility of the need for change and the various elements of the plan for change. This he does, not as an "expert" with all the answers, but as a mediator between the changee and his environment, pushing for the articulation of changee goals and an evaluation of current behaviors relative to these goals. This strategy results in a form of reality testing on the part of the changee under protected confidential conditions in which he is free to experiment at both the intellectual and muscle levels. The change agent exerts influence by virtue of his consistent charge to the changee to "test his behavior" against reality. Since the changee's environment is part of his reality, he must necessarily come to grips with the issue of "What are the consequences of my behavior for others and, in turn, what are the consequences of their reactions for me?" The dilemma inherent in these issues provides the motivation for undertaking programs of change on the part of individuals once the relevance and credibility of the answers are recognized.

The agent of change who pursues the 9/9 change strategy attempts to do so within the context in which the problem exists; i.e., he attacks the problem in its natural habitat rather than in a setting of his own making under artificially imposed conditions. This may be within the family context if the problem has its genesis there or within some other reference group with which the changee identifies and to which he is committed. The relearning of behaviors, therefore, may involve a number of people other than the changee proper; but to the extent that these others contribute to current and future changee behavior, they represent a part of the reality with which the change agent must be prepared to deal. Ultimately, the change agent would hope to create the conditions under which the changee can begin to assess reality and its implications for himself. To do so, however, requires that the changee have an opportunity not only to re-evaluate his situation as it relates to the situation of the rest of society, but an opportunity to practice and experiment with new behavioral patterns as well. It is only in this way that the changee will be able to generalize from the experiences he has during change to his workaday world. In turn, the change agent who pursues the 9/9 course will find that it is necessary to share his power equally in order to attain the amount of involvement and participation necessary on the part of changees to result in their commitment to the program.

Thus, the 9/9 agent of change serves as a representative of society who intervenes into the social life of the changee much as the psychoanalyst intervenes into the mental life of his patients. By sharing power of decision with the changee he is able to reinterpret changee behavior in terms of changee goals and to create conditions for evaluating behavior by the nature of his interventions. He employs a problem-solving approach to the integration of conformity and commitment and exhibits a maximal concern for both as the essential elements for enduring change.

## Strategies of Change and "Views of Man"

Implicit in the whole notion of change discussed here is the idea that the individual correctional worker controls the probabilities of success in the change process. This is so because, as we have said, the assumptions the change agent holds about change and how it should be effected directly influence the type of change strategy he will employ. Thus, assuming that change is the objective of corrections, it is no wonder that one finds so many different perceptions and interpretations of the task at hand and the resulting blurring of the professional image. This is merely a symptom of the failure of correctional personnel to articulate an agreed-upon objective, supported by a set of definitive assumptions and principles. One of the first tasks which must be confronted toward this end is a clarification of the correctional "view of man."

While it would be unrealistic to contend that the assumptions that various agents of change hold with respect to the means for effecting change are uncolored by personal needs and dynamics, this is a less important consideration than the basic view of man which the correctional person holds. The logic of this position is that we tend to respond to people on the basis of the "theories" we have about them. As might be expected, the views of man which underlie each of the change strategies discussed earlier differ in some very fundamental ways.

**The 9/1 view of man.** Essentially, the view of man which would necessitate the adoption of a change strategy predicated on strict formal power, close surveillance, and the use of rewards and punishments is that man is primarily a hedonistic, pleasure-seeking animal who can be motivated by either the possibility of rewards or by fear of punishment. As such, he is seen as having little personal integrity and sense of responsibility, poor judgment, few of the more advanced social needs such as those for affiliation or achievement, and little capacity for controlling his own fate. He is seen as dependent, passive, and indifferent and, therefore, in need of a "firm" hand to get him moving in the right direction. This is, of course, basically an authoritarian point of view which becomes translated into power-oriented actions by the agent of change.

**The 1/9 view of man.** In many respects, the 1/9 view of man constitutes a reaction to the culturally older 9/1 view. It represents an abhorrence of the notion that man is primarily pleasure-seeking and indifferent, but seems to retain many of the ideas that he is dependent and incapable of controlling his own fate. The upshot of this mixture is a view that men who deviate from the norms of their culture are basically good, but ill socially and psychologically. Implicit in this view is the idea that, because of their dependence and lack of self-control, they must be helped by others if they are ever to overcome their inadequacies. As such, this view of man requires a strategy which emphasizes the dependability of the change agent as a person who is interested in and accepting of people in trouble and who, at the same time, has a capacity to understand them that they themselves lack. In an extreme form, this view of man may result in the assumption of a "holier than thou" posture on the part of change agents as they deal with "exceptional cases." In its less extreme form it would seem to place relatively greater emphasis on the psychodynamics of individual changees than on the social determinants of deviant behavior.

**The 1/1 view of man.** The 1/1 view of man, much as the 1/1 strategy of change, reflects a change agent's feelings of disenchantment and frustration with his professional world. As such, it tends to be pessimistic in character and focuses on the notion that people are what they are, regardless of others' attempts to help or change them. Man is seen as a free agent, who is good or bad as a matter of genetic chance and who, alone, can decide to pursue programs of change or nonchange. Many of the elements of irresponsibility and truncated social needs found in the 9/1 view of man are also represented here; but the assumption of independence (if not counterdependence) is made by the 1/1 change agent, rather than the dependent characterization subscribed to by 9/1 and 1/9 agents. To a great extent, this view of man belies the change agent's own feelings of alienation as much as those of the offender. In extreme instances, this view may even be bolstered by an adherence to the somewhat unsophisticated position of genetic endowment, as epitomized by the Jukes and Kallikaks, or to such premises as the "criminal mind" in an attempt to rationalize away change agent responsibility for changee behavior.

**The 5/5 view of man.** This view of man employs a compartmentalized assessment of people with the result that an assumption of innate "goodness" is made, on one hand, coupled with a perceived need for leadership, on the other. The vast majority of people are seen as followers, and this idea reflects a basic distrust of their capacities to lead themselves. Thus, the 5/5 view of man, unlike those already described, incorporates and places major emphasis on the social needs of individuals to "belong" and to have meaningful affiliations with people they can trust and respect. Thus, deviant behavior is attributed to "misidentification" with deviant leaders on the part of changees who have gotten in with the "wrong crowd." Man is viewed as malleable on the basis of his need for gratifying relationships which, when used constructively, can become the source of motivation for change and more adaptive behavior. Such a view requires a strategy which can effectively initiate and sustain a "personalized" relationship between the change agent and the changee. The 5/5 change agent, in effect, pits his leadership against that of less socially acceptable leaders. It is perhaps symptomatic of the view that a major source of concern to the 5/5 change agent is whether or not he is being "conned" by the changee.

**The 9/9 view of man.**    Unlike the views of man associated with other change strategies, the assumptions underlying the 9/9 strategy attest to the basic similarities of all men. While individual differences are recognized, they are not used as the basis for explaining deviant behavior or conforming behavior. Rather, man is seen as a social animal motivated by the desire to achieve and to behave responsibly, while at the same time valuing both his independence and dependence and his capacity for fate control. He is seen as a learner who finds ways of satisfying these basic needs on the basis of experience with his particular reference group or culture. Thus, deviant behavior under this view is attributed to deviant learning and the problem of change is seen as one of relearning more appropriate means of need satisfaction. Neither the needs nor the capacities of individuals are discredited, as such; rather, the conditions for learning are seen as the prime determinants of behavior and the generalized need for mature functioning is seen as the only motivation necessary to prompt relearning. This view requires a strategy which facilitates learning by way of providing the means for an effective translation of valid social principles into changee awareness and behavior. That is, it requires change agent skills in creating the conditions for "discovery" on the part of changees within those realistic limits of society which bind us all.

**"Views of Man" and the Self-fulfilling Prophecy.** It can be seen that each strategy of change has as its genesis a distinctly unique view of man. Each of these, if correct, would call for unique procedures. Therefore, 9/1 change relies on the basic process of coercion; 1/9 on a process of self-maximation; 1/1 on spontaneous remission; 5/5 on the dynamics of identification; and 9/9 on a process of internalization.[6] As such, each of these processes is set in motion by the agent of change; and each may meet with some degree of success. While each success experience may serve to reinforce the agent's view of man, he should also be aware of his assumptions and their relevance for the self-fulfilling prophecy. Since we all know that it is possible to *cause* what we expect to happen to actually occur in our relations with others, the correctional change agent should ask himself why he finds people dependent or irresponsible or sick or in need of a leader. It may be that we view man many times not so much as he is but as we are. To the extent that this is true in the field of corrections, the profession will grow no more than its most articulate spokesman.

## SUMMARY CONSIDERATIONS

Thus, we have tried to present a wide range of correctional practices as they exist and are currently being employed. It seems self-evident that, given such a wide divergence of assumptions and practices, the field of corrections cannot help being characterized by professional ambiguity, duplication of effort, and antithetical pursuits. Moreover, this will continue to be the case until some unifying principle can be discovered which will allow a new input of theory and experimentation. We suggest that the canopy of correctional change represents such a unifying principle and that under it the profession and its workers can grow. Therefore, the challenge of corrections, it would seem, lies at the interface of conformity and commitment.

# NOTES

SOURCE: *The Journal of Criminal Law, Criminology and Police Science*, 57 (December 1966), 493–503.

1. Theodore R. Sarbin, "Role Theory," in Gardiner Lindzey, ed., *Handbook of Social Psychology, vol. I* (Reading, Mass.: Addison-Wesley Co., 1954).

2. Robert R. Blake and Jane S. Mouton, *Managerial Grid* (Houston, Texas: Gulf Publishing Co., 1964).

3. The word *conformity* as used here refers to conformity on the part of a changee to a set of social standards, however derived. *Commitment* is defined as the subjective feeling on the part of the changee that his conformity to such standards is desirable and necessary. Commitment should not be confused with "incarceration," the usual definition of the term in the correctional field.

4. Albert D. Biderman and Herbert Zimmer, *Manipulation of Human Behavior* (New York: John Wiley, 1961); Warren G. Bennis, *et. al.*, *The Planning of Change: Readings in the Applied Behavioral Sciences* (New York: Holt, Rinehart & Winston, 1961).

5. Kurt Lewin, *The Relative Effectiveness of a Lecture Method and a Method of Group Decision for Changing Food Habits* (Ames: State University of Iowa Child Welfare Research Station, 1942); J. M. Levine and J. Butler, "Lecture vs. Group Discussion in Changing Behavior," *Journal of Applied Psychology*, 36 (1952), 29–33; L. Coch and J. R. P. French, "Overcoming Resistance to Change," *Human Relations*, 1 (1948), 512–32.

6. The change processes of coercion, identification, and internalization have been previously identified and discussed at length by Herbert Kelman, and are summarized in his article, "The Induction of Action and Attitude Change," *Proceedings of the Fourteenth International Congress of Applied Psychology* (1961). (Editor's note: see also, Herbert C. Kelman, "Compliance, Identification, and Internalization: Three Processes of Attitude Change," *Conflict Resolution*, 2 [1958], 51–60.)

# 16

## SOME NOTES ON TREATMENT THEORY IN CORRECTIONS

### Don C. Gibbons†

Some years ago Ernest Greenwood discussed some relationships between social science and social work.[1] In that essay he stated the ideal form that a technology of social work should take. He indicated that social work would operate with diagnostic typologies that define the nature of the problems for treatment. "Diagnosis" would then constitute a process by which a given problem would be classified as falling within a type in the diagnostic scheme. A well-developed practice field would also employ a typology of treatment procedures linked to the diagnostic device. Together, these sets of principles would constitute the "practice theory" of the field. Greenwood also issued a call for collaborative research between social scientists and social work practitioners which would be designed to convert social science theory into practice theory. The end product of such research would be a relationship between social science and social work similar to that between medicine and certain fields of basic science, such as physiology, biochemistry, and bacteriology.

Correctional treatment of criminals and delinquents is commonly identified as a legitimate area of social work practice. Accordingly, Greenwood's analysis can be applied to corrections in order to indicate the direction in which that field should go if it is to become a technology based on scientific knowledge.[2] Thus, in a well-developed correctional profession, a diagnostic model or typology shared by all treat-

† Don Gibbons is a professor in the Department of Sociology at San Francisco State College.

ment workers would be applied to offenders. The determination of the "treatment problem" for any specific offender would involve locating that individual within a set of diagnostic categories. In turn, treatment would involve the manipulation of that person's behavior and attitudes in some manner specified within a body of statements of strategy or theory linked to the diagnostic typology. Further, the training of workers would include the communication of the diagnostic models and treatment principles to trainees.

At present, correctional work does not show this structure to any pronounced degree. Instead, what is now most characteristic is the use by treatment workers of crudely articulated behavioral theory which holds that most offenders are emotionally maladjusted and in need of intensive individual therapy. Such theory systematically ignores an abundant amount of sociological theory and research which indicates that many forms of unlawful conduct arise out of strains and defects in the social order, to which illegal behavior is a "normal" response. Although some of the work of such investigators as Cohen, Cloward and Ohlin, Sutherland, Sykes and Matza, and others has begun to creep into discussions of treatment, this material is not prominent in comparison to the mass of psychological material in correctional literature.

Moreover, it is not simply that etiological theory in corrections shows little sensitivity to sociogenic variables in deviant behavior. In addition, most current theory does not take full account of variations among types of offenders. There is mounting evidence to indicate that neither a psychogenic nor a sociogenic image of offenders is sufficient to encompass the variety of behavior patterns represented by the total population of law violators. A satisfactory description of offenders would involve the delineation of a number of criminal and delinquent types. Some of these patterns of illegal behavior are characterized by personality problems and other characteristics identified in psychogenic models, while others are not.

As for treatment techniques, the use of unshared and largely intuitive procedures by different workers is predominant. These tactics are frequently vague and ambiguous, even to the worker, and they are not based upon the available empirical evidence regarding the nature of offenders.[3] Instead, they are compounded out of gross behavioral theories and speculative hunches arrived at by trial and error in the work setting.

In considerable part the use of crude behavioral theories and intuitive treatment procedures is a reflection of the kind of training characteristic of correctional workers. This is usually some kind of generic social work training. Unfortunately, generic principles of social work do not provide specific guides as to how the correctional worker should operate in particular situations. For example, consider the kinds of statements made about "relationship" as a key to effective casework. Doubtless the establishment of a relationship is important, but the really difficult questions have to do with the specific kind of relationship that is required in order to effect changes in criminal behavior, the techniques by which such a specific relationship may be established, and the special problems that arise in correctional settings in establishing treatment relationships. The literature is not particularly helpful on such points. In summary, generic principles applied to corrections do not indicate in any very precise way the tactics that can be expected to rehabilitate offenders.[4]

Diagnostic models are not usually involved in the training of correctional social workers. Trainees do not customarily come face to face with a solid body of information about the nature and etiology of criminality or the variations among offenders. Moreover, rehabilitative theory based upon diagnostic models is virtually nonexistent and is not part of correctional training. As a consequence, "treatment" is now largely a situation in which "someone does something to someone else."[5] That something which is done may or may not be related to the problems of the offender. Moreover, relatively little is known about the effectiveness of those things that are done in the name of treatment.[6]

Of course the preceding is an exaggerated description of the present state of affairs. Signs of progress in the direction of empirically sound and effective correctional practices can be seen in recent issues of professional journals. Some analyses of treatment strategies[7] and some materials on delinquent and criminal typologies[8] offer encouragement. Also, some rather good research material is now accumulating on the effects of specific programs of treatment upon offenders.[9] Finally, there are a few state correctional systems in which research evaluation of programs has become a permanent part of operation. In California in particular, both the adult and the juvenile correctional systems are involved in the study of the impact of programs upon offenders, who are classified according to diagnostic devices developed there. No doubt much will be learned from such research.[10]

In spite of these promising signs, there is more that could be done in order to accelerate the development of sound correctional techniques and practices. It is the thesis of this paper that explicit attention should be given to constructing a clear, detailed, and comprehensive conceptualization of treatment based upon a set of empirically grounded diagnostic types. This theory would spell out those kinds of manipulation of the offender which are required in order to modify his behavior patterns so that he may become a law-abiding citizen. Such theory could be used in the training of correctional workers so that intuitive and unshared tactics might give way to standardized and describable practices.

This paper offers only a bare beginning in this direction.[11] The comments below include a discussion of several possible diagnostic models for adult offenders along with some statements about strategies for the treatment of the types specified in one of the models. However, this is only a first approximation of a developed body of treatment theory. For one thing, the business of articulating treatment hypotheses for a range of offender patterns is too complex to be accommodated within a brief paper. More important, it is not possible at present to specify in detail the complete list of behavior patterns which exist in the real world of offenders. However, if the development of treatment theory waits until a set of diagnostic types is produced in which the supporting evidence is overwhelming, it will wait forever. In addition, even though the present data are incomplete, more is known about criminal patterns than is sometimes recognized.

## Possible Diagnostic Models

Where can suitable diagnostic models be found? This section considers two typologies that might serve as diagnostic models. It should be noted that this essay is restricted to treatment theory for adult offenders, although the basic view outlined here is relevant to juvenile delinquents as well.

One typology that has much to recommend it has been presented by Schrag,[12] who has summarized a sizable body of research data indicating that there are four patterns of inmate roles oriented around certain focal issues in the prison community. He identifies these as the "prosocial," "antisocial," "pseudosocial," and "asocial" role patterns.

"Prosocial" inmates are those who have committed violent personal crimes, who have few prior criminal convictions, whose criminality is response to situational stress, and who verbalize proadministration norms in prison. "Antisocial" inmates show extensive delinquency records, recidivistic histories, and antiadministration attitudes. They are usually property offenders who regard crime as a livelihood. They tend to be products of criminalistic families who live in urban, lower-class neighborhoods. "Pseudosocial" inmates have been involved in subtle, sophisticated property offenses. They exhibit no delinquency record and have above-average educational and social backgrounds. They are frequently from parental backgrounds of inconsistent discipline and family disharmony. In prison they exhibit shifting loyalty attachments as they attempt to "work both sides of the street." That is, the pseudosocial inmate is the "politician" who operates as a manipulator of both the inmates and the administration. Finally, the "asocial" inmate exhibits a pattern of bizarre offenses, frequently accompanied by violence, high recidivism, and a history of early behavior disorders. He is egocentric, with poorly developed loyalty relationships to either inmates or administrators. He is a frequent troublemaker in the institution and is usually the product of a parental background of severe rejection.

Schrag's analysis is the product of research investigation

rather than speculation. One major implication of this material is that the search for criminal types is worth pursuing, for it may be that role patterns observed in prisons represent situationally specific manifestations of variations among offenders which can be discovered in a variety of different settings, such as probation case loads, prisons, and parole or other correctional situations.

One effort to define a set of criminal types not specific to any particular correctional milieu has been made by the present author.[13] This typology identifies thirteen offender types in terms of "definitional dimensions" of offense behavior, attitudes, and self-definitions. In addition, it specifies "situational correlates," or background characteristics for the defined types. No claim is made that this classification is inclusive of all adult criminals, but it is argued that it would include a sizable portion of the total population of offenders.

This is not the place for a detailed discussion of the derivation procedures by which this typology has been developed, but it should be noted that the typology has been drawn out of the existing research literature. For example, it includes as one type the "naïve check forger," defined in part in terms of characteristics identified in Lemert's investigation of naïve forgers.[14] On the other hand, limitations in the existing data have required that these statements about offender types be supplemented by intuitive "hunches" from case record material and elsewhere so that the empirical accuracy of some of the descriptions in the typology is indeterminate.

The comments about treatment strategies in the next section are organized around the second typology rather than around Schrag's categories. However, the two are related. For example, it is likely that the quasi-professional property offender and the joyrider-auto thief represent patterns that frequently emerge in antisocial inmates in prison. Similar relationships probably exist between other types in the two systems.

Although the complete typology includes thirteen patterns of offender behavior, some of these are of little importance in discussions of treatment, for they are infrequently found in the group of conventional offenders. These types are the "professional thief," the "professional 'heavy' criminal," the "upper-class fringe violator," and the "white-collar criminal." From this point on, this paper will omit consideration of these four patterns.

Space limitations preclude an extended discussion of the elements and variables in the typology, but in table 1 the defining characteristics of the types are briefly indicated.[15] The prison role-type parallel of each pattern is indicated in Table 1.

## TABLE 1
### DEFINING CHARACTERISTICS OF OFFENDER TYPES

| Type | Offense Pattern | Self-Definition Attitude |
|---|---|---|
| *Semiprofessional property offender* (Antisocial) | Robbery, burglary, larceny, and allied offenses; unskilled repetitive crime with small profit | Self-definition as a criminal, but as a victim of society; hostile toward police and correctional authorities |
| *Auto thief-joyrider* (Antisocial) | Repetitive auto theft for pleasure; "car clouting" and other auto offenses for profit not included | Self-definition as a criminal, and as tough, manly; concerned with others' perception of him as a "tough guy" |
| *Naïve check forger* (Prosocial) | Passing bad checks, usually without skill; often passes checks while drinking | Self-definition as noncriminal, and as a person burdened with personal problems |
| *Embezzler* (Prosocial) | Illegal conversion of property from a position of financial trust | Self-definition as a noncriminal, as different from "real criminals"; rationalizes acts as not really criminal |
| *Personal offender* ("one-time loser") (Prosocial) | Crimes of violence under situational stress —murder, manslaughter, assault | Self-definition as a noncriminal, but as deserving of punishment; no pronounced antisocial attitude |

| | | |
|---|---|---|
| *Psychopathic assaultist* (Asocial) | Offenses against persons or property or both, characterized by violence in "inappropriate" situations | Self-definition as a criminal, but as a victim of the treachery of others; views others as generally untrustworthy |
| *Violent sex offender* (Prosocial) | Sexual assaults upon physically mature females, characterized by extreme violence, mutilation, etc. | Self-definition as noncriminal |
| *Nonviolent sex offender* (Prosocial) | Sex offenses—such as child-molesting—usually with immature victims; statutory rape and similar offenses not included | Self-definition as a noncriminal; frequently rationalizes himself as Christian and his offense as not sexual but "educational" |
| *Heroin addict* (Antisocial) | Use of heroin or other opiate; property offenses as source of income for purchase of drugs | Self-definition as a criminal, but sees criminal status as unjust; holds that drugs usage is a relatively harmless personal vice |

### Diagnostic Models and Treatment Strategy

The following comments constitute an initial attempt to specify some directions for treatment of the criminal types included in Table 1. The intent is to suggest directions for further development rather than to lay out a set of detailed recipes for treatment. In the interest of brevity, the discussion of treatment tactics is handled in two ways. First, summary analysis of treatment strategies for all of the types is presented in Table 2, in which some of the major dimensions

### TABLE 2
### TREATMENT DIMENSIONS AND DIAGNOSTIC TYPES

*Semiprofessional property offender*

| | |
|---|---|
| Formal treatment program ... | Guided-group-interaction form of therapy in group composed of other "antisocial," "right guy" offenders |
| Adjunct program .......... | Vocational training or educational program |
| Goal ..................... | Modification of attitudes toward police, work, crime, and society; development of "prosocial" attitudes |
| Periods .................. | Institutional group therapy carried on most intensively during last few months of incarceration and continued during parole |
| Frequency ............... | Intensive in the prerelease period, with group meeting at least several times a week |

*Auto thief-joyrider*

| | |
|---|---|
| Formal treatment program ... | Guided-group-interaction form of therapy in group composed of other "antisocial," "right guy" offenders, but with some members who have been non-joyriders |

## TABLE 2, Continued

Adjunct program . . . . . . . . . . .Recreational program with active participation in athletics

Goal . . . . . . . . . . . . . . . . . . . .Demonstration of inappropriateness of "tough guy" criminal activity, aid to offender in developing a self-image which is tough and masculine but consistent with socially acceptable behavior

Periods . . . . . . . . . . . . . . . . . .Same as for semiprofessional property offender

Frequency . . . . . . . . . . . . . . .Same as for semiprofessional property offender

*Naïve check forger*

Formal treatment program . . .Client-centered individual therapy, group therapy in groups composed of other forgers, or both

Adjunct program . . . . . . . . . .Alcoholics Anonymous

Goal . . . . . . . . . . . . . . . . . . . .Breaking down the offender's rationalizations for forgery, discouraging dependent behavior, building up a fund of acceptable solutions to problems

Periods . . . . . . . . . . . . . . . . . .Intensive treatment if on probation or institutionalized, continued during parole, including group treatment, at least in part, and involvement in Alcoholics Anonymous during parole

Frequency . . . . . . . . . . . . . . .Several times a week

*Embezzler*

Formal treatment program . . .Intensive treatment not usually required; superficial assistance from time to time from treatment workers; isolation from more criminalistic types of prisoners

## TABLE 2, *Continued*

Adjunct program . . . . . . . . . . Assignment to clerical or other service position in the institution

Goal . . . . . . . . . . . . . . . . . . . Preservation of the offender's prosocial self-image and attitudes

Periods . . . . . . . . . . . . . . . . . During parole some help in adjusting to altered social and economic status

Frequency . . . . . . . . . . . . . . . Infrequent—once a week or less

*Personal offender* ("one-time loser")

Formal treatment program . . . Similar to that for embezzler

Adjunct program . . . . . . . . . . Assignment to institutional position

Goal . . . . . . . . . . . . . . . . . . . Similar to that for embezzler

Periods . . . . . . . . . . . . . . . . . Intensive treatment during parole

Frequency . . . . . . . . . . . . . . . Infrequent—once a week or less

*Psychopathic assaultist*

Formal treatment program . . . Some form of group treatment combined with intensive psychiatric counseling

Adjunct program . . . . . . . . . . None specific

Goal . . . . . . . . . . . . . . . . . . . Development of "normal" personality structure; resocialization of essentially undersocialized person, including development of loyalty attachments, role-taking abilities

Periods . . . . . . . . . . . . . . . . . Intensive treatment during entire period of incarceration and parole

Frequency . . . . . . . . . . . . . . . Relatively intense—several times a week

*Violent sex offender*

Formal treatment program . . . Psychiatric therapy conducted by psychiatrist or clinical psychologist

## TABLE 2, *Continued*

Adjunct program . . . . . . . . . .None specific

Goal . . . . . . . . . . . . . . . . . . . .Modification of bizarre sexual orientations

Periods . . . . . . . . . . . . . . . . .Intensive treatment during entire period of incarceration and parole

Frequency . . . . . . . . . . . . . . .Relatively intense—several times a week

*Nonviolent sex offender*

Formal treatment program . . .Intensive psychiatric therapy, particularly at initial stage of incarceration; possibly supplemented with group treatment in group of nonviolent sex offenders at later stage of prison term

Adjunct program . . . . . . . . . .None specific

Goal . . . . . . . . . . . . . . . . . . . .Modification of offender's self-image of inadequacy and sexual impotency; breaking down rationalizations regarding deviant sex acts; directing offender toward more aggressive and dominant relations with adults, particularly with his spouse

Frequency . . . . . . . . . . . . . . .Relatively intense—several times a week

*Heroin addict*

Formal treatment program . . .Individual therapy designed to deal with personality problems, along with guided group interaction designed to modify group-supported norms and attitudes regarding drug use and criminality

Adjunct program . . . . . . . . . .Vocational or educational program

## TABLE 2, *Continued*

Goal ....................Modification of "antisocial" attitudes, particularly attitudes
toward drug use, law enforcement agencies, and drug addiction treatment programs;
reduction of severe personality problems

Periods ..................Individual treatment and withdrawal from use of narcotics
during early period of incarceration; group treatment toward end of prison term and
in parole period

Frequency ...............Relatively intense—several times
a week

or aspects of treatment are indicated and in which comments
are made about different offender patterns. Second, some relatively detailed remarks are made about one of the offender
patterns in order to illustrate treatment theory in greater
detail.

Most of the dimensions in Table 2 require no explanation.
However, the distinction between formal treatment and adjunct programs is not self-evident. By "formal treatment" is
meant those programs directly aimed at modification of characteristics of offenders—such as unfavorable attitudes toward
work or criminalistic self-images—which are responsible for
deviant behavior. "Adjunct programs" are those parts of the
correctional process which are not directed specifically at the
modification of attitudes, but which do play an auxiliary role
in rehabilitation. Vocational training is a case in point. Persons are not criminals because of a lack of job skills but
rather because of unfavorable attitudes toward work. Treatment should be directed toward modification of such attitudes.
However, those offenders who exhibit negative attitudes
toward work frequently have poor work habits and are
deficient in vocational skills. In such cases, vocational training
could play an important part in the rehabilitation of the individual, provided that he also undergoes attitude modification.

The discussion below, concerning treatment policies for "semiprofessional property offenders," is designed to indicate the kind of extended analysis that could be made about other types as well.

### Semiprofessional Property Offenders

Persons who exhibit repetitive careers of relatively unskilled property crime and pronounced "antisocial" attitudes are relatively common among offenders, particularly in correctional institutions. Such criminals are usually from urban, lower-income slum areas where patterns of criminality are widespread. They often show backgrounds of family neglect, unstable work records, juvenile delinquency, and involvement in frequent petty offenses.

In many programs, semiprofessional property criminals are placed in some kind of intensive, individual treatment on the assumption that they need "insight" into their "problems." A corollary of such treatment is that if he gets an understanding of his problems, the offender will then be able to behave in a law-abiding fashion. It might be that intensive individual therapy would improve the mental health of such offenders, just as some amount of psychotherapy might be beneficial to many law-abiding citizens, but it is unlikely that this is the most effective strategy for the treatment of semiprofessional property offenders. These individuals exhibit a well-developed structure of "antisocial" attitudes, including hostile views of the police, antitreatment views, antipathy toward conventional work roles, and a sense of injustice which holds that they are the victims of a corrupt society in which everyone has a "racket." Moreover, these attitudes are group-shared and group-supported. They are, of course, the kind of attitudes specified in the inmate code as "proper." The treatment problem in the case of semiprofessional property offenders centers around the substitution of prosocial attitudes for the kinds enumerated above.

How is this to be accomplished? The most realistic strategy is probably a form of group therapy along the lines of "guided group interaction."[16] There the effort is made to

change group attitudes by encouraging offenders to exert
pressure upon each other to exhibit prosocial views. In such a
program, the role of the therapist tends to be that of a kind
of parliamentarian, rather than of a technical psychiatric
expert who uncovers personality problems. In guided group
interaction, an offender is likely to verbalize more acceptable
attitudes as a result of peer group pressures rather than of
"insight." In effect, the offenders in the therapy group represent both the patient and the therapist or agent of change.

Existing programs of this kind are most commonly found
in institutions, rather than in probation or parole settings.
However, the argument for group treatment should be
equally valid for these other situations. It would be highly
desirable to continue this form of treatment outside of the
institution. Indeed, the major technique of treatment for
parolees of the semiprofessional offender variety would be
group therapy. In this instance, however, the optimal treatment recommendation may have to be tempered by other
considerations. Many communities are not prepared to accept "novel" experiments which encourage fraternization
among parolees, even though the assumed risks of such innovations may be grossly exaggerated in the public mind.

Many semiprofessional criminals exhibit extremely spotty
work records, poorly developed work habits, and negative
attitudes toward work. One part of the treatment problem involves changes in attitudes toward work, so that the offender
will verbalize sentiments other than those implied in the statement that "only slobs work." However, it may be argued that
attitude change alone will not be sufficient to ensure parole
success. Favorable work attitudes may not insulate an offender from illegal behavior unless he also has an opportunity
to engage in noncriminal employment. On these grounds,
there is much to be said in the case of semiprofessionals for
vocational training as a valuable adjunct to treatment.

An additional, related point is that the combination of group
treatment and vocational or educational training should be designed to adjust the criminal to the realities of life outside
the walls. Offenders cannot realistically look forward to
interesting, highly paid jobs upon release even when they have

received vocational training. For some semiprofessional criminals, law-abiding jobs will not pay as well as crime, but such consequences as additional and more lengthy prison terms make the criminalistic alternative to law-abiding behavior unprofitable. It is this view of the choices open to the offender which must be made clear to him.

There is no claim that group treatment represents a cureall. What is argued is that, relative to alternative forms of treatment, group therapy is likely to result in lower recidivism rates and better adjustment. Nevertheless, recidivism rates among semiprofessional offenders are likely to remain rather high regardless of the kind of treatment used. Numerous obstacles lie in the way of effective group programs in institutions, particularly in maximum security prisons. For example, the inmate social system is organized in such a way as to exert pressure upon inmates to exhibit consistently antisocial attitudes. The inmate group has effective sanctions which it can employ to force "deviant" inmates to behave properly, that is, to discontinue participation in treatment programs. One of two responses to these pressures is likely to occur. The inmate may withdraw entirely from therapy programs when faced with a loss of status among other inmates, or he may attempt to "beat the system" by entering into treatment in a kind of sham performance designed to "con" the administrators. Yet it is possible that the inmate system is not as consistently "antitreatment" in organization as has sometimes been suggested in the literature,[17] and changes in the prison system might be effected to lessen the impact of associational patterns among inmates upon therapy. Nonetheless, such changes have yet to be developed and implemented.

Another impediment to treatment in institutions is that administrators can provide few opportunities for inmates to practice prosocial behavior. Ideally, therapy should be accompanied by outside-the-therapy-group activities in which inmates are encouraged to act out law-abiding citizen roles. The possibilities for such activities in prison seem limited indeed.

A final difficulty with group treatment, or any other therapy with semiprofessional offenders, is that treatment does not

alter the nature of the environmental pressures that contributed to criminal behavior in the first place. Instead, the parolee
goes back into a community in which opportunities for work
and other environmental problems continue unchanged. For
this reason alone, extremely high rates of success cannot be
expected. It may be that a drastic alteration in recidivism
among lower-income, slum-area offenders depends upon some
rather profound changes in the nature of American society.

## SUMMARY

This paper has directed attention to deficiencies in the
treatment theory with which correctional agents now attempt
to rehabilitate offenders. The discussion has indicated that
formalized diagnostic models are needed in order that a body
of explicit and detailed statements of strategy specific to different problems of treatment may be developed. Several
diagnostic models have been suggested, along with some terse
statements of treatment strategy for various diagnostic types.
The diagnostic models and treatment hypotheses presented
here fall considerably short of ideal, but most of the correctional literature is even more inadequate. The purpose of
this essay was to point to directions for further development.
If the general argument has the result of stimulating more
attention to problems of diagnostic typologies and treatment
theory, the aims of the paper will have been accomplished.

## NOTES

SOURCE: *Social Service Review*, 36 (September 1962), 295–305.
1. Ernest Greenwood, "Social Science and Social Work: A Theory of
   Their Relationship," *Social Service Review*, XXIX (March 1955),
   20–32. See also his "Attributes of a Profession," *Social Work*, II
   (July 1957), 45–55.
2. For a discussion of some complexities involved in the professionaliza-
   tion of corrections which are ignored in the present paper, see Donald R. Cressey, "Professional Correctional Work and Professional
   Work in Correction," *NPPA Journal*, V (January 1959), 1–15.
3. For a discussion of some deficiencies in current treatment theory,

see Don C. Gibbons and Donald L. Garrity, "Some Suggestions for the Development of Etiological and Treatment Theory in Criminology," *Social Forces,* XXXVIII (October 1959), 51–58.

4. The following are representative cases of "generic" statements on treatment: Harleigh B. Trecker, "Social Work Principles in Probation," *Federal Probation,* XIX (March 1955), 8–10; David Dressler, *Practice and Theory of Probation and Parole* (New York: Columbia University Press, 1959), 124–70.

5. Some evidence of the inadequacies of conventional social work training for corrections can be found in Lloyd E. Ohlin, Herman Piven, and Donnell M. Pappenfort, "Major Dilemmas of the Social Worker in Probation and Parole," *NPPA Journal,* II (July 1956), 211–25.

6. One brief résumé of the evidence on the effectiveness of treatment is found in Don C. Gibbons, "Comments on the Efficacy of Criminal Treatment," *Canadian Journal of Corrections,* II (April 1960), 165–74. See also Daniel Glaser, "Scientific Evidence on the Prison Potential," paper delivered at the American Correctional Association Congress of Corrections, Columbus, Ohio, September 27, 1961. (Editor's note: see Daniel Glaser, *The Effectiveness of a Prison and Parole System* [Indianapolis: Bobbs Merrill, 1964].)

7. Some samples of recent statements on treatment which are guided by an explicit theoretical rationale are: Donald R. Cressey, "Contradictory Theories in Correctional Group Therapy Programs," *Federal Probation,* XVIII (June 1954), 20–26; Donald R. Cressey, "Changing Criminals: The Application of the Theory of Differential Association," *American Journal of Sociology,* LXI (July 1955), 116–20; Lloyd W. McCorkle, Albert Elias, and F. Lovell Bixby, *The Highfields Story* (New York: Henry Holt & Co., 1958); LaMar T. Empey and Jerome Rabow, "The Provo Experiment in Delinquency Rehabilitation," *American Sociological Review,* XXVI (October 1961), 679–95; Richard L. Jenkins, M.D., *Breaking Patterns of Defeat* (Philadelphia: J. B. Lippincott Co., 1954).

8. Clarence C. Schrag, "A Preliminary Criminal Typology," *Pacific Sociological Review,* IV (spring 1961), 11–16; Clarence C. Schrag, "Some Foundations for a Theory of Corrections," in Donald R. Cressey (ed.), *The Prison* (New York: Holt, Rinehart & Winston, Inc., 1961), 346–57; Don C. Gibbons and Donald L. Garrity, "Definition and Analysis of Certain Criminal Types," *Journal of Criminal Law, Criminology and Police Science,* LIII (March 1962), 27–35; Don C. Gibbons, "Problems and Prospects of Delinquent Typology," *Sociological Inquiry,* XXXII (spring 1962), 235–44; John W. Kinch, "Continuities in the Study of Delinquent Types," *Journal of Criminal Law, Criminology and Police Science,* forthcoming.

9. See Gibbons, *op. cit.*

10. For results to date, see California, Department of the Youth Authority, *Current Status Report of Research Activities* (Sacramento, 1961).

11. The author is indebted to Peter G. Garabedian for a critical reading of an earlier version of this paper and for a number of suggestions which have been incorporated into this draft.

12. Schrag, *op. cit.*

13. Gibbons and Garrity, *Journal of Criminal Law, Criminology and Police Science,* LIII, 27–35.

14. Edwin M. Lemert, "An Isolation and Closure Theory of Naive Check Forgery," *Journal of Criminal Law, Criminology and Police Science,* XLIV (September–October 1953), 296–307.

15. For a résumé of the research data on which these types are based, see Gibbons and Garrity, *Social Forces,* XXXVIII (October 1959), and *Journal of Criminal Law, Criminology and Police Science,* LIII, 27–35. This typology is obviously an oversimplification of the actual characteristics of offenders, for, as the typology is stated here, it does not provide categories for classifying actual offenders who exhibit versatile offense careers. Additionally, the statement of the typology in table 1 is somewhat terse. However, these are difficulties which could be overcome in an extended discussion of typologies and treatment. The typology presented in table 1 is detailed enough to serve the purposes of the analysis in this brief paper.

16. Not everything now called group therapy would be included within the scope of group therapy as used here. That is, there are many programs called "group therapy" which are actually individual treatment in a group setting. In these the orientation is toward providing individual offenders with insight into deep-seated personality problems. The essential aims of such programs are the same as those of intensive individual therapy. Such programs should be distinguished from group therapy, in which principles of group interaction are employed for the purposes of changing behavior and in which treatment problems are seen as group-shared and group-supported.

   For an incisive discussion of the confusion of different forms of group therapy, see Cressey, *Federal Probation,* XVIII, 20–26.

17. Stanton Wheeler, "Socialization in Correctional Communities," *American Sociological Review,* XXVI (October 1961), 697–712; Peter G. Garabedian, "Western Penitentiary: A Study in Social Organization" (Ph.D. dissertation, University of Washington, 1959).

# 17

## THE NATURE AND EFFECTIVENESS OF CORRECTIONAL TECHNIQUES

*Donald R. Cressey†*

### INTRODUCTION

The criminological and penological literature contains two principal conceptions of "correctional techniques." The older conception considers as correctional techniques those general systems and general programs used for handling criminals and assumed to be somehow reformative. Thus, imposition of either physical or psychological pain, in any of a variety of settings, continues to be viewed as a general system for correcting criminals. Similarly, one rationale for introducing and maintaining general programs such as probation, parole, and imprisonment has been that these programs are or will be more "correctional" than the programs used in the past. A newer conception of "correctional techniques," however, places more emphasis on the specific methods used in attempts to change individual criminals. While descriptions of such methods are by no means as precise as descriptions of medical techniques, an analogy with clinical medicine is made, with the result that utilizing the methods is called "treatment" or "therapy." Thus, within a parole or probation organization, the agents may help offenders find jobs, order them to stay out of saloons, or counsel them on psychological problems of adjustment. Because each of these maneuvers is assumed to have some efficacy in changing criminals into noncriminals, each is viewed as a treatment or correctional technique. Similarly, prisoners may be enrolled in prison schools, ordered to work, given vocational counseling and training, or engaged in

† Donald Cressey is Dean of the College of Letters and Science at the University of California at Santa Barbara.

individual or group psychotherapeutic interviews. These specific programs also are viewed as techniques.

This paper will be devoted to closer identification of these two conceptions of correctional techniques, to discussion of the problems involved in measuring the effectiveness of "techniques" defined in either the first or the second sense, and to exploration of possible reasons for reluctance to define "correctional techniques" more precisely.

## GENERAL SYSTEMS AND PROGRAMS

During the past two centuries, the principal societal reaction to criminality in the United States has been punitive. Punishment for criminals is pain or suffering intentionally inflicted by the state because of some value the pain or suffering is assumed to have. In administration of the criminal law, we have assumed that one value stemming from infliction of pain on offenders is reformation or, in a newer terminology, "rehabilitation" or "correction" of those offenders. Other values, such as deterrence, are also assumed, but it is the idea that punishment reforms which makes the infliction of pain a correctional technique in the broadest sense of the term. Consistently, the general programs used for implementing the punitive reaction to crime also have been viewed as correctional techniques. Physical torture, social degradation, restriction of wealth, and restriction of freedom are among the programs used for inflicting pain on criminals. At present, the most popular techniques of this sort are restrictions on wealth (fines) and restrictions on liberty (imprisonment).

Strangely, in the criminological literature, practically no space is given to discussion of the reformative value which the imposition of fines is assumed to have. Of seven recent criminology textbooks, two discuss only casually the possible rehabilitative effect of fines,[1] and five scarcely touch the topic at all.[2] Discussion of inflicting pain by imprisonment is a different matter. From the time of its invention, the prison has had its loud supporters and loud critics.

As a general program for dealing with criminals, the prison, like the mental hospital, performs an integrating function for society.[3] This function, in turn, is assumed to have two principal aspects. First, the prison is expected to restore society to the state of equilibrium and harmony it was in before the crime was committed. "Undesirables," "deviants," "nonconformists," "outlaws," etc., are segregated behind walls. Second, the prison is expected to contribute to social integration by reducing the occurrence of future crimes. This latter aspect of the prison's integrative function is performed in two different ways. On the one hand, crime rates are assumed to be kept minimal both by the deterrent effects of imprisonment and by the effect that imprisoning men has on reinforcing the anticriminal values of the society doing the imprisoning.[4] On the other hand, imprisonment is expected to reduce crime rates by changing criminals into noncriminals. It is the last goal of prisons which gives imprisonment, as a general program, the character of a "correctional technique."

It must be emphasized that support for continuing the punitive reaction to crime or for specifically implementing this reaction by imprisonment is always based on some value which punishment in general, or the specific kind of punishment inflicted by the fact of incarceration, is *assumed* to have. We do not have any objective scientific evidence that inflicting pain on criminals is an efficient system for maintaining, or restoring, social integration. We do not *know* that imprisoning men deters others, reinforces anticriminal values, corrects criminals, or in some other way promotes social solidarity. Neither do we *know* that inflicting other kinds of pain corrects criminals or, generally, integrates society. Moreover, we do not *know* that inflicting pain by imprisonment or some other means is an *inefficient* system for achieving the desired ends.

In recent years, there has been a distinct trend away from the notion that inflicting pain reforms criminals. Also, it is now fashionable to argue that prisons do not correct and that, therefore, they should be abolished[5] or so modified that they become hospitals rather than places of punishment.[6] But neither the trend nor the fashionable arguments are based on scientific evidence that punishment is not effective as a general correctional technique. This is true simply because there never has been an acceptable measure of "efficiency." How much integration is necessary before a society is integrated? How low must a recidivism rate be before it can be said to be minimal? This kind of fairy-tale question can lead only to fairy-tale answers: "some," "enough," "lower than at present."

Currently, it is possible to argue, for example, that recidivism rates are high and that this has resulted because punishment is not inflicted with enough certainty or severity. It also is possible to argue that the rates are low (lower than they would be if . . .) because we have been using some punishment, at least. Alternatively, it can be argued that the rates are high because punishment is being used, and that the rates are low because punishments have been becoming less severe. No study has ever demonstrated that one of these arguments is more cogent than the other.

Moreover, even if a fixed bench mark of some kind could be established and we could discern that the recidivism rate moved above or below it after some general program was introduced, we still could not attribute the increased "efficiency" or "inefficiency" to the change of program. For example, measuring the effectiveness of parole, as compared to the effectiveness of the earlier system of determinate sentences, is complicated by variations in use of probation and by variations in the nature of parole itself. Also, a finding that recidivism rates are higher or lower *after* the introduction of a parole program can easily be attributed to any of numerous conditions which might have occurred simultaneously with the introduction of the program. Among these are differential arresting, sentencing, and prison practices, and differentials in the total populations from which criminals are selected.

The above comments refer only to some of the difficulties involved in measuring the effect of general programs on recidivism. When we attempt to evaluate the effects on the entire society, the difficulties are compounded. For example, there is no way of knowing whether crime rates are higher today, when punishments appear to be relatively mild, than they were some years ago, when punishments were more severe. Accordingly, we cannot know whether punishment does or does not deter criminals or reinforce anticriminal values. The numerous essays pointing out the inadequacies of statistics on crime agree on at least one point: We have no measure of the crime rate; we have only what are said to be "indices" of it.[7] The "indices" we use, however, such as "crimes known to the police," are not indices at all, for the relationship between the set of statistics used as an "index" and the true crime rate cannot be determined. Since there is no way to determine how many crimes are committed, we can only guess that crime rates are increasing, decreasing, or remaining the same, and we can only guess that an "index" bears some constant relationship to what is happening to the true crime rate. This vagueness, in turn, makes it necessary for us to use only nonscientific or pseudoscientific data as bases for arguments to the effect that a general system, such as punishment, or a general program, such as imprisonment, is or is not effective. Thus, a statement that the prison is a failure because it has not efficiently performed its integrating function must be based on humanitarian, political, or other nonscientific grounds, for there can be no scientific data underlying the statement. Neither is there any scientific evidence that the prison has been a "success" in this regard.

## SPECIFIC METHODS

By adopting the newer, more restricted conception of "correctional techniques," we do not necessarily avoid the methodological difficulties involved when general systems and programs are taken as the unit of observation. Statements regarding the effectiveness of specific procedures which are assumed to implement some general system for handling criminals, such as punishment, or which are part of some general program, such as imprisonment or parole, are subject to reservations which are identical to those placed on statements about the systems and programs themselves. This is evident from the fact that we can only assume that a specific technique such as "psychotherapy" or "strict discipline" is or is not corrective.

Currently, academicians and the members of professions involved in correctional work ordinarily assume that any *real* correctional technique is nonpunitive in nature. Only a generation ago, it was common to assume that a specific correctional technique was a method for implementing society's punitive reaction to crime, but the popular assumption at present is that a technique for inflicting punishment cannot be corrective. Because of this assumption, we are rapidly coming to substitute the words "treatment" or "therapy" for the words "correction" or "reformation." Saying that a method is a treatment or therapeutic technique is, then, simply a way of saying that the users of the technique do not make the traditional assumption that intentional infliction of pain is corrective. Psychotherapy, vocational education, counseling, and even direct financial assistance are viewed as "corrective" principally because they are nonpunitive, not because they have been demonstrated as effective methods for changing criminals into noncriminals. There is no scientific evidence that any nonpunitive correctional technique of this kind is either more or less effective than were punitive techniques such as "teaching discipline," "instilling fear of the law," and "breaking the will."

The paucity of scientific data on effectiveness or ineffectiveness of specific methods for dealing with individual criminals is not owing merely to oversight or lack of scientific interest in evaluation. On the contrary, many taxpayers have sincere interests in determining whether or not their money is well spent, and social scientists have keen interests in evaluating the effectiveness of techniques which are consistent, or even inconsistent, with some theory of crime causation they might hold. Explanation of our lack of clear conclusions about various techniques is difficult and complex. Perhaps we have few clearly evaluative studies for the same reason that we have no crime statistics which are clearly valid: We cannot afford to let them appear.[8]

## DILEMMAS OF EVALUATIVE RESEARCH

Precise research on the "success" of either general programs of crime control or more specific methods of correction furnishes information which is the basis for public esteem and professional reputation, as well as information about the correctional technique being evaluated. These two are very different. Personal and organizational needs supplement the societal needs being met by administration and utilization of various correctional techniques. For example, by utilizing or advocating use of particular techniques in correctional work, a person may secure employment and income, good professional reputation, prestige as an intellectual or scholarly authority, the power stemming from being the champion of a popular ideology, and many other personal rewards. An agency organized around administration of a technique may fill such needs for dozens, even hundreds, of employees, and may itself have more general, organizational needs for survival. Hence, evaluative research results which would show that the technique is ineffective and would, thereby, seriously threaten the agency or the personnel must be avoided if possible.

There are two principal ways to avoid the possibly unfavorable consequences of evaluative research. The first, and simplest, method is to ensure that such research is not initiated either by the persons utilizing the technique or by outsiders. Few personnel administering correctional programs in prisons or in parole agencies, for example, have either the research training or the time necessary for evaluating the effectiveness of their work. Further, practical correctional workers are likely to screen carefully the sociologists, psychologists, and, most of all, newspaper reporters who want to poke around in their bailiwick. This is necessary. Unsympathetic researchers or reporters are almost certain to "misunderstand" some of the events and conditions they observe, and a "scandal" could wreck the chances of doing *any* correctional work. A currently more popular method for avoiding any unfavorable consequences of evaluative research, however, is to permit or even undertake the research, while ensuring that any results will be subject to interpretation as "inconclusive."

In the past decade, we have in the United States witnessed tremendous growth of interest in research which would evaluate various action programs dealing with human relations—in mental hospitals, factories, governmental bureaus, correctional agencies, and other organizations—and it is now almost essential that one "be in favor of" evaluative research if he is to maintain a reputation as a good correctional worker or theoretician. This presents the personnel utilizing correctional techniques with a dilemma. On the one hand, one's reputation depends in part upon his being in favor of evaluative research. On the other hand, such research might threaten the very existence of an agency and damage the reputations of the personnel. Fortunately, there is a solution to the dilemma. Stated simply, it is to ensure that any research results can be interpreted as "conclusive" if they favor continued utilization of the technique and as "inconclusive" if they do not. For example, it is important that we be able to attack a research study on methodological grounds, pointing out that it really did not measure the effects actually being produced by the technique in whose administration we have a personal stake. Ultimately, evaluative research furnishes grounds for public opinion and, in the case of public agencies, at least, grounds for legislative action. Accordingly, if we really "believe in" our techniques, we will, as good Americans and good public servants, "fight for them."[9] One way to do this is to ensure that any adverse administrative or budgetary decisions based upon the research can be countered by an exposé of a poor or incomplete research design. In a sense, we attack research methods in the behavioral sciences as being too imprecise, while at the same time maintaining research conditions which make precision impossible.

Even the behavioral scientists themselves are not immune. Because of personal investments, academic theoreticians (like the writer) are likely to argue that criminals are being corrected by any technique which is, or seems to be, consistent with a favored theory of crime causation or of personality change. For the same reason, personnel of agencies devoted to rehabilitating criminals are likely to maintain that criminality is reduced by whatever it is that they are doing. Moreover, the implication is likely to be that crime is caused by whatever it is the agency is trying to correct. Administrators of a prison containing a school, a work program, individual psychotherapy, a recreational program, and strict discipline will almost inevitably maintain a "multiple-factor" notion regarding crime. They can scarcely do otherwise, for some external groups having strong interests in the prison maintain that crime is caused by educational "factors," others maintain that it is caused by economic "factors," others by personal or psychological "factors," still others by group "factors," and so on. The administrator must attempt to satisfy, or pacify, each of these groups. He is directed to believe that all the various techniques are necessary for the rehabilitation of a maximum number of inmates. He cannot risk abandoning any of them, for to do so might seriously threaten his budget and his personal prestige in the community. Consequently, it is highly desirable that any study designed to test the effectiveness of one of the techniques be subject to interpretation as "inconclusive," no matter how carefully or scientifically it is conducted.

For example, a research study which seemed to show that attending a prison school had little or no effect on the reformation of criminals would not necessarily lead to abandoning the school program. Rather, the "intangible benefits" of education probably would be enumerated, or, more likely, the study would be attacked on the ground that some variable, such as selection of the "least amenable" prisoners for education, was not controlled. In our society, education is a Good Thing, and schools must be maintained in prisons and justified as corrective ("good" men are educated; therefore, to make bad men good, educate them), whether or not there is any scientific evidence of their effectiveness.

Most of the difficulties arising in attempts to measure the effectiveness of correctional techniques stem, then, from failure to define precisely what a correctional technique is. This failure, in turn, seems to be a consequence of the fact that the groups controlling correctional agencies maintain widely di-

vergent theories about crime causation and about what the
agencies should do. Agency personnel cannot go "all out" to
test one group's theory if doing so subjects them to severe criticism from that or another group. Since we do not *know* how
to change criminals, we can only experiment with different
techniques. Yet, as we have indicated, the fact that agencies
are owned by persons with vested interests in their operation
means that no experiment can be definitive.

This system for perpetuating criminological and penological
ignorance has a highly useful function: it narrows the areas in
which disagreement can occur. "Inconclusive" studies of the
effect of correctional programs serve a useful purpose by harmonizing widely divergent ideological and theoretical commitments held by the many persons who must deal with criminals. Personnel such as police, guards, social workers, judges,
industrial foremen, teachers, clubwomen, district attorneys,
ministers, psychiatrists, and baseball coaches have very different notions about how to correct criminals, but these differences cannot result in embarrassing public denunciations or
even serious private disagreements so long as no precise evidence favorable to one or the other group arises. Just as
vague, common-sense, and "umbrella" terms are useful to in-
terdisciplinary crime commissions and research teams because
they reduce the area about which disagreement can be expressed (thus indicating high degrees of consensus when, in
fact, no one knows what his colleagues are talking about), so
vague definitions of "correctional techniques" and vague systems for evaluating the effectiveness of such techniques are
useful because they decrease the range of points on which
disagreements can occur.[10]

## A VOCABULARY OF ADJUSTMENT

Personnel maintaining either theoretical or practical interests in the control of crime and delinquency have developed a
rich vocabulary of motives for justifying as "corrective" whatever it is they are doing. Perhaps we developed the vocabulary
during a period when concern for precise evaluation was not

great, and continue it in order to "show" that any research on the effectiveness of our favored technique or program is inconclusive. So that this vocabulary can be illustrated, let us assume that a state has passed a law requiring all its parole agents to be registered psychiatrists who will use professional psychiatric techniques for rehabilitating parolees. Let us assume further that the required number of psychiatrists is found and that after ten years, a research study indicates that introduction of psychiatric techniques has had no statistically significant effect on recidivism rates—the rates are essentially the same as they were ten years earlier. The following are ten kinds of overlapping themes which are likely to be popular among the personnel with personal interests in continuing the program.

1. "You can't use rates as a basis of comparison—if only *one* man was saved from a life of crime the money spent on the program is justified."

2. "Even the New York Yankees don't expect to win all their ball games; the program certainly *contributed* to the rehabilitation of *some* of the clients."

3. "Recidivism is not a good criterion of efficiency; 'clinical observation' indicates that the criminals handled psychiatrically are 'better adjusted' than were the criminals going out of the system ten years ago and that even the repeaters are 'less serious' repeaters than were those of a decade ago."

4. "Psychiatric techniques for rehabilitation never were tried; the deplorable working conditions made success impossible—there was not enough time, case loads were too big, and salaries were so low that only the poorest psychiatrists could be recruited."

5. "You can't expect any system in which the criminal is seen for only a few hours a week to significantly change personalities which have been in the making for the whole period of the individual's life and which are characterized by deeply hidden, unconscious problems; we can only keep chipping away."

6. "For administrative reasons, the program was changed in midstream; good progress was being made at first, but the

program was sabotaged by the new administrator (governor, legislature)."

7. "The technique was effective enough, but the kind of criminals placed on parole changed; ten years ago the proportion of criminals amenable to change was much greater than at present."

8. "Had the technique not been introduced, the recidivism rates would be much higher than at present; the fact that there is no difference really indicates that the technique has been very effective."

9. "There are too many complex variables which were not controlled in the study; a depression (prosperity) came along and affected the recidivism rate; the newspapers gave so much publicity to a few cases of recidivism that parole was revoked even in many cases where genuine progress toward rehabilitation was being made."

10. "The study is invalid because it used no control group, but it has pointed up the need for *really* scientific research on psychiatric techniques; we must continue the program and set up a ten-year experimental study which will reassess our potential, locate some of the transactional variables in the patient-therapist relationship, determine whether some therapists have what we may term 'treatment-potent personalities' and others have what we are tentatively calling 'recidivistic creativity,' identify whether the catalystically oriented therapeutic climate is self-defeating when occupied by reagent-reacting patients, and measure the adverse effects of post-therapeutic family-warmth variables on favorably prognosticated and emotionally mature dischargees."

Each of these ten themes has an equivalent which is used if the research findings are in the reverse direction. Suppose the mythical research study indicates that after the ten-year program, the recidivism rates *are* significantly lower than the rates in the earlier period. Persons using the above vocabularies are then likely to accept the validity of the study. But this does not mean that popular vocabularies for justifying existing programs in the face of adverse research findings will not be brought into play. On the contrary, supporters of some other technique, perhaps one in use before the ten-year program was started, can now use the same vocabularies:

1. "In the ten-year period, the proportion of men amenable to change was much greater than in the prior period; the parole board cracked down and placed only good risks on parole, so the change would have occurred even if the technique had not been used." (See number 7 above.)

2. "Although the technique was the one officially used, I happen to know that many of the workers informally used methods which are consistent with *my* theory rather than with the theory officially designated as the one to be implemented." (See numbers 4, 5, and 6 above.)

3. "There are too many complex variables which were not controlled in the study: the criteria for revoking paroles were changed, a depression (prosperity) was in effect ten years ago, and many parole violations were overlooked merely to prove the effectiveness of the program." (See number 9 above.)

4. "If the technique, rather than something quite incidental to it, were effective in changing criminals, an even larger proportion of the criminal group would have been rehabilitated; a medical cure is specific to a disease and cures it." (See numbers 1, 2, 3, and 8 above.)

There is no need to elaborate this list. Additional slogans to match each of those given to justify research which shows no significant differences could be enumerated.

The themes we have listed, or variations on them, are heard wherever correctional work is being evaluated. Probation and parole workers argue that probation and parole have never been tried. Prison workers argue that probation has drained off the "good convicts." Psychotherapists in any system argue that the punitive and custodial aspects of the program make it impossible to do effective work or, alternatively, that one (two, six, twenty-seven) therapists should not be expected to have much effect on a criminal population of 2000 (1000, 500, 100).

Significantly, variations on these themes could be used, and probably were used, in reference to correctional systems in which the primary instruments expected to induce change in criminals were techniques for inflicting pain.

To a large degree, these arguments are the consequence of labeling as "correctional" almost anything convicted criminals are expected to do. This is most easily discernible in prisons where whatever is done with prisoners to keep them occupied and/or productive and quiet is likely to be called a correctional measure. In the 1920's and early 1930's, prisoners were expected to work in prison factories, and these work programs were said to be rehabilitative. In the depression years, when the prison factories declined and prison populations increased, inmates were enrolled in prison schools. Enrollment in academic or vocational education classes became a correctional technique. Shortly after smoking privileges, canteen privileges, radios, and television are introduced—perhaps for humanitarian or custodial reasons—they are viewed as part of the correctional program. When psychiatrists, social workers, psychologists, and sociologists were employed to occupy some of the inmates' time and, further, to drain off some of the "rumbles" caused by disturbed inmates, thus contributing to a quiet, smooth-running prison, their services came to be labeled as correctional or rehabilitative. Even the salary of a man who supervises an institution's food and sanitary services is likely to be charged to the "care and treatment" (corrections) budget.

The same kind of observation can be made of general noninstitutional programs and of specific techniques within these programs. When prisons are overcrowded and inmates are, therefore, assigned to prison farms, camps, road-building crews, or parole, we argue that such assignment is a correctional technique. Alternatively, we keep inmates out of prisons by suspending sentences and requiring recipients of this action to file a monthly report with a probation officer, naming this a rehabilitative device. Not too long ago, a parole agency might equip its officers with guns and order them to "correct" parolees by watching them carefully. In more modern agencies, we hire only men with college degrees and ask them to do something (unspecified) different from that done by guncarrying parole officers; this something, also, is corrective.

## SOME THEORIES OF PERSONALITY, CRIME, AND CORRECTION

If correctional work were scientific, each correctional technique would be established on a rational basis. We would be reasonably sure that men commit crime in certain describable circumstances and not in others, and then we would set out to modify these crime-producing circumstances. Utilization of each correctional technique would be an experiment designed to test the validity of a theory of crime causation. Stated in another way, from a theory of crime causation, we would predict that certain techniques would work and others would not. If the technique were carefully administered under experimentally controlled conditions but yet did not change criminals, we would be able to conclude either that (a) the theory on which the technique was based is wrong, or (b) the technique used was not consistent with the theory. Because correctional work is carried out under the kind of conditions we have already described—conditions which can scarcely be characterized as scientific—we are unable to draw either conclusion. The techniques in use certainly are not derived from precise statements of criminological theory.

Yet, there is a possibility that some order can be imposed on our rather disorderly conduct. Perhaps in the long run, we will find that some technique introduced for nontheoretical reasons "works." If this occurs, then we can, by working backward, develop a plausible theory of crime causation. "If practical programs wait until theoretical knowledge is complete, they will wait for eternity, for theoretical knowledge is increased most significantly in the efforts at social control."[11] Although the various techniques currently in use were not necessarily introduced for theoretical reasons, we can discern, at least, that some of them are fairly consistent with standard theories of personality, crime causation, and rehabilitation.

At present, there are two general and popular, but contradictory, principles for the correction of criminality. These two principles—the "group-relations principle" and the "clinical principle"—are, in effect, theories of rehabilitation. Some correctional techniques are somewhat consistent with one or the other of them, some with both, and some with neither. The two principles are the logical outgrowths of two alternative theories of crime causation. These theories of crime causation, in turn, are applications to a specific kind of behavior, criminality, of two even more general theories of the relationship between personality on the one hand, and social relationships, on the other. We shall briefly identify the two theories of personality and the two criminological theories and then shall proceed to the two principles or reformation.

As Stanton and Schwartz have pointed out, behavioral scientists at one pole think of the "organization" of social interaction and "personality" as two facets of the same thing.[12] The person is viewed as a product of the kinds of social relationships and values in which he participates; he obtains his satisfactions and, in fact, his essence, from participation in the rituals, rules, schedules, customs, and regulations of various kinds which surround him. Moreover, the person (personality) is not separable from the social relationships in which he lives. He behaves according to the rules (which are sometimes contradictory) of the large organization, called "society," in which he participates; he cannot behave any other way.

On the other hand, behavioral scientists at the opposite pole think of the individual as essentially autonomous, and they consider his interaction with rules and regulations of society and other organizations as *submission* rather than participation. "Personality" is an outgrowth of the effect that the "restrictions" necessary to organization have on an individual's expression of his own, pristine, needs. These behavioral scientists emphasize "individual self-determination" and make a distinction between the "real" or "natural" part of the person and the "spurious," "artificial," or "consensual" part. The former is viewed as primary, free, and spontaneous; the latter (obtained from the social relationships making up society) is formal, secondary, and restrictive.

Certainly the two theories of the relationship between personality and culture are more complex than this simple statement implies, and probably few behavioral scientists maintain one or the other of them explicitly and with no qualifications. But these two ideas, in form even more garbled and unqualified than we have used, have made their way into correctional work and have become the basis, indirectly, at least, of correctional techniques.

Consistent with the first general theory is criminological theory which maintains, in essence, that criminality is behavior which the person in question has appropriated from the social relationships in which he has been participating. Crime, like other behaviors, attitudes, beliefs, and values which a person exhibits, is the *property* of groups, not of individuals.[13] Criminality is not just the product of an individual's contacts with certain kinds of groups; it is, in a very real sense, behavior which is "owned" by groups rather than by individuals. A man who participated exclusively in organizations of social relationships (groups, societies) which had a monopoly on criminality would exhibit criminal behavior, just as a person who participated exclusively in groups owning only law-abiding behaviors would be law-abiding. But since most organizations own both criminal behavior and law-abiding behavior ("honesty is the best policy, *but* business is business"), the behavior exhibited by any member of the organization will depend upon his *differential participation* in one or the other of the behaviors owned by the organization. The "differential association" theory is a good example of criminological theories of this kind.[14]

Consistent with the second general theory of personality is criminological theory maintaining, essentially, that criminality is a personal trait or characteristic of the individual exhibiting the behavior. An extreme position is that criminality is a biological phenomenon. Much more popular is the theoretical position that criminality is a psychological defect or disorder, or a "symptom" of either. The criminal is one who is unable to canalize or sublimate his "primitive," individualistic, antisocial impulses or tendencies,[15] who may be expressing symbolically in crime some unconscious wish or urge arising from early traumatic experiences with the "restrictions of society,"[16] or who suffers from some other individual psychological trait or condition. In any case, criminality is the *prop-*

*erty* of the individual exhibiting it. Perhaps the criminal is "unable to accept the restrictions of society;"[17] perhaps his experiences in social relationships have given him unconscious urges which, when expressed, are criminalistic and beyond his control; perhaps they have built up in him a deep resentment of authority, latent hostility, or free-floating aggression. The essential notion here is that a "healthy" personality is one which does not own criminality because it has been permitted freely to express itself in numerous alternative ways.

The group-relations principle of reformation is based on the first polar type of theory about the relationship between personality and culture and the first kind of criminological theory. The basic notion is that attempts to change the criminal behavior of a person must be directed at modification of the groups owning the behavior. If the behavior of a man is an intrinsic part of the groups to which he belongs, then attempts to change that behavior will succeed only if the groups are somehow modified. While this principle is generally accepted in modified form by sociologists and social psychologists, there has been no consistent or organized effort to base techniques of correction on it. Many correctional practices and programs arising in the past one hundred years, however, have been indirectly, at least, consistent with it. Only in this way has the theory that changing the social relationships of offenders will modify criminality been implemented.

Among the more general programs which are, implicitly, consistent with the group-relations principle are probation and parole, where the offender is to be integrated into sets of social relationships in which criminality as a way of life is truly taboo. Similarly, even imprisonment as we now know it may be viewed as an unsuccessful system for attempting to force criminals to become members of organizations which do not own criminality, but, instead, own anticriminal behavior.

Within probation and parole systems, a precise, scientific technique which is consistent with the group-relations principle has yet to be invented. Rather than descriptions of techniques, we find statements that the individual is to be rehabilitated by "gaining his confidence and friendship," "stimulating his self-respect," "manipulating his environment," "providing a supportive atmosphere," or "changing his group relations." It is necessary to know how confidence is secured, how self-respect is stimulated, how the environment is to be changed, what a supportive atmosphere is and how it is to be created, and how group relations can be changed.[18]

The same difficulty arises in connection with techniques used within prisons. Academic and vocational education are consistent with the group-relations principle to the extent that they are directed toward changing the offender's postinstitutional group relationships. Conceivably, this is successful in some cases. A popular but apparently fallacious assumption is that passing through an educational course, such as eighth-grade arithmetic, should make bad citizens (prisoners) good, because passing through such courses is a characteristic of good citizens. But it may be hypothesized that such courses are "correctional" only to the degree that they change inmates' postrelease associations. Similarly, vocational education courses are often assumed to correct inmates by imparting vocational skills to them, thus enabling ex-convicts to earn a living "so they do not have to return to crime." But the implication of the group-relations principle is that training men to be, say, bricklayers will not automatically correct their criminality. Conceivably, however, the newly acquired skill might in a few cases have the effect of directing inmates into essentially anticriminal social relations upon discharge.

Prison labor is subject to the same kind of analysis. Ordinarily the assumption is that nonpunitive labor of almost any kind will instill in inmates "habits of industry" so that in the postrelease period, they will work in acceptable occupations and will not commit crimes. This assumption is similar to earlier assumptions that punitive labor, or punishment of almost any kind, will "tame" the criminal and make him lawabiding. Alternatively, we can assume that work in prisons is corrective largely to the extent that it is conducive to changes in social relations upon discharge, but it also contributes to the morale of inmates so that they are psychologically better equipped for making such changes.[19] It is at least plausible that in some cases, possession of work and social skills learned in prison affects the ex-convict's social mobility and that, as he moves from the status of an unskilled worker, an uneducated person, or an unemployed person to another status, his social relationships change in such a manner that his attitudes toward legal norms change.

Individual and group psychotherapy are rapidly becoming popular correctional techniques, both in prisons and in probation and parole. In individual psychotherapy, the psychological needs of individual inmates are of primary consideration, and the assumption is that correction of any psychological disorder or problem the inmate may have will change his criminality. Alternatively, adherents of the group-relations principle assume that individual psychotherapy is effective in changing criminality to the extent that it serves as a stimulant or inducement to changes in social relationships. The criminal's psychological problems may be relieved, but this has little or no effect on his reformation unless his relationships with the groups owning the criminality he has been exhibiting are modified. Conceivably, interaction with a psychotherapist is just as effective in stimulating such changes as is interaction with a teacher, tradesman, or work-crew foreman.

Group therapy as a correctional technique is not necessarily consistent with the group-relations principle. Rather, a popular assumption is that group therapy, like individual therapy, corrects criminality by correcting individual psychological disorders.[20] The emphasis in the "group work" of correctional agencies, such as probation offices, usually is on the role of the group in satisfying the psychological needs of an individual[21] or in some way enabling the individual criminal to rid himself of undesirable psychological problems. There is almost unanimous opinion that group therapy is an effective technique for treating mental patients, principally because isolated and egocentric patients are assimilated into the clinical group.[22] But the group-relations principle implies that for correcting criminals there must be more than this; and in treatment based on this principle, the aim is not mere reduction of isolation and belligerence of prisoners as they operate in the prison situation (although this is important to the smooth operation of the institution) but the provision of positive opportunities for integration into groups which own an abundance of anticriminal values and behaviors. Again, interaction in a clinical group might be considered effective as a correctional technique to the extent that it gives the participants experiences in the role of a law-abiding person and to the extent that these experiences carry over to affect the kind of social involvement the participants experience when they become ex-convicts.

The clinical principle of reformation is consistent with the second type of theory about personality and the second kind of criminological theory. If criminality is an individual disorder, then, like a biological disorder, it should be corrected on a clinical basis. Consistent with the most extreme position is the notion that the criminal's anatomy or physiology is to be modified through lobotomy, castration, modification of glandular functioning, or something else. Much more popular is the theory that the individual disorders producing criminality are psychological in nature and are, therefore, to be corrected through psychological attention. But in either case, the implication is that criminality should be corrected or treated clinically. In a sense, criminality is viewed as analogous to an infectious disease like syphilis—while group relationships of various kinds are necessary to the disorder, the disorder can be eradicated in a clinic, without reference to the conditions under which it was acquired. "Individualized treatment" usually refers to an attempt to correct some characteristic of the *individual* which is believed to underlie his criminality.

Individual psychotherapy, as a system for correcting criminals, is perhaps the best example of a current correctional technique based upon the clinical principle. Similarly, social casework has been greatly influenced by psychiatry, and as a result, many of the "diagnoses," "prescriptions," and "therapies" recommended or administered by social caseworkers attached to courts, prisons, and other agencies dealing with criminals are in clinical terms.

Because criminality is an expression of psychological disorders, it is to be corrected by elimination of the disorders. But because the disorders, in turn, spring from the restrictions society has placed on "free" individuals, correction of them must be in the form of modifying the impact of the restrictions on the individual. Although this might have reformation of society as one of its implications, individual criminals are to be corrected by giving them relief from the restrictions—in the form of "ventilation," "catharsis," "acting out," and other devices for removing "tensions," "aggression," "unconscious tendencies and wishes," and other individual disorders. If criminality is an expression of an individual disorder, then attempts to change criminal behavior will succeed only if this disorder is remedied. Many of the correctional techniques and programs arising in recent times have been indirectly consistent with this principle, as well as with the group-relations principle.

Probation and parole, as general programs, permit criminals more freedom than is possible if they are incarcerated, and, therefore, these systems reduce the intensity of the war between the individual and his society. Since criminality is an outgrowth of "undue" restriction of the individual by society, it is not logical to restrict the criminal further in attempts to correct him. Probation and parole are, then, corrective, even if they are only less restrictive than imprisonment. Similarly, in recent years, adherents of the clinical principle have emphasized the importance of making the prison itself less restrictive than formerly, presumably on the assumption that a "relaxed discipline" or "therapeutic climate" will enable inmates better to "act out" and in other ways adjust to the restrictions of society.

As is the case with the group-relations principle, scientific techniques for implementing the clinical principle within probation and parole systems have not been invented. We learn that offenders are to "gain insight," "relieve emotional tensions," "sublimate," etc.; but we do not know precisely how this is to be done. Similarly, we must know how, or whether, these processes produce anticriminality or, at least, noncriminality. Even if we had a precise statement of how to rid criminals of emotional tensions, for example, this action might have little to do with changing the criminality of behavior.

Most "correctional techniques" used in prisons are consistent with the clinical principle only in very indirect ways. It may be hypothesized that academic and vocational education are effective only to the extent that they permit the individual to express himself, sublimate antisocial tendencies, or escape from the restrictions on an uneducated person. It is not sufficient merely to implant knowledge or vocational skills; the education in a few cases might be effective because it alleviates, partially at least, the criminals' personal psychological problems. Similarly, labor in prisons is corrective largely to the extent that it enables individual inmates to escape from the rather harsh, restrictive, unstimulating environment which characterizes many institutions.

Individual therapy and group therapy are, of course, consistent with the clinical principle and have been introduced into correctional work by adherents of the second type of personality theory. Group therapy, for example, both enables and forces the participants to "get beneath the surface," "adjust to reality," identify their individual traits in terms such as "resentment of authority," "feelings of guilt," "frustration," and "oedipus complex," and to dissipate the "tensions" and "anxieties" arising from such traits.[23] In the words of one writer, "the future of group therapy in correctional work is bright because it offers help to a greater number of individuals and permits the release of pent-up hostility and aggression which, among more aggressive groups, frequently breaks out in open conflict."[24]

## CONCLUSIONS

The foregoing discussion has led to the rather obvious conclusion that most of the "techniques" used in "correcting" criminals have not been shown to be either effective or ineffective and are only vaguely related to any reputable theory of behavior or of criminality. To a degree, this is a consequence of the kinds of theories we have, as well as of the vested interests practical men and others have in the administration of specific kinds of programs. Many of the techniques consistent with the group-relations principle and the theory on which it is based could not be implemented in a society where correctional workers, like other men, work only an eight-hour day and forty-hour week. And many of the "diagnoses"

which are consistent with the clinical principle and its theory
call for techniques and/or programs which no correctional
agency could possibly afford. What is needed is a correctional
technique which is explicitly based on a theory of behavior
and of criminality and which can be routinely administered
by a rather unskilled worker in the framework of the eight-
hour shift. Caution is needed, however. Insulin and electric
shock treatment is more popular in state mental hospitals than
is individual psychotherapy, but this greater popularity is not
necessarily attributable to the fact that shock therapy is more
effective or more consistent with behavioral theory. Rather, it
probably is popular because it can be both routinely and
cheaply administered.

# NOTES

SOURCE: *Law and Contemporary Problems*, 23 (autumn 1958), 754–71.
  1. Robert G. Caldwell, *Criminology* (New York: Ronald, 1956), 427;
     Walter C. Reckless, *The Crime Problem*, 2nd ed. (New York: Apple-
     ton, Century, Crofts, 1955), 559.
  2. Harry E. Barnes and Negley K. Teeters, *New Horizons in Criminol-
     ogy*, 2nd ed. (Englewood Cliffs: Prentice Hall, 1951); Ruth S. Cavan,
     2nd ed. *Criminology* (New York: Thomas Y. Crowell, 1955); Mabel
     A. Elliott, *Crime in Modern Society* (New York: Harper, 1952);
     Edwin H. Sutherland and Donald R. Cressey, *Principles of Criminol-
     ogy*, 5th ed. (Philadelphia: Lippincott, 1955); Donald R. Taft, *Crimi-
     nology*, 3rd ed. (New York: Macmillan, 1956).
  3. Talcott Parsons, "Suggestions for a Sociological Approach to the
     Theory of Organization, II," *Administrative Science Quarterly*, 1
     (September 1956), 225.
  4. See Emile Durkheim, *The Division of Labor in Society* (Glencoe:
     Free Press, 1949), 70–110.
  5. John Bartlow Martin, *Break Down the Walls* (New York: Ballantine
     Books, 1954).
  6. Benjamin Karpman, "Criminality, Insanity, and the Law," *Journal
     of Criminal Law and Criminology*, 39 (January–February 1949), 584.
  7. See, for example, Max Grünhut, "Statistics in Criminology," *Journal
     of the Royal Statistical Association*, 114 (1951), 139; Thorsten Sellin,
     "The Significance of Records of Crime," *Law Quarterly Review*, 67
     (October 1951), 496, and, "The Measurement of Crime in Geo-
     graphic Areas," *Proceedings of the American Philosophical Society*,
     97 (1953), 163.
  8. See Donald R. Cressey, "The State of Criminal Statistics," *NPPA
     Journal*, 3 (July 1957), 230.
  9. At least one school of thought maintains that public employees are
     not mere "servants" or agents of public purpose; they are, on the

contrary, expected to have their own views of their mission and of appropriate policy. See Monypenny, "The Control of Ethical Standards in the Public Service," *Annals of the American Academy of Political and Social Science,* 297 (1955), 98.

10. Cf. Cressey, *op. cit.,* 241.
11. Sutherland and Cressey, *op. cit.,* 3.
12. Alfred H. Stanton and Morris S. Schwartz, *The Mental Hospital* (New York: Basic Books, 1954), 37–38. See also, Donald R. Cressey, "Rehabilitation Theory and Reality, II, Organization and Freedom," *California Youth Authority Quarterly,* 10 (summer 1957), 40.
13. Dorwin Cartwright, "Achieving Change in People: Some Applications of Group Dynamics Theory," *Human Relations,* 4 (1951), 381.
14. Sutherland and Cressey, *op. cit.,* 74–81.
15. Sheldon and Eleanor T. Glueck, *Delinquents in the Making* (New York: Harper, 1952), 162–63; Ruth Jacobs Levy, *Reductions in Recidivism Through Therapy* (1941), 16, 28.
16. Edwin J. Lukas, "Crime Prevention: A Confusion in Goal," in Paul W. Tappan (ed.), *Contemporary Correction* (New York: McGraw-Hill, 1951), 397.
17. Lloyd W. McCorkle, "Group Therapy in the Treatment of Offenders," *Federal Probation,* 16 (December 1952), 22.
18. In the writer's statement on how to change criminals in a manner consistent with the differential-association theory, it was necessary to *assume* that "small groups existing for the specific purpose of reforming criminals can be set up by correctional workers and that criminals can be induced to join them." Donald R. Cressey, "Changing Criminals: The Application of the Theory of Differential Association," *American Journal of Sociology,* 61 (September 1955), 116.
19. Sutherland and Cressey, *op. cit.,* 522.
20. Donald R. Cressey, "Contradictory Theories in Correctional Group Therapy Programs," *Federal Probation,* 18 (June 1954), 20.
21. See the discussion by Robert G. Hinckley and Lydia Hermann, *Group Treatment in Psychotherapy* (Minneapolis: University of Minnesota Press, 1951), 8–11.
22. See Marshall B. Clinard, "The Group Approach to Social Reintegration," *American Sociological Review,* 14 (April 1949), 257; S. R. Slavson, *An Introduction to Group Therapy* (New York: The Commonwealth Fund, 1943), 1; William C. Menninger, *Psychiatry in a Troubled World* (New York: Macmillan, 1948), 316.
23. See McCorkle, *op. cit.;* S. R. Slavson, "Group Psychotherapy in Delinquency Prevention," *Journal of Educational Sociology,* 24 (1950), 45; Justin K. Fuller, "Group Therapy for Parolees," *Prison World,* 14 (1952), 9–11.
24. L. C. C. Kesselman, "Book Review," *International Journal of Group Psychotherapy,* 2 (1952), 194.

# 18

## SOME REFLECTIONS ON THE ROLE OF CORRECTIONAL RESEARCH

*Alfred C. Schnur†*

### INTRODUCTION

Laws are broken millions of times each year. As one consequence, thousands of convicted law violators are turned over to correctional agencies. For what proximate and ultimate purposes have these thousands been convicted? Just what is to be done with them? Society does not seem to know. Except for apparent satisfaction with measures short of extermination or life quarantine for most offenders, there seems to be no clear-cut agreement as to ends and means to ends. Almost all the objectives ever propounded and almost all the measures ever applied in dealing with nonconformists since the beginning of recorded time are still employed today in the management of law violators. Consequently, many different and often incompatible purposes are served, and many different and conflicting techniques are utilized.

Although society does not seem to know what it really wants, correctional agencies are, nonetheless, obliged to make decisions. Both by their action and inaction, these agencies necessarily define objectives and the means of attaining them with the resources provided and within the constraints imposed by society. Thus, albeit fortuitously, correctional agencies profoundly affect, not only the convicted law violator, but free society, since virtually all convicted law violators eventually re-enter free society.

Correctional agencies have a tremendous range of discretion in their management of convicted law violators, and al-

† Alfred Schnur is a professor at the School of Police Administration and Public Safety at Michigan State University.

though they never have the benefit of society's consensus in exercising this discretion, they frequently incur its adverse criticism. Ironically, there seems to be a general unawareness that much of the confusion and inconsistency in correctional objectives and the vacillation in implementing these objectives is directly attributable to society's indecision regarding the criminal and its failure to provide the means to utilize existing knowledge or to acquire further knowledge of the variables of crime to permit optimal treatment.

## SOME LIMITATIONS OF RESEARCH

As research has helped in so many other areas, so in corrections can it help to solve the problems of defining and achieving objectives in the treatment of convicted law violators. The role of correctional research, however, is fraught with possibly serious misunderstanding. It is not a panacea for correctional problems—although some correctional administrators expect it and some "researchers" claim it to be. In and of itself, it will not, for example, eliminate recidivism, nor should it be expected to do so. The correlations (and intercorrelations) of the variables of recidivism may, of course, be revealed through research, as may the conditions under which recidivism increases and decreases; but whether this knowledge, if discovered, should be used and how it should be used are matters involving values which correctional policy makers and budget makers—not research scientists—must decide. The research scientist can help only by indicating the implications, the consequences, the costs, and the compatibility of possible decisions. In other words, research, alone, cannot actually make decisions regarding correctional means and ends; but research is the only way in which the knowledge necessary for rational decisions can be secured.

Research, too, will not always turn up manipulatable explanations for consequences. For example, previous criminal record has been found sufficiently often to pass the one-per-cent test of statistical significance to be generally accepted as one

of the variables associated with recidivism. It is, however,
obviously a variable about which nothing can be done, as
such, in the case of a man with an extensive criminal record.
This is also the case with another variable—the age at which
the first crime was committed. Both of these variables represent accomplished, unalterable facts and cannot be undone.
But they both constitute, along with other factors, clues of
pertinence in making decisions about placement in various
treatment programs and in estimating risks of recidivism, if
and when the offender is released from a correctional institution.

Although objective findings disclosed by research may be
unpleasant, this does not alter the fact of their existence, their
consequences, or their truth. Many ideas based on these findings, however, are found "unworkable," not because of any
inherent fault, but because hostile individuals tamper with the
necessary conditions for their proper operation. Examples of
this are often seen when, as a consequence of prison riot or
other scandal, personnel representing the new penology are
employed to institute reforms. Unfortunately, not all of the
new staff may truly reflect the new penology, and not all of
the old staff reflecting the old penology may be replaced.
Those who are devotees of the old penology may busy themselves with sabotaging new ideas by failing to carry out orders,
by initiating conflicting policies, and by creating situations to
discredit and embarrass the new staff. By these intrusions,
they may prevent the creation of the necessary conditions for
the utilization of the new penology.

Research which confirms the popular is often popular; that
which does not is frequently discredited on emotional grounds.
For example, let us assume that research has discovered that
whipping men for their misbehavior has a beneficial effect
upon the recidivism rate. This conclusion would probably be
accepted or rejected upon the basis of whether or not one
did or did not believe in whipping, on grounds quite unrelated
to its effectiveness as a correctional instrument. There would
probably be individuals who would not whip, no matter how
effective it might be discovered to be, because they just did

not want to whip. This, of course, would not alter the effectiveness of whipping as a corrective device.

Another source of difficulty for researchers is the desire of most laymen for definite answers, not statements of probability. Statistical analysis, however, produces only the latter. These conclusions are, nevertheless, exact in a scientific, if not a lay, sense, and they advance knowledge by enhancing the accuracy of decision-making and promoting greater understanding and control of the variables of correction. In the prediction of parole and postparole behavior, for example, although the devices produced by research leave much to be desired, they do augur the possibility of tremendous advancement, since even these inferior instruments have never failed to surpass the common-sense decisions of the men who have tried to best them.

Research is neither moral nor immoral. It is amoral. Its findings can just as easily be used to defeat as to achieve any currently selected correctional ends. There is nothing about research, as such, that ensures that its findings will be properly understood and interpreted, or even used to serve one particular goal. As a case in point, let us consider the research that has been conducted on parole and postparole behavior. This is probably the most frequently researched area in corrections—at least the most published. The researching of the variables of parole and postparole behavior has produced a variety of instruments that can be used—and misused—in achieving particular correctional goals—say, the minimizing of recidivism. Many of these do a sufficiently good job in forecasting to pass the one-per-cent test as well as the five-per-cent test of statistical significance. This means that correctional research has enabled such accurate forecasting of parole and postparole behavior that its explanation on the basis of luck (chance) is too remote for rational men to accept.

This knowledge can, of course, be used in widely divergent ways. A parole board can use this information to reduce the recidivism rate of parolees to a minimal level, for example, by releasing only those men who are almost certain to be successful, allowing the rest to serve out their sentences. This may, of course, increase the over-all recidivism rate of the correctional system; but it will also make the parole board and its parole supervision system appear to be very good, in one sense, because they would be dealing only with successes. This appearance, naturally, would be specious, being simply a reflection of selection (i.e., men with built-in probabilities of success, whether paroled or not) and having nothing to do with any causation that might be credited to the parole board action or parole supervision.

On the other hand, a parole board can use the same information to maximize recidivism by releasing only men who are almost certain to fail. Although such use is not probable, it could happen particularly if, by a curious set of circumstances, there were one parole board member, or a whole parole board, who would like to discredit parole in the public eye through high failure rates.

As a third possibility, a parole board might have so much faith in parole that it would regard it as the only mechanism by which men should be released from prison. As a consequence, it would seek to grant parole to as many men as possible. Feeling that the public would tolerate only a certain amount of parole violation, however, it would first determine the critical point and use this and the violation rate as guides for its decisions.

To reject men for parole on the basis of their probability of success may not, incidentally, be the way to minimize the over-all recidivism rate for the whole correctional system. It may very well be the case that the man with a low probability of success on parole would have an even lower probability of success if not paroled. Since parole boards only determine the timing of one kind of release and do not usually have the power to remand men to life quarantine, since virtually all men are released at the expiration of sentences, the relevant question, if minimizing recidivism is the objective, is to determine when and how men should be released to maximize lawful behavior, and then to act accordingly.

Most parole-prediction instruments are built out of zero order correlations, without regard to intercorrelations. This could lead, through misinterpretation, to misuse. For example, the age at release has often been found to be related to success after release—the older, the better. This might result in older men being given preference in release simply because they are older. This is what could happen by using studies that have not addressed and solved the problems of intercorrelations. Such arbitrary misuse of the zero order correlations would be a gross error, since other studies that have considered intercorrelations have found that the association between age and success disappears when previous criminal record is held constant—that is, the relationship between age and recidivism is simply a reflection of previous criminal record (which, of course, may be a reflection of something else not yet included in research studies of the variables of recidivism). Too much has frequently been attributed to these zero order relationships. Until there are adequate studies conducted using more meaningful data with multiple-correlation analysis of an appropriate type, zero order relationships must be understood as being possibly no more than mere indicators of recidivism. This does not mean that such findings are not useful as selection instruments, but only that the basis for explanation and selection may be simply the score indication, and not the factor upon which the score is based.

Some of the unfounded criticisms of prediction instruments are simply a consequence of their misuse—not a fault of the instrument, but a fault of the users who drew conclusions that were not warranted. For example, some have interpreted a high success score for parole as indicating a lesser need for close supervision than a lower score. Such a high score could, however, just as well mean a high probability of success only if there is close supervision. Since studies of parole have not researched the relationship of supervision to success, it is premature to use these prediction tables as supervision guides. For all we now know, men with low success scores may have low scores because they are of the type that are likely to be oversupervised, not because they are of the type that are likely to be undersupervised.

## SOME POSSIBLE RESEARCH AREAS

The correctional process—probation, institutions, parole—is operated in relative ignorance today. The convicted law violator is subjected to this process because of his inability to adjust to the professed norms of society. The correctional worker does not know how to secure an adjustment for him, as is evidenced by the inexact estimates that have been made of the effectiveness of the correctional process. Correctional decisions are made upon the basis of blind hunch, faith, intuition, whim, dramatic circumstances, and so-called common sense, when they should be made upon the basis of the *uncommon* sense that emerges from a statistical analysis of data describing the offender and the process. The kind of analysis that has been successful in enabling rational decisions to be made in other areas of life cannot be made in the correctional process, however, because the research that is needed has simply not been done.

No research has been done to date that enables us either to say that one treatment program is better than another or to look at a convicted law violator and say this is the treatment he needs. There is no evidence that probation is better than institutions, that institutions are better than probation, or that parole is better than escape. (There are, for example, many dramatic instances of escapees who, having successfully reformed themselves without benefit of casework, have attained distinguished positions in their communities.) At the present time, there is no evidence that being arrested and being subjected to the correctional process aborts criminal careers or has a deterrent effect upon other potential criminals. There might even be less crime if nothing were done about it. Research could possibly shed some light, but no research conducted to date answers these questions.

Much research has been done to differentiate successful from unsuccessful probationers and successful from unsuccessful parolees. As a consequence of this research, it is possible to answer the question: How do successes differ from failures?

But it is not possible, because of the way the research has been conducted, to say that the particular treatment researched is better or worse than some other program. Nor is it possible to say, now that it is known how the successes and failures differ, how the chances for success can be increased or decreased, because the factors that have been studied cannot be manipulated—they have already arranged themselves and cannot be altered in any way. In fact, in one state where prognosis is required, it is possible to make the prognosis before the convicted law violator comes to prison as accurately as if it were made the day before he left prison, because none of the experiences within the prison are taken into account in distinguishing between successes and failures. The predictive factors are things that occurred in his life before he ever came to prison and are things about which nothing can be done.

Recommendations for expensive treatment have frequently been made. Although some convicted law violators may require such treatment, it would probably be wide of the mark for many others. Instead of trying to give all convicted law violators a little of every kind of treatment in the hope that some exposure to it will be effective, effort should rather be made to determine what treatment is best, under what conditions, and for what type of person, so that each may get enough of the kind of treatment he needs—if treatment is his need—for it to take effect. These things can be objectified and studied if the effort is taken.

What is needed is ongoing research of a character that analyzes all the effects of all the presently available treatment techniques for all those undergoing treatment. This analysis is the only kind of analysis that will enable decision makers to act intelligently. Such research, however, will not answer the question: What is the best thing to do with this man? It will only tell what is the best thing to do with what is now being used.

The only adequate way to ascertain the relative value of the various kinds of treatment now in operation is to take a number of offenders at the earliest point of contact before conviction, preferably at the arrest level—earlier, if there were any way of doing it—and begin scientific observations. The offenders should be closely studied, differentiated into types, and followed forward for a number of years subsequent to the cessation of any legal control over them by the state. Since sentencing practice is such a haphazard procedure at present, it is to be expected that most of the various treatment types will be represented in nearly all of the dispositions available to the court and in all of the varieties of subsequent treatment given these offenders. Such a research project should exercise no control over the management of the offender with respect to the kinds of experiences that he will have, but should rather be concerned with rigorous observation. An easy, but empty, objection to such a procedure is that by the time such research has been completed, corrections will have moved ahead and will be using new and different procedures. Although change in the correctional process is to be desired as the years roll by, it is the observation of practitioners in the field that the Declaration of Principles, enunciated in 1870 at the first Congress of Correction in Cincinnati, has not yet been fully effected.

This analysis of the treatments which are being used at the present time should be supplemented by experimental research of treatment techniques not now being used, so that the old can be abandoned, changed, or amplified, and the new adopted, as indicated by their effectiveness as drawn from an adequate research analysis.

The lack of meaningful research regarding the merits of the various kinds of treatment constitutes an inhibiting factor in the progressive development of prison administration. Those who are dissatisfied with current prison operational methods and who feel that they should reflect our growing knowledge of human behavior in noncorrectional settings are at a loss to prove the validity of their beliefs. Conclusive evidence, one way or the other, is not currently available. The consequence is that the new penology and the old penology are discussed with heat at professional meetings, and decisions are made, not upon the merits of the situation, but upon the basis of who is in authority and whether or not persons can be converted to a particular belief upon no more than faith.

One valuable kind of research that is gaining popularity is an analysis of the prison community as such. This subject is probably as pertinent a consideration in determining the effectiveness of a particular treatment program as is the structure of the civilian community that is trying to implement it. It is possible—even probable—that, given the same personnel and program, but given divergent structures in the prison community, the success consequences of a particular program would vary. The social interactions among inmates and between inmates and civilians need further consideration in conducting treatment evaluation research.

Correctional authorities are losing much valuable material and information by not instituting parallel research evaluation programs to determine the adequacy of each new idea put into practice, for there is no other way of gauging an idea's worth. An enterprising organization would be well advised to experiment with new ideas on a small scale, with research to determine the merits of each, rather than sweepingly to overhaul its whole correctional program before the worth of the proposed innovations has been established.

Standards of evaluation with reference to other than recidivism rates are also needed. For example, the full implications of an industrial operation within an institution should be investigated to ascertain whether or not other activities could be more beneficially carried on in its stead. Thus, if it costs an institution more to manufacture an item than to purchase it on the open market, the institution might well apportion the inmate time, staff, and equipment to other activities that would be more worth while from a financial standpoint as well as from one of successful adjustment after release.

One of the main deficiencies of correctional research is that so many projects are conducted as though no research had been done before, as though the researcher were ignorant of previous research. The only contribution of much correctional research, therefore, is to confirm earlier research findings. This may have a disguised value, however, since certain comparisons with respect to the stability of predictive variables can then be made. But these comparisons cannot be made without serious qualification. There is some variation in the definition of what constitutes success and what constitutes failure, and enough variation in the particular factors studied, the way in which the factors are defined, the time period, and the kind of samples studied to render the results of different studies not strictly comparable. It has been observed, however, that even where the studies are sufficiently similar for comparisons to be made, certain factors are negatively related with success in one study, positively related in another, and unrelated in yet another. It has also been observed that some factors are never significantly associated with success in any study and that some factors are always related with success in every study. A useful analysis for future research would, therefore, be to compare the findings regarding particular factors and to state the limitations of the comparisons. It might be profitable to set up as adequate a research design as possible, with as objective definitions as possible of the variables included in these studies, with as much benefit taken of new statistical techniques as possible, to see whether such general comparisons can be confirmed. It would be more valuable if this could be done by several different investigators, in different jurisdictions, during the same time interval, in exactly the same way—and the results could then be compared.

Perhaps what is needed as much as research of the field variety is an investigation and analysis of the research that has been done—the questions that have been asked, the answers, and the associations that have been established. This would constitute a springboard for future research. At the present time, there is no place in which correctional research findings are co-ordinated, no easy means of referring to the findings on particular factors. The findings from correctional research today, where ascertainable, represent a veritable crazy quilt. If it were possible to map out the correctional process in all its variations and then mark the points that have been researched and the significance of the findings, there would doubtless be great embarrassment at the meager results of the characteristic sporadic *ad hoc* studies. If all of the correctional research that has been done could have been concentrated upon the total correctional process within one system, we would probably be in a better position than we are today with our present piecemeal knowledge. It is always true, of course, that research projects raise more questions than they answer; it is a shame, however, that the ratio of answers is so small for the field of corrections.

This is not to say, of course, that the research that has been done to this point, if utilized, would not improve correctional operations today. Some of it certainly would. In fact, this haphazard pattern has produced several interesting observations that would not have been possible had research been concentrated upon one system. Certain variables have been studied with reference to almost similar problems in many of the states of the United States and in many of the Western European countries. It is interesting to note that the association between almost similar variables and almost similar definitions of adjustment has been in the same direction, and upon occasion, the coefficients have been identical. Of course, this is something that could have happened by chance. It is quite unlikely, however (and, of course, this could be tested statistically), that essentially the same findings should have emerged in so many places by chance. Analysis may reveal certain universals for prediction systems. At least, variables would be suggested that should be included in any future project attempting to make analyses.

## SOME OBSTACLES TO RESEARCH

Correctional research, of course, has all the problems involved in other research in human behavior. It has, moreover, the problem of contending with the peculiar control over the research data exerted by official agencies. Correctional researchers, in addition to the task of resolving the problem they are addressing, also are confronted with the task of piercing the iron curtain of a certain kind of officialdom. Research really should be easier to conduct in correctional settings than elsewhere because the convicted law violators that constitute the data are controlled; but because officialdom defines the ways in which the data under control can be handled, correctional research is often made unnecessarily difficult. Much research that could have been very meaningful has been frustrated because the original research design was altered by the correctional agency—often with the explanation (excuse) that such activity would either be disturbing to the security of the institution or damaging to the treatment program of the institution.

Chief, perhaps, among the many obstacles to the acceptance of correctional research is the fact that many agencies are defensive about their work. The characterization of their efforts as ineffective or unwarranted is interpreted as a personal affront. Consequently, they resist research findings unless they accord with their preconceived notions.

Some correctional administrators, on the other hand, are interested in research—that is, until they learn what it costs and how long it takes to secure answers. They are impatient and unwilling to pay the freight. Upon occasion, correctional administrators are so disturbed by a problem, an impending explosion, that they feel forced to turn to research for help. But then they want their answers yesterday, and they want them cheap. Research, however, cannot be tailored to meet the emotional needs of a desperate administrator. Scientific methods cannot be short-circuited. There are no bargain days for methodology.

Each classification used in preparing data constitutes a hypothesis. The validity and reliability of classifications affect the research conclusions. How reliable and valid are the classifications recorded by the correctional personnel? How much of the variation in data is to be explained by variation in the men who prepared the records, rather than by variation in the variable itself? The typical records found in correctional systems are practically useless for research purposes. They are often not worth the time and money it takes to analyze them. The lack of standards in recording is strikingly apparent when one is dealing with a recidivist with experience in several different prisons. The current prison observes him, prepares records, makes a diagnosis, and plans treatment. While much of this is in process, the current institution is awaiting the receipt of records about him from the other institutions in which he has been confined. When the various records are compared, there is so little consistency, it is often to be wondered if all these institutions were dealing with the same person. Human nature does change, but there are certain things that should remain constant from one setting to another.

Research utilizing existing records has demonstrated the inadequacy of such records, not only for research purposes, but for administrative purposes. The decisions made by administrative agencies in working with these convicted law violators are at least as important as the uses made of these data for research purposes. Record-keeping systems need tremendous overhauling to serve either administrative or research purposes. Possibly many of the erroneous common-sense generalizations made by men of experience are reflections of not just faulty thinking or the impossibility of analyzing a large number of variables mentally, but also the inadequacy of the data from which the common-sense observations are drawn.

Among the many inadequacies of correctional agency record data is the sheer absence of information. Often, when analyzing a case record, it is impossible to ascertain whether the reason for missing data is that the question was not asked, the question was inapplicable, or no information was available. The reasons for the absence of data, as well as the fact of its absence, are pertinent to research analysis. Researchers require assurance that the same questions were applied to all the cases. When there is no information in the record, there is an area of doubt.

Conclusions drawn from case studies merely represent a lower and more haphazard form of statistical analysis. Case studies of adequate quality are useful as a basis for designing a quantitative assessment of a problem. Often, however, case studies are not useful because persons making them are not sufficiently rigid and objective in securing data. Case studies that are not good enough for statistical processing really are not good enough for any kind of generalizing. Data that can be defined can be communicated and thereby be made publicly accessible. Such data can be analyzed. Data that are only privately accessible and cannot be defined cannot be made a basis for drawing reliable conclusions. Case studies tend to be interpreted according to the bias and training of the observer and not according to the data. It is very easy to find what one chooses to find in case studies. This does not mean, of course, that case studies should not be carried out; they should be carried out, however, only as a preliminary to statistical analysis.

Much statistical research has little significance because some people have been so eager to apply formulae to problems that they have not taken sufficient time to make a qualitative study of the problem. Time should be taken for study before developing formulae. Too often, many things are learned about a problem after the project has begun and it is too late to change the research design and start over; and many ideas of this type are never followed up because so many correctional research projects are one-shot efforts.

## SOME CAVEATS AND CONCLUSIONS

Some correctional agencies are reluctant to sanction research because of the many unqualified comparisons made of the success rates reported by research in various jurisdictions and the widespread conclusion that the success rate is an adequate indication of the relative worth of correctional agencies. Such comparisons, of course, are often unwarranted because success rates are affected by many variables that have nothing to do with the competence of personnel or the adequacy of the agency's program. Variations in success rates among different jurisdictions as reported by different researchers may simply be reflections of differences in the definition of success in the different studies, or differences in the adequacy of the data collected. Some studies have definitions of success so strict that if they were applied to the average man on the street, he would probably be classified as a failure. Other studies classify a man as a success if he has not been convicted of a crime subsequent to his release from the treatment program. If two jurisdictions were compared on success rates alone, the jurisdiction that had the researcher with the more rigorous definition would probably have a lower success rate than the one with the less stringent definition, even if the former had the better program. This would be even more probable if the researcher with the more rigorous definition of success also had intensively investigated to see if the men were successful and the researcher with less stringent definition relied solely upon the law enforcement records for his information. Differences in success rates may be more a reflection of differences in the definitions and in the thoroughness of research than a reflection of the relative effectiveness of various agencies in minimizing recidivism.

Ranking agencies in effectiveness on the basis of success rates may not even be warranted when the researches are conducted with the same definitions and the same thoroughness. This could be the case if some agencies had more offenders who were difficult-treatment types than the others had. This might affect success rates more than variations in quality of treatment. In order to compare agency effectiveness in various jurisdictions, it would really be necessary that the persons undergoing treatment in the various jurisdictions be social twins with respect to factors pertinent to success and failure. The treatment itself should be the only variable.

Total success rates reveal very little. What kind of people were these successes and failures to start with? For example, the higher or lower success rate of one probation department when compared with another may merely reflect a difference in judicial sentencing practice. One probation department may appear to be more successful simply because one judge was more cautious than another in granting probation. Possibly the more cautious and selective the judge, the higher the total success rate will be. Similarly, the probation department that operates in a community with a strict police department is more likely to have a case load with a large proportion of less serious offenders than the probation department that operates in a community with lax law enforcement. Consequently, cases of the former will have higher built-in probabilities of success—i.e., they will be more likely to be successes, no matter what kind of supervision they are given on probation.

Research reports should include a detailed description of the program that has been studied and of the setting in which it operated. This increases the value of the report and facilitates fairer comparisons of similar programs operated by different agencies. Too often it is assumed that if programs have the same name they are the same. Some correctional systems have programs in name only, and others have well-developed programs. A detailed description of just what the program is makes it possible for findings to be interpreted more meaningfully.

Despite the confusion of means and ends that characterizes corrections, research can be conducted that can facilitate the formulation of more rational decisions in the management of law violators. Although much more is needed and many problems in its conduct and the utilization of its findings are yet to be solved, completed correctional research has unquestionably advanced the understanding, prediction, and control of the variables of recidivism and has helped in the determination and the achievement of correctional goals.

# NOTES

SOURCE: *Law and Contemporary Problems*, 23 (autumn 1958), 772–83.

# PROBLEMS OF ORGANIZATION
## WITHIN THE PRISON

# INTRODUCTION

The next five selections revolve around the common theme of conflict, and, more specifically, the conflict that arises from the organizational character of contemporary correctional institutions. Though there are many "problems of the organization," such as the recruitment and retention of competent staff, interest here is focused on organizational conflict for several reasons. For one, conflict is so prevalent in the correctional organization that it sometimes obscures from the eyes of observer and staff member alike the existence of co-operation, co-optation, and other social processes in the prison setting. Secondly, many of the problems generated by organizational conflict impinge directly upon the major task of the institution. The defensive barriers that result from role conflicts among staff members, as well as the barricades arising from conflicts between staff and inmates, tend to be destructive of staff member interaction and communication. And thirdly, conflict within an organization is a major though often overlooked source of organizational change, even in the change-resistant correctional institution.

Much of the conflict within correctional institutions arises out of the bifurcation of organizational goals. Custody and treatment are presented as simultaneous, albeit sometimes differentially evaluated, goals for achievement, yet their achievement requisites tend to be contradictory. In his second contribution to this volume, selection 19, Zald explores these divergences in organizational goals and the resulting conflicts in role expectations, relying upon data collected from the institutions presented in selection 10. He bases his analysis on a "power-balance" model of conflict, which describes the pattern of conflict within a given institution by locating the sources and net distribution of salient power. Zald concludes tentatively that the intensity of organizational conflict depends in part upon the incompatibility of the two major goals of "keeping them" and "treating them," upon the extent of interdependence among the major power groupings of staff members, and upon the extent to which the organizational tasks have become routinized and ritualistic.[1]

In selection 20, Weber gives us further insight into the problem of organizational conflict by documenting somewhat phenomenologically the role conflicts encountered between professional and nonprofessional staff members of five juvenile institutions. The division of labor between professional and nonprofessional appears to be sound when one examines the formal level of organization. At the informal level, however, where the world of day-to-day relations exists, there is a tendency for the division to become a significant barrier to effective interaction between members of the two groups. In some of its aspects, the barrier is similar to that encountered between staff and inmate groups. Because of differences in value orientations, educational backgrounds and other sociocultural factors, the members of one group may have difficulty in understanding the functions and ultimate goals of members of the other group. In time, this absence of personalized understanding can lead to perceptions of the other as threatening to one's own values and goals, and in many cases even to one's position in the organization. As a response to these perceptions of "other," the staff member may become hostile, protective, or isolative, all of which interferes with constructive interstaff relations, and ultimately the primary goal of the organization suffers.

Grusky, in selection 21, approaches the study of role conflict in correctional organization through an analysis of the conflicts engendered among the officials of a prison camp by the introduction of a new formal goal. Grusky notes that, while inconsistencies in organizational goals may create role conflicts, the formal status of a given member of the organization will be fundamentally influential in determining the kind and intensity of conflict he experiences and the manner in which he responds to it. Supervisory and other administrative personnel will be expected to support all formal goals of the organization, at least publicly, regardless of any goal inconsistency. Lower-echelon personnel, on the other hand, may enjoy a greater latitude of expression. In addition, there is the constant possibility of personnel succession or replacement as a factor influencing adjustments to role conflict. In any organization, any member can be succeeded; when this happens an entirely new pattern of conflict and conflict responses can emerge, especially if the succession involves management personnel. Grusky was fortunate enough in his study to be present before, during, and after the occurrence of a major instance of administrative succession, and he was able to document the impact of the succession upon the established patterns of conflict adaptation.

Selection 22, by Cressey, examines again the problem of conflicting demands on organizational members which arise from diverse organizational, professional, and personal values. Concentrating his analysis on the "first line of contact" with the correctional client, Cressey compares the ambiguities and strains of role experienced by the guard in custody- and treatment-oriented prisons. In both cases the ambiguities and strains are great, but they are especially severe (sometimes functionally debilitating) in the treatment-oriented institution. And the more truly treatment-minded, in practice as well as principle, the organization becomes, the more painful and confusing are the guard's experiences of role conflict. In this setting the traditional role of the guard as a "turnkey" or "policeman" is not appropriate, and yet he lacks the necessary qualifications for acceptance as a purveyor of treatment. But, although he is properly neither turnkey nor therapist, he continues to serve as the first and most frequent line of interaction with the inmate.

The first four selections of "Problems of Organization Within the Prison" all seem to depict the prison as an organization of nearly total conflict. As Robert Presthus once pointed out, the evidence suggests that "the dedicated organization man is perhaps rarer than we have assumed."[2] This is not to say that conflict is an unexpected part of social organization. But correctional and other "totalized" institutions seem to be somewhat unique in the extent and nature of their internal conflicts. And, as the four selections demonstrate, excessive conflict can preclude achievement of the central goal of altering unacceptable behavior.

In selection 23, Ohlin offers some means to reduce role conflict in correctional organizations. Essentially, his suggestions consist of such methods as participative leadership, decentralized decision-making and task-force planning. The key to the solution of the problem is *involvement*. If all staff members can have free access to all information, can participate in all decision-making which will affect them in any way, and can feel they are members of an integrated, participative team effort, they are less apt to perceive differences in values as personally threatening and more likely to honestly attempt achievement of organizational goals. But the participative atmosphere must be real; efforts to fool middle- and lower-echelon personnel into compliance by using participation as a "gimmick" are seldom successful for any length of time.[3]

Of course, as several of the selections illustrate, the problem of role conflicts cannot be fully alleviated until the more basic contradictions in organizational goals are resolved. And resolution of these issues will entail a clear and unadulterated choice between either retributive, vengeance-oriented or therapeutic, change-oriented reactions to criminal behavior.

## NOTES

1. On this point of routinization and ritualism in task activity, see Daniel Glaser, *The Effectiveness of a Prison and Parole System* (Indianapolis: Bobbs Merrill, 1964), 137–39.
2. Robert V. Presthus, "Editor's Commentary," *Administrative Science Quarterly*, 4 (July 1959).
3. For a comprehensive discussion of these management techniques, some suggested sources are: Douglas MacGregor, *The Human Side of Enterprise* (New York: McGraw-Hill, 1960); Rensis Likert, *New Patterns of Management* (New York: McGraw-Hill, 1961); and, Mason Haire, editor, *Modern Organization Theory* (New York: John Wiley & Sons, 1959).

# 19

# POWER BALANCE AND STAFF CONFLICT IN CORRECTIONAL INSTITUTIONS

*Mayer N. Zald†*

Many observers have noted that correctional institutions are conflict-prone organizations. Powelson and Bendix,[1] and Weber,[2] among others, have described in detail the conflicts that develop between professionally trained treatment personnel—psychiatrists, social workers, and psychologists—and lay personnel—cottage parents, attendants, or guards. These conflicts arise out of the incompatible requirements of custodial and treatment goals. A custodial goal requires the staff to attempt to control and contain clients and leads to punitive control techniques and to authoritarian staff-inmate relations; whereas a treatment goal requires the staff to attempt to encourage positive individual change and, given contemporary theories of treatment, leads to an emphasis on nonpunitive control of inmates and to permissive and close staff-inmate relations. Since correctional institutions vary in the relative dominance of custody and treatment in their goals, it seemed likely that institutions might differ in their level and pattern of staff conflict. Using data from a comparative study of five correctional institutions for delinquents,[3] we attempt in this paper to account for some of these differences.

The goals of a correctional institution for delinquents can be located on a continuum[4] whose poles are custody and treatment, and will probably not be at either pole of the continuum, since society usually requires some attempt to implement both goals. Different positions on the goal continuum are reflected in the role requirements and role strain on the

† Mayer Zald is an associate professor in the Department of Sociology at Vanderbilt University.

staff.[5] Furthermore, and this is our main point, the position of an institution's goals on the continuum is a determinant of the *level* of conflict and of the *pattern* of conflict among the organization's employees.

As in any organization, conflict in correctional institutions occurs when there is competition for control of the operating practices and policies of the institution. This may include competition for control of the rules and policies governing staff-inmate relations or, more subtly, for control of the frame of reference used to define situations. Conflict within large-scale organizations is usually nonviolent and often covert, because membership in an organization restricts the legitimacy of property destruction, interpersonal violence, and overt refusal to follow directives. When we speak of conflict in correctional institutions, therefore, we are speaking of felt but not accepted frustrations or goal blockages of particular employees or groups of employees created by practices of other groups within the organization.

While conflict may develop over salaries and working conditions or out of personality incompatibility, here we are concerned with the conflicts specific to correctional institutions for delinquents and caused by their goals and structure. Briefly, we see the *level* of conflict in an institution as a function of several factors: (1) the extent to which organizational goals lead staff groups and individuals to pursue incompatible policies, (2) the degree of ambiguity in the relation of administrative means to organization ends, (3) the extent to which organizational behavior cannot be routinized but instead requires continuous choice and new decisions, and (4) the degree of interdependence of staff groups.

We conceive of the *pattern* of conflict as a function of the power balance among staff groups (such as cottage parents, social service workers, and teachers), the degree of interdependence and intercommunication among groups, and the differences in attitudes and values of these groups. Basic to our concept is the notion that the power of groups is related to the goals of the organization. In custodial institutions cottage parents are likely to have more power, and operational policies will be directed toward maintaining their position; in treatment institutions social service workers are likely to make many of the major decisions.

Organizational conflict was one of several problems investigated in this comparative study.[6] Both public and private and large and small institutions were included in the study. The goals of the institutions studied were at different points along the continuum. Questionnaires were completed by employees (staff) and inmates; historical documents and official records were examined; and observations of organizational procedures and extended unstructured interviews with key executives were conducted. In this paper we rely primarily on data obtained from the staff questionnaire and on observations and extended interviews.

First we briefly describe each of the five institutions studied to provide the reader with a perspective on the data. Second, we discuss the hypothesis pertaining to the level, of amount, of organizational conflict. Third, we present a paradigm for predicting patterns of staff conflict and data which test these predictions. Finally, we consider the implications that our discussion of conflict in treatment institutions has for organizations in general.

## DESCRIPTION OF INSTITUTIONS

The position of the goals of each institution on the continuum, the institution's size, and its control (public or private)[7] are presented in Table 1. We now briefly characterize

TABLE 1
CHARACTERISTICS OF INSTITUTIONS STUDIED

| Goals | Size | |
|---|---|---|
| | *Small* | *Large* |
| Custodial | | *Dick Industrial School* |
| | | 260 boys |
| | | 65 staff members |
| | | Public |

TABLE 1, *Continued*

| | | |
|---|---|---|
| Mixed | *Regis Home*<br>56 boys<br>13 staff members<br>Private | *Mixter Training School*<br>400 boys<br>177 staff members<br>Public |
| Treatment | *Inland School*<br>60 boys<br>40 staff members<br>Private | *Milton School for boys*<br>200 boys<br>177 staff members<br>Public |

the major orientation of each institution to provide a background for the data pertaining to conflict.

*Dick*[8] Industrial School stressed *discipline* in its program and had the most custodial goals of the institutions in the sample. Its rehabilitation program was summed up in its motto "Firmness, Fairness, and Faith," and the superintendent, a former state legislator and physical education instructor, felt that a program of hard work and discipline was more effective than any clinical treatment program. In fact, he insisted that he would not hire professionally trained social workers, because he thought they would disrupt institutional discipline. All persons working with boys were allowed to punish them physically, and major sanctions were applied to those who ran away—their heads were shaven and they were beaten with a paddle; they were put into an isolation cell and given only bread and water, and in addition were started over again on their term of confinement.

Although some efforts had been made to broaden the vocational training program, no other aspect of Dick's program had changed in recent years. The institution continued to operate with traditional means of rehabilitation—discipline, hard work, and limited education—governed by a basically custodial set of decision criteria.[9]

*Regis,* run by a Catholic *religious* order, and *Mixter,* a *mixed*-goal institution which had benign custodial policies, were located close together on the center of the goals continuum. We consider Mixter to be closer to the center of the continuum because of its multiple emphasis on custody *and* treatment. On the other hand, Regis was operated more like a residence and was not confronted to any great extent with the problem of implementing multiple goals of custody and treatment.

Regis was a small institution which stressed care and guidance in its official goal statements and attempted to provide a controlled environment for its clients. The boys went to school at some twenty schools throughout the city in which Regis was located, and the staff considered one of their prime objectives to be that of helping the boys to do better in school.[10]

The superintendent of Regis, though willing to have professional treatment personnel on his staff, insisted that their orientation be sympathetic to that of the religious order. In practice this meant that Freudian orientations were suppressed because the Freudian orientation was believed to be overpermissive, especially with regard to sexual behavior. In some respects, however, the program of Regis resembled that found in treatment institutions, since attempts were made to provide a wide range of activities which the boys would enjoy.

Where Regis was a small, private institution, which could select its clients and could send a boy back to court if he did not obey the rules, Mixter was the largest public institution in its state and was for some counties their last resource in handling delinquents. Mixter was often criticized by its neighboring citizenry and the press because of its high truancy rate. Mixter was benign in its custodial policies, refusing to allow its staff to use repressive sanctions. Its other major emphasis was on containing and controlling the clients, which limited it to low-risk rehabilitational programs.

The superintendent of Mixter, an educator who had been employed in both military and civilian prison systems, felt that he had continually to accommodate himself to custodial pressures, both from relevant external publics and from many of his staff members. Internally, the head of cottage life, who had a consistently custodial perspective,[11] was perceived by staff members and executives to be second in command to the superintendent, although not officially so designated.

Compared to the three other institutions, Milton and Inland were both institutions with predominantly treatment goals. *Milton* was a medium-sized public institution that stressed the therapeutic *milieu* technique, attempting to rehabilitate the delinquent through his relationships with the staff and through a carefully planned educational program. To implement its milieu treatment philosophy, it had established cottage committees composed of cottage parents and social service workers to discuss and make decisions about the program of each client. Although officially a social service worker was in charge of each committee, a high degree of consultation was maintained.

The superintendent at Milton was a former journalist and state administrator. Although he was strongly committed to treatment goals, his major functions were to maintain a sound relationship with various external groups and to promote harmony among the employees. Major internal control was given to a psychiatrist, who was in charge of all staff-inmate activity, and who was deeply committed to the milieu philosophy. Because Milton was a public institution, it had to be somewhat more custodial than Inland, but its directors considered its custodial goal to apply explicitly only to a few extreme cases.

*Inland* focused on *individual* treatment in a one-to-one relationship with a professional as its major rehabilitative tool. Its chief executives considered Inland to be best fitted for the care of psychoneurotic adolescents who needed to be away from home, and definition in terms of psychological need rather than legal status.[12] A majority of its clients, however, were court-committed delinquents.

The superintendent, a former minister and teacher of sociology, and the assistant superintendent, a clinical psychologist, were both firmly committed to treatment goals, although the superintendent sometimes supported a more custodial orientation in public relations programs over the judgment of treatment personnel. Since the superintendent defined his major role externally and had tense relationships with the staff, major internal control fell to the assistant superintendent.[13]

To summarize, our final ranking of goals of the institutions places Dick's goals at the custodial end of the continuum—at least compared with the goals of other institutions in this sample. Regis' goals come next, followed by Mixter's, which are here considered to be just to the custodial side of the center of the continuum (mixed-goal). Milton and Inland are clearly treatment institutions. The fact that one focuses on milieu treatment whereas the other focuses on individual treatment will be shown to be of major importance in accounting for the pattern of conflict.

## LEVEL OF INSTITUTIONAL CONFLICT

We predicted different levels of conflict for institutions with different goals. In institutions with predominantly custodial goals, criteria of effectiveness—such as low runaway rates—are easily established; programs are highly routinized; and staff interdependence is low, centering mainly around transferring clients from one supervisor to another. We would thus expect little conflict among the employees of institutions with custodial goals. As a correctional institution takes on treatment goals, however, professional treatment personnel must be added to the staff. Their perspectives often clash with those of custodial personnel. Furthermore, criteria of effectiveness are difficult to establish for treatment goals, since the success of rehabilitation can be established only over a long period of time and the efficacy of alternative policies and ways of handling delinquents are difficult to determine. Mixed-goal institutions are, therefore, likely to have a higher level of conflict than more custodial institutions. Even when institutions have predominantly treatment goals, the difficulties of establishing objective criteria of success and of dealing with the behavior problems of inmates lead to a continuing debate over means. Similarly, the individualized planning and lack of routinization required by treatment programs result in constant discussion and decision-making. Disagreements requiring adjustment occur continually. In predominantly treatment, as in mixed-goal, institutions, therefore, conflict is likely to be high.[14]

In order to obtain a quantitative measure of conflict, members of the staff of each institution were asked, "On the whole, would you say there is any tension between the following pairs of groups?"[15] The pairs listed were: (1) "teachers and social service workers," (2) "social service workers and cottage parents," (3) "cottage parents and teachers," and (4) "employees and the superintendent."[16] Respondents checked a five-point scale ranging from "a great deal of tension" to "no tension at all."[17] (Percentage distributions for each pair in each institution are presented in appendix A.)

In order to establish the over-all conflict level within each institution we excluded the "no" responses[18] and computed conflict indices by combining the amount of tension for pairs.[19] Two index scores were computed: the first index score included all four judgments of tension made by respondents; the second index score excluded the tension perceived between employees and the superintendent—it is a measure of intergroup tension. Conflict index scores are presented in table 2.

TABLE 2

COMBINED INDICES OF LEVEL OF CONFLICT

| Conflict index | Dick | Regis | Mixter | Milton | Inland |
|---|---|---|---|---|---|
| All pairs | 1.79 | 1.83 | 2.11 | 2.40 | 2.20 |
| All pairs except superintendent | 1.78 | 1.94* | 2.11 | 2.58 | 1.98 |

* Based on only two pairs, (1) cottage parents and social service, and (2) Regis Home and schools.

These computations show that Dick and Regis tended to have lower tension index scores than Mixter, Milton, and Inland, thus tentatively confirming our hypothesis. Although size may account for some of the variation, the differences among the institutions cannot be attributed only to the size of the institution.[20] Dick had a larger staff than Inland but had a lower tension level; while Mixter was larger than Milton yet tended to have a slightly lower conflict level. Furthermore, although Mixter had over four times as many staff members as Inland, its combined tension level for all pairs was approximately the same as that of Inland. Comparing Regis and Inland, we find that the level of conflict appears to be similar, if we exclude the superintendent-employee pair from the data. The data from Regis, however, are not really comparable, since they are based on only two pairs, one of which is not internal to the institution.

Our observational impressions tended to confirm these findings about the level of perceived tension. Especially at Dick, conflict was muted, and in conversations with staff it was difficult to elicit comments on the amount or issues of conflict. At Inland, Milton, and Mixter the staff readily supplied the investigator with comments about the sources of conflict. Moreover, as noted earlier, field observations indicated that at Inland superintendent-staff relations were tense, while at Milton superintendent-staff relations showed little tension or conflict. The quantitative indices reflect these differences. Scores on the second index are lower than on the first index at Inland and are higher at Milton, reflecting the different degrees of tension between superintendent and employees at the two institutions.

The quantitative data are supported by our observational impressions. We conclude that the more custodial institutions in our sample did have a lower level of conflict than the mixed-goal or treatment institutions.[21]

## PATTERN OF CONFLICT

### A Power-Balance Model

The position of an institution's goals on the continuum is related not only to the level of conflict but also to the power balance and patterns of conflict among the staff. If teachers, cottage parents, and social service workers have somewhat divergent goals or perspectives within an institution, then conflict is most likely between those who are unable to control the situation and those who are perceived as being in control of the situation.

Our basic model of patterns of conflict in correctional institutions for delinquents, which we call the power-balance model, is as follows: Since custodial institutions give more power to cottage parents and to custodial perspectives than do treatment institutions, we expect teachers and social service workers in custodial institutions to be in conflict with cottage parents but not with each other. The benign custodial institution, that is, the mixed-goal institution on the custodial side of the continuum, is likely to have a pattern of conflict similar to the custodial institution, differing only in that conflict is more intense. On the other hand, in individual-treatment institutions we expect teachers and cottage parents to be in conflict with social service workers but not with each other. In a milieu institution, where there is a greater sharing of power between cottage parents and social service workers and a team concept of organization, we expect teachers to conflict with cottage parents and social service workers, but there should be little conflict between cottage parents and social service workers. The model is summarized in the paradigm in table 3, which gives our predictions for the level of conflict for each pair of staff groups in the various institutions.

TABLE 3
PARADIGM OF CONFLICT PATTERNS: PREDICTED
LEVELS OF CONFLICT AMONG COTTAGE
PARENTS, SOCIAL WORKERS,
AND TEACHERS

|  | CONFLICT PAIR | | |
|---|---|---|---|
| INSTITUTIONAL TYPE | Cottage parents and teachers | Cottage parents and social service | Teachers and social service |
|  | CONFLICT LEVEL | | |
| Custodial and benign custodial | high | high | low |
| Individual treatment | low | high | high |
| Milieu treatment | high | low | high |

Two preconditions underlie this model, and when these preconditions are violated exceptions to the predicted patterns may occur. First, it is assumed that conflict requires some minimal interdependence among groups, the lower the interdependence, the less the conflict. If groups have little intercommunication, however, their members may not recognize the conflict even though the groups may be interdependent. For example, in a custodial institution teachers may have a more rehabilitative orientation than cottage parents, but, since teachers are isolated, their feelings of being frustrated by cottage parents may not be apparent to others.

Second, teachers, social service workers, and cottage parents are assumed to have conflicting perspectives and values. Organizational adaptation, however, may lead to the selection and socialization of personnel so that they accommodate to the dominant perspectives. For instance, the cottage parents at Inland and the social service workers at Dick had perspectives which supported the dominant orientation. In such cases conflict with dominant groups is not expected.

To evaluate the utility of our model, we must examine the actual power balance among staff groups in the sample. We must also examine the amount of conflict between each of the pairs in a given power balance (e.g., how much tension was perceived between themselves by the cottage parents and the social service workers). We have used an arbitrary criterion of 30 per cent or more in the "high" or "some" tension category for either partner to the conflict as representing high conflict. For instance, if 30 per cent of the teachers in an institution perceive high conflict with cottage parents but only 10 per cent of cottage parents perceive conflict with teachers, it is still considered to be a high-conflict situation. Field observations are also used both to examine the issues of conflict and its form of expression, and to validate our questionnaire data.

### The Power-Balance Model Tested

First, we must examine evidence for the assumption that power balances differ in institutions with different goals. Elsewhere we have discussed in detail the power balance actually found among staff groups;[22] here we touch only on the major trends. In general the data confirm our assumption of a relationship between institutional goals and the power of staff groups.

Table 4 presents the proportions of staff attributing high influence to cottage parents, teachers, and social service workers (counselors, social workers, psychologists).[23] It is clear that social service workers at the treatment institutions, Milton and Inland, were seen as having high influence by a larger proportion of staff than at other institutions. There is a decline in the perceived influence of cottage parent groups from Dick, the most custodial institution, to Inland, where individual treatment was stressed. At Milton, under the milieu principle, cottage parent influence was high. It is also clear that teachers were perceived as having little influence in any of the institutions.

## TABLE 4
### STAFF PERCEPTION OF POWER BALANCE

PER CENT OF STAFF PERCEIVING GROUPS
AS HAVING HIGH INFLUENCE

STAFF GROUPS

| | Dick (N=62) | Regis (N=9) | Mixter (N=155) | Milton (N=108) | Inland (N=37) |
|---|---|---|---|---|---|
| Cottage parents | 50 | 33 | 34 | 70 | 8 |
| Teachers | 23 | .. | 11 | 17 | 19 |
| Social service | 38 | 22 | 49 | 76 | 76 |

In table 4 there seems to be one exception to our assumption. At Mixter, the benign custodial institution, the internal ordering of groups indicates that a larger proportion of staff (49 per cent) perceived social service workers as having great influence than perceived the cottage parents (34 per cent) as having great influence. This must be seen, however, in the setting of the general policies and distribution of executive power at Mixter. There the head of cottage parents was second only to the superintendent in perceived power; twice as many employees perceived the head of cottage parents as having great influence as perceived the training director (the nominal second in command) or the head of social service as having great influence. Thus, while it is true that cottage parents were limited by rules and regulations, custodial definitions still reigned, although enforced through the head of cottage parents. While social service staff members might have been able to influence decisions about a boy's program, they had little official control over when a boy went home, and the social service department as a whole did not shape policy. Although the education and status of the social service worker carried some weight in any particular case, in terms of general policy, custodial cottage life requirements predominated. The influence pattern at Mixter was that which might be expected in an institution with goals near the center of the continuum.

Let us now look at the predicted and actual patterns of conflict in Dick, Mixter, Milton, and Inland. (Regis is excluded from this analysis, since it did not have teachers.) The results are summarized in table 5. Eight out of twelve predictions were correct: at Dick only one prediction was correct, at Mixter all three were correct, and at Milton and Inland two predictions in each were correct. The pattern of conflict in each of the institutions will now be discussed in detail. As we will show, three of the incorrect predictions resulted from the failure of the data to satisfy the predictions of the model, not from an inadequacy in the model.

*Dick.* From the power-balance model of conflict we expected social service workers and teachers in Dick, the custodial institution, to be in conflict with cottage parents but not with each other.

Although the general level of conflict at Dick was low, 40 per cent of the teachers perceived "some" or "high" tension with cottage parents and 30 per cent perceived "some" or "high" tension with social service. Neither cottage parents (9 per cent)[24] nor social service workers (0 per cent) perceived tension with the teachers. Furthermore, there was lit-

TABLE 5
SUMMARY OF PREDICTED AND ACTUAL
CONFLICT PATTERNS

| | CONFLICT PAIR | | |
|---|---|---|---|
| INSTITUTION* | Cottage parents and teachers | Cottage parents and social service | Teachers and social service |
| | CONFLICT LEVEL | | |
| *Dick* | | | |
| Predicted | high | high | low |
| Actual | high | *low*† | *high* |
| *Mixter* | | | |
| Predicted | high | high | low |
| Actual | high | high | low |
| *Milton* | | | |
| Predicted | high | low | high |
| Actual | high | *high* | high |
| *Inland* | | | |
| Predicted | low | high | high |
| Actual | low | *low* | high |

* Regis is excluded because it did not have three conflict pairs.
† Instances where predicted and actual outcomes are different are in italics.

tle perceived tension between cottage parents (18 per cent) and social service (0 per cent).[25] Thus, only the prediction of conflict between cottage parents and teachers turned out to be correct. However, by considering the amount of interdependence and the perspectives of staff groups, the deviations from the model in the other two cases can be explained.

What conflicts there were at Dick between teachers and cottage parents were based on the teachers' greater permissiveness and interest in rehabilitative educational activity. These differences were evident in at least three areas of organizational activity: (1) cottage parents stressed control of client movement while teachers tended to be lax in their watchfulness; (2) teachers felt educational activities should be given priority over work activities;[26] and (3) teachers felt some cottage parents were too harsh with the boys. These are standard custodial-treatment conflicts and need not be discussed further.

How do we account for the low conflict between cottage parents and social service and the higher conflict between social service and teachers? The issues between social service workers and cottage parents were, surprisingly, the reverse of what we would expect. For example, one cottage parent complained that the social service director and the chaplain did not spend enough time with the boys. He felt the boys needed counseling and wanted information which was not being provided by social service. The social service director, a former clothing salesman, and the chaplain supported custodial and disciplinary policies. These accommodations to the institution may also help to explain the conflict teachers felt with social service workers. Teachers and social service workers were, however, of similar educational and status backgrounds and interacted informally with each other. Little conflict was evidenced during the period of field observation, and it is not possible to conclude definitely that the nonrehabilitative orientation of the social service workers frustrated teachers' objectives.

It is likely that the accommodation of social service workers to the institution prevented the predicted pattern of conflict between cottage parents and social service workers from occurring at Dick. Since the social service director and the chaplain did not support a more permissive and rehabilitative program, a precondition for the operation of the power-balance model was not met. Moreover, the isolation of both teachers and social service workers from cottage parents minimized the emergence of overt conflict.

*Mixter.* Mixter was a benign custodial type of institution, and, although the over-all level of conflict was higher than at Dick, the pattern of conflict was expected to follow that predicted for custodial institutions. As predicted, teachers (57 per cent) and social service workers (88 per cent) conflicted with cottage parents (15 per cent, 30 per cent), while teachers (28 per cent) and social service workers (13 per cent) had little conflict with each other.[27]

While, as at Dick, teachers perceived tension between themselves and cottage parents, overt conflict was not high, and cottage parents perceived less tension than did the teachers.

The teachers had little formal or informal contact with the cottage parents and also had little influence in the institution. Furthermore, since they had little contact with the cottage parents, their only source of information about cottage parents was from the boys—who tended to tell "atrocity tales." They tended to work their seven-hour day and have little other involvement in Mixter, the issues of conflict between teachers and cottage parents being the traditional custodial issues.

By contrast, social service workers were in constant contact with the cottage parents and cottage-life department, and, although some social service staff supported the custodial program, the conflicts with cottage parents were more clearly evident than those of the teachers. Conflict between social service workers and cottage parents had been even more virulent during an earlier period, and this had led the superintendent to require that social service workers spend two hours a week in the cottages in order that they might learn to work with the cottage parents. To some extent, this led to an accommodation of the social service workers to the cottage parents, because the increased communication allowed them to appreciate the point of view of the cottage parents, not just of the boys. Few resources relevant to cottage parents were controlled by social service workers; therefore there was no reason for the cottage parents to accommodate to the social service workers. The conflicts between social service workers and cottage parents were also less than they might have been, because the head of cottage parents and his assistants handled many disciplinary problems without involving the social service workers. If the social service workers had been brought into these cases more often, they might have sided with the boys.

The pattern of conflict at Mixter conformed closely to what we expected. An important difference between Dick and Mixter, which helps account for the emergence of the predicted pattern of conflict at Mixter, lies in the greater power of social service staff. Mixter's social service workers were perceived by cottage parents as a competing power, while at

Dick social service workers did not present a threat to the dominant definitions or policies.

*Milton.* The power balances at Mixter, Dick, and Regis differed sharply from those at Inland and Milton in that the power of social service and the importance of treatment goals were clearly established. Our model of conflict led us to expect little conflict between social service and cottage parents at Milton, because they shared power and made joint decisions, while we predicted high conflict between teachers and both cottage parents and social service workers. The data indicate high conflict between all three groups:[28] teachers (67 per cent) and cottage parents (32 per cent); cottage parents (48 per cent) and social service (89 per cent); and social service (67 per cent) and teachers (67 per cent).

The conflict between teachers and the cottage committees —social service workers and cottage parents—was clearly the result of the low power of the teachers. The teachers had not been fully incorporated into the structure implementing the milieu treatment philosophy and thus were unable to influence the decisions of the cottage committees directly. The teachers felt that often, when a boy was sent back to the cottage for disrupting the school, the cottage committees would neither discipline the boy nor tell the teachers what action had been taken. As a result, they felt that they were left without adequate information. On the other hand, some cottage parents felt that teachers sent boys back to the cottages too quickly and were not patient enough with the boys.

More important for evaluating the adequacy of our model were the factors contributing to the maintenance of conflict between cottage parents and social service workers. The difficulty of integrating all cottage parents into the milieu structure seemed to be an important factor. Although the cottage parents in charge of each cottage, the cottage mothers, and the day cottage parents worked closely with social service staff, cottage parents who worked in the afternoon and evening had to deal with large groups of boys armed only with an injunction to "understand before you act." The head cottage parents and recreation men sometimes helped the other cottage parents in the evening, but the afternoon and evening cottage parents were not in close contact with members of the social service staff. In general, then, it was difficult to bring all cottage parents into committee structure.

Another factor contributing to the maintenance of tension was the inability of this institution to pay adequate salaries to cottage parents, making it difficult to attract personnel with compatible attitudes. While Inland used only college men, Milton's larger size and its location prevented it from relying on college men alone; nor did the executives think this would be desirable.

Finally, the very operation of the cottage committees contributed to the maintenance of tension. Disagreements and differences in perspective were easily brought into the open and expressed. Differences of opinion about the role of discipline and authority were thus projected into sharp focus.

However, the cottage committees had been effective in lowering the over-all level of conflict at Milton. Staff members reported that the institution was much more stable at the time of the study than it had been several years earlier, when the "professionals" and the cottage parents were in open conflict. Many staff members claimed that the higher level of conflict between social service workers and cottage parents at an earlier time had been reflected in tension among the boys; in recent years there had been a decline in fighting, property destruction, and general "acting out."

There was a direct relationship between the length of service of cottage parents at Milton and the tendency to perceive tension: Of the eight cottage parents who had worked at the institution for less than one year, only two perceived high tension; of the nineteen who had worked there between one and six years, eight perceived high tension; while of the eight who had worked there more than six years, seven perceived high tension. It is possible that the cottage parents with seniority had been sensitized to perceive tension by the older issues and conflicts. Although our data indicate that there was still conflict, it appeared to be less virulent than previously and was more often a disagreement over means than the earlier disagreements over basic aims.

Unification of the cottage committee also had changed somewhat the bases of differentiation in the institution, and, therefore, the bases of conflict. Although social workers and psychologists retained their professional identities, to some extent they gave up their departmental identities. The new lines of differentiation were between cottage teams. Within the limits defined by the institutional schedule and facilities, each cottage established its own rules of procedure and did its own programming. Since the cottages had different age groups and diagnostic problems, different procedures were felt to be necessary for each cottage. Cottage parents were encouraged to adapt formal procedures to their special needs. The organization into cottage committees meant that, instead of the professionals uniting against the nonprofessionals, the professionals faced each other across the boundary of the team, and identifications within the cottage committees were not uncommon. Conflicts of this sort among professionals did not affect the operation of the individual cottage committees and, therefore, as compared to departmental conflicts, might be expected to contribute less to institutional instability.

*Inland.* Because of Inland's focus on individual treatment we expected its teachers and cottage parents to conflict with social service workers but not with each other. The data indicate that there was little conflict between cottage parents (0 per cent) and teachers (18 per cent), while there was high conflict between teachers (56 per cent) and social service staff (50 per cent).[29] Contrary to our prediction,[30] however, there was little conflict between social service (0 per cent) and cottage parents (0 per cent). The model is thus only partially supported.

Conflict between teachers and social service at Inland involved issues central to an educational, as opposed to a psychotherapeutic, approach to rehabilitation. Although conflict had been somewhat lowered by indoctrinating teachers into psychodynamic theory, the "old guard" continued to believe that the clinical orientation was overly permissive and failed to establish occupational and life goals for the boys. Clinical focus on the resolution of psychological problems de-emphasized educational goals. Furthermore, even though the teachers admitted that the small size of classes at Inland was ideal for teaching, some continued to feel that their lack of authority and ability to discipline led to constant classroom disruptions and misbehavior.

While the teachers at Inland were in conflict with the social service staff, as expected, they were not in conflict with the cottage parents. Both teachers and cottage parents had little power in the institution, and, since they were not interdependent, there was little basis for strain or tension. Field observation revealed no overt conflict between cottage parents and teachers.

Why, contrary to our prediction, was there little conflict between social service and cottage parents? The field observations indicated that cottage parents did feel themselves to be under strain; the strain, however, did not evidence itself in overt conflict for two reasons. First, conflict was avoided by hiring young cottage personnel who accepted the clinical, permissive orientation. Second, cottage parents tended to have closer informal relationships with the social service workers than with the teachers. Moreover, in contrast to Mixter, the weekly meeting of cottage parents and social service workers contributed to the accommodation of the cottage parents to the social service workers. The status of the social service workers, the youth of the cottage parents, and the clear-cut treatment goal minimized conflict.

Although the social service workers had close informal relations with the cottage parents, they had no responsibility for the supervision of cottage parents or the management of the cottages. Disciplinary problems were handled by the assistant director or the head of cottage life; as a result social service workers were freed from decisions which might have led them to conflict with the cottage parents. At Inland, then, the pattern of conflict departed from that predicted by our model largely because the cottage parents did not have a custodial orientation.

## SUMMARY AND CONCLUSIONS

Two major conclusions may be drawn from this analysis of the level and pattern of institutional conflict. First, we may tentatively conclude that the level of conflict in correctional institutions is a function of their multiple goals, their vaguely specified means, the degree of interdependence of employee groups, and the degree of routinization. Mixed-goal and treatment institutions had a higher level of conflict than more custodial institutions.

Secondly, we have demonstrated the utility of a power-balance model of conflict in accounting for the patterns of conflict in correctional institutions. In eight out of twelve cases the conflict level between pairs was predicted by the power-balance model of conflict. In three of the cases in which the model was not successful in predicting the actual level of tension, its failure appears to have been, not the result of the model, but of the data to satisfy the preconditions of the model. That is, since social service workers at Dick accepted the dominant custodial perspectives and cottage parents at Inland accepted treatment perspectives, the necessary precondition of divergent values was not met. In the case of Milton we failed to take into account the effect of heightened interdependence in raising the potential of conflict and the persistence of divergent views when few criteria were available to establish the efficacy of alternatives. Although the model cannot be applied without knowledge of the relation of organizational adaptations to the preconditions of conflict, such as staff interdependence and divergent values of staff groups, the power-balance model can be a useful tool in predicting the patterns of conflict. A word of caution may be in order, however; power balance among groups is directly related to differences in institutional goals. The pattern of conflict reflects the over-all power balance among executives as well as the power balance among specific groups.

## The Problem-solving Organization

Consideration of the conflict over means that existed in the two treatment institutions leads us to a view of organization and organizational conflict which has not been well conceptualized in the literature. Much has been written about the advantages of involving lower-level staff in decision making.[31] In situations in which rational criteria exist and in which routinized programs are possible, such involvement of lower-level personnel may be partly a fiction or at best feasible only for a limited range of decisions, for in organizations with routinized techniques major decisions are usually made in the higher echelons. To be effective, however, treatment institutions, particularly those operating on a milieu principle, may be forced to allow decision making to occur on lower levels.

In this respect, milieu institutions depart sharply from our usual conception of bureaucratic organization, which assumes that routinized procedures are used and that the discretion of lower-level personnel is sharply circumscribed. From this point of view bureaucracies are considered as tools or machines for achieving ends. If the environment of such organizations were relatively stable and technology did not change, organizations would operate routinely.

Such a model, of course, is rarely approached; changes in the sources of supply, in the amounts and kinds of market demands, in the labor market, and in technology require organizational adaptation. Nevertheless, even granting the pervasiveness of informal organization, some organizations, for periods of time, may operate relatively routinely. Furthermore, many of these adaptational problems may have few or no consequences for the rank and file of the organization. We would suggest that the philosophy of milieu treatment requires such institutions to be continually solving problems, and the rank and file of the organization must be involved in this process.

Treatment institutions in general, and milieu institutions in particular, must continually adapt resources to the therapeutic needs of their inmates. Techniques of handling inmates and programs for each inmate must be established and co-ordinated among staff members. Techniques must be changed as inmates change and react to staff behavior. In other words, the organization is not turning out a standardized product with standardized means; neither the tasks nor the techniques lend themselves to uniform definition.

Individualized planning and programming require a larger staff to participate in the making of decisions. Lower-level staff must be consulted so that they can provide information for decisions, and also to ensure staff motivation to carry out organizational policy. In treatment institutions the absence of objective indices of staff performance requires staff members to be committed to goals if executives are to be sure that organization goals are pursued. In a factory, on the other hand, objective indices of production allow control from above without great commitment of lower-level staff—production failures can be met by sanctions. One way to ensure staff motivation is to involve them in the decision-making process, but involving lower-level staff in decision making may open up a wide range of problems for debate.

A third factor contributing to the problem-solving nature of milieu treatment organizations is the interpersonal basis of all service to inmates. As compared with organizations that turn out material products or offer only limited and specific services, the operation of milieu institutions, and correctional institutions in general, is based on interpersonal relationships. If these relationships are to be used for treatment gain, the organization must take into account the personalities and special competencies of, and attachments between, staff members and inmates. Where in many large-scale organizations the personalities and attachments of lower-level staff are considered to be irrelevant to organizational decisions, in treatment institutions staffing patterns and assignments must take into account and utilize the relationships existing between staff members and inmates. Personal criteria, therefore, enter into the realm of organizational decisions. On the executive level of many large-scale organizations, of course, such factors are likely to play a role, but in milieu institutions personality and interpersonal relationship factors are likely to enter into decisions even at the lowest level of the staff.

What are some of the consequences of operating as a continually problem-solving organization? Since there have been few, if any, studies of organizations from this point of view, we can only speculate. First of all, in a problem-solving organization, at least as exemplified by milieu treatment institutions, decision-making must be decentralized. If executives are actually to involve lower-level staff, more than token consultation must take place—real power to take action must be delegated. By careful selection and training of personnel, executives can ensure that lower-level staff members make decisions in accordance with over-all policy and goals. Despite this, some decisions will be made which the executive would have made differently. Paradoxically, the organization must give up control over some areas to achieve organizational goals. Failure to delegate control over decisions may result in cynicism and staff apathy. Executive control must take the form of specifying the intent and aims of policy and setting the limits of staff discretion.

Secondly, problem-solving organizations are likely to be conflict-ridden organizations. The opening up of organizational decisions to discussion and debate raises, or maintains, the level of conflict in the institution. Even if overt conflict is raised or maintained in problem-solving organizations, however, some kinds of tension may be lowered—those tensions that result from feelings of injustice and misunderstandings and that lead to subversion of goals and avoidance of rules. In any event, the conflict that results in a milieu treatment institution with carefully selected and trained personnel is likely to be different from that of the mixed-goal institution. First, basic disagreement about goals is less likely and conflict and debate operate more to adjust disagreements about means to the agreed ends. Secondly, greater involvement on the part of lower-level staff can be used to further and promote organizational activities. Although the milieu institution or the problem-solving organization may have a high level of conflict, it may be that the conflict is of a kind that works in the service of institutionalized goals rather than as a brake and impediment to organizational effectiveness.

## APPENDIX A
## PERCEPTION OF TENSION BETWEEN GROUPS
### (IN PER CENT)

| Conflict pair | Dick (N = 62) | Regis (N = 9) | Mixter (N = 155) | Milton (N = 108) | Inland (N = 37) |
|---|---|---|---|---|---|
| Cottage parents and teachers | | | | | |
| High tension* | 3 | .. | 7 | 9 | .. |
| Some tension | 13 | 22† | 16 | 37 | 8 |
| Little tension | 29 | 44 | 32 | 32 | 49 |
| No tension | 37 | 33 | 23 | 5 | 27 |
| Not answered | 18 | .. | 25 | 17 | 16 |
| Cottage parents and social service | | | | | |
| High tension | 2 | .. | 8 | 10 | .. |
| Some tension | 15 | 33 | 27 | 41 | 8 |
| Little tension | 27 | 33 | 26 | 28 | 46 |
| No tension | 37 | 33 | 15 | 9 | 32 |
| Not answered | 19 | .. | 25 | 12 | 14 |
| Teachers and social service | | | | | |
| High tension | 3 | .. | 1 | 9 | 8 |
| Some tension | 7 | .. | 14 | 35 | 27 |
| Little tension | 29 | 56‡ | 37 | 33 | 43 |
| No tension | 44 | 44 | 23 | 9 | 11 |
| Not answered | 18 | .. | 26 | 13 | 11 |
| Employees and superintendent | | | | | |
| High tension | 3 | .. | 8 | 3 | 27 |
| Some tension | 15 | 11 | 12 | 12 | 22 |
| Little tension | 29 | 67 | 36 | 42 | 24 |
| No tension | 37 | 22 | 21 | 30 | 14 |
| Not answered | 16 | .. | 21 | 14 | 14 |

Probability $< .05$ for each of the first three pairs, $> .05$ for the last pair; determined by Difference in Proportions Test, comparing those checking "little tension" or more at Dick and Regis with those in similar categories at Mixter, Inland, and Milton.

* "High tension" combines "a great deal" and "considerable" tension.
† Regis Home and schools substituted here.
‡ Social service and director substituted here.

# NOTES

SOURCE: *Administrative Science Quarterly*, 6 (June 1962), 22–49.

1. Harvey Powelson and Reinhard Bendix, "Psychiatry in Prison," *Psychiatry*, 14 (February 1951), 73–86.

2. George H. Weber, "Conflicts between Professional and Non-Professional Personnel in Institutional Delinquency Treatment," *Journal of Criminal Law, Criminology and Police Science*, 48 (May–June 1957), 26–43.

3. This study is part of a larger study of correctional institutions for delinquents being conducted under the direction of Robert D. Vinter and Morris Janowitz at the University of Michigan under a grant from the National Institute of Health (M-2104). The data reported here are drawn from my "Multiple Goals and Staff Structure: A Comparative Study of Correctional Institutions for Delinquents" (Ph.D. dissertation, University of Michigan, 1960). I am indebted to the Elizabeth McCormick Memorial Fund of Chicago, which also supported the study, and to Harrison White, Charles Perrow, and Anthony Kallet for their comments on an earlier draft of this paper.

4. For a discussion of the differences between custodial and treatment mental hospitals see Milton Greenblatt, R. York, and E. L. Brown, *From Custodial to Therapeutic Care in Mental Hospitals* (New York: Russell Sage Foundation, 1955).

5. For a discussion of differences in role requirements in prisons see Donald R. Cressey, "Contradictory Directives in Complex Organizations," *Administrative Science Quarterly*, 4 (June 1959), 1–19. See also Oscar Grusky, "Role Conflict in Organization: A Study of Prison Camp Officials," *Administrative Science Quarterly*, 3 (March 1959), 452–72; and George H. Weber, "Emotional and Defensive Reactions of Cottage Parents," in Donald R. Cressey (ed.), *The Prison: Studies in Institutional Organization and Change* (New York: Holt, Rinehart and Winston, 1961), 189–228.

6. For a statement of the hypotheses of the larger project see Robert D. Vinter and Morris Janowitz, "Effective Institutions for Delinquents: A Research Statement," *Social Service Review*, 33 (June 1959), 118–30.

7. See Zald, *op. cit.*, 48–54, for a description of the process of selecting institutions for the study and a comparison of our sample to the universe of institutions. For the measurement of institutional goals see *ibid.*, 84–114. To recapitulate briefly the selection process and the measurement of goals, institutions were initially selected on a reputational basis so as to maximize comparison of custodial and treatment institutions. An attempt was also made to have both public and private and large and small institutions in the study so that these important variables could also be taken into account. The purpose of our selection was to emphasize comparison, not to represent the universe of institutions. The reputations of institutions, our initial criterion for selection, are obviously composites of goals and oper-

ating programs. To measure goals independently, we used official documents, executive perspectives on goals, and staff perceptions of goals. Placement of an institution on the goals continuum was dictated by the interrelation of all three measures for each institution.

8. The first two or three letters of each name refer to some salient aspect of the institution's program (serving as a mnemonic device). False names are used to preserve anonymity, which was guaranteed.

9. Of the three public institutions in our sample, Dick was the only one not under some form of civil service; all staff members could be politically appointed (except for the teachers who were under merit service). Although there is not a direct relationship, it is likely that the more urbanized a state and the more educated its residents, the greater the chance that it has an effective civil service *and* institutions with treatment goals. Put another way, it is unlikely for treatment goals to find support in a poor and "backward" state.

10. Since there was no attempt to contain delinquents at Regis, its inclusion in the study might be questioned. In order to have a variety of institutions of different sizes and goals a small institution emphasizing containment was sought. Since none was available, excluding Regis would have left an important gap in our comparisons. Its small size allows us to make comparisons with Inland, and its emphasis on respect, obedience, and education reflects a parallel with older concepts of rehabilitation; it must, however, be considered as a special case. The important comparisons are between Dick, Mixter, Milton, and Inland.

11. While Regis had no operating departments and Dick was just slightly departmentalized, Mixter, Milton, and Inland were fully departmentalized.

12. Inland called itself a "residential treatment center," indicating its attempt to change identification and affiliation from that of a correctional institution to that of an institution dealing with psychological problems of adolescent boys.

13. On the inside-outside dichotomy in the executive role in treatment institutions see Zald, *op. cit.*, 128–29, 143–54; also R. D. Vinter, "Juvenile Correctional Institution Executives: A Role Analysis" (mimeographed; Ann Arbor, 1958).

14. Initially we expected conflict to be lower both in institutions having a predominantly treatment and predominantly custodial orientation, hypothesizing that conflict was a function just of multiple goals. During the exploratory phases of the research we recognized the difficulty of resolving conflict in treatment institutions and modified our hypothesis.

15. Of course, it is true that conflict may exist without perception of tension. If conflict is defined as direct competition for scarce goods or values, it is conceivable that conflict could exist without tension (psychological frustration), as in a game. However, if tension occurs between two groups, it is highly probable that it is based on some sort of conflict of interest. Furthermore, in common usage the two are often identified together. We use perception of tension as an indicator of underlying conflict.

16. The same type of conflict question was used by Basil Georgopoulos and Arnold Tannenbaum in "A Study of Organizational Effective-

ness," *American Sociological Review,* 22 (1957), 534–40. They found that conflict as measured by this type of question was inversely related to productivity, organizational effectiveness, and organizational flexibility in the divisions of a package delivery company.

17. The data to be presented are based on self-administered questionnaires which all staff members were asked to complete; 85 per cent or more of the staff who were asked to fill in questionnaires in each of the institutions filled them in, though not always completely. The questionnaire was distributed after the research staff had been around the institution for at least a week. Staff members were guaranteed anonymity.

18. There was a high rate of "no" responses on the tension questions, partly because many staff members were unwilling to comment on the amount of tension between groups of the staff of which they were not a part.

19. In computing the index, "a great deal of tension" is assigned a weight of 5, "considerable tension" a weight of 4, and so on. The equation for the index is given by $T = \dfrac{\Sigma P_r W}{N_{pa}}$ where $T$ is tension level, $P_r$ is proportion, $W$ is weight, and $N_{pa}$ is the number of pairs. To illustrate for one pair, if 15 per cent check "a great deal of tension" (5), 60 per cent check "considerable tension" (4), and 25 per cent check "some tension" (3), the score for that pair would be 3.90.

20. Georgopoulos found a statistically significant positive correlation of .53 between size and tension (personal communication).

21. This conclusion should not be taken to imply that all treatment institutions will always have high levels of conflict. Small institutions, especially, which are able to select personnel carefully, may avoid intense forms of conflict. Furthermore, conflicts over working conditions and other factors may change the level of conflict of an institution.

22. Mayer N. Zald, "Organizational Control Structures in Five Correctional Institutions," *American Journal of Sociology,* 68 (November 1962), 335–45.

23. Respondents were asked: "How much influence does each of the following groups have in making decisions about *how the boys should be handled?*" A five-point scale was used.

24. Wherever a percentage in parentheses follows a member of a conflict pair, it refers to the proportion in the group who perceive "some" or "high" tension with the other group.

25. At Dick there were 11 cottage parents, 10 teachers, and 2 social service workers who filled in the questionnaire.

26. A general complaint of the school involved the institution's overemphasis on production. The principal of the school felt that clients too often were taken out of school to work on the farm. Sometimes whole classes would be put to work and sometimes just a few boys would be taken out, interrupting teachers' lesson plans and making it difficult to keep the boys at the same rate of progress. At all the institutions teachers complained about classroom interruptions, but, where in Mixter, Inland, and Milton boys were taken out of school to participate in social service activity, at Dick they were taken out to work.

27. At Mixter there were 35 cottage parents, 14 teachers, and 8 social service workers who filled in questionnaires.

28. At Milton there were 38 cottage parents, 9 teachers, and 9 social service workers who filled in questionnaires.

29. At Inland there were 7 cottage parents, 9 teachers, and 4 social service workers who filled in questionnaires.

30. As Harrison White has pointed out in a personal communication, a larger proportion of teachers than any other group in all of the sample institutions tended to perceive high conflict, while the proportion of cottage parents perceiving conflict was always less than any other group—regardless of the partner to the conflict. On the one hand, the teachers' overperception of conflict may reflect their isolation and sense of powerlessness. On the other hand, cottage parents' underperception of conflict may reflect their lower education and working-class origins, rendering them both less aware of interpersonal strain and less committed to ideological positions regarding appropriate institutional means.

31. For instance, Peter F. Drucker, *The Practice of Management* (New York: Harper & Row, 1954).

# 20

## CONFLICTS BETWEEN PROFESSIONAL AND NONPROFESSIONAL PERSONNEL IN INSTITUTIONAL DELINQUENCY TREATMENT*

*George H. Weber*†

In an effort to provide better diagnostic and treatment services for juvenile delinquents committed to their care, many institutions, in recent years, have added people from a number of professions to their staffs. These usually include social workers, teachers in special education, psychologists, psychiatrists, and recreational therapists. In institutions, these people are frequently known as the "professional staff." They are employed for the study and treatment[1] of delinquents and the consultation with and guidance of other staff members.

In this latter function, the professionals may be asked by the administration to advise those workers who supervise and manage the everyday living experiences of the delinquents, such as getting up, going to bed, personal hygiene, eating, playing, and working. Within the institutions, these workers are commonly known as the "nonprofessional staff" (as differentiated from the professional staff)[2] and usually include cottage parents, vocational and work supervisors, and maintenance workers.

This division of work, with its theoretical consistency and its apparent applicability, would seem to be acceptable to both groups, as it is consistent with the currently accepted principles of delinquency treatment, personnel practice and education. It is a plan which should allow the professionals an opportunity to increase their practical knowledge of delinquency and to apply the specific skills of their work to the delin-

† George Weber is Chief of the Division of Program Design in the Bureau of Work Programs, U.S. Department of Labor.

quents and the institution. It is a plan which should also give the nonprofessionals an opportunity to increase their theoretical knowledge of delinquency and to receive some specialized help with some of their difficult problems.

In actual practice, however, this plan may encounter sharp difficulties in acceptance and functioning. Conflicts may emerge when professionals and nonprofessionals attempt to bring their specialties together. Value orientations, statuses and roles, and ideas of delinquency causation and treatment, undoubtedly, will differ in each group. Problems are likely to arise from the conceptions that each group has of itself and each other in each of these different areas.

The material for this paper was secured from two private and three public institutions for delinquents and was gathered over a period of three years. The method of the study was that of participation and observation. The data were gathered by four people, including the writer, who worked in these institutions in either a professional or nonprofessional job. The institutions varied in the number of delinquents in residence from about thirty to nearly four hundred. The proportion of professionals to nonprofessionals varied from 2 per cent to 37 per cent. With the exception of two institutions, the nonprofessionals preceded the professionals in the setting.

In all institutions studied, conflicts were in evidence. In some, the conflicts were more intense, continuous, and dramatic than in others. In all the institutions, some co-operation transpired between the professionals and nonprofessionals and the author does not wish to imply that all these conflicts occurred to the same degree in every institution or that they were continuous. However, conflicts were a significant aspect of the relationships existing between the professional and the nonprofessional in all the institutions studied.[3]

## VALUE ORIENTATIONS

The professionals and nonprofessionals held different values regarding their own and the other's work. The professionals often stressed humanitarianism and service. They thought of themselves as primarily providing a service to the delinquents and they believed that, when they went into a particular case or group for study, they should assume full responsibility for it within their specialty. The professionals thought of themselves as co-operative, as sharing and exchanging information and ideas, as respecting the integrity of others and the right of others to express themselves. Keen observations and a reflective and critical approach to problems were held in high regard by them. Formal education and training, as such, were also respected by this group.

The professionals saw the nonprofessionals as holding two sets of values. One view regarded the nonprofessionals as being a hard-working, simple group of people, usually generous and kind to the delinquents in their care, and good-intentioned in their relationships and dealings with the other staff members. They saw them as valuing sincerity, friendliness, and courage, simplicity and industry. The other view regarded the nonprofessionals as strict disciplinarians who demanded hard work and obedience from the delinquents. They thought that they were rigid in their viewpoints, antagonistic toward professionals, and reluctant to take any suggestions concerning their work. Here they regarded the nonprofessionals as valuing formal and restrained behavior, compliance, and authoritarianism. In both of these conceptions, the professionals saw the nonprofessionals as having very little importance in working with problems concretely and had little regard for a theoretical approach to these problems. A psychiatrist alluded to several of these points when he was discussing a cottage mother's management of a boy:

Mrs. S. wants Bobby punished for his stealing, immediately. She isn't interested in studying it more fully. She says that "if he did it, he should be punished and then he has paid his debt." If anyone expresses any other ideas on it, she feels her position is seriously threatened. If pressed on the matter, she'll take her feelings out on the boy.

On another occasion a psychologist, referring to the uncritical methods of the nonprofessional, said:

It seems that many of the cottage parents have worked out rather simple schemes for dealing with behavior problems. It apparently makes them more comfortable, even though it may be harmful to the boys. It's difficult to approach them about these things because you are apt to break down whatever relationship you have.

The nonprofessionals emphasized kindness, firmness, the ability to get along with people, and hard work as necessary qualities for work with delinquents. They viewed the immediate, the concrete, the practical, and action—the "getting something done"—as important. Broad experience and intimacy with the problems of working with delinquents were considered indispensable by them. The nonprofessionals considered themselves responsible for the general development and welfare of all the boys.

The nonprofessionals regarded the professionals as generally pseudointellectual and theoretical. They also regarded the professionals as valuing material wealth and education. The nonprofessionals often pointed to the higher salaries given to the professionals for work they believed was "easier." They believed that the professionals valued leisure and comfort for themselves above that of the delinquents and that they tended to be authoritarian in their relationships with others. The apparent leisure and comfort of the professionals was referred to by a cottage parent when she said:

It's fine and easy for you people working up in the administration building to come at eight o'clock, leave at five, and have a half-day off on Saturday, but we cottage parents are with the boys all the time. If we aren't, one of our helpers is.

Another comment by a vocational supervisor illustrates this situation:

We don't feel they (the professionals) understand or appreciate our job. It's easy enough for them to sit up in the main office in a nice soft chair and behind a fancy desk. They only have to deal with one boy at a time and he is putting his best foot forward most of the time when he is up seeing them. He knows they have a lot to do with the paroles.

The nonprofessionals charged the professionals with confusing "book learning" with workable knowledge, and of ranking such learning above the nonprofessional's practical experience. They contended that this theoretical background and professional training, while important to the professional, actually hindered their grasp of the total situation at times.[4] This was being considered by a maintenance worker when he remarked:

> That guy who calls himself a psychologist is so busy studying what he calls psychopathology and working in therapy that he doesn't know the rest of the world the kid lives in. The way he is going about things, it doesn't look like he's going to have much chance to learn about it.

A psychologist, reflecting on this point, commented:

> The psychologist trained primarily in the psychology of the individual, the social worker trained mainly for case work, and the psychiatrist trained primarily in the diagnosis and treatment of the individual patient are not prepared to deal with the complex problems which the therapeutic management of groups presents. This is no reflection against them, unless they assume they are specialists in something they obviously are not.

Although many nonprofessionals saw the professional as emphasizing a theoretical background and professional training for work with delinquents in practice, the nonprofessionals viewed some as smooth operators without "real know-how," hiding their ineptness and, at times, some hostility behind good manners and the prestige conferred by schooling.[5] They also saw the professionals as placing power and status over democratic practices. A maintenance worker's comment illuminates the nonprofessional's view of some aspects of the professionals' relations to others.

These professional people talk about democratic practices and group processes, and that we have just as much to say about things as they do but I haven't seen it operate that way. Not only do they try to tell us what to do, but the case workers and the others are right next to the superintendent's office and they're telling him what to do. They have been off to school and while they haven't learned much, they have learned how to operate. When you give them a tough kid to deal with, they can't tell you what to do that's of much account—saying nothing about taking the kid on themselves.

Conflicts of values between professionals and nonprofessionals may be further illustrated by an episode in the parole planning for a delinquent. It shows that these conflicts can have a detrimental influence on the adjustment of the delinquents.

Don was a fifteen-year-old boy who had been committed to the "Boys' Training School" for petty stealing. His father had died and his mother had deserted him. While he had been severely deprived of parental love and childhood friendships, his maladjustment was not extreme. His development at the school during his year of residence was excellent. His major activities included study in the academic school, where he excelled in the sciences, and work in the school infirmary as an orderly.

Don had been offered two placement plans. One placement was in the home of a dentist and his wife, who were interested in adopting the boy and giving him educational opportunities to the limit of his capacity and interest. The other placement was in the home of a farm family, who could offer him a good home but could not give him the education or the material advantages of the dentist's home.

After discussing these possibilities with the social worker, Don also talked about it with his science teacher, cottage mother and a nurse. The teacher encouraged him to accept placement with the dentist emphasizing the educational opportunities. The nurse encouraged him to do the same. She emphasized the possible material advantages of the dentist's home, the opportunity of making the right kind of friends, as well as the educational opportunities. The cottage mother, however, thought that he should choose the farm family because it was her opinion that they really wanted him and would love him more than the dentist and his wife. She also expressed the opinion that farm life was good and would present fewer temptations than life in the city.

When Don attempted to reconcile these different points of view with his own ambivalence about any type of placement, he became anxious, tense and restless. He went to see the social worker about his confusion; she accepted his indecision and said it was unfortunate that he had been given so much advice.

After this conference Don talked with some boys who overheard a heated argument between the nurse and his cottage mother. They informed Don that the nurse had flatly informed the cottage mother that her own preference, as well as that of the science teacher, was for his placement in the dentist's home. The boys also told Don several other things: that the nurse insisted that the farm family only wanted to exploit him as a laborer; that the cottage mother had denied this, and pointed out that while he would have to do his share of the work, they had excellent farm machinery and some hired help and that the cottage mother had countered that the dentist only wanted the boy as a show piece to follow in his footsteps.

Don became increasingly uneasy and confused. That night he ran away.

The teacher and nurse, as members of the professional group which valued education, social and economic status, favored the dentist's home for Don. The nonprofessional, in this case the cottage mother, attached the values of honesty and independence of rural life and favored the farm placement. This conflict in values, with Don caught in the middle, had damaging results for him.

## CONCEPTIONS OF STATUS AND ROLE

The professionals thought of themselves as being primarily responsible for the study of delinquents for diagnostic and planning purposes. While they acknowledged the value of the nonprofessionals' diagnostic observations and opinions for institutional and postinstitutional planning, the professionals maintained that this area of responsibility was essentially theirs.

In addition to their diagnostic studies and planning duties, the professionals believed that they should devote a large portion of their time to treatment. For example, they gave suggestions for structuring the delinquent's environment to the nonprofessionals or offered some form of individual or group treatment to the delinquents. If they aided the delinquent by structuring his environment, the professionals usually worked with other professionals and nonprofessionals; if they offered some form of treatment, they worked immediately with the individual delinquent or group of delinquents.

The professionals' conception of their work also included assisting the delinquent to bridge the gap between the institution and outside world by proper orientation upon entry, by communication with relatives and officials during his stay, and follow-up studies with parole agencies after he left.

The professionals thought of the nonprofessionals as primarily guiding and supervising the delinquents. They thought the nonprofessionals were: 1) too restrictive with the delinquents, 2) did not try to understand the delinquents, and 3) resisted the professional's ideas and recommendations. While the professionals recognized that the nonprofessionals had some duties in connection with diagnostic studies and program planning, they regarded such duties as minor. The idea that the nonprofessionals were too restrictive is exemplified by the remark of a social worker.

> That's what's the matter with these people, they are too hard on the kids. They want to make them follow a rigid and exact pattern which is their idea of being good. They don't want to hear what we have to say about management of the boys because so often it goes against their whole way of doing their job.

The rejections of the professionals' recommendations by the nonprofessionals was pinpointed by a psychiatrist when he said:

I have been working with the D's (cottage parents) for approximately a year. I don't believe they have any intention of modifying their cottage management. I don't believe they ever will. We used to get open resistance from them; now it's passive resistance. For example, the strap was used openly, but now you never see a strap around; however, anyone who has anything to do with their cottage knows it's still being used.

A social worker commented further on this problem:

I sincerely believe that we cannot move any faster in creating a good treatment program for the boys than some of the staff (non-professionals) are willing and able to move. I also believe in helping them to move forward but after awhile, it seems a little foolish to try to help some of these people become good rehabilitative workers.

On the other side of the picture, the nonprofessionals saw themselves as the backbone of the institution. Their constant intimate relationship with the delinquent was believed to be the major part of the delinquent's institutional program and they felt responsible for the boy's total welfare while in the institution. They believed that their duties in this connection were performed in an interested, definite, firm, and consistent manner. A typical attitude was reflected by a cottage parent who said:

We ran this institution well for many years. I'm pretty sure that we did a better job with the boys than is done now with all this high-priced help. We are still doing a good job; if it weren't for us, this place couldn't run.

Whether a staff member is married and/or has reared a family seems to play a role in the staff conflict over the care and treatment of delinquents.[6] A nonprofessional's comment shows this:

I ought to know something about this. I raised five kids of my own and they are all doing all right. That is more than you can say for some of those young fellows up there in the office who are passing out the word.

On this same point a professional remarked:

> The trouble with our cottage parents and vocational super-
> visors is that they think they can treat these delinquents like
> they treated their own youngsters. They don't realize that
> these boys may be quite different. Nor do they recognize
> that, by thinking of these boys as they thought of their own
> children, they may get quite personally involved.

Occasionally some nonprofessionals saw themselves as having even broader duties, and they assumed responsibility for
the delinquent's welfare outside the institution. This took the
form of unofficial parole planning and, at times, unofficial
parole supervision. In one institution, after a cottage mother
had unofficially written to the relatives of a boy asking them
to come and get him, as he was ready for placement, she said:

> Social work is fine, I guess, but there is too much red tape
> to it, or they make it that way. There's no reason to keep a
> boy waiting six weeks when he is ready to go and his rela-
> tives are ready to take him, just to make a lot of agency
> referrals. These referrals are for the purpose of studying
> the home to see whether it is alright or not, but what differ-
> ence does it make? If it is alright, fine. If it isn't, they can
> seldom find another place for an "adolescent delinquent", as
> they say. So the boy is ready and waiting. If he doesn't get
> some satisfaction about placement, he soon will go downhill
> fast and all the good we have done for him will go, too.

There are some similarities in the way in which the professionals view their duties and the way in which nonprofessionals view them. For their part, the nonprofessionals considered the professional's duties as centering around: (1) the
delinquent's admission into the institution; (2) initial diagnostic and planning activities; (3) communication with relatives
and outside agencies; (4) considerable counseling on situational problems and limited special treatment work with delinquents; (5) some consultation work with staff members;
(6) planning with the administration; (7) planning the parole

of the boy and (8) liaison work with the parole authorities after the delinquent leaves the institution.

The nonprofessionals formally conceded the diagnostic duties to the professionals, but they believe that diagnosis has only general implications in shaping a boy's program and probably very little significance for them in their areas of work.

A cottage parent's statement makes this clear:

> I like to talk with others about the boys and plan for them because there is always a lot one person misses or fails to do. I do not appreciate having some person push an opinion of a boy's character and intelligence on me that they may have formed in a few hour's time. I've worked with some of these boys a long time and I think I know them, too. I've tried different ways with them (professionals), now I just listen and then go ahead and do it my own way.

The necessity of having the professional's diagnosis was questioned by the nonprofessionals. The professionals' means of communication was criticized.

A farmer of an institution had this to say:

> I work with boys all day long, every day. I know a boy, what he is like and what he's not like, what he can do and can't do. Just the other day, without me saying a thing, a boy told me all about his home and he cried. I can't put it in the language that those people in the administration building can— that is, put it up so that nobody but them can understand it— but I know this boy. That outfit up at the administration sees a boy for a few hours and they think they know the whole story and then want to tell us in language we can't understand. And besides the kids come back to us all upset about these tests they give 'em.

The nonprofessionals were reluctant to concede the advisory or consultation role to the professionals. While there was some overt harmony, underlying negative feelings were strong. This underlying resentment was pointed out by a vocational supervisor who said:

I wouldn't mind this long-haired bunch up in the offices who have their education, but when they feel like they have been called on to give it to me too, I don't want it.

The superintendent of one of the institutions of this study who himself was a professional remarked:

The ordinary run-of-the-mill professional clings to his theory too much, and unfortunately, theory is frequently too abstract to be directly applicable to concrete problems. As a result, the cottage parents and others do not have too much confidence or respect for them.

In considering this problem, the social worker talked about professional workers without experience:

People with some professional education bring some valuable knowledge to their job, but they would be better off if they could appreciate themselves a little more realistically. You know, they haven't really learned what is needed to do their job, and all that it implies. Unfortunately, many of them feel compelled to give advice and suggestions. I guess they feel they have to justify their existence on the staff.

The work of the professionals which involved the delinquent's admission into the institution was generally accepted by the nonprofessionals; however, the cottage parents thought that considerable orientation and intake work needed to be done with the delinquents once they reached the cottage. They also accepted the role of the professionals in communicating with relatives and outside agencies, but some difficulties arose in this connection because the cottage parents would give different information to visiting parents from what the social workers and other professionals did.

The nonprofessionals were troubled by the part professionals played in planning the institution's treatment program. They felt left out.[7]

The nonprofessionals also felt they were by-passed when it came to parole planning and actual placement. They thought their ideas did not receive adequate consideration. They also complained about delays in placing a boy once he was given parole.

Many conflicts occurred over these divergent ideas of statuses and roles.[8] Those stemming from the diagnosis and treatment of the boys were also found to be serious.

John had been in the Training School for approximately two weeks. During this period, his time had been largely taken up by his orientation program and diagnostic studies of him by the staff. The cottage parents had been orienting him to institutional and cottage life and had been observing him in a variety of situations. The psychologist had given him several tests. He had been seen by the psychiatrist, physician, dentist and social worker.

At the end of these two weeks, a staff meeting was called and each member who had contact with John came with a report of his findings. A professional chaired the meetings and the other professionals consumed the majority of the period with their discussion and recommendations. This was particularly so with the psychologist and psychiatrist, who became involved in a discussion about the nature and extent of the boy's anxiety and the defenses he had available for its control. The social worker raised the point of the historical development of this anxiety and its significance for programing.

After these lengthy discussions, the conference progressed to the point of concrete program planning. John was brought into the group at this time to participate in the planning. While he previously discussed his desires and wishes regarding his institutional program with his social worker, his inclusion here was an effort to have him share more directly in matters concerning his future. John expressed his interests and wishes to the staff. He said he wanted to be assigned to the tailor shop because he wanted to learn the trade.

John left the group and his cottage mother questioned assigning him to Mrs. F. at the tailor shop because she did not believe John was especially interested in tailoring and she knew that the disciplinary control of the boys in the tailor shop was poor. She said she thought he had been attracted to tailoring by reports from the grapevine that this shop allowed more freedom than some others. She acknowledged John's anxiety but emphasized his aggressive behavior in the cottage and urged that he be considered for a work placement that offered more disciplinary control.

The professionals listened to her, respectfully, but no one responded to her ideas. Rather, they discussed other aspects of John's program.

John's case was summarized by the chairman, and his assignment to the tailor shop was included without comment. John's staff conference was finished; everyone returned to his place of work.

Several days later, the woman in charge of the tailor shop reported that John had not reported to the shop as assigned and she wondered what had happened. John's absence was investigated. It appeared that the complete rejection of the cottage mother's proposal and the lack of further discussion of it at the staff meeting had made her angry; she had deliberately sent John to another assignment.

When the cottage mother attempted to participate in the planning for John's program, she indicated that she conceived of herself as having responsibilities for planning delinquents' programs. The professionals, reserving this role for themselves, rejected the cottage mother's participation. The cottage mother retaliated by ignoring the job assignment for John that the professionals arranged.

## THE CONCEPTS OF DELINQUENCY AND DELINQUENCY TREATMENT

Generally, the professionals viewed delinquency as deviant behavior resulting from the interaction of etiological, predispositional factors with situational variants. They saw this behavior as emerging from the interplay of many elements in which the boy's conscious activity was only one of these involved. They believed that institutional treatment stemming from a constructive institutional milieu, as well as individual and group treatment, provides the boys with rehabilitative experiences and would help them modify their behavior.

The professionals were found to hold the delinquent responsible for his behavior, within a certain framework, but they did not morally evaluate it. Rather, they tried to understand the motivations for this behavior and if some appropriate therapeutic measures were available, they would recommend it. If the professionals thought it was indicated, they would participate in the treatment.

To the nonprofessionals, the professionals seemed inconsistent in their thinking about treatment. The professionals talked about many of the delinquents being activity- and action-oriented rather than thoughtful and verbal in their behavior, and thus the major way of treating them was to provide a variety of constructive everyday corrective environmental experiences for them. Yet the professionals continued to see boys in office interview situations. When this was explained to the nonprofessionals on the basis of diagnostic and special treatment work for selected cases, the nonprofessionals countered with: 1) weren't the factors of comfort, easiness, and simplicity entering the professional's decisions, 2) if their (the nonprofessionals) environmental treatment was the most effective approach to the delinquents, why the salary, status, and other differentials between themselves and the professionals.

Many nonprofessionals assumed that all similar surface behavior had the same dynamics or meaning. Thus they were confused when the professionals recommended dissimilar attitudes and activities for what the nonprofessional thought were like delinquents.

The criteria for selecting boys for individual or group therapy seemed confusing to the nonprofessionals, thus such questions as: "If good for some boys, why not for others? I've got a couple over in my shop that need something. I don't see why they weren't included." With little insight as to what the professionals were attempting to accomplish, the nonprofessionals were skeptical, suspicious, and at times opposed to therapy.

The majority of the nonprofessionals had not formalized their thinking about delinquency causation; however, many of them believed that delinquent behavior was historically and situationally determined. They believed that present situations and past experiences played an important part in bringing about delinquent behavior, but that, once institutionalized, the delinquent would become penitent, see the error of his ways, and of his own free will choose socially constructive goals despite his present obstacles and past experiences.

To the professionals, the nonprofessionals appeared inconsistent and ambiguous in their thinking about treatment. The nonprofessionals talked of past experiences and the current situation as factors in behavior but said that if only the delinquent "would make up his mind, he could do what is right, because after all, he knows right from wrong. If he doesn't know right from wrong, then punish him because a child always learns to leave a hot stove alone after he is burned often enough." At times, they assumed that "if a boy has been mistreated, all you have to do is be nice to him and treat him right, and he will be O.K.". In this instance they viewed treatment as being synonymous with kindness. Some of these inconsistencies are apparent in the case of Jim.

Jim was transferred to the "Boys Training School" from the state orphanage because he was "incorrigible". Following the orientation and study period, the staff met to discuss the results of these findings and to plan for his stay at the school. The professionals generally agreed that the boy was suffering from an insidiously developing schizophrenic condition, that his controls over his intense anxiety and hostility were crumbling and that his contact with reality was weak and intermittent. They viewed his judgment as severely impaired and anticipated bizarre hostile behavior from him. Their general recommendations included an environment of acceptance, security and supportive psychotherapy.

The cottage-father listened to these analyses and proposals. He appeared to have difficulty with the terminology but understood it well enough to disagree in principle. He went on to describe several concrete episodes of Jim's behavior in which Jim had torn some plastic tile from the floor of the hall and had collected all the dirty socks he could find and put them in his locker. He further pointed out that when he had confronted Jim with this "nonsense" that he could stop it if he wanted to, especially if there was some penalty attached to such behavior, Jim agreed. The house-father commented that while the medical diagnosis might be "true" he still regarded

Jim's behavior as rising from a wish to be "ornery" and that it could be changed "if people would put their foot down on him".

Some bizarre behavior borders on the normal. To the untrained observer, it is frequently difficult to determine where one stops and the other starts. Although Jim's cottage parent could understand the schizophrenic condition of Jim in theory, he could not recognize or accept it as it occurred in Jim's daily living. Perhaps he had known many boys who did some of the very things Jim had done, and they were relatively normal.

He was intimately aware of Jim's actions, but he did not have a diagnostic frame of reference that he could bring to bear on this behavior and thus was unable to understand Jim's condition as being anything else than simple orneriness.

## SOME NEGATIVE EFFECTS OF THE CONFLICTS[9]

These conflicts had significant detrimental effects on the system of social relationships as a whole as well as on the groups and individuals involved.[10]

In some of the institutions, conflicts between these groups resulted in the system of social relationships becoming so disorganized that constructive interaction among the staff was nearly impossible. For example, some of the institutions required all the professionals and nonprofessional people working with a particular delinquent to attend his staff meetings; however, many of the nonprofessionals could not "find time" to attend the meetings even though their work load or schedule of duties had not noticeably increased. In other institutions, the professionals and nonprofessionals avoided meeting each other informally, as in the cafeteria and the staff recreation rooms.

Both professional and nonprofessional groups were disturbed by internal frictions. At times, dissensions pitted the vocational teachers and maintenance workers against the cottage parents and the social workers against the psychologists and psychiatrists.

In all of the institutions, a varying number of staff members set up devices to protect themselves and withdrew from some of the normal and expected activities. This, of course, reduced constructive interaction. In one institution the professionals spent much of their time in research, although this was not included in the duties of their job. At another institution, the professionals tended to ignore the organizational problems, and discussed instead the theory of their various fields. At several institutions, the professionals carried on exhaustive discussions regarding individual cases of delinquents and the institution's problems, but they rarely advanced beyond diagnosis of a delinquent or criticism of the administration and the nonprofessionals.

The nonprofessionals also had a variety of protective devices. Only one cottage parent would work when both were scheduled to work; the other would be upstairs resting. They would force particularly difficult boys into recreational activities outside the cottage rather than follow the professional's recommendations for providing activities for them at the cottage, where the situation at the time was expected to be less complex.

Staff members, in their efforts to work in these situations and adapt to them, may become maladjusted. Anxiety, feelings of discouragement, aggressive and psychosomatic reactions were not uncommon responses among many of the workers in these institutions.

Situationally, these reactions appeared related to the staff conflicts as well as to the nature and intensity of the children's behavior.[11]

Some staff members sought "one-sided" solutions outside of the institution by feigning co-operation with the institution's efforts to achieve co-operation. For example, in one institution a group of dissatisfied nonprofessionals appealed directly to the commissioner of the institution's administration concerning their complaints. In several institutions, a powerful cadre of nonprofessionals worked undercover for a change of administration through special interests groups. They wanted to be rid of the present administration and many of the professionals. This group complained about the professionals "meddling with

our discipline." In another institution, the professionals, thinking that the administration failed to support their ideas and
recommendations, worked secretly to gain a change in the
administration.

Further along this web of subterfuge, the "acting out" of
certain staff members worked against the institutions' goals.
For example, at several schools, the professionals left work
early, commenting, "What's the use of staying? We can't get
any co-operation anyway." Yet they always accepted full-time
pay. In another institution, a few of the professionals appropriated books from the library, rationalizing that "I might as well
get something out of this job," and "You couldn't get anyone
around here interested in learning about this."[12] A farmer at
one institution was highly critical of administrative laxness
concerning intergroup conflicts. He declared vehemently that
people should be made to "toe the line or get out." Gradually
his criticism waned and he would sarcastically remark, "I'm
running my own little playhouse now, I expect others to run
theirs. That's the only way a guy can get along here." A short
time later he was caught stealing some livestock from the
school.

As a result of these staff conflicts, the delinquent is frequently damaged rather than helped. Many delinquents came
to these institutions from homes with extremely disturbed family situations where their needs for a secure and stable family
life were ignored or where the parents were highly inconsistent. As a result, many delinquents developed devious means
of satisfying their needs. They very shrewdly evaluated the
social situations about them. They detected weaknesses, and
they exploited and manipulated the situation for their personal
ends. This behavior-attitude had played a strong role in their
delinquency in the first place and was one of the behavioral
tendencies that the institution tried to modify. Yet this was
quite impossible if the delinquent was exposed to an institutional environment where the surroundings were similar to
those which had contributed to his unhealthy condition.

John, a delinquent at a Training School, was denied a holi-
day pass to his home by his cottage parent because he had

persistently been intimidating younger boys and, whenever possible, beating them. Aware that there were differences of opinion regarding treatment methods between the social worker and the cottage parent, John went to see the social worker, complaining that he was restricted from his pass unfairly and that the cottage parent was "down on him" and that "he had just been playing with the other fellows." The social worker was sympathetic and after the boy left, she discussed it with the chief social worker. He took it to the superintendent who, in turn, asked to see the cottage parent. The cottage parent, threatened by this apparent display of power by the professionals, said that "he thought maybe a pass would be the thing to help him". Later, in talking with his associates, the cottage parent bitterly denounced the professionals.

Many delinquents are shrewd and devious in their actions. John was such a boy. By manipulating some staff members, who fell unwittingly into his trap, he got his pass. The conflict of status and role here between the professionals and nonprofessionals is evident again; a conflict over treatment methods is also indicated. John was aware of these conflicts and cleverly exploited them to his own advantage, and continued his delinquent way of dealing with the world.

## SOME RECOMMENDATIONS TO RELIEVE THESE CONFLICTS

Education is obviously not a cure-all, but the professionals might profit from training programs that provided them with a broader frame of reference, and sensitized them to the practical functioning of an organization. If properly administered, such training should help them empathize with a greater variety of people. While the colleges do teach the professionals many things, there is a lot that the institution itself can do to add to this teaching process. In-service training, internships, and residences at institutions for delinquents would be of considerable help.[13]

In order for the professional to understand the role of

the nonprofessional, it might be well for him to work as a participant-observer in the various nonprofessional jobs during the early period of his employment. However, such a procedure would probably be difficult for many professionals to accept. In one of the institutions studied, the administration and the heads of professional departments agreed to provide this type of experience for the newly hired professionals. At first it was intimated to the professionals that one week's close sharing of cottage life would aid greatly in their orientation. Later they were told that such a period of observation and participation was expected, and that as soon as they were ready the process would begin.

Of the nine professionals to whom this opportunity was extended, three began it and only one completed the activity. When those who did not attempt it or failed to complete it were faced with their failure to participate, various excuses were made.

"I was too busy with other activities."

"After all, I'm not studying to be a cottage parent."

"Just how do you conceive of my role here?"

"My wife needed me at home at night."

"I can learn just as much by testing a boy as I can by watching him in a cottage."

This procedure and reasons for the expected participation had been previously explained to them.[14]

Concomitant with the experience of being a participant-observer in a variety of nonprofessional jobs the professional should meet with the nonprofessional of each job to learn of the activities and problems of the job from the standpoint of the nonprofessional. In such arrangements the professional would, of course, profit from constructive departmental and administrative leadership.

The total institution should be made aware of a new staff member's arrival in advance along with the position he is to fill and the role he is expected to play. Upon arrival he should be introduced to the other staff members, including nonprofessionals. Many times the new staff member needs some early reassurance, support, and friendly guidance in his efforts to work himself into the institution. In several of the organizations, efforts were made in this direction, but in the others very little was done. Such procedures are as necessary for the nonprofessional as they are for the professional.[15]

The nonprofessionals need systematic frames of reference to use in shaping their experiences and firsthand familiarity with delinquents into an organized repertoire of knowledge and skills which provide them with new vantage points from which to view and work with the delinquents. This might be provided by in-service training.[16]

The nonprofessionals may need to take part in regularly scheduled classes in connection with their work. The classes should be small and carried on by conference and discussion rather than by lecture. The subject matter of these classes should be focused on the personality of the delinquents and the behavior of groups in an institutional setting. Also, the nonprofessional worker should become familiar with some of the terminology and theoretical background that professional people use in approaching the problem of delinquency. This does not mean that the nonprofessional must be trained as a theorist but that he must have some understanding of this as it relates to his job.

The institutions need to refine and intensify their recruitment, selection, and orientation procedures for both the professionals and nonprofessionals. In many cases this means that, in addition to sponsoring various programs to increase the efficiency of these procedures, the institutions must also raise wages and improve working conditions.[17]

Within the institutions, the administration as well as the professional and nonprofessional staff must always strive to keep the various channels of communication functioning. Administrative-department head conferences and departmental, along with interdepartmental, meetings can facilitate this. Various institutional service committees, e.g., staff recreation and library committees, might prove effective vehicles. An institutional planning board made up of equal numbers of professionals and nonprofessionals could help in planning the overall policies of the school and might have some value in decreasing the number and intensity of conflicts between the two groups.[18]

In addition to these attempts to structure situations that would be conducive to harmonious staff relationships, the institution must provide regular procedures through which conflicts can be managed. Different conflicts would require different types of action. Sometimes administrative action would be clearly indicated, as in the case in pay and hours, or unsatisfactory working conditions. In many cases, however, it would appear that the people with conflicts need an opportunity to meet, discuss, and try to "work through" their differences and problems, either individually or in groups, with an experienced, capable institutional worker who has a broad grasp of the situation.[19]

It should be remembered, however, that the routine employment of in-service training, conferences, or committee meetings will not ensure the resolution or prevention of conflicts. None of these are a "package approach" to all situations. Rather, they provide several ways to work toward these ends. It takes a sympathetic and interested administration and some desire on the part of employees to improve staff relationships. Excellent leadership on the part of those working directly with the conflicts is required if any of these means are to be realized at their fullest potential.[20] Hostilities, anxieties, suspicions, resistances and negativisms are involved in any of these approaches if they are employed intensively.[21]

In one institution, a cottage mother expressed her hostility toward a teacher by criticising her teaching methods. Actually, the teacher's methods were good but the cottage mother was jealous of the friendly feelings and loyalty that the boys from her cottage were expressing to the teacher. This problem grew until each worker was openly criticising the other. The psychologist was asked by the superintendent to work this out with them. In that institution, he assumed this role at times.[22]

The psychologist talked with each individual for approximately an hour on two different occasions about these problems. After these talks, it appeared that a meeting including both workers could help in the resolution of this matter. Each agreed that such a meeting might be helpful. The meeting took place at a mutually convenient time and place. It progressed well until the schoolteacher pointed out one too many critical things about the cottage mother's attitude to her boys. In spite of the psychologist's efforts to help the cottage mother express her thoughts and feelings regarding this problem, she left the meeting in a defensive rage.

In retrospect, a number of critical considerations can be raised. Was the joint meeting premature? Had the psychologist moved too quickly in his effort to have the two people talk over their mutual problem? Should he have tempered the teacher's remarks? Instead of encouraging the cottage mother to express her feelings, should the psychologist have used different techniques in coping with the cottage mother's reaction? For example, should he have supported her in this crisis? Or should he have focused the discussion more on facts than on the thoughts and feelings of the cottage mother and teacher?

The psychologist then saw the cottage mother the following morning. At first she was defensive and self-righteous. Following this, she began to express some guilt about her "walking out." The psychologist listened and accepted her expressions and then purposely focused the discussion on the more immediate problem. After another meeting with the cottage mother and the teacher individually in which each vented considerable hostility toward the other, a joint meeting was tried again. This meeting was a success in the sense that they were able to express their ideas and feelings and could accept those of the other in working out their mutual responsibilities and relationships to the boys.

The overt and readily apparent aspects of any institutional problems have their deeper counterparts in the personal problems of the staff members. Often the institutional problems of anxiety, jealousy, hostility, and competitive feelings stem in part from the personal and individual feelings of the staff members and are aggravated by them. The institutions for delinquents, because of their social structure and delinquent population, were fertile battlegrounds upon which the individuals brought their personal tendencies into play. Thus, this problem has both the individual as well as the institutional aspects.[23]

A case in point is that of Mr. M., who was a rigid, caustic, and driving trades instructor. He was often officious about administrative unfairness. Also, he was ambivalent in his attitudes towards people in positions of leadership and authority. Mr. M. did his best work and seemed most comfortable when he was given encouragement and support by his supervisor. Under optimum institutional conditions, the approach was enough to offset his tendencies to be overly critical of people in superior positions.

Shortly after Dr. H. joined the staff of this institution as a psychologist, he attended a meeting of department heads. Mr. M's supervisor was one of those in attendance. Techniques of supervision were considered by the group during this meeting. Mr. M's supervisor asked Dr. H. what caused people to be "hard-headed". Without questioning the supervisor further, Dr. H. replied, "Sometimes people do that to defend themselves against their real feelings." The supervisor accepted this without question and then proceeded to discuss another subject. Several days after this department head's meeting Mr. M. became irritable, critical and uncompromising with his boys. His supervisor, in talking with Mr. M., commented that Mr. M's attitude must be caused by something else—perhaps anger toward the boys of this class.

This interpretation made Mr. M. angry and he replied sarcastically that it sounded like a psychological idea. At lunch and after school that day he was very outspoken against all of the professionals as he talked with others. Some of what he had to say had its contagious effect and was carried to the school's administration. Following this, the superintendent talked with Dr. H. and the supervisor to learn about the situation and how to correct it. Mr. M. learned of this meeting and suspicioned that plans were being made against him. As a result he became more defensive and exceedingly critical of others.

The general procedure used to attack these problems will influence the techniques used by the individuals who cope with a particular problem. However, the skill and knowledge of the person who works with the problems will probably be the dominant factors in determining the choice of procedures.

However, whatever the procedure or technique may be, the groups and individuals must be helped to recognize and face some of the more important conflicts. They must be shown how to explore those conflicts and learn about their causes including their own contributions to them, and they must work these problems through to a better level of understanding and work relationships.

# NOTES

Source: *Journal of Criminal Law, Criminology and Police Science,* 48 (May–June 1957), 26–43.

* I wish to thank Dr. Melville Dalton for his guidance and suggestions in the prosecution of the research on which this paper is based.

1. "Treatment," as used in this paper, denotes all the systematic efforts which are carried on within an institutional setting to assist in the rehabilitation of the delinquent. This includes general environmental arrangements, as well as individual and group treatment.

2. The titles "professional" and "nonprofessional" accentuate the differences between the two groups and appear to facilitate conflict rather than co-operation. It is an unfortunate differentiation. For an analysis of the difficulties in defining a profession, see M. L. Cogan, "Toward a Definition of Profession," *Harvard Educational Review,* 23 (winter 1953), 33–50.

3. Carl R. Doering describes some similar professional and nonprofessional conflicts in a penal system in Foreword to *A Report on the Development of Penological Treatment at Norfolk Prison Colony in Massachusetts,* edited by Carl R. Doering (New York: Bureau of Social Hygiene, Inc., 1940). For conflicts between psychologists, psychometrists, and social workers on the one hand and the house officers on the other, see particularly pages xi and xii.

4. The specialist's limitations have been described by others: Harold J. Laski, "The Limitations of the Expert," *Harpers,* 162 (December 1930), 102–6; Robert K. Merton, "The Machine, The Worker and The Engineer," *Science,* 105 (January 24, 1947), 79–81; Wilbert E. Moore and Melvin M. Tumin, "Some Social Functions of Ignorance," *American Sociological Review,* 14 (December 1949), 788–89.

5. This problem raises several questions: 1) Was the professional's education, on which he leaned for support in his work, relevant to and adequate for carrying out his assignments? 2) Was the web of conflicts so complex that the education could not be utilized?

6. In one institution where this was a point of conflict, 50 per cent of the professionals were or had been married, while 97 per cent of the nonprofessionals are or had been married. In another institution it was 42 per cent of the professionals and 84 per cent of the nonprofessionals.

The age differences also appeared to be important in the conflict between the two groups. In one institution the average age of the professionals was thirty years while that of the nonprofessionals was forty-one years. In another institution the average age of the professionals was thirty-four and that of the nonprofessionals was forty-six. Statistically, these are highly significant differences. Together with the other data, they suggest that age differences and experiental disparities in family and parental roles were very important factors in the dissimilar orientations of the two groups toward the delinquents.

7. Status and role conflicts of the professionals are not limited to these institutional settings. Ruth Emerson, writing on "Standards in Medical Social Work," an article in *The Hospital in Modern Society*, a symposium edited by A. C. Bochmeyer (New York: The Commonwealth Fund, 1943), 346, says, "That there is too great a diversity of opinion among executives as to the nature of the return to the hospital, which should be expected from the activities of the social service department, seems indubitable. To some, the social worker is a glorified, and yet not altogether satisfactory, bill collector. She is sent on miscellaneous errands and asked to perform various institutional tasks for which there is no provision in the personnel of the hospital budget. Her position in some institutions is to be classed somewhere between that of the cash girl in a department store and the telephone clerk at the information desk."

Further, in this regard, the professional-nonprofessional conflicts of this study bear many similarities to the staff-line conflicts of industrial organizations reported by Melville Dalton in "Conflicts Between Staff and Line Managerial Officers," *American Sociological Review*, 15 (June 1950), 342–51.

In an unreported research by the author on fifty psychiatric aides, similar status and role conflicts were observed between the aides on the one hand and the physicians and particularly the nurses on the other.

8. One of the most important components of a healthy and vigorous staff morale is the opportunity the staff has to express their ideas and to contribute suggestions concerning the institutional program, particularly on those matters which involve them. For evidence of the motivational effects of group decision, see Kurt Lewin, "Group Decision and Social Change" in T. M. Newcomb and E. L. Hartley (eds.), *Readings in Social Psychology*, (New York: Henry Holt and Company, 1947), 330–45; D. MacGregor, "Conditions for Effective Leadership in the Industrial Situation," *Journal of Consulting Psychology*, 8 (March–April 1945), 55–63; and Robert Tannenbaum and Fred Massarik, "Participation by Subordinates in the Managerial Decision Making Process," *Canadian Journal of Economics and Political Science*, 16 (August 1950), 408–18.

9. This not to imply that only negative and destructive phenomena are associated with conflict, although this is the focus here. For a theoretical discussion of the positive as well as the negative aspects of conflict see Georg Simmel, as translated by Albion W. Small, "The Sociology of Conflict," *American Journal of Sociology*, 9 (1903–1904), 490–525.

10. As in society, there were those who took difficulties and conflicts in their stride; however, frustration, anxiety, and other reactions were widespread. Some of these problems in society are characterized by Karen Horney, *The Neurotic Personality of Our Time* (New York: W. W. Norton and Company, 1937).

11. Information was given about these points in a paper entitled, "The

Emotional Reactions of People Working with Emotionally Disturbed and Delinquent Children," by Ralph W. Coltharp and George H. Weber, presented at the 1951 Mid-Continent Psychiatric Association, Kansas City, Missouri.

12. For a discussion of this problem on a broader scale, see Lawrence S. Thompson, *Notes on Bibliokleptomania* (New York: The New York Public Library, 1944).

13. The current program of the Training Branch, Juvenile Delinquency Service, United States Children's Bureau, is important in this respect. Under their leadership special training in the field of corrections is being planned to assist various specialists working in the field of delinquency control. For example, a program was offered to university teachers and prospective teachers of social work at the University of California, Berkeley, in the summer of 1956. See "Projects and Progress," *Children,* 3 (January–February 1956), 37.

14. The theoretical bases for the importance of being able to take the role of the other in interpersonal relations is set forth in George H. Mead, *Mind, Self and Society,* (Chicago: University of Chicago Press, 1934), 360–76. For the practical application of this idea to training in industry see Alex Bavelas, "Role Playing and Management Training," *Sociatry,* 1 (June 1947), 183–90. The work that has been done to improve the relationships between supervisors and workers in industry is suggestive in regard to improving the relationships between the professionals and nonprofessionals in institutions for delinquents. N. R. F. Maier, *Principles of Human Relations,* (New York: John Wiley and Sons, 1952), describes how supervisors are taught to consider problems from the worker's point of view, to look at the various possible motives underlying the worker's behavior, to encourage the worker's self-expression, and to develop solutions to problems with the work group. The effects of employee participation in decision-making on production in industry are presented by Lester Coch and J. R. P. French, Jr., "Overcoming Resistance to Change," *Human Relations,* I (1948), 512–32.

15. The importance of incorporating the new worker into an organization is described by Delbert C. Miller and William H. Form, in *Industrial Sociology* (New York: Harper and Brothers, 1951), 676–97, and Edwin E. Ghiselli and Clarence W. Brown, in *Personnel & Industrial Psychology* (New York: McGraw-Hill Book Company, Inc., 1955), 378–410, and Margaret L. Newcomb, Eleanor Gay, and Barry L. Levin, "A Training Program for Social Work Students in a Psychiatric Clinic," *Social Case Work,* 34 (May 1953), 204–11.

16. In respect to the general problems of training nonprofessionals for training schools see Susanne Schulze and Morris Fritz Mayer, "Training for House-Parents and Kindred Personnel in Institutions for Juvenile Delinquents," 44–71, in *Training Personnel for Work with Juvenile Delinquents* (Children's Bureau Publication No. 348, 1954). The work of Bernard H. Hall, *et al., Psychiatric Aide Education* (New York: Grune and Stratton, 1952), is significant in a related field with similar problems.

17. This is particularly true for the nonprofessional. For the house-parent's problems in this connection see Morris F. Mayer, "The House-Parents and the Group Living Process," 97–117 in Susanne

Schulze (ed.), *Creative Group Living in a Children's Institution* (New York: Association Press, 1951).

18. The position of one side cannot possibly be clearly understood by those on the other side unless frequent communication occurs. For a vivid illustration of this truism see Alexander H. Leighton, *The Governing of Men* (Princeton: Princeton University Press, 1946). For the importance of communication for effective integration of any group see Fritz J. Roethlisberger, *Management and Morale* (Cambridge: Harvard University Press, 1941), 62–63.

19. Should the spontaneous, informal day-to-day efforts of the staff to resolve their conflicts prove ineffective, administrators would undoubtedly find procedures of voluntary conciliation more acceptable to the members of the professional and nonprofessional groups than compulsory measures. In the area of labor and management it is interesting to note that most members of the Minnesota "fact-finding" commissions favored voluntary as opposed to compulsory arbitration in regard to labor relations problems. The "fact-finding" commissions are appointed under the Minnesota Law to place certain limitations on strikes; see Jack Stieber, "Minnesota Labor Relations Acts—An Opinion Survey," *Harvard Business Review*, 27 (1949), 665–67.

20. For discussions of leadership see Chester I. Barnard, *The Functions of the Executive* (Cambridge: Harvard University Press, 1938); George C. Homans, *The Human Group* (New York: Harcourt Brace and Company, 1950), 415–40; and Leon H. Richman, "Sound Administration: The Key That Unlocks," in Susanne Schulze (ed.), *Creative Group Living in a Children's Institution* (New York: Association Press, 1951), 18–34.

21. Though outside of the framework of this discussion, it should be recognized that many times the problem of conflict between professionals and nonprofessionals in institutions serving delinquents cannot be resolved by dealing only with the groups or individuals who experience the problems. In addition, determinants of conflict outside of the institution such as economic or political conditions must be included in this problem-solving process. Harold L. Sheppard, in an article, "Approaches to Conflict in American Industrial Sociology" (presented at the Congress of International Sociological Association, Liege, Belgium, 1953), stresses this point in respect to industrial conflict.

22. For the general rationale underlying this psychologist's approach to the workers, see Nathaniel Cantor, *Employee Counseling* (New York: McGraw-Hill Book Co., 1945), 73–131; Carl R. Rogers, *Client-centered Therapy* (New York: Houghton Mifflin Company, 1951), 19–64; and Elliott Jaques (ed.), "Social Therapy," *Journal of Social Issues*, 3 (1947).

23. See in this connection the special symposia, *American Journal of Sociology*, 42 (May 1937) and 45 (November 1939); Sigmund Freud, *Group Psychology and The Analysis of the Ego* (London: the Hogarth Press and the Institute of Psychoanalysis, 1948), and Fritz Redl, "Group Psychological Elements in Discipline Problems," *American Journal of Orthopsychiatry*, 13 (1943), 77–81.

# 21

## ROLE CONFLICT IN ORGANIZATION: A STUDY OF PRISON CAMP OFFICIALS*

### *Oscar Grusky†*

The official goals of an organization determine in large part the types of role expectations associated with the positions that make up the social structure of the system.[1] If an organization is assigned[2] a new major goal, and if this goal is in conflict with what formerly was the only primary goal of the system, then we would expect that conflict between the goals would create new stresses for many members of the organization. These two or more sets of conflicting role expectations, defined by the organization as legitimate by the fact that they are derived from an official goal, create role conflict.[3]

The increasing emphasis on quasi-environmental, rehabilitation, or "milieu" treatment programs in organizations such as prisons and mental hospitals, which formerly have had primarily custodial goals, presents a situation containing the necessary ingredients for such role conflict. In this paper we are primarily concerned with the effect of the conflicting goals of custody and quasi-milieu treatment in a small Midwestern prison camp (Camp Davis) on role conflict among the officers and staff.

Associated with the goal of custody in a prison or mental-hospital setting are staff role expectations that typically involve a general distrust and suspicion of inmate or patient behavior.[4] Consequently in traditional custodial prisons, for example, the officials and inmates are characteristically hostile to one another and show a relatively low level of interaction. On the other hand, associated with the goal of quasi-milieu treatment

† Oscar Grusky is an associate professor in the Department of Sociology at the University of California at Los Angeles.

is a distinctly opposite set of role expectations for officials. The guard or the attendant in a treatment-oriented setting is encouraged to trust the inmate or patient, to interact often with him, and in general to be emotionally supportive.[5] The two goals, then, prescribe conflicting expectations for guard or attendant behavior. The assumption implicit in the custodial goal affirms that the function of the organization is to protect the community by keeping the prisoner in the organization. He is correspondingly labeled as "dangerous," deserving of punishment, and unfit for the "outside world." In contrast, the assumption implicit in the treatment goal affirms that the function of the organization is to protect the community by "rehabilitating" the prisoner. He is correspondingly seen as "mentally ill" or "neurotic" and hence to a considerable extent not really responsible for his past actions. He is deserving of "individual treatment" by which his personal needs can be cared for and his ego healed.[6]

The conventional prison or mental hospital where the custodial goal is the primary objective can be characterized as a formalistically oriented bureaucracy, which like Gouldner's punishment-centered bureaucracy entails continuous enforcement of official regulations resulting in a considerable amount of inmate (or patient) resistance as well as highly formalized relationships between the officials and the inmates.[7] On the other hand, the prison organization or mental hospital where quasi-milieu treatment is a major goal contains the structural elements of a formalistically oriented bureaucracy combined with a pattern of social relationships in the organization which represents a process of a radically different nature. Institutionalization of a highly supportive staff-inmate relationship, which derives from the promulgation of the treatment goals, is characteristic of an indulgency-oriented bureaucratic pattern.[8] Thus from the point of view of the organizational structure as a whole the conflicting goals, i.e., custody and treatment, set in motion conflicting organizational processes.

Although conflict between an organization's basic objectives may create the underlying conditions necessary for role conflict, other factors will be instrumental in determining both the essential nature of the conflict for the role occupant and the type of adaptation to the role conflict that is possible. Formal position in the hierarchy of the organization is of fundamental importance in determining the extent of the conflict experienced. The occupants of the elite authority roles in most organizations are expected to demonstrate greater loyalty to the organization's goals (be they incompatible or not) than are other staff members. Moreover, the elite are commonly responsible for maintaining the integration of the organization and hence are likely to be subjected to a greater variety of internal pressures than are the nonelite. Finally, the elite are more likely to be responsible for negotiations with other social systems which impinge on their organization and thus are more exposed to forces from these systems than are the other officials.

With respect to the prison system that was the object of our research, we hypothesized as follows:

(1) Role conflict among the prison camp officials stemmed directly from the conflict between the organization's formal goals of custody and treatment.

(2) The differences in the formal hierarchical position of the supervisor and the other staff members should produce different types of role conflict and correspondingly different types of adaptation to the conflict.

## THE SUPERVISOR[9]

The chief administrator of a prison organization is traditionally granted extensive independent authority. At Camp Davis the supervisor was at all times the center of a highly centralized authority system. No guard or other officer was permitted to make a policy decision without first consulting him. And in time of an emergency, such as an escape, his immediate notification was required even if he was not on duty.

The formal responsibilities of the supervisor involved policy-making with respect to both of the camp's two major goals—custody (maintaining discipline and control over the inmates) and treatment ("rehabilitating" them). During any given time the supervisor's decisions played a crucial role in creating con-

ditions consistent with one goal or the other. If he stressed
discipline by establishing new restrictive rules and hence cur-
tailing the inmates' freedom, he would be seen as decreasing
the probability of achieving the quasi-milieu treatment goal,
since such a policy would serve to increase inmate resentment
toward the officials. On the other hand, if he was overly permissive in his policies, discipline and control would break
down and he would not be able to sustain the custodial goal.

The mutual interdependence and the contradictions implicit
in the camp's goals served both to create and to intensify three
major problems confronting the supervisor.[10] First, the guards
were differentially committed to the two goals: some preferred
emphasizing their custodial duties at the expense of their treatment responsibilities; others preferred emphasizing treatment
and neglecting discipline. The problem for the supervisor was
to maintain an integrated staff in the face of the divisive pressures generated by the two conflicting goals. The supervisor
himself considered this to be his most pressing problem.

> Well, strangely enough the biggest problem I've had is not
> with the inmates but with people that work for you. [What
> do you mean?] Well, it's kind of a long story. I've had
> trouble from the officers—not so much from their using poor
> judgment on handling something in camp, although that has
> come up, but more from personality traits. Some are intolerant
> and show it. They use poor discretion—talking about other
> officers in front of inmates. They've been either too lax or too
> custodially-minded. [And that's not what you want?] I want
> somebody who strikes a happy medium.——is a good exam-
> ple.——[the counselor] is the opposite. He's too treatment-
> minded and overlooks custodial affairs. The camp has over-
> looked relations with the community. For the sake of the whole
> program you've got to be custodially minded. You've got to
> show concern for protecting the people around here. We've
> had officers that have taken things home from the camp—
> which is strictly against the rules. Likewise they've brought
> things in to inmates that they shouldn't.

The two goals, moreover, helped to set the conditions for
the creation of an informal system of social relationships

among the guards, which in turn reinforced their incompatibility and increased the supervisor's integrative problems.

The second problem was that of reconciling the conflicting demands made by officials of the State Corrections Agency—demands which were often incompatible, though authoritative:

A good example would be that the Prison Camp Division [of the State Agency] demands that you must "shake down" inmates [search their person and their belongings] a few times a year while the Treatment Division feels you shouldn't disturb an inmate's personal belongings.

The position of the camp in the formal organizational structure of the State Corrections Agency was such that the supervisor was administratively responsible to separate divisions of the agency for each of the camp's goals. Thus we see that conflict in the organizational goals, abetted by the organizational structure, created a situation where mutually conflicting demands were continually made on the supervisor on the policy-making level. Whereas in a typical prison camp it is perfectly in keeping with the supervisor's role to favor policies such as shaking down inmates, using inmate informants, and watching the inmates' behavior very closely, the same policies automatically became a source of potential strain in this treatment-oriented setting.

Thirdly, the incompatible goals complicated relationships with the nearby community.

The community feeling is a problem. There's been a lot of antagonism. The facilities are run down; it's been run down all the time. [What do you mean community feelings are a problem?] Newspapers will come out and advocate that we close the camp and put a fence around it—without that problem the supervisor has to worry about security and he can't be as lax or lenient as he might be. If you don't keep that in mind and do something to hurt the community you're done. [Uh huh.] There's a formal organization made up to fight the camp. Every once in a while a petition will start around. [A nearby city] has been the worst agitator right around the camp area . . . I see their [the community's] opposition as a threat to the camp. [Oh?] There's a continual pressure by them and if enough pressure is applied they can require the camp to be closed.

The common antagonism of communities to correctional institutions was intensified by the fact that the camp was a minimum security camp where escape was relatively easy and where "treatment" was being attempted. (When the treatment goal is not understood, there is a distinct possibility that the process of treatment may be seen as coddling the inmate and thus be distorted to play on the fears of the community.) The supervisor's problems in this regard were aggravated by the fact that the camp was defined as experimental and as a result was very much in the limelight. The balance of power in the correctional system of the state between the faction emphasizing the goal of custody and the faction emphasizing treatment was influenced by the presumed success or failure of the camp. As a result pressures from the representatives of the two major factions in the State Corrections Agency tended to be intensified, so that the supervisor was always "on the spot."

The adaptation of the supervisor to the role conflict generated by the contradictory goals might be labeled "administrative neutrality," to connote an orientation of affective impartiality with respect to the two major policy areas. The supervisor, though a social worker by training, was neither strongly protreatment nor strongly procustody, as this comment suggests: "Another thing I found out is that you *can* be custodially minded as well as treatment-minded. You don't have to be one or the other."

The administrative neutrality response was effective in several ways. First of all, it enabled the supervisor to maintain at least adequate relations with representatives of both factions of the Corrections Agency. It also facilitated his being accepted by the staff, an acceptance which he could not have achieved if he had been overcommitted to either of the conflicting objectives. Moreover, the administrative neutrality adaptation tended to increase the relative power position of the supervisor in an already highly centralized authority structure. Because he was neutral, both the custodially oriented staff members and the treatment-oriented staff members were compelled to operate through him to extend their influence successfully in the camp.

The supervisor's position with regard to the formal treatment program was one of accepting ultimate responsibility, yet manifesting a relative lack of involvement in its day-to-day program. For example, he never sat in on any of the small group-therapy sessions. This lack of overcommitment to treatment permitted him to set policies which were consistent with the administrative neutrality orientation. In short, it allowed him to operate impartially and hence to balance the incompatible demands of the goals of custody and those of treatment.

## THE GUARDS

Associated with role conflict is a lack of consensus in the organization concerning approved behavior in situations that are morally conflicting. In Camp Davis, as we have indicated, this lack of consensus lay in the conflict between the goals of custody and of treatment. For the guards the conflict stemmed principally from the fact that the objectives of quasi-milieu treatment required a different set of decision-making criteria than did the custodial objectives. If an inmate in a traditional prison system violates the rules, the guard simply writes up a "ticket" and the inmate is punished by a central disciplinary court or a disciplinary officer. However, if the same violation occurs in a treatment-oriented prison organization, it complicates the guard's response and creates conflict, for he must decide whether he ought to write up a ticket or whether, for treatment reasons, he ought to let the inmate "express his emotions." The directive to use the latter criterion is contained in this policy statement by the supervisor:

And you can, of course, be stern or security-minded and still keep the respect of the men. If you bear in mind to be fair—don't tell them one thing and do something else. And, uh, let them blow their top off once in awhile—if a man says s.o.b. to you, let him, but don't overdo it.

The nucleus of the conflict lies in the obvious ambiguity of the phrases "once in awhile" and "but don't overdo it." Each situation then must be judged uniquely by the particular guard, and a precarious balance must be maintained with regard to the treatment and custodial expectations associated with the guard's role. The very vagueness and impreciseness of the expectations associated with the goal of quasi-milieu therapy heightens the guard's dilemma.

Two modes of adaptation to the situation were found among the four guards. Two of the guards (to be called "custodially oriented guards") responded by emphasizing the application of custodial criteria, and two (to be called "treatment-oriented guards") responded by emphasizing the application of treatment criteria. Hence, the opposite goals and the ambiguity of expectations derived from them created a corresponding bifurcation in the orientation of the guards.[11]

Even the terminology of the custodially oriented guards reflected their orientation. The camp was a "penitentiary" and the offenders were labeled "inmates" or "cons." The treatment-oriented guards, in contrast, referred to the inmates as "men," "campers," or occasionally "boys." Both of the custodially oriented guards decried the lack of discipline in the camp.

> I think discipline is necessary; possibly something similar to military discipline would help. [Do you think there's enough discipline here now?] Possibly enough if it was enforced strictly as it should be. Off the cuff, [he] told me that everyone has his own idea about how a penitentiary [he uses this word] should be run. He feels one should make an example of the inmate who disobeys the regulations by destroying state property or by lack of personal hygiene. He thinks more military-like inspections should be held—giving punishments and rewards to the inmates periodically. He says he'd be stricter now with the inmates except that the camp supervisor is against it. [Notes on a postinterview conversation.]

Not only did they recommend greater discipline in order to decrease the influence of treatment criteria, and thus decrease the ambiguity of their role expectations, but they believed that the inmates agreed with their orientation in this regard:

> Most inmates would rather have a strict discipline. They know where they stand—don't like one officer writing up one thing and another officer overlooking the same thing.

All of the ambiguity implicit in their role, however, could not be resolved simply by stressing custodial criteria. Although the two guards could and did avoid participating in the formal aspects of the treatment program, and did interact less with the treatment-oriented guards,[12] they could not completely reject the treatment goals, for to do so would have resulted in sanctions against them. Moreover, although this adaptation involved, at the least, latent resistance to the treatment aims,[13] the very existence in the camp of a treatment program provided them with a distinct source of gratification. Unlike the guards in many prisons, all the guards in the camp had a considerable number of friendly associations with the inmates. Since it was the treatment program that helped facilitate such associations, even the custodially oriented guards experienced these rewards, as this guard noted:

> Well, there's a whole lot of satisfaction in keeping this many unstable characters in line. [Uh huh.] And, well, after a man's been here six months, having him come to you and tell you you've helped him and helped straighten him out—that happens quite often.

Naturally such personally satisfying events only complicated the problem for the custodially oriented guards. Committed as they were to a strong emphasis on discipline, an ambivalent orientation toward the treatment program could serve only to intensify their role conflict.

On the other hand, the treatment-oriented guards were faced with stresses of a different sort. The role of one of them was formally defined as having both counseling and guard functions attached to it. He was responsible for organizing and maintaining the treatment program and for providing individual counseling to the inmates. At the same time he was responsible for performing strictly custodial functions such as making a periodic count of the inmates. The former duties were the most time-consuming; hence this role, more than any other, officially represented the treatment goals of the camp.

The counselor-guard, being overcommitted to the treatment aspects of his role, saw the other duties as hindering his effectiveness.

> The number one problem is the dual role of counselor and guard that I play. This is in terms of getting a positive feeling toward me so they [the inmates] will upon their own choosing come to see me.

The tireless efforts of the counselor-guard and his almost missionarylike zeal enabled him to expand the treatment program to new areas of camp life.[14] A sizable part of his efforts was devoted to gratifying the inmates by being extremely permissive. This policy on occasion included overt rejection of certain custodial requirements and did not increase his popularity among the custodially oriented staff, though it did make him popular with the inmates.

> I try not to let them see that this is a rigid bureaucracy;—I try to let them see it as a flexible community. That is why on these rules I do very little on strictness; for example, I don't just tell them there are yard limits, period. I tell them about them and say if you want to go beyond the yard limits, see me and we'll see what we can do. [Have you ever let anybody go beyond the yard limits?] Sure, plenty of times, but if —[the head of the Prison Camp Division] saw me he'd have my neck. Sometimes the rules are so rigid in these places that it hampers us in helping these guys.

The other treatment-oriented guard, though somewhat less committed to the treatment aspects of his role than the counselor-guard (he had no formal counseling functions) demonstrated a similar pattern. Only the two treatment-oriented guards on the staff, for example, led any group therapy sessions and, correspondingly, they tended to have much closer relations with the inmates than did the other guards.

The adaptation of the treatment-oriented guards, like that of the custodially oriented guards, could not entirely alleviate the ambiguity implicit in their role. The former could not fully reject the custodial expectations associated with their role just as the latter could not completely reject the treatment expectations. Thus both were left with strong feelings of ambivalence.

## THE EFFECTS OF ADMINISTRATIVE SUCCESSION

Role adaptations which are appropriate at one period of time in an organization's history may not be appropriate at another time. One important source of change in an organization is succession, the process of replacement of key officials in the formal or informal network of relationships in the organization. Succession is a vital organizational phenomenon because it is inevitably disruptive, that is, it always creates some temporary disequilibrium in the organization. The effects of succession are, of course, variable. The more highly bureaucratized an organization is, for example, the less severe the consequences of succession are likely to be.

We have seen how the position of the supervisor and the guards helped promote their particular type of adaptation to the problems largely created by the incompatibility of the organizational objectives, custody and treatment. Now let us examine the impact of succession on these adaptations to role conflict.

The administrative changes that occurred consisted of the replacement of the camp supervisor and one of the custodially oriented guards. There is evidence that suggests that these personnel changes were related to a power struggle in the upper echelons of the Corrections Agency between the faction representing custody and that representing treatment. The new supervisor was selected by the faction favoring custodial treatment and was therefore committed to its point of view. An adaptation of administrative neutrality was therefore not structured as a potential response for him.[15] The new supervisor, confronted with a role in which he had had no previous experience and being relatively uncommitted to the quasi-milieu treatment goal, responded by formalizing relationships in the organization. The most important changes which he instituted involved the substitution of formal rules for informal ones. After being in charge of the camp for about a month, he inaugurated a list of fifty-two rules that the inmates were instructed to abide by rigorously.[16] It was, of course, not the great number of rules themselves (for very few of the rules were new) but the rigidity implicit in the nature of the rules which became symptomatic of the development of a new type of relationship between the staff and the inmates. Under the administration of the former supervisor there had been relatively few standardized rules, thereby legitimating relatively individualized and informal relationships between the guards and the inmates. With the appointment of the new supervisor this informality was replaced by impersonal and formalistic relationships between the inmates and the staff promoted by this set of rules. Hand in hand with this policy went an increasing emphasis on closer supervision and stronger security controls. Policies which were consistent with the ideology of custody quickly supplanted the earlier pattern, in which both treatment goals and custodial objectives had had equally important roles in guiding decision-making.

The hostility of the inmates to the new policies culminated in a crisis two weeks after the new rules were initiated, when a group of inmates perpetrated damage amounting to $400 to two Conservation Department trucks. The escape rate shortly thereafter rose to its highest point in the two-and-one-half-year history of the camp, as did the number of inmates who were voluntarily and involuntarily transferred out of the institution.[17]

Three general factors within the camp's staff contributed to the organizational strain: (1) the decline of the old informal groups among the staff, (2) the inability of the new supervisor to enlist the staff's co-operation in enforcing the new policies because of his overcommitment to the custodial goal, and (3) the lack of direct communication channels from the inmates to the guards to the supervisor, resulting in a lack of immediate knowledge by the chief policy maker of the impact of his decisions.

The fact that new personnel were replacing key staff officials in a small, highly integrated social structure meant that new informal alignments had to be made among the staff. The addition of both a new custodially oriented guard and a new custodially oriented supervisor upset the previous balance. The treatment-oriented guards responded to this minority position by becoming more cohesive and remaining apart from the other officials.[18] As a result the supervisor found it difficult to implement his policies. The treatment-oriented guards often did not enforce the new rules, whereas the custodially oriented guards did enforce them, as this incident illustrates:

[A treatment-oriented guard] is griping about the rules, suggesting that they just can't be followed in a place like Davis. He recounts the time last night when he saw three guys playing cards. [Only two are allowed to play at one game.] He knew he was supposed to write them up for it, but he didn't. Instead he just told them to break it up [Notes, September 17, 1956].

The inconsistencies in the administration of the new policies naturally produced anxiety, puzzlement, and concern on the part of the inmates with regard to their expected orientation toward the new regulations, as indicated in this exchange between an inmate leader and a treatment-oriented guard:

*Inmate:* Now what about this visiting rule that cuts down visiting hours, is that gonna be enforced?
*Guard:* No.
*Inmate:* [Puzzled] Well, how do we know which rules are gonna be enforced and which are not? Why you may not write us a ticket and someone else will—how are we going to know what to do? Like going into the kitchen for coffee—it's against the rules now, but some guys do it and get away with

it. . . . Y [a custodially oriented guard] just doesn't come
around unless to catch somebody and write him a ticket—now
how will he stand on the rule?

The newness of the supervisor—the fact that he had not
been acquainted either with the staff or with the inmates—
resulted in his lacking any emotional ties to past staff policies
that had become traditional in the camp. Moreover, once the
supervisor had initiated his strongly custodially oriented policies, little informal interaction occurred between him and the
treatment-oriented guards. This in turn resulted in an even
greater decrease in the influence of treatment criteria on camp
policies and also promoted a general lack of substantive
knowledge on the part of the supervisor as to the impact of
his policies on the inmates. Since the treatment-oriented guards
had interacted more often with the inmates, they had functioned as a major source of information—information to which
the former supervisor, because of his neutrality, had had access but which was unavailable to the new man because of
his custodial orientation.

In summary, the process of succession intensified the role
conflict of the staff members. The new supervisor's strong
commitment to custody made it more difficult for him to implement the treatment expectations which were still defined
as legitimate, though de-emphasized informally, in the organization. The treatment-oriented guards, feeling compelled to go
so far as to promote rule violations because of their strong
commitment to the milieu-treatment goal, became extremely
insecure. And, finally, the custodially oriented guards found
themselves in a situation that minimized the possibility of maintaining friendly relations with the inmates, relations which
had been defined as an important part of the treatment goal
and which in the past had been a source of gratification for
the guards themselves.

## MILIEU THERAPY AND THE ADMINISTRATION
## OF TREATMENT SETTINGS

Role conflict, as we have used the term, is created in a formal organization whenever two conditions are met: (1) two or more inconsistent patterns of role expectations and behaviors are attached to a single position in the system, and (2) both patterns of expectations are defined by the organization as legitimate. A person's perception of such an inconsistency in role expectations and behavior is excluded, in this definition, as a necessary ingredient of role conflict, although if the role conflict is extreme it is very apt to be a concomitant. The legitimacy of a given set of role expectations associated with a position is often tied very closely to the types of objectives of that social system. At Camp Davis a basic factor in the role conflict of the officers and staff was shown to be the conflict between the organization's goals of custody and quasi-milieu treatment.

But a more general question arises. Does the goal of milieu or quasi-milieu therapy necessitate certain types of organizational arrangements and hence generate particular types of organizational problems? Since organizations which have formally initiated programs of milieu therapy differ greatly in their size and in the degree of bureaucratization and emphasis placed on their programs, as well as in other important characteristics, generalizations about these settings, and especially generalizations based on a single case study, must, by their very nature, be tentative ones.

Nevertheless, the milieu-therapy goal does appear to promote certain characteristics and it is desirable to identify these. Therapeutic milieus, such as those found in some mental hospitals,[19] the Orthogenic School,[20] Pioneer House,[21] Wiltwyck,[22] and some prison camps all exhibit certain similar basic features. Milieu therapy apparently has important implications for the authority structure of the organization, the relative status of its members, its reaction to administrative succession, and the organization's resistance to becoming highly bureaucratized. To be more explicit, our observations suggest that the milieu or quasi-milieu-therapy goal tends to enhance the status of the primary members of the organization. By primary members we refer to those members, such as patients in mental hospitals and inmates in prison settings, who represent the *raison d'être* of the organization. Milieu-therapy programs help to make the patients or inmates central to the organization. Its resources are mobilized to rehabilitate them and change their attitudes rather than merely to maintain the organization. Milieu-therapy programs thus are implicitly optimistic and dynamic. Moreover, the success of the organization in achieving its treatment goal is evaluated in terms of the response of the primary members. Do their attitudes change? Do they become rehabilitated? In this sense, then, the positive nature of the goal, in contrast for example with the more protective, negative, and system-maintaining character of the goal of custody, favors promoting the status of the primary member. The positive therapeutic function of such an elevation in status, however, may be the source of potential dysfunction for the organization. In raising the relative status of the primary member, the morale of the lowest-level staff member, such as the attendant, the guard, or the housekeeping staff, may be adversely affected by his suffering a relative loss of status. By comparative standards the guard and the attendant ordinarily feel they have more status than the inmates or patients. Milieu-therapy programs may tend to reduce their status.

Milieu-therapy programs also promote more interaction between the staff members and the primary members. By defining the primary members as important, the ideology associated with milieu therapy also operates to encourage intimate relationships between the officials and the primary members, as Schwartz has suggested: "Thus, a therapeutic milieu facilitates the staff's understanding of and sensitivity to the patient; it provides opportunities to learn about the patient as a person."[23]

The organization becomes fully (in a quasi-milieu-therapy program, somewhat less fully) oriented toward the satisfaction of the needs of the primary members. Much flexibility, protection from "traumatic handling," relatively free expression of emotions, and what Redl and Wineman call "routines which relax," typify an organization geared to providing nurture and a minimum of organizationally induced frustration. Such an organizational program has distinct implications for its authority structure. Since achievement of the milieu-treatment goal requires constant and close contact with the primary members and since every person who interacts with the primary members may influence the course of development of that treatment, all the members of the organization are, in a general sense, therapists. Thus authority with respect to the implementation of treatment tends to become highly decentralized. This is consistent with an increase in primary member authority, which is symbolized by the patient government programs in mental hospitals where the milieu-treatment goal has been instituted. Such a decentralization trend is ideologically promoted by stressing the importance of democratic decision-making as a therapeutic factor in the treatment setting. The primary member is seen as being thwarted if he cannot participate in the decision-making and therefore likely to become more hostile to the authorities and less likely to benefit by the therapy.

One of the important positive functions of this decentralization of authority is that those who are responsible for making decisions about the primary members are the ones most likely to have the greatest amount of substantive knowledge upon which to base their decisions because of their close contact with them. On the other hand, the decentralization operates to promote intimate contacts between the staff and the primary members and may, therefore, make administrative succession a more disruptive phenomenon than would otherwise be the case.[24] In addition, the delegation of authority downward to the lower echelons may function to create intrastaff antagonism such as that found at Camp Davis. Such antagonism is inapposite to the needs of a therapeutic milieu, which requires a satisfied and contented staff. Schwartz has pointed out that staff morale is of basic importance:

> When personnel have high morale—that is, function with enthusiasm, derive satisfaction from their work, are motivated to participate with patients, . . . the probability is that they will contribute to patient improvement. Conversely, when personnel have low morale—that is, are discouraged, uninspired, dissatisfied, withdrawn, hopeless about patients and ineffective in their activities—the probability is that they will tend to keep the patients ill.[25]

The most general and inclusive characteristic which milieu and quasi-milieu-therapy goals tend to influence directly in an organization is its predilection for bureaucratization. A system of rules, impersonality, functional specialization, and a hierarchy of authority are the essence of bureaucratic structure.[26] The degree of development of each of these characteristics in any formal organization, we assume, will partly be a function of the nature of the organization's official goals. At Camp Davis the goal of custody operated to promote the development of bureaucracy, whereas the goal of quasi-milieu treatment operated to hinder this process. The custodial goal was consistent with the establishment of formal rules, clear lines of authority, differentiation of function, and maintenance of social distance, particularly between inmates and officials. The quasi-milieu-treatment goal, in contrast, militated against bureaucratic direction. The treatment expectations encouraged the guard to treat the inmate as an individual, and to be both kindly and warm. They clearly specified that the inmate was not to be treated "as a number," that is, not in an object-oriented, impersonal manner. Both formal rules and impersonality were thereby overtly discouraged. Correspondingly the normal lines of authority and channels of communication were also somewhat altered. The proliferation of the treatment goals tended to make the inmates more powerful, more important, and more influential than is the case in most prison settings.[27] With the decline in formal rules went a decline in the guard's formal controls. The implementation of treatment goals tended to encourage decentralization with respect to the actual implementation of treatment duties, although it encouraged centralization of policy-making.

Finally, the treatment goal discouraged functional specialization in that it tended to make each of the officials a therapist in addition to his other roles. The guard became more than simply a custodian. He became defined as a protector, friend, confidant, and therapist or counselor. In so far as the treatment goal promoted multiple roles for the guards, it hampered the specialization process.

In sum, the custodial goal tends to place the organizational needs for stability, routinization, and order ahead of the needs of the individuals in the system. Conversely, the quasi-milieu-treatment goal tends to promote the satisfaction of personal needs at the expense of organizational discipline and control. The officials of the prison camp, caught up in a system in which these two contradictory bureaucratic processes were operating, were prone to role conflict. If it is generally true that the milieu-treatment goal functions to hinder the process of bureaucratization, then it may be that the consequences of administrative succession for such settings are likely to be much more severe than in organizations with other types of formal goals.

It may appear from what we have said that nothing but dysfunctional consequences for the organization can result from the implementation of milieu or quasi-milieu therapy. Actually nothing could be less true. Our research indicated, for example, that the quasi-milieu-treatment goal functioned to promote co-operative behavior on the part of the inmates generally and especially on the part of the inmate leaders. When the Camp Davis inmates were compared with inmates at a control institution that did not have the milieu-treatment goal, the former were found to have much friendlier attitudes toward their staff and were much more favorably oriented to their institution than was the case with the latter, to a statistically significant extent. And unlike those at other prison institutions, the inmate leaders at Camp Davis were found to be highly co-operative in their relationships with the prison camp officials. The evidence suggested that the formal mechanisms of control displaced by the implementation of the quasi-milieu-treatment goal were apt to be substituted for by equally (and possibly more) effective informal control techniques.[28] As the functional theorists in sociology have affirmed, a phenomenon may produce *both* adaptive and nonadaptive responses.

# NOTES

SOURCE: *Administrative Science Quarterly,* 3 (March 1959), 452–72.

* The author gratefully acknowledges the helpful comments of Morris Janowitz, of the University of Michigan, and Donald R. Cressey, of the University of California, Los Angeles. He would also like to express his appreciation to the Camp Davis staff and inmates and to the State Correctional Agency officials who made this research possible.

1. By role we mean a set of behaviors which are expected of people who occupy a certain position in a social system. The expectations are commonly shared attitudes about what the person in the role ought to or ought not to do.

2. The decision to adopt a new goal for the organization may occur in the following three ways, or in a combination of them: (1) if the organization is in a hierarchy of organizations, as in this study, the official goal is assigned by a higher-level organization (in this case, the State Corrections Agency); (2) if the organization is independent, the elite of the system may arbitrarily decide to adopt a new goal; or (3) the members of the organization may consensually make the decision.

3. For a good up-to-date summary treatment of role conflict, cf. N. Gross, *et al., Explorations in Role Analysis* (New York: John Wiley & Sons, 1958), especially chapter XV.

4. Cf. Donald Clemmer, *The Prison Community* (Boston: Christopher, 1940); and S. Kirson Weinberg, "Aspects of the Prison Social Structure," *American Journal of Sociology,* 47 (March 1942), 717–26. For mental hospital settings, cf. Ivan Belknap, *The Human Problems of a State Mental Hospital* (New York: McGraw-Hill Book Co., 1956); and F. Pine and D. J. Levinson, "Two Patterns of Ideology, Role Conception and Personality in Mental Hospital Aides," D. C. Gilbert and D. J. Levinson, "Role Performance, Ideology and Personality in Mental Hospital Aides," and H. L. Smith and D. J. Levinson, "The Major Aims and Characteristics of Mental Hospitals"—all in M. Greenblatt, D. J. Levinson, and R. H. Williams (eds.), *The Patient and the Mental Hospital* (Glencoe: Free Press, 1957).

5. Cf. M. Greenblatt, *et al., From Custodial to Therapeutic Patient Care in Mental Hospitals* (New York: Russell Sage Foundation, 1955), 1–34.

6. Although this picture is purposely somewhat overdrawn for any *particular* prison setting or mental hospital, it is accurate in its essentials.

7. Cf. Alvin Gouldner, *Patterns of Industrial Bureaucracy* (Glencoe: Free Press, 1951).

8. This "indulgency-oriented" process is similar to what Gouldner also calls a "mock bureaucratic" pattern. *Ibid.*

9. Some descriptive information about Camp Davis should be noted at this point. The institution contained approximately sixty-five male inmates, ranging in age from seventeen to twenty-eight years, their offenses being of all types except sex offenses. The camp is a minimum security institution—there are no walls and the guards are not armed. The formal part of the treatment program consisted mainly of weekly sessions of small group-therapy meetings, during which the inmates' personal problems were aired and discussed in a relatively nondirective manner.

10. Seeman suggests that leadership positions in organizations automatically create contradictory demands and hence predispose role conflict. Cf. M. Seeman, "Role Conflict and Ambivalence in Leadership," *American Sociological Review*, 18 (August 1953), 374.

11. Although we are stressing organizational factors in this paper, obviously degree of commitment to one goal or the other is also influenced by personality predispositions. Cf. S. A. Stouffer and J. Toby, "Role Conflict and Personality," in T. Parsons and E. A. Shils, *Toward a General Theory of Action* (Cambridge, Mass.: Harvard University Press, 1952).

12. As suggested earlier, the staff interaction patterns, like the role expectations, were bifurcated along the same custody-treatment dimension. Hence the treatment-oriented guards interacted primarily with each other and the custodially oriented guards did likewise. The supervisor in general maintained his neutral position by interacting with both, although he tended more toward the treatment clique, partly because his middle-class background and college education equipped him with values more consonant with theirs. The custodially oriented guards, unlike the other guards, did not have any college training.

13. Sometimes the resistance was more than latent, as these comments about the treatment program by a guard suggest: "Too bad they couldn't devote a little more time to it. [Do you think it does any good?] In a few cases, yes. [The rest?] Well, a lotta guys just try to impress someone by going; they're not as sincere as they could be. A lot of times I think it's used to get a quicker parole."

14. In many respects he was similar to Wilensky's general missionary types. Like the missionary he felt somewhat persecuted, and "Authorities or Higher-Ups" or "Non-believers" in treatment were anathema to him, as these quotes suggest:

"Also, I have heard staff members say and make negative remarks about the program—such as the group discussions being nothing more than bull sessions, which is true in a certain amount if meant as communication, but they were referring to it in a derogatory manner. I think these are generally the things that make my job difficult."

"I also dislike the feeling of not being able to trust some of the people—higher-level staff members—I work with."

Moreover, like the missionary type, he worked extremely hard and selflessly, spending many more extra hours in camp than any of the other staff personnel. Cf. H. Wilensky, *Intellectuals in Labor Unions* (Glencoe: Free Press, 1957), 114–17.

15. Cf. A. Gouldner, *op. cit.*, part II.

16. Even the tone of the language used in the new regulations was harsh

—particularly so in the frame of reference of a relatively indulgent prison setting. For example: "When you sit down to a meal you must remain seated until you are through with the meal," "You must stay inside the yard limits," etc. In the three-page list of rules the following terms were used: "You must"—18 times, "No"—4 times, "You are not permitted"—2 times, "Don't"—3 times, "Keep"—2 times, other, similar terms—8 times, and 6 separate words or phrases were underlined for emphasis.

17. Specific details of the consequences of the succession can be found in O. Grusky, *op. cit.*, chapter VII.

18. This aloofness was also promoted by the fact that the two saw one of their number as the legitimate successor.

19. Cf. Belknap, *op. cit.*; Greenblatt, Levinson, and Williams, *op. cit.*; A. Stanton and M. Schwartz, *The Mental Hospital* (New York: Basic Books, 1954); Greenblatt *et al.*, *op. cit.*; and M. Jones, *The Therapeutic Community* (New York: Basic Books, 1953).

20. Cf. B. Bettelheim, *Truants from Life* (Glencoe: Free Press, 1955).

21. Cf. F. Redl and D. Wineman, *Children Who Hate* (Glencoe: Free Press, 1951), and F. Redl and D. Wineman, *Controls from Within* (Glencoe: Free Press, 1952).

22. Cf. W. and J. McCord, *Psychopathy and Delinquency* (New York: Grune and Stratton, 1956), 123–76.

23. Cf. M. Schwartz, "What Is a Therapeutic Milieu?" in Greenblatt, Levinson, and Williams, *op. cit.*, 132.

24. This decentralization is probably more characteristic of the smaller milieu-therapy settings, such as the Orthogenic School, Wiltwyck, and Camp Davis. The larger mental hospitals may experience the decentralization problem within a ward and at the same time experience the reverse and more conventional bureaucratic problem in the hospital as a whole, which is likely to be highly centralized. In the case of the bureaucratic problem the top administrators must make their decisions without detailed knowledge of the situation, since their "high" position does not allow for direct contact with the specific operations of the hospital.

25. Cf. Schwartz, *op. cit.*, 139.

26. For a statement that emphasized these four factors, see Peter Blau, *Bureaucracy in Modern Society* (New York: Random House, 1956), 19.

27. There was considerable evidence that the major formal mechanisms of social control were replaced by informal controls, such as informal co-optation of the inmate leaders. Cf. O. Grusky, "Treatment Goals and the Behavior of Inmate Leaders: A Study of an Experimental Prison Camp," *American Journal of Sociology*, 65 (July 1959), 59–67.

28. Cf. Grusky, "Treatment Goals and Organizational Behavior," chapters V and VI.

# 22

## CONTRADICTORY DIRECTIVES IN COMPLEX ORGANIZATIONS: THE CASE OF THE PRISON*

*Donald R. Cressey†*

American prisons have changed from relatively simple institutions with punishment and custody as objectives to more complex organizations with difficult and contradictory goals. Such change has required alteration in the kinds of direction and supervision given employees. In early prisons the organizational goal was fairly clear and the role of the employee was correspondingly precise. A bureaucratic hierarchy of ranks operating through an established set of punishment-enforced rules ensured that discipline was maintained among inmates and among employees. Guards, as the workers in the system, were expected to handle inmates without favoritism and without giving special consideration to the problems of individual prisoners. Supervisors in turn were expected to treat guards alike and to see that they enforced the disciplinary rules for inmates. Thus a set of rather precise rules for inmate behavior had as its corollary a rather precise set of rules for the behavior of employees. In this system administrative judgment of the quality of a guard's work was based on a single criterion, the degree to which he conformed to the rules for his behavior. A guard who followed the rules was evaluated most highly.

Because of changes in prison goals, guards in modern prisons are expected to do more than stand guard. Even in the type of institution which continues to emphasize custody, called here the "custodially oriented prison," humanitarian

† Donald Cressey is Dean of the College of Letters and Science at the University of California at Santa Barbara.

concern for the welfare of inmates and external demands that inmate labor be utilized have effectively deprived the personnel of many means of control. The goal of such institutions has shifted from mere custody to humanitarian custody or productive custody. Thus inmates cannot be kept docile by severe punishments or severe deprivations; neither can a large number be kept in solitary confinement. Custodial control is to be maintained among prisoners who must be handled humanely and permitted to work together and in other ways consort with each other. Guards then are to maintain discipline and follow rules for doing so, but they also are to ensure that antagonism, hostility, and unco-operativeness are not aroused in inmate populations even though these have been granted a degree of freedom which could be used to initiate riot or rebellion.

In the other principal type of modern prison, called here the "treatment-oriented prison," the role of the guard has been even more sharply bifurcated. Here guards must preserve some measure of order and discipline, since this is essential to a prison's custodial goal, but they must also contribute to accomplishment of an institutional therapy or individualized-treatment goal. Generally speaking, the latter goal can be achieved only if guards are instructed to relax in custodial and disciplinary matters, to take the personality needs of each inmate into account, and to individualize the handling of inmates accordingly.[1] These practices are viewed either as constituting treatment itself or as means of assisting (or at least not hindering) the treatment practices of professional personnel such as social workers and psychologists.

The shift in prison goals has therefore had as one of its effects the introduction of conflicting directives for employees in both major types of institution. In the course of a year spent partly in a custodially oriented prison and partly in a treatment-oriented prison, we were able to observe these conflicting directives by studying the criteria used to evaluate the performance of guards in both systems. Generally, guards in the custodially oriented prison were expected to enforce rules and maintain discipline while at the same time minimizing friction among inmates or between inmates and staff. In the treatment-oriented institution guards were to contribute to inmate rehabilitation by relaxing, being non-directive, and showing concern for inmate personality problems, but they were also expected to maintain order, keep inmates productively employed, administer justice, and see that escapes did not occur. These conflicting directives made it necessary to use multiple criteria in evaluating guard performance and made the guard's job an extraordinarily difficult one. One consequence in the custodially oriented prison was low employee morale and the highest employee turnover rate of any state institution, and a consequence in the treatment-oriented prison was high morale and the lowest institutional turnover rate.

## MULTIPLE CRITERIA

The use of multiple criteria in judging worker performance always makes it necessary for the employee to make judgments about committing himself to the task or tasks which have been set for him. As Ridgway has said, "Without a single over-all composite measure of performance, the individual is forced to rely on his judgment as to whether increased effort on one criterion improves over-all performance, or whether there may be reduction on some other criterion which will outweigh the increase in the first."[2] The use of multiple criteria is therefore either implicitly or explicitly based on the assumption that the individual worker will commit his "efforts, attention, and resources in greater measure to those activities which promise to contribute the greatest improvement to over-all performance."[3] For maximum organizational efficiency theoretical criteria must be specified so that additional effort in one area will yield desirable results in over-all performance.

There are two principal systems for specifying theoretical conditions in which conformity by a worker will be evaluated as desirable over-all performance, to be rewarded and encouraged. One is to standardize procedures and work tasks in explicit sets of rules. In this kind of system individuals who commit themselves explicitly to form and procedure are rewarded even if such commitment means a decline in achievement of success measured by some other criterion, such as quality of the end product. Even if multiple criteria are used in judging performance, a worker employed under these conditions will be able to discover that conforming to standardized procedures will be most highly rewarded. He will be able to discern, for example, that commitment to routinized forms is highly desirable even if one stated criterion for measuring his worth is an acceptable end product.

The other system is to evaluate workers on the basis of clearly specified results which they are expected to accomplish. This system encourages ingenuity and, at the same time, "assures the standardization necessary for bureaucratic operation."[4] The worker here commits himself to creation of the desired, specified, standard, end product, even if such commitment means deviation from supervisors' conceptions of how the end product is to be produced. Workers will somehow learn that over-all performance is judged on the basis of end product, even if one stated criterion for measuring achievement is conformity to standardized rules of procedure.

A high rating on over-all performance depends, then, upon the worker's ability to discover these two systems and, when multiple criteria are used in evaluations, to exercise discretion regarding the tasks to which energy will be committed. However, one of the most significant things about the two prisons studied was that neither provided even theoretical criteria which guards could use in order to gain over-all ratings of excellence. As indicated below, in both institutions multiple and contradictory criteria were used in such a way that it was impossible for guards to discern whether it would be profitable to commit themselves to following rules, to accomplishing a desirable end product, or to some combination of these two.

In the custodially oriented prison this situation was a consequence of administrative inability to specify the appropriate means for achieving the desired end result—minimum disorderliness among inmates—and at the same time stressing that dedication to these means would bring the greatest rewards. In the treatment-oriented prison it was a consequence of administrative inability either to measure the effect of an employee's activity on production of the end product specified as desirable—reformation of inmates—or to specify appropriate means for achieving this goal. Stated in another way, administrators in the custodially oriented prison stressed the importance of means, not end product, yet they were unable to specify the desirable means; whereas in the treatment-oriented prison administrators emphasized that competence was to be judged on the basis of end results, but in making evaluations of employees they were unable to use as a criterion either end product or degree of commitment to routines. In both organizations use of multiple criteria under such conditions of open discretion stemmed from the administrative view of the nature of inmates.

## THE CUSTODIALLY ORIENTED PRISON

In the custodially oriented prison inmates were officially viewed as dangerous, scheming, conniving men in need of close surveillance. Accordingly one important administrative task was minimization, to the fullest extent possible under the law and the humanitarian concern of external groups interested in the institution's operation, of inmate freedom. Rules that set the limits of inmate freedom precisely were therefore specified, and one major set of criteria used for evaluating guard performance was the extent to which the inmate rules were enforced. The chief custodial administrator had the following to say in a speech to new guards:

> You are here to enforce the rules of the institution. Every rule. You must enforce every rule. If we thought that one of these rules was not needed, we would throw it out. We go over them every now and then and decide whether they should be changed. We did that about five years ago—went over with all of the departments the rules that applied to them. So don't fail to enforce a rule, even if you think it is nonsense. It is there for a reason. Don't blow hot and cold; enforce the same rule in the same way every day. Come in and see me or see a

lieutenant if you think the rule doesn't make sense. We will take it up. But if it is there, enforce it.

This general rule for guard behavior was a corollary of the general rule to inmates that all rules were to be obeyed. Similarly, slightly less general rules for all employees, such as, "escapes shall be prevented at all costs," were corollaries of less general rules for inmates: "No inmate shall escape." Correlated also were the specific lists of rules pertaining to each guard's post. A shop guard might be instructed that no inmate was to be permitted to smoke in the shop, while inmates were instructed that smoking was not permitted. Then, if an inmate escaped or smoked, there had been a rule violation by both an inmate and an employee. A bureaucratic chain of command designed to enforce the personnel rules was well developed and had as its ultimate objective the enforcement of rules for inmate conduct. In essence guards were expected to guard, and supervisors were expected to see that this task was accomplished.

Because of this emphasis on rules for enforcing rules it was difficult to find a guard activity that was not regulated from above. We could find no system of rules or rule enforcement for guards which was equivalent to the "mock bureaucracy" or the "representative bureaucracy" described by Gouldner for a factory.[5] Guards' duties were defined in such a way that only rarely could an employee do something which was not either in accordance with, or a violation of, rules. Such activities as going to the toilet, whistling, laughing, talking, and smoking were among the actions about which regulation from above was sought, for guards as well as inmates. Generally speaking, guards were expected, while in the institution, to place themselves completely at the disposal of the administrators, to be used as the latter saw fit.[6]

A second important administrative task in this institution was minimization of the number of disgruntled inmates. When complete physical incapacitation of the governed is impossible, and when government is by a small minority, consent of the majority to be governed must somehow be obtained. Rules must be enforced, but enforcement must not be so rigid and arbitrary that the governed are stimulated to riot or rebel. In contemporary conditions of imprisonment, where inmates do not consent to be governed and cannot be physically segregated, numerous near-equivalents of physical incapacitation have been devised. For example, incentives and rewards, such as parole, "good time" allowances, and trustee status, are granted principally to inmates who have remained isolated from others. In this way psychological solitary confinement has been substituted for the physical solitary confinement characterizing early prisons.[7] In addition, caution must be exercised in what is called the enforcement of rules. Although the set of rules for inmates serves as advance notice that nonconformists will be punished,[8] rules and punishments must be administered in such a way that both the conditions of imprisonment and the punishments are accepted by a maximum number of inmates. Such acceptance will minimize the probability of revolt, riot, and even individual rebellion. Positively this means that the rules must be enforced in a manner which does not make inmates disgruntled; guards must use discretion and common sense in enforcing rules. An administrator had the following to say about the undesirable action of an employee whose duty it was to enforce the rule that inmates shall not, among other things, write to criminals or criticize the administration in their letters:

> He was letting a few things through so we talked to him about it, and right away he started just sending letters back with a little slip saying "rejected" or "rewrite." And when that happens, of course, everybody gets upset and you have all these disgruntled inmates on your hands.

In the custodially oriented prison the conflicting directives to guards and the conflicting criteria for judging their competence were directly related to these two principal administrative tasks. Guards were to secure strict conformity to institutional rules and, at the same time, were to exercise common sense in order to maintain conditions in which a minimum number of inmates would become disgruntled and potentially

rebellious. In the words of one administrator, "The good
guard is the one who gets the best discipline with the least
friction." Although both were directives to commit one's
energy to form and procedure, it is significant that precise
rules for minimizing the amount of inmate disgruntledness
were not given the guards. The result was that guards could
rely neither on "following the rules for enforcing inmate
rules" nor on "using common sense in enforcing inmate rules"
in order to gain high over-all ratings. This was observed in
two principal contexts.

First, the administrative view of inmates as dangerous and
conniving puts emphasis upon detection and prevention of
*potential* as well as actual inmate rule violation. The general
order to enforce inmate rules was complicated by its implication that guard action was to be ex post facto. A guard who
took the order literally could only watch and wait, in much
the way traffic policemen sometimes hide behind billboards
waiting for violations. Since such action in the prison would
grant inmates an opportunity to gamble on the advantages
of nonconformity against the disadvantages of possible detection and punishment, enforcing inmate rules had to be interpreted to mean that guards were to be alert to *potential*
violations. They could not be instructed that absence of trouble
on individual posts was the desired end product, to be
achieved by individually initiated means, including the exercise of common sense, because absence of trouble on a post
could mean that a guard had entered into a conspiracy with
inmates and had created a condition potentially dangerous to
institutional security.[9] A supervisory system for observing and
testing the alertness of guards—for testing the degree of their
commitment to form and procedure—was therefore necessary.
But the presence of alertness tests always assumes that rules
are completely explicational and that discretion or common-
sense procedures are not expected. Since this was not the
case in the prison, a guard's use of common sense to prevent
inmates from becoming disgruntled became a potential source
of a demerit, not of a reward. Stated in another way, a guard's
alertness to expectations regarding his duty to keep inmates
from becoming disgruntled could not be tested, for explicit

rules defining this duty could not be formulated; and deviating (in an attempt to keep inmates from becoming disgruntled) from the specified rules could be taken as a sign of nonalertness, not of competence.

It became impossible then for guards to find a principle for committing their energy to following rules, to using common sense and discretion, or to an acceptable combination of the two. If a guard enforced the rules by formally reporting all inmate misconduct or potential misconduct to a central disciplinary court, the relatively high frequency of such reports when he was on duty was likely to be taken as evidence of poor performance, with demerit as its consequence. Conversely if he were detected exercising discretion and overlooking violations or potential violations of minor rules, he also might receive a demerit, in this case for not being alert to potential danger. The ensuing problem for guards is illustrated in the following three statements:

> I think the big problem in here is the problem of counselors. You hear in the schoolroom [in-service training] up there that we are supposed to be counselors to these men and everybody is talking about how you have to be a counselor, you have to help them and such things as that. But if you get caught talking to an inmate, it's murder. They see you talking to an inmate and they think that you're trying to help him get over the wall or smuggle in some whiskey or something like that. Now, that just isn't right. I think that we ought to be counselors. I agree with that. But I think that in order to be counselors we've got to be trusted, and they just don't trust the officers. They don't want them to do any thinking themselves.
>
> They always think there is something wrong with what you do. Like talking to inmates. I talk to them all the time. I have to talk to them. How in hell are you going to get anything done if you don't talk to them? I find out about them, whether I can trust them and things like that by talking to them. Then the lieutenant comes in and you aren't supposed to be talking to them. To hell with them. I just keep on talking to them. Of course, on my job it's a little different, because I have only a small bunch of inmates. But how are you going to get to know them if you don't talk to them?

A probationary guard was assigned to one of the shops for a day's tour of duty so he could learn the rules of the shop. The old guard to whom he was assigned gave him the following lesson, among others.

> Now, especially when you are on probation, what you are going to hear is that you shouldn't talk to these inmates. That's the rule. But you've got to talk to them. You and I know that you can't get along with them unless you talk to them. If they come up to you with something, well, you've got to talk to them about it. You can't just scare them away. But you have to watch out to see that you do it wisely and see that the lieutenant doesn't catch you at it. Just like in here I have to be over there around the corner to see what in hell the inmates are doing, and at the same time if the lieutenant comes in and I'm over there in the corner talking with them or something, to see that they don't get in a fight or something like that, then I'm on the carpet for not being alert and saluting the lieutenant or the deputy warden when they come through.

Secondly, the two facets of the guard's role logically called for two very different administrative reactions to guard deviation, but guards could discern only one response. As is illustrated in criminal law theory and procedures, in our culture the reaction to deviation viewed as *deliberate* is one of punishment and close surveillance, whereas the reaction to deviation perceived as *unintentional*—as due to ignorance or inability to conform—is education and therapy.[10] It follows that when the guard's role is primarily a simple one of following orders, writing conduct reports, and participating in a show of force, deviation will be perceived as *deliberate uncooperativeness,* with punishment as a consequence. But when the role is viewed primarily as a more complex one of using finesse, subtleties, discretion, and other individualized measures to keep inmates contented, deviation must be assumed to be the *unintentional* consequence of ignorance, with education as a consequence. In the custodially oriented prison the bifurcated role of the guard obscured the distinction between these two responses. Significantly the organizational structure designed to repress inmates made it impossible for administrators and supervisors to respond in clearly nonpunitive terms to guard deviation resulting from expectations that they would properly use discretion and common sense.

In order to gain employment in the custodially oriented prison guards had to (1) pass a written examination and be certified by the state personnel department; (2) survive interviews with the warden, an administrative assistant, and the deputy warden; (3) survive a check into their personal lives by parole agents in their home communities, and (4) pass a six-month probationary period during which they were under very close scrutiny by all the supervisory personnel. Such a formidable screening device should eliminate the unfit and incompetent—men who are *unable* to perform the duties of a guard as these duties are perceived by supervisors—and it was presumed to do so. No complaints were voiced to the investigator about the system of selection or about the quality of the candidates from among whom the selections were made.

Opinions were voiced, however, about the civil service system that conferred job tenure on guards as soon as they passed their probationary period. Despite the fact that all custodial administrators had begun their employment as guards and had thus once been on probation themselves, they often complained that once a guard had passed probation he became negligent in his duties, "because he knows we can't fire him." The first words spoken by a captain to the investigator during his first day at the institution included something like, "I have more trouble with the guards around here than I have with the inmates." "Trouble" with guards was found to include perception of their conduct as *deliberate* refusal to enforce inmate rules and to keep order. If screening procedures keep out the obviously unfit, then not performing one's duties must be viewed as due to deliberate laziness, deliberate indifference, or deliberate insubordination.

But guards were also expected to use discretion and common sense, and their deviation from this administrative expectation was viewed as stemming from *inability* to meet expectations rather than from deliberate unco-operativeness. Consistently *education* rather than punishment was the device used for correcting the deviation. Supervisors and administrators attempted to give this guidance both in on-the-job consultations and in more general in-service training sessions. However, the judicial system which necessarily had to be used for handling those deviations that were perceived as deliberate made it difficult for the guards to view the supervisory consultations as anything but devices for administering demerits, and they viewed the education received in in-service training sessions as unrelated to everyday institutional practices.

The rigid system for screening guards, with the consequent assumption that most guard deviation was deliberate, made it necessary to handle employee deviations from the rules (both those coinciding with rules for inmates and those for coordinating employee behavior—such as rules specifying the type of dress and the time at which one should arrive for work) by a procedure similar to that used in "strict liability" cases in criminal law.[11] In such criminal law cases the traditional differential in response to intentional and unintentional deviations is abandoned, for criminal intent is *assumed* to be present. Offenders are held liable for their conduct regardless of their intentions. For example, in statutory rape (intercourse with a female younger than the age of consent) a man's honest belief that the girl was above the age of consent does not preclude a finding of guilty. Most traffic violations are handled under the same principle. Generally speaking, the strict liability procedure is used in criminal law for determining guilt in those types of cases in which *mens rea* would be difficult to prove and in which the prohibited behavior is administratively undesirable but not highly reprehensible.

Use of the strict liability procedure in the custodially oriented prison was administratively important because it emphasized the impersonal nature of security rules, the necessity for employee unity, and the importance of organizational integration. Use of the procedure also minimized the number of extenuating circumstances which guards could use as defenses against charges of rule violation. For example, guards could not defend tardiness with excuses indicating that they did not intend to be tardy. When twenty-nine employees were late because of a severe snowstorm, each was given a demerit—a total of three such demerits in a year was punished by a suspension without pay. Similarly guards who were not considered alert by a lieutenant passing their post were given demerits, just as were guards caught deliberately violating the rules in some way. Demerits for not being alert were, in fact, sometimes awarded without the guard's knowledge.

In criminal law strict liability procedures are used only for handling deviations from precise rules such as those specifying speed limits and the age of consent. In the custodially oriented prison, however, this procedure was used to handle deviation from expectations of supervisors regarding the proper use of discretion and common-sense handling to prevent inmates from becoming disgruntled. As indicated earlier, the rules regarding such expectations were necessarily imprecise. Because the rules were imprecise, deviation in turn was necessarily unintentional, not deliberate. A guard could not deliberately violate a rule (making himself a candidate for punishment) because he could not be told what the rule was. Yet there was no alternative to assuming, as in strict liability procedures, that such deviations were deliberate. Supervisors could use only negative evidence in estimating a guard's competence. As indicated, they were obligated to give demerits when they caught a guard violating security rules by using discretion or common sense in the handling of inmates. A guard could not be rewarded for doing his duty; he could only be downgraded if he did not conform to the rules designed to ensure that he would be alert and would enforce rules for inmates. Accordingly the educational devices used in responses to expectations that guards would minimize inmate disgruntlement necessarily were double-edged—in on-the-spot consultations guards were educated regarding proper conduct, but the fact that they had deviated from prescribed rules was, under strict liability procedures, ground for punitive action in the form of a demerit.

In these circumstances a guard could not do anything in the hope that it would bring him a high rating; low ratings could be avoided by doing nothing, by staying out of sight. Guard reactions took three principal forms, which cannot be discussed here: apathy, deliberate misconduct, and deliberate concealment. These of course were precisely the reactions which the system of close supervision was designed to prevent.

## THE TREATMENT-ORIENTED PRISON

Contradictory directives for guards were even more apparent in the treatment-oriented prison. In this institution guards were expected both to guard and to use discretion in enforcing rules, just as they were in the custodially oriented prison. The principal difference was the objective of the exercise of discretion—to aid in treatment rather than to reduce disgruntlement. Although this institution's walls, gun towers, bars, locks, and rules revealed official concern for protecting society by repressing inmates, the stated policy was "to co-ordinate all the institution's facilities in a program of individualized treatment." Official emphasis, therefore, was on the goal of rehabilitating inmates, who were not viewed as dangerous, conniving men, but rather as "clients" who needed the nonpunitive treatment services which the institution could provide.

The behavioral theory officially used was a mixture of humanitarianism, middle-class values, and psychiatric principles. One significant point of view was that conformity to prison rules is an undesirable restriction of inmates who need opportunities for self-expression and "acting out."[12] Inmate deviation from rules within the institution, like criminality itself, was often considered a consequence of *inability* to conform rather than as intentional and deliberate violation. Accordingly it was the duty of guards to respond therapeutically—to understand inmates and to help them with their problems, to avoid being rigid or punitive. Decision-making was decentralized so that guards could handle inmates individually and could informally reward those showing signs of improvement. Thus, the discretion which guards in the custodially oriented prison were to use as a means for preventing inmates from becoming disgruntled was to be used here for rehabilitating inmates.

It was impossible, however, for administrators to use a guard's contribution to inmate rehabilitation as the only index of his competence. There were two principal reasons for this.

First, although inmate rehabilitation was an explicit goal of the organization, it was impossible to measure the institution's success in this regard. Numerous preinstitutional and postinstitutional conditions affect recidivism rates, making it impossible to correlate either high or low recidivism rates with institutional activities.[13] More specifically the contribution of any one guard to the rehabilitation or recidivism of inmates could not be measured. In judgment of guard competence, emphasis was placed on the production of a desired end result, rehabilitated inmates, rather than on adherence to specified procedures for achieving this goal. But because the rehabilitative effectiveness of a guard could not be measured, the guard in association with inmates who became rehabilitated could not be given higher ratings than guards who had supervised inmates who became recidivists.

Second, the administrators' commitment to democratic values, such as equality and justice and to the subsidiary organizational goal of protecting society from inmates required that they secure inmate compliance with rules. From the professional or treatment standpoint, guards were to act as referral agents for the professionally trained staff and were to handle inmates' minor emotional problems themselves. As indicated, this meant that guards were to be receptive, passive, and relaxed. But like employees of the custodially oriented prison, guards were also expected to guard. While they were to be relaxed and professional so as to contribute to inmate rehabilitation, they were also to maintain order and see that inmates performed work tasks that had to be accomplished if the institution were to continue operating.[14] Although institutional policy stressed inmate welfare and rehabilitation, guards were expected to contribute to the welfare of the institution and to the protection of society.

In this situation rules stating that guards should relax and, in so doing, contribute to inmate rehabilitation could not be explicitly stipulated or enforced. In other organizations the fact that a worker's contribution to the desired end product could not be measured might have shifted emphasis in personnel supervision toward a system of evaluation on the basis of adherence to form and procedure, rather than on production of a standardized product. It was impossible to use this system in the treatment-oriented prison, however, because it is impossible to break down into a set of "rules for therapeutic action" the expectation that each inmate will be handled according to his individualized needs for treatment. Guards could not be given an explicit set of treatment rules to follow any more than guards in the custodially oriented prison could be given a set of rules for minimizing the number of disgruntled inmates. They could only be instructed to be professional, to relax, and to use discretion in handling inmates. Accordingly their performance could not be evaluated by determining the degree to which they conformed to form and procedure.

Furthermore the administrative commitment to create a relaxed, therapeutic climate made it impractical to use as criteria of worth either the guard's skill in enforcement of inmate rules or adherence to rules for the *custodial* behavior of personnel. In the first place, an explicit body of custodial rules for inmates, to be carefully enforced by guards, would have vitiated the official view that the inmate was essentially a sick person in need of help or treatment rather than a bad man in need of punishment or close surveillance. In the second place, an explicit body of rules for the custodial conduct of guards could not be formulated or enforced, because it was principally in reference to custodial relationships that guards were to relax. The nonprofessional supervisors who were expected to diffuse treatment values to guards also were expected to achieve the institution's custodial goal. But positive instructions for handling guards in a manner which would contribute to the therapeutic climate were as difficult to formulate and communicate as were positive instructions to the guards for handling inmates therapeutically.

Supervisors were, generally speaking, expected to do nothing which would make the guards tense or rigid, and this meant that they could not precisely formulate, let alone enforce, even custodial rules for guards. Thus the expectation that guards would contribute to the treatment of inmates deprived supervisors of punishment-enforced (bureaucratic or rank) authority to secure compliance with routines which either they or the administrators considered desirable from a security standpoint. And the fact that neither supervisors nor guards were treatment specialists meant that supervisors did not have the professional or technical authority to secure compliance with professional expectations regarding treatment. Consequently the supervisors' authority was neutralized; they could scarcely judge a guard as either *unwilling* to do his job, which would make him the subject of punishment, or as *unable* to do his job, which would make him the subject of education and therapy. One result was a system in which supervisors maintained with workers personal, friendly, neighborly, and equalitarian relations based on criteria other than work performance rather than formal, bureaucratic, authoritarian, supervisory, professional, or other relations ordinarily existing between managers and workers.

The relaxed supervision thus created pleasant working conditions but also complicated the criteria to be used in judging guard competence. Each guard had to decide for himself the degree to which either relaxation or custodial rigidity was to be used in particular circumstances. On treatment grounds guards were to overlook inmate deviations, but on custodial grounds they were, at the same time, to secure inmate compliance with rules. If they enforced discipline and insisted on inmate orderliness, they risked undesirable diagnosis as rigid, punitive, or neurotic, because such enforcement theoretically interfered with individualized treatment. But if they relaxed to a degree that institutional security and organization seemed to be threatened, then they risked undesirable diagnosis as lazy or unmotivated. One consequence was widespread inability of guards to discover the theoretical conditions under which additional effort in one area of behavior would yield desirable ratings on over-all performance.

# CONCLUSION

In both a custodially oriented prison and a treatment-oriented prison multiple and contradictory criteria were used to evaluate the performance of guards, but a system which enabled the guard to commit himself to one activity in order to improve his over-all rating was not provided. In the custodially oriented prison he had to follow rules, but he also had to violate the rules in order to keep inmates from becoming disgruntled. In the treatment-oriented prison he was to be relaxed and therapeutic in order to rehabilitate inmates, but at the same time he was expected to preserve institutional orderliness.

These conditions seem to be inherent in the kind of internal organization that is necessary if a prison is to achieve the multiple and somewhat contradictory goals which society sets for it. Prisons differ significantly, if not uniquely, from other organizations, because their personnel hierarchies are organized down to the lowest level for the administration of the daily activities of men. The guard, who is the lowest-level worker in a prison, is also a manager. He is managed in a system of regulations and controls from above, but he also manages, by a corresponding system of regulations, the inmates who are in his charge. Essentially because he is a worker, he cannot be given full discretion to produce a desired end product such as inmate docility or inmate rehabilitation, and essentially because he is a manager his activities cannot be bureaucratized in a set of routine procedures.

# NOTES

SOURCE: *Administrative Science Quarterly*, 4 (June 1959), 1–19.
* This paper, read at the annual meetings of the American Sociological Society in August 1958, is based on field research conducted between July 1955 and September 1956, when the author was attached to the Center for Education and Research in Corrections, University of Chicago. The results of this research project are now being prepared

for early publication and are being integrated with the results of other research conducted at the center during the years 1953–56. The author is greatly indebted to Lloyd E. Ohlin, director of the center, to Donnell M. Pappenfort and Herman Piven, who were research assistants, and to the Russell Sage Foundation, which financed the center.

1. See Donald R. Cressey, "Social Organization of Correctional Institutions" (paper read at the annual meetings of the American Sociological Society, 1956); and "Rehabilitation and Reality, II, Organization and Freedom," *California Youth Authority Quarterly*, 10 (1957), 40–47.

2. V. F. Ridgway, "Dysfunctional Consequences of Performance Measurements," *Administrative Science Quarterly*, 1 (1956), 240–47.

3. *Ibid.*

4. Peter M. Blau, *Bureaucracy in Modern Society* (New York: Random House, 1956), 66.

5. In the first type of bureaucracy the rule is neither enforced by management nor obeyed by the workers, and in the second there is mutual *acceptance* of the rule, so that deviation from it can be viewed as due to ignorance or carelessness rather than to willful resistance. Alvin W. Gouldner, *Patterns of Industrial Bureaucracy* (Glencoe: Free Press, 1954), 181–206, 215–19.

6. Herbert A. Simon, "Inducements and Incentives in Bureaucracy," in Robert K. Merton, Aliso P. Gray, Barbara Hockey, and Hanan C. Selvin, *Reader in Bureaucracy* (Glencoe: Free Press, 1952), 331. In the custodially oriented institution framed copies of a state statute providing that the warden may conscript the aid of any citizen to assist in maintaining order in the prison were posted in conspicuous places. The lesson for guards was intended to be: A warden who has authority to draft men on the street, without regard for their personal preferences or opinions, in order to maintain order certainly can utilize the lives of *employees* in any manner he sees fit. The chief custodian made this point explicit in his talks to new guards.

7. This practice has developed as a response to denial of administrative power to confine most inmates in solitary and, positively, to insistence that inmate labor be used efficiently, at least in the maintenance of prisons. See Richard A. Cloward, "Social Control in the Prison," in Cloward, *et al., Theoretical Studies in Social Organization of the Prison* (*Social Science Research Council*, Pamphlet #15, 1960), 20–48; and Donald R. Cressey and Witold Krassowski, "Inmate Organization and Anomie in American Prisons and Soviet Labor Camps," *Social Problems*, 5 (1957), 217–30.

8. Gouldner has specified this as an important condition necessary to obtaining consent. *Op. cit.*, 168–71.

9. This is one of the principal devices guards in some prisons use to control inmates and to get along with their superior officers. See Lloyd W. McCorkle and Richard Korn, "Resocialization Within Walls," *Annals of the American Academy of Political and Social Science*, 293 (1954), 88–98; and Gresham M. Sykes, "Corruption of Authority and Rehabilitation," *Social Forces*, 34 (1956), 257–62.

10. Gouldner has observed this principle in operation in the relationships between management and workers in a factory. *Op. cit.*, 159–61, 176–80, 215–19, 232–34.

11. See Jerome Hall, *General Principles of Criminal Law* (Indianapolis: Bobbs Merrill, 1948), 279–322.

12. See Donald R. Cressey, "Rehabilitation Theory and Reality," 40–47.

13. This inability to measure the effectiveness of crime prevention and corrections programs is extremely important to personnel engaged in the administration of criminal justice and even to workers in theoretical criminology, for it enables men with vastly different ideologies and theoretical conceptions to work together. See Donald R. Cressey, "The State of Criminal Statistics," *National Probation and Parole Association Journal*, 3 (1957), 230–41; and "The Nature and Effectiveness of Correctional Techniques," *Law and Contemporary Problems*, 2 (1958), 754–71.

14. See Cressey, "Social Organization of Correctional Institutions."

# 23

# THE REDUCTION OF ROLE CONFLICT IN INSTITUTIONAL STAFF*

## Lloyd E. Ohlin†

Correctional institutions throughout the United States today are undergoing a process of transformation. They are changing from relatively simple institutions with punishment, custody, and security as objectives to much more complex organizations with such difficult goals as vocational training, education, and personality and value reorganization superimposed on the older custodial expectations.

Such changes require fundamental redefinition of the roles which institution staff members must play, the relationships they maintain with one another and with their charges, and the various activities of their jobs. Basic conflicts are bound to occur in the process. Nowhere is this more clearly apparent than in the dilemma experienced by cottage staff, or houseparents, in juvenile institutions.

Older forms of correctional organization were based on highly authoritarian systems of relationship created to achieve the goals of custody and moral regeneration. The institutions operated through an established set of rules, the violation of which called for predictable forms of punishment. Classification took the form of grading offenders in terms of custodial risk.

In such systems the clarity of the objectives was matched by the clarity with which the role of houseparent was defined. He was expected to treat his charges all alike without regard to favoritism or special considerations arising out of individual need. Only in this way, it was thought, could order be main-

† Lloyd Ohlin is a professor of sociology at the New York School of Social Work, Columbia University.

tained and justice be done. The houseparent who secured the greatest rule conformity by punishing rule violators consistently and impartially was evaluated most highly by the administration.

## SOURCES OF CONFLICT

The current movement from this type of institution to one in which treatment interests are dominant precipitates a form of role conflict for cottage staff members. Where custodial requirements are minimized and treatment is stressed, they are faced with a dual obligation. On the one hand, they must continue to preserve order and discipline, since this is essential for keeping the institution going and a necessary precondition for effective treatment. On the other hand, they must individualize the handling of their charges according to the unique personality problems of each, so as to aid rather than hinder the therapeutic efforts of the professional staff.

The houseparent in this situation is confronted with a dilemma. The only way he knows of preserving order is to secure conformity to a set of rules which are clearly understood by all members of his cottage. His commitment to democratic values of equality and justice impels him to enforce these rules by punishing violators appropriately. However, he is told that punishment may often make treatment more difficult and that the proper attention to individual needs would make it unnecessary. He is torn between a recognition that an unenforced rule is no rule at all and an interest in abetting treatment efforts.

In most institutions the houseparent in this situation has little training and receives little help from his superiors. Ordinarily his supervisors are persons with greater seniority who have risen from the ranks. Frequently, though they have learned to talk about the houseparent's role in terms of its treatment obligations, they actually evaluate performance in relation to the houseparent's ability to run a quiet and orderly cottage. Constant referrals of disciplinary problems from a particular cottage mean to the supervisor that the houseparent is not doing a good job, an assumption based on the belief that if the houseparent understood his charges he could prevent disciplinary infractions. The effect of this type of evaluation is to reinforce the houseparent's control-treatment dilemma.

In most training schools too the houseparent receives little help from professional staff members. The latter work from a central office and carry case loads of individuals scattered throughout the institution. They are not routinely faced with the problem of maintaining group control within a cottage. They tend to become isolated from the disciplinary responsibilities faced by the houseparent and to feel unprepared for and uninterested in intervention in problems of order or security. Interested primarily in therapy, they tend to assess the houseparent's disciplinary action in relation to its effect on the offending individual without regard to its consequences for other members of the cottage. They strongly resist the tendency of administrators and cottage staff supervisors to place primary emphasis on the maintenance of routine, order, and custody.

### Trapped Houseparents

The inevitable result of these various expectations of the houseparent is to produce considerable conflict between staff units—cottage, supervisory or administrative, and professional. The confusion arising as to the division of authority and responsibility is quickly aggravated and exploited by those juvenile offenders who are most opposed to the institution's goals.

Faced with the necessity of maintaining order and discipline within the cottage without anyone outside knowing of trouble, many houseparents resolve the dilemma by forming friendships with the natural leaders among their charges.[1] Through conferring special privileges and rewards on these persons the houseparent secures their help in controlling the activities of his other charges. This makes him vulnerable to threats of disciplinary violation unless he meets the young people's demands for control over cottage affairs. Thus, the most rebellious and hostile young persons become dominant and exact conformity from their more tractable peers.

The houseparent who is trapped in such a situation is apt to struggle to regain control through occasional inconsistent attempts to enforce his rules to the letter by meting out severe punishments for infractions. There follows a rash of runaways, riots, property destruction, and other rebellious behavior which cannot be hidden. Soon the old order is restored.

## A PROBLEM

I have thus far described only a few of the major aspects of role conflict among houseparents in modern institutions for juvenile offenders. Many other pressures and counterpressures operate in this situation, and many variations exist in its form and content. I have, however, delineated the background against which one institution—the New York State Training School for Girls—set about trying to resolve the dilemma in the houseparent's problem of maintaining a quiet, orderly, but treatment-oriented cottage. The following description of this experiment and its effects derives from searching discussions with the superintendent and the members of his staff and from personal observation.

A change of management in this institution in 1953 resulted in a stronger emphasis on professional treatment goals. This transformation was directed by an experienced administrator trained in social work and committed to the values of his profession. He assembled a group of social workers to implement his program. The process of change was facilitated by a high turnover in cottage staff in the first year of the new administration, which made it somewhat easier to set up and enforce new role expectations for both cottage and professional staff.

In the beginning of the new administration the role definition for houseparents at this institution closely paralleled the conflicting expectations described in the preceding general statement. Cottage staff members were supervised by a small group of "seniors," former houseparents carrying supervisory and administrative functions. The seniors made up the institution's "home life department," a referral center for all administrative and disciplinary problems with which the cottage staff felt unable to cope. They provided the houseparents with guidance in carrying out their jobs and evaluated their performance. Though the seniors had acquired an ability to talk in terms of treatment objectives, their evaluations in effect reflected the degree to which the houseparents maintained discipline and order within the cottages and achieved an involvement of the girls in their care into institutional routines.

A houseparent's failure to fulfill these expectations was interpreted as a mark of incompetence and an evidence of inability to adopt a "treatment" orientation toward individual girls. As a result the houseparents felt that their requests to supervisors for support of disciplinary actions were handled in an inconsistent and unpredictable fashion. They could secure little guidance in resolving their basic dilemma—how to maintain a quiet cottage without interfering with individual treatment objectives when confronted with a group of girls largely hostile to the institution's purposes and informally organized for achieving their own ends.

The houseparents also felt unable to get full understanding of the nature of their problem or help in resolving it from the institution's social case workers. These formed a separate unit and were assigned their cases on an individual basis after the initial intake examination. Though they made numerous efforts to confer with the houseparents, communication centered about special problems of individuals. The case worker was not prepared to deal with the houseparent's relationship with an individual girl as a part of the total context of relationships in the cottage. As a consequence the emphasis on solving problems of group discipline through understanding the treatment needs of the individual case only intensified the houseparent's basic conflict and sense of inadequacy.

The organizational arrangement made for division of responsibility and resulting confusion in regard to treatment and disciplinary decisions. It thrust back on the houseparent the basic task of resolving the role dilemma and tended to produce considerable hostility among the three staff units.

The case workers were not kept informed of what others were doing to persons in their case load. They felt that both the seniors and the houseparents failed to work effectively because they were not basically oriented to treatment objectives and were not making an effort to understand and deal with the actions of individuals in relation to their treatment needs.

The houseparents' hostility reflected feelings of being abandoned and left to face their role problem without adequate understanding and support from their superiors. Under the pressure of day-to-day situations they resorted to devious ways of resolving their anxiety on an intuitive basis, but with relatively little success. Some retreated to a fixed and rigid set of rules which they enforced uniformly with whatever disciplinary tools were available to them within the cottage, while others developed cajoling relationships with their charges. In both cases the adjustment indicated an abandonment of treatment goals within the cottage.

The girls generally responded to this state of confusion and divided responsibility by manipulative tactics in which they sought to play various staff members off against one another. The houseparents shopped around for acceptable prescriptions in individual cases of misbehavior by presenting their problems alternately to the seniors and the case workers, frequently playing off one against the other. No single unit had access to all information known about an individual girl. Each unit pursued different objectives, collected different types of information about the girls, and arrived at different assessments of what ought to be done. The resulting intrastaff conflicts provided ample reason for the new administration to be concerned about their effect on both the custodial and treatment objectives of the institution.

## AN EXPERIMENT

In the face of these conditions the superintendent and his staff of social workers concluded that much more intensive and close supervision of cottage activities by professionally trained persons should be arranged. Consequently, the home life department and the case work service unit were combined into an integrated "cottage service department," with a trained social worker as director. Each social worker was assigned to supervise the activities of the girls and staff in two cottages.

At the present time twelve of the sixteen cottages are under the authority of a social-work supervisor. The four remaining cottages are supervised by seniors, who also carry general troubleshooting responsibilities on the shifts to which they are assigned. The social workers have line authority over the staffs in the cottages under their direction and are expected to provide them with direct support and guidance in the handling of the girls. They are also required to provide treatment to the girls in these cottages.

This reorganization of the institution's structure firmly locates ultimate responsibility with the supervisors for all administrative, disciplinary, and treatment problems in the cottages. The social-work supervisors are also expected to provide routine evaluations and recordings on the work of the cottage staff. As a matter of practice, though they carry final authority for decisions, they make a conscious effort to share decision-making with the cottage staff and to delegate authority to those houseparents who can safely and willingly assume it.

The effort is to present a united front to the girls of the cottage. Where a difficult disciplinary action has to be taken both the houseparent and the supervisor jointly present the decision to the offending girl. The supervisor refrains from openly countermanding inappropriate decisions reached by a houseparent but attempts to use the incident to prepare the houseparent for more adequate handling of similar cases in the future.

### Relocation of Power

The net effect of this change has been to relocate power in the hands of the supervisors, unify the authority structure, decentralize treatment and disciplinary decision-making to the various supervisory units, provide for professional attention to the total range of cottage problems, and preserve central control and continuity in the handling of individual cases.

The change was met by a considerable amount of initial hostility by houseparents. Some were afraid that they could not measure up to the social workers' expectations of them. Others felt that supervision by treatment-oriented social workers would challenge the disciplinary and treatment measures which they had evolved to maintain order. This hostility gradually turned to enthusiastic acceptance as the houseparents found that they could share the total range of their problems with their new supervisors, that the supervisors were ready to help with the complicated decisions posed by the necessity to carry on control and treatment simultaneously. The houseparents found that the basic role conflict with which they had been struggling was no longer theirs alone but could now be passed on or at least shared with the social-work supervisor.

Though the behavior of the girls improved during the integration experiment, the superintendent and his staff were primarily concerned with a "desire to increase, expand, and refine treatment techniques." In evaluating the results, consideration must be given to the experiment's effects on relationships among the staff, between the staff and the girls, and among the girls themselves.

## THE RESULTS

Insufficient time has elapsed for more than a brief observation of the apparent consequences. Furthermore, resources have not been available to support the independent, objective, and probing type of inquiry which is necessary to assess fully the impact of this staff reorganization at all levels of institutional activity. The following indications, therefore, drawn primarily from staff observations and reactions, should be viewed only as preliminary and suggestive:

1. In the structural change which took place, what has hap-

pened to the customary institutional role relationships between social case workers and houseparents?

The clear reorganization and clarification of the location of power, authority, and decision-making have resulted in a redefinition of the duties of the social worker, making them more nearly coextensive with those of the houseparent. Problems of administration, cottage organization, and discipline have been added to the social worker's traditional concern with individual treatment.

The cottage staff has passed on its role dilemma to the new social-work supervisor. The houseparents are no longer expected to have the competency derived from training, philosophy, or experience to solve the basic conflicts of cottage life. According to the social-work supervisors, as a result of these changed expectations the houseparents are happier, more amenable to suggestions, less rigid in their relationships with the girls, more interested in understanding the girls' treatment needs, more flexible in disciplinary decisions, and more concerned with acquiring a reputation for running a well-adjusted cottage.

This concern with campus reputation indicates an interest on the part of the houseparents in conforming to a developing unified concept of their role. It also shows some willingness to be identified with the girls in the cottage, as well as with the supervisor, in a shared conception of achieving a "good cottage."

In general, a very marked increase in staff harmony has occurred through the minimizing of the basic sources of misunderstanding, competition for control, and factional pursuit of different objectives inherent in the former separation of role obligations.

2. What has happened by virtue of this organizational change to the traditional social-work relationship with the client?

Clearly a stronger authority identification has been built into the new role of the social worker. The social workers have expressed the opinion that the new role offers greater opportunities for treatment than formerly and that there is nothing inconsistent in the various duties or activities of this role from the standpoint of treatment effectiveness. The social-work supervisors have said that the girls do not restrict the information they offer about their problems any more than they did formerly. In fact, the girls seek out the social workers even more frequently and volunteer personal information just as freely.

The social workers report, moreover, that new sources of information drawn from the affairs of cottage life have been opened to them which have enhanced their ability to deal with the individual girl's personal problems. They are now able to relate these problems more successfully to the content of the girl's daily experience in her cottage. This has minimized misrepresentations in the girls' communications to them and has permitted more effective use of the realities of cottage experience as a treatment resource.

The administration places special emphasis on the contribution of the staff reorganization to the staff's ability to present a united front to the girls in the institution. The opportunity for the girls to exploit communication failures between houseparents and social workers has been largely eliminated. The new structural arrangement has greatly facilitated the exchange and sharing of information, thus blocking the girls' ability to manipulate staff and exploit staff misunderstandings as a way of solving or evading personal problems.

3. What has been the effect of the staff integration on the girls' relationships with one another and on their subsequent careers?

An adequate answer to this question would require much more intensive investigation of attitudes and relationships among the girls. While it seems clear that the new system has helped to lessen manipulative and deviant responses on the part of the girls in their relations with staff members, it is not clear how much the decrease in misbehavior is simply due to the greater control potential in the new staff arrangement rather than to greater acceptance and internalization of staff values on the part of the girls.

Possibly the increased centralization of authority among

staff has been matched by a greater centralization of relationships among the girls and a heightening of the effectiveness of their informal controls over one another's behavior. The relatively untroubled smoothness with which the new integration has occurred suggests that the basic accommodations which formerly existed between the girls' informal organization and the official system have not been materially altered. The ease with which "acting-up" members are being controlled to preserve a good-cottage reputation suggests the presence of a fairly well-structured arrangement of roles set by the girls themselves. This would mean that the girls' values as opposed to administrative values are still intact, thus blocking effective internalization of official values except by the "squares" who already have them anyway.

## OBSERVATION NEEDED

The foregoing comments on the girls' relationships can only be advanced as a possible hypothesis of the girls' response to staff integration. Currently no evidence is available to provide a clear picture. Observations point to many advantages in the new staff organization from an administrative point of view. It greatly facilitates the management and control of the institutional population. It seems to offer greater opportunities for staff to pool their observations to arrive at more realistic treatment decisions in individual cases. Information is not yet available, however, to determine whether the benefits to the staff in their handling of the girls and in their relations to other staff members are matched by benefits to the girls in their peer experiences and in their subsequent careers.

The results thus far appear to be highly desirable and to point to the general success of the experiment. They also suggest the need for more intensive observations of the girls' responses.

# NOTES

Source: *Children,* 5 (March–April 1958), 65–69.
* Based on a paper presented at an advanced seminar in authoritative settings at the New York School of Social Work in December 1956.
1. Gresham Sykes "The Corruption of Authority and Rehabilitation," *Social Forces,* 34 (March 1956), 257.

# A FINAL NOTE

# 24

## THE READER IN THE THICKET
### (The Groundkeeper's Case)

*Richard Korn†*

Leo Rosten, social scientist and author, creator of the inextinguishable H-Y-M-A-N K-A-P-L-A-N, once offered his personal test of fiction: "It never happened but it's all true . . ."

In the old days most of the inmates—I should have said patients—came from this county. Each county had its own place for its people in those days—and the whole county had less than the town of Rutland today. I knew them all, so you might say that each one of them was different in some way. But there was one you might call a little more special than the others. He was not only simple—nowadays they call it retarded—he was also a little "off." But they kept him here for fifteen years or more before they decided he was daft on top of dull.

He didn't seem all that odd to me either, in the beginning. Maybe I knew him too well. When I first saw him, before he came here, he was just another kid in town. He was an orphan —not a full orphan, just half. But it was all the same, because his father left town right after the mother died. His dad was one of those summer colored workers from the South. Came up here, married one of the colored girls in town—she was somebody's maid—and right off got her in a family way. She died when the boy was a few years old. The father stayed around long enough to see the kid into the orphanage and then went South. For a number of years he'd come back to work summers, and he'd spend time with his boy in the evenings wherever the kid was boarded at. In those days they boarded

† Richard Korn is an assistant professor at the School of Criminology at the University of California, Berkeley.

them out early. The last summer he came was when the boy was six or seven. After that he stayed away for good. A few years later it turned out the boy was simple—so they shipped him here.

He was the quietest kid you've ever seen—never said a word to anyone, never even opened his mouth. He'd just do what he was told until he got tired of it and then he'd stop and smile with those big white teeth until a person would just have to give up. That's when everyone decided he was simple. When nothing would work. After a while they all got the idea that he couldn't understand anything and there was no use in talking to a boy who never said anything. Not that there's anything special about that *here*. We have lots of people who don't talk —idiots and the like. But he was different. He just didn't look all that stupid. You *know* that look. He didn't have it. And it made me wonder.

One Sunday I had to do some pruning work on the bushes by the river. You can see them from here—they're the oldest and thickest and thorniest in New England. They make a kind of natural fence between the grounds and the river—that's why we never cut them down. A few steps inside and a person would be invisible in there—if he could stand the thorns. You could hide a regiment in that thicket. I never got deeper than a yard or two myself. Well, there I was, pruning, when I hear this voice. From in *there*.

I guess I didn't care about the thorns just then. I got down and wiggled myself in, a foot a minute. It was awful slow, because of the thorns—a person in a hurry could stab himself to death in there. It got darker by the inch—but I had the voice for direction.

I must have crawled for half an hour. Then I saw him. He was standing up in a kind of hollow inside the thicket—later I found he made it himself, lashing one branch against the other. He was standing there, holding a thick, heavy book, *declaiming* to himself. He was not only talking—he was *reading*.

It was then I made my big mistake. All I could think of was, *I've got to show them—the doctors.* They have to see it—and hear it. So I didn't even wait to make out the words. I just wiggled my way out as quickly and quietly as I could and ran to the main house to find the resident. That was my second mistake. It was Sunday, you see—after visiting time—and the resident had turned in for his afternoon nap. I must have banged on his door for ten minutes before he opened it. Then I just poured it out.

All he did was stand there and stare. The first thing he said was, "You have blood all over your face." I explained again about the thicket, but he just didn't seem to understand. I finally calmed myself down—I saw he was more interested in me just then than in what I had to say—and told him the whole story again. The second time around he must have realized that I was in my right mind. But by then he had lost interest. He looked over toward his bed and yawned. Then he said, "This doesn't seem like much of an emergency. Can't it wait until Monday?" I was still pretty peppery in those days. Doctors were still new then—and this one was young enough to be my grandson. I said, "No. It couldn't wait until Monday."

It took him another fifteen minutes to get himself ready. It was getting dark by then. When we finally got to the thicket I couldn't be sure of where I had come out. I picked a spot and started threading myself in. When I figured I was in deep enough I began moving to the right. Ten, maybe fifteen yards. Nothing: no hollow, no boy, no book—and no sign that anybody had ever been there. Then I worked my way back toward the left and did the same thing. No sign of anything in that direction either. I must have been inside for half an hour. Then, outside, I heard the resident whistling to himself, to let me know that all this was pretty damn foolish. So I got out of the bushes and we went hunting for the boy. We found him in his dormitory, bright as a copper penny—not a scratch or a mark on him.

Right off the resident began to fire questions at him. What was his name, and what day was it, and where is he, and how about that book, and what was he doing in those bushes? The boy just stood there and smiled that smile of his. Then the resident took out a piece of chewing gum and held it out to him, saying "Gum?" The boy reached for it, and the resident pulled it away. "Say, 'Gum,'" he said, moving his jaw up and down, showing the boy how to do it. The boy just stood there. Then the doctor held out the gum to me and said, "Say gum." I said, "Gum" several times—and he gave me the gum. I popped it in my mouth, saying gum, gum, rolling my eyes like I was enjoying myself to beat hell. Then the doctor held out another piece to the boy, right close to his mouth, and tried to get him to say gum. The boy looked at the gum like he wanted it real bad. He wanted it so bad you could see the saliva dripping from his mouth. But he didn't make a sound. The resident was pretty disgusted. By then there were about ten boys around us, yelling, "Gum!" The resident straightened up, gave us both a dirty look—one for me, another for the boy—tossed the stick of gum into the nearest open mouth, and walked off.

The next day the chief resident called me into the office. He began by telling me how glad they were that I showed so much interest, et cetera, et cetera, me being the oldest and *in some ways* the most experienced man on the staff, et cetera, et cetera, but there were some things the younger people understood better, not because they were smarter, but because they had been to school, et cetera. Then he came to the point and said that the boy's record and all his tests *proved* that he couldn't talk, so there was no use in trying to make him. When he saw by my face that I wasn't convinced, he pulled down a book and read to me where it said that idiots can't talk. Then he closed the book and waited for me to agree.

I told him that I appreciated their appreciation, and respected their schooling, which is why, like a damn fool, I had sent for the resident in the first place, and that book learning is all very well, *but the boy could talk*. He could not only talk, I said, he could *read*. "Damn near as good as you, Doctor," I said.

He didn't say anything after that, so there we both were, trying to be polite and not saying what we both had on our minds. Finally I just stood up and went out. From that day to this I never said a word more about it.

But I wasn't through with it—even if they were. From then

on I was that boy's shadow. Especially when he was out on the grounds. I never saw him with the book—so I figured he must have kept it in the bushes. I shadowed him everywhere for the next few months—but never once did he go near the thicket. Then something began to dawn on me. I noticed that whenever I followed him, he'd never once turn back to look at me. Even when he couldn't help hearing my steps behind him. What would *you* do if you heard somebody behind you? You'd look to see *who* it was, and *why*. The only time you wouldn't do that was if you didn't want the person to *know you knew*. Pretty good reasoning for an idiot, don't you think? Pretty good—but not good enough. One day I checked my idea out. I started shadowing him as usual, then quietly faded back and went to the main house, and got up on the roof with a pair of binoculars. Sure enough, he kept up the mouse and cat business of not looking back for a while. Then he finally glanced around, saw that I was *not* there and started looking for me! He looked pretty near everywhere—except the roof.

I waited. He circled the grounds once more. Then, quick as a snake, he was in the thicket. I made a mental note of the place he went in. Ten minutes later I was creeping after him. I knew something about my quarry now—I've done a little deer stalking in my time—even so, I was lucky. He'd even allowed for being followed in there. He'd move a little bit, then he'd wait and listen. But I'd allowed for that too. Whenever he stopped, I stopped—whenever he moved, I moved. Then I heard a new sound. He was tying branches together, making his little hollow. I wiggled closer, covered by the noise he was making. Finally he was finished. He waited another long spell. Then he started to dig. The earth came up easily: that solved the mystery of the book. He pulled it out of the hole. It was wrapped in a thick tarpaulin. Then he did an odd thing.

He rolled the tarp into a kind of ball—not quite a ball, more like a rug bunched together—and then stood it against a branch where it supported itself like a turned-over V on its two ends. Then he took off his hat and put it on top of the V. Next he picked up the book and started to read, out loud. He was reading to *it*—the figure he had made! I had the strangest feeling I knew what the story would be about.

It was a child's story all right—a kind of fairy tale. About a little black prince who was taken out of his father's castle and made to do slave work for the bad people. He slaved for years, and never told anybody who he really was. Then, one fine day, his father, the king, came back to get him, leading a great shining army.

I guess I'd heard about all I wanted to hear. I came out of my hiding place and went to him. He gave an awful cry and hugged the book to him. He was about thirteen then, but still very small, and I loomed over him, like the bogeyman come true. Then I realized I just didn't have any idea about what to do next. So I just stood there, looking down at him, getting more and more uncomfortable, and feeling more and more like an intruder who had turned somebody else's dream into a nightmare. I reached out, very gently, to take the book—and he held it tighter, looking up at me with big wet eyes. It was wrapped in a brown paper cover. He sure didn't want to let go of it and I didn't have the heart to pull it out of his arms. So we just stood there like two wax figures, while I tried to figure out what to do. Then I looked closer at the cover, and saw some handwriting on it. It was his father's name, written in big, fancy letters, but so faded you could hardly make it out.

At about that time we both understood that I wasn't going to do anything. He knew this at once, somehow, because all at once he broke out in that big white smile. Then I started to giggle—and then there were *two* idiots instead of one, laughing up a storm, like we shared the funniest secret in the world. Then, just as free and relaxed as you please, he wrapped the book up in the tarp, dropped it carefully back into the hole, flashed me another big smile—and was gone through the bushes. Somehow I didn't have any inclination to dig it up to see what it was. Without saying anything, we seemed to have made an agreement. And that was that.

I was not about to break it, then or later, and maybe that was my third mistake. Because it was that book, in the end, that got him into this big trouble. Nothing happened for six or seven years. Then, one day, this psychologist—we'd just started having psychologists—was walking near the river, just as I had done. He must have heard the boy. And just as I had done—he must have been very curious or very athletic—he sneaked into the bushes, and listened. I still can't understand why the boy let him get so close. Anyway, he lay there in the bushes, waiting until the story was over. Then he stepped up and asked to see the book. He must have been very firm about it—he must have been shocked when he saw who it was, because nobody had even gotten the boy to talk. Anyway, he either demanded the book or pulled it out of the boy's hands —and the boy let him take it. That's when we found out what it was.

It was an old Sears-Roebuck catalogue. When the psychologist saw what it was, he handed it back to the boy and told him to read from it again. The kid must have really been scared. Because, right away, he started to reel off one of his stories about the little black prince, every now and then turning a page, as if he was reading. He might have seen somebody do that once—or maybe he thought that was what reading was.

Anyway, when the psychologist tried to get him to read the actual words and he couldn't—which proved, I guess, that he couldn't read—the psychologist took the catalogue back and read an actual page to him. Something about different kinds of pants. The boy wouldn't believe it, and kept shaking his head. Then he tried to grab the book back—and that's when the fun began. It took the psychologist and two men to drag him to where they could get a strait-jacket on him. The psychologist wasn't much help because his arms were bitten in twelve places.

That's when they decided he was crazy as well as simple. A few days later they figured they'd have to send him to the other place up north, though by then he'd calmed down enough to be let out of the jacket. Somehow the boy found out that he was going to be shipped. That afternoon he was missing. I was one of the ones sent to look for him. It didn't take me very long—I guess I knew where to look. He was in the water, all right, with the tarpaulin all sort of wrapped around him. I wonder if he thought he could get across the river on it.

## NOTES

SOURCE: *Issues in Criminology*, 2 (Spring 1966), 1–6.

# BIBLIOGRAPHY
(Additional Readings in Correctional Organization)

Barker, Gordon H., and W. Thomas Adams, "The Social Structure of a Correctional Institution," *Journal of Criminal Law, Criminology and Police Science,* 49 (January–February 1959), 417–22.

Belknap, Ivan, *Human Problems of a State Mental Hospital* (New York: McGraw-Hill Book Co., 1956).

Bennis, Warren G., Kenneth D. Benne, and Robert Chin (eds.), *The Planning of Change: Readings in Applied Behavioral Sciences* (New York: Holt, Rinehart & Winston, 1961).

Berk, Bernard, "Organizational Goals and Inmate Organization," *American Journal of Sociology,* 71 (March 1966), 522–34.

Blau, Peter M., and W. Richard Scott, *Formal Organization: A Comparative Approach* (San Francisco: Chandler, 1962).

Briggs, Dennie L., "Convicted Felons as Social Therapists," *Corrective Psychiatry and Journal of Social Therapy,* 9 (third quarter, 1963), 122–27.

Brim, Orville G., Jr., and Stanton Wheeler, *Socialization After Childhood: Two Essays* (New York: John Wiley & Sons, 1966).

Caudill, William, *The Psychiatric Hospital as a Small Society* (Cambridge: Harvard University Press, 1958).

Clemmer, Donald, *The Prison Community* (Boston: Christopher, 1940). Reissued edition, with a foreword by Donald R. Cressey (New York: Holt, Rinehart & Winston, 1958).

Cloward, Richard A., *et al. Theoretical Studies in Social Organization of the Prison* (New York: Social Science Research Council, Pamphlet No. 15, 1960).

Conrad, John P., *Crime and Its Correction: An International Survey of Attitudes and Practices* (Berkeley: University of California Press, 1965).

Cressey, Donald R., "Contradictory Theories in Correctional Group Therapy," *Federal Probation,* 18 (June 1954), 20–26.

——, "Social Psychological Foundations for Using Criminals in the Rehabilitation of Criminals," *Journal of Research in Crime and Delinquency,* 2 (July 1965), 49–59.

—— (ed.), *The Prison: Studies in Institutional Organization and Change* (New York: Holt, Rinehart & Winston, 1961).

——, and Witold Krassowski, "Inmate Organization and Anomie in American Prisons and Soviet Labor Camps," *Social Problems,* 5 (winter 1957–58), 217–30.

Empey, LaMar T., and Jerome Rabow, "The Provo Experiment in Delinquency Rehabilitation," *American Sociological Review,* 26 (October 1961), 679–95. See also: Gordon, Whitney H., "Communist Rectification Program and Delinquency Rehabilitation Programs: A Parallel?" and, Empey and Rabow, "A Reply to Whitney H. Gordon," *op. cit.,* 27 (April 1962), 256–58.

Empey, LaMar T., Maynard L. Erickson, and Max L. Scott, "The Provo Experiment in Delinquency Rehabilitation: Fifth Annual Progress Report, 1963–64," Brigham Young University, mimeographed, n.d.

Eztioni, Amitai, *Complex Organizations: A Sociological Reader* (New York: Holt, Rinehart & Winston, 1964).

Fisher, Sethard, "Social Organization in a Correctional Community," *Pacific Sociological Review,* 4 (fall 1961), 87–93.

Fox, Lionel W., *The English Prison and Borstal Systems* (London: Routledge & Kegan Paul, 1952).

Galtung, Johan, *Fengsels Samfunnet (The Prison Community)* (Oslo: Universitetsforlaget, 1959). In Norwegian.

Garabedian, Peter G., "Social Roles and Processes of Socialization in the Prison Community," *Social Problems,* 11 (fall 1963), 139–52.

——, "Legitimate and Illegitimate Alternatives in the Prison Community," *Sociological Inquiry,* 32 (spring 1962), 172–84.

Garrity, Donald L., "Some Implications of Prison Organization for Penal Objectives," *The Howard Journal,* 11 (1964), 166–79.

Giallombardo, Rose, *Society of Women: A Study of a Women's Prison* (New York: John Wiley & Sons, 1966).

Gibbons, Don C., *Changing the Lawbreaker: The Treatment of Delinquents and Criminals* (Englewood Cliffs, N.J.: Prentice-Hall, 1965).

——, "Comments on the Efficacy of Criminal Treatment," *Canadian Journal of Corrections,* 2 (April 1960), 165–74.

Glaser, Daniel, *The Effectiveness of a Prison and Parole System* (Indianapolis: Bobbs-Merrill, 1964).

——, "Effectiveness of the Federal Correction System," *Federal Probation*, 28 (December 1964), 3–6.

Goffman, Erving, *Asylums* (Garden City: Doubleday & Company, 1961).

Göransson, Hardy, *Some Aspects of the Swedish Prison System* (Stockholm: Regent Bocktrycken, 1955).

Greenblatt, Milton, Daniel G. Levinson, and Richard Williams (eds.), *The Patient and the Mental Hospital* (Glencoe: Free Press, 1957).

Grusky, Oscar, "Organizational Goals and the Behavior of Informal Leaders," *American Journal of Sociology*, 65 (July 1959), 59–67.

——, *Treatment Goals and Organizational Behavior: A Study of an Experimental Prison Camp.* Unpublished Ph.D. dissertation (Ann Arbor: University of Michigan, 1957).

Hartung, Frank E., and Maurice Floch, "A Social Psychological Analysis of Prison Riots: An Hypothesis," *Journal of Criminal Law, Criminology and Police Science*, 47 (May–June 1956), 51–57.

Hazelrigg, Lawrence E., "The Accuracy and Relevance of Staff Perceptions of the Inmate in the Correctional Institution," *Journal of Criminal Law, Criminology and Police Science*, 58 (June 1967), 204–10.

Irwin, John, and Donald R. Cressey, "Thieves, Convicts and the Inmate Culture," *Social Problems*, 10 (fall 1962), 142–55.

Jenkins, Richard L., *Breaking Patterns of Defeat* (Philadelphia: Lippincott, 1954).

Johnston, Norman, Leonard Savitz, and Marvin E. Wolfgang (eds.), *The Sociology of Punishment and Correction* (New York: John Wiley & Sons, 1962).

Jones, Maxwell, *The Therapeutic Community* (New York: Basic Books, 1953).

Kirby, Bernard C., "Measuring the Effects of Treatment of Criminals and Delinquents," *Sociology and Social Research*, 38 (July 1954), 368–74.

Klare, Hugh, *The Anatomy of Prison* (London: Hutchison, 1960).

Makarenko, Anton R., *The Road to Life: An Epic of Education* (Moscow: Foreign Languages Publishing House, 1955).

McCleery, Richard, *The Strange Journey* (Chapel Hill: University of North Carolina Extension Bulletin, 1953).

——, *Policy Change in Prison Management* (East Lansing: Michigan State University Government Research Bureau, 1957).

——, "Conflict and Accommodation in a Penal Institution," paper presented at the Annual Meeting of the American Political Science Association, 1958.

McCorkle, Lloyd W., and Richard Korn, "Resocialization Within Walls," *Annals of the American Academy of Political and Social Science*, 293 (May 1954), 88–98.

McCorkle, Lloyd W., Albert Elias, and F. Lovell Bixby, *The Highfields Story* (New York: Holt, Rinehart & Winston, 1958).

Morris, T., and P. Morris, *Pentonville: A Sociological Study of an English Prison* (London: Routledge & Kegan Paul, 1963).

Novick, A. G., "Training School Organization for Treatment," *Proceedings, National Association of Training Schools and Juvenile Agencies*, 54 (1958), 72–80.

Ohlin, Lloyd E., *Sociology and the Field of Corrections* (New York: Russell Sage Foundation, 1956).

——, and Donnell Pappenfort, "Crisis, Succession and Organizational Change," mimeographed paper, 1956.

——, and William C. Lawrence, "Social Interaction among Clients as a Treatment Problem," *Social Work*, 4 (April 1959), 3–13.

Peizer, Sheldon B., E. B. Lewis, and R. W. Scollon, "Correctional Rehabilitation as a Function of Interpersonal Relations," *Journal of Criminal Law, Criminology and Police Science*, 46 (1956), 632–40.

Perrow, Charles, "Reality Shock: A New Organization Confronts the Custody-Treatment Dilemma," *Social Problems*, 10 (spring 1963), 374–82.

Polsky, Howard, *Cottage Six—The Social System of Delinquent Boys in Residential Treatment* (New York: Russell Sage Foundation, 1956).

Powelson, Harvey, and Reinhard Bendix, "Psychiatry in Prisons," *Psychiatry*, 14 (February 1951), 73–86.

Rapoport, R., and E. Skellern, "Some Therapeutic Functions of Administrative Disturbance," *Administrative Science Quarterly*, 2 (1957), 84–85.

*Readings in Correctional Change* (Austin: University of Texas School of Law, Southwest Center for Law and the Behavioral Sciences, n.d.).

Reckless, Walter C., "The Impact of Correctional Programmes on Inmates," *British Journal of Delinquency*, 6 (September 1955), 138–47.

Schnur, Alfred C., "The New Penology: Fact or Fiction?" *Jour-

*nal of Criminal Law, Criminology and Police Science,* 49 (November–December 1958), 331–34.

Schrag, Clarence C., "Leadership Among Prison Inmates," *American Sociological Review,* 19 (February 1954), 37–42.

———, "A Preliminary Criminal Typology," *Pacific Sociological Review,* 4 (spring 1961), 11–16.

Simpson, Jon E., Thomas G. Eynon, and Walter C. Reckless, "Institutionalization as Perceived by the Juvenile Offender," *Sociology and Social Research,* 48 (October 1963), 13–23.

Stanton, Alfred H., and Morris S. Schwartz, *The Mental Hospital* (New York: Basic Books, 1954).

Sternberg, David, "Synanon House—A Consideration of Its Implications for American Corrections," *Journal of Criminal Law, Criminology and Police Science,* 54 (December 1963), 447–55.

Street, David, Robert D. Vinter, and Charles Perrow, *Organization for Treatment: A Comparative Study of Institutions for Delinquents* (New York: Free Press, 1966).

Stürup, Georg K., *The Treatment of Criminals at Herstedvester, Denmark.* The Issac Ray Award Lectures presented at the University of Pennsylvania, Schools of Law and Medicine, November 1966.

Sykes, Gresham M., "Men, Merchants and Toughs: A Study of Reactions to Imprisonment," *Social Problems,* 4 (October 1956), 130–38.

———, "The Corruption of Authority and Rehabilitation," *Social Forces,* 34 (March 1956), 257–62.

———, *The Society of Captives: A Study of a Maximum Security Prison* (Princeton: Princeton University Press, 1958).

Tittle, C. R., and D. P. Tittle, "Social Organization of Prisoners: An Empirical Test," *Social Forces,* 42 (1964), 216–21.

*The Offender: An Answer to the Correctional Manpower Crisis.* Proceedings of a Workshop on The Offender as a Correctional Manpower Resource, Institute for the Study of Crime and Delinquency, Asilomar, California, September 1966.

Vinter, Robert D., and Roger Lind, "Staff Relationships and Attitudes in a Juvenile Correctional Institution" (Ann Arbor: University of Michigan School of Social Work, 1958).

Wallace, Robert, "Ecological Implications of a Custody Institution," *Issues in Criminology,* 2 (spring 1966), 47–60.

Ward, David A., *Prison Rule Enforcement and Changing Organizational Goals.* Unpublished Ph.D. dissertation, University of Illinois, 1960.

——, and Gene G. Kassebaum, *Women's Prison: Sex and Social Structure* (Chicago: Aldine Publishing Company, 1965).

Weeks, H. Ashley, *Youthful Offenders at Highfields* (Ann Arbor: University of Michigan Press, 1958).

Wheeler, Stanton, "Social Organization and Inmate Values in Correctional Communities," *Proceedings, American Correctional Association,* 1959, 189–98.

Wolfgang, Marvin E., "Age, Adjustment and the Treatment Process of Criminal Behavior," *Psychiatry Digest,* 25 (July 1964), 21–35, and (August 1964), 23–36.

Yablonsky, Lewis, "The Anticriminal Society: Synanon," *Federal Probation,* 26 (September 1962), 50–57.

Zald, Mayer N., "Organizational Control Structure in Five Correctional Institutions," *American Journal of Sociology,* 68 (November 1962), 335–45.

—— (ed.), *Social Welfare Institutions: A Sociological Reader* (New York: John Wiley & Sons, 1965).

# INDEX

# ANCHOR BOOKS

## GOVERNMENT AND POLITICAL SCIENCE

# ANCHOR BOOKS

SOCIOLOGY

# Sociology (continued)

# Sociology (continued)